BEYOND THE PASS

BEYOND THE PASS

Economy, Ethnicity, and Empire in Qing Central Asia,

1759–1864

JAMES A. MILLWARD

STANFORD UNIVERSITY PRESS
Stanford, California
1998

Stanford University Press
Stanford, California
© 1998 by the Board of Trustees
of the Leland Stanford Junior University
Printed in the United States of America
CIP data appear at the end of the book

To the memory of Celia and Richard Millward

For Madhulika

In his attempt to cross Xinjiang's Taklamakan Desert in 1895, Sven Hedin found his men to be more of a liability than an asset. When sandstorms threatened and water grew low, he forged ahead while they lost hope, drank camel urine, and died in the sand.

My experience in writing this book could not have been more different—all the way, I have been borne along by the help and encouragement of others. This was especially the case in China, where I conducted the bulk of the research for this book in 1990 while affiliated with the Institute for Qing History Studies at People's University in Beijing. I was extremely fortunate in having as my advisors Cheng Chongde and Hua Li, who on that and subsequent occasions have shared with me their deep knowledge of the Qing frontiers, steered me to the important literature, and introduced me to other scholars in the field of Xinjiang history. The sheaves of letters they wrote gained me a warm welcome among their colleagues in Mongolia, Ningxia, Gansu, and Xinjiang as well as around Beijing, and thus made this book possible. I am thankful as well to Dai Yi and Ma Ruheng at Renda and to Ma Dazheng and the staff of the Zhongguo Bianjiang Shidi Yanjiu Zhongxin for similar help.

During my research year in China, the following scholars gave generously of their time and expertise: in Beijing, Chen Yongling, Lin Yongkuang, Wang Xi, Zhang Yuxin, and especially Wu Fengpei, who is truly a national treasure; Hao Weimin and Jin Feng (Altan Orghil) in Hohhot; Chen Yuning, Lai Cunli, Ma Ping, and Yang Huaizhong in Ningxia; Wang Xilong in Lanzhou; Ji Dachun, Feng Xisi, Li Sheng, Miao Pusheng, Pan Zhiping, Qi Qingshun, Xu Bofu, and Zhou Xuan in Urumchi. Qin Weixing spent the days of Qorban shepherding me around Urumchi, for which I am eternally in his debt. It is a pleasure also to thank Abdulğeni, Chao-ge-tu, Kämäl, Li Shoujun, Mollaniaz, Xie Zhining, and Zhang Shiming for smoothing the way at various points. My friends Sun Hong, Wan Jun, Wang Hengjie, Wang Tong, Wang Yi, and Zhang Xuehui made Beijing seem like home; other friends and colleagues, Sabine Dabringhaus, Mark Elliott, Blaine Gaustad, John Herman,

Melissa Macauley, Nancy Park, Steven Shutt, and Paola Zamperini made even the Renda dorm feel homey—a considerably more difficult task—and taught me a great deal of history in the process.

　While I made my first written reconnaissances of the material I brought back from China in a dissertation for Stanford University, the guidance of Albert Dien, Harold Kahn, and Lyman Van Slyke kept me on track. Hal Kahn's thoughts have been particularly helpful in explaining to me what I was writing about; passages in his letters often described my work better than I could myself, and not a few terms first employed by him have found their way into my vocabulary. Pamela Crossley, Mark Elliott, James Hevia, Jonathan Lipman, Toby Meyer, Celia Millward, Sue Naquin, Peter Perdue, Evelyn Rawski, and Morris Rossabi have carefully read, corrected, and commented on all or portions of this book in various drafts. Their comments have been of great help, though I have probably implemented too few of their suggestions. I have also profited from discussions with Dorothy Borei, Alison Futrell and the Rome/Qing comparative imperialism seminar at Arizona, Kato Naoshi, Laura Newby, Shinmen Yasushi, Sugiwara Jun, and Nakami Tatsuo. My editors at Stanford University Press, Pamela MacFarland Holway and Stacey Lynn, and my copy editor, Erin Milnes, have been both sharp-eyed and pleasant to work with. Muriel Bell offered support and encouragement for this project from its inception, for which I extend my gratitude. Others, too, have made important contributions to this project, whether they know it or not: Kahar Barat, Carol Benedict, Philippe Forêt, Giu Renquan, Jake Haselkorn, John Olsen, Caroline Reeves, Joan and Daniel Sax, Jan Stuart, Kaneko Tamio, Hoyt Cleaveland Tillman, Mike Winter-Rousset, and Dick Wang. Meera and Sushma Sikka have kept me sustained at key stages with (aptly named) gobi paratha.

　I am grateful for research access and assistance provided by the Number One Historical Archives in Beijing; Yin Shumei's graceful approach to problems was always appreciated, and her good humor brightened many grim days otherwise illuminated only by the pallid glow of a microfilm reader. In Japan, Hamashita Takeshi welcomed me into his seminar and facilitated access to the collections of the Tōyō Bunka Kenkyūjo. I also consulted the collections of the Tōyō Bunko and Keio University, as well as the British Library, the library of the School of Oriental and African Studies, Stanford University Green Library and the Hoover Institution, Widener and Harvard-Yenching Libraries, the University of Arizona Oriental Library, Georgetown University Lauringer Library, and the Library of Congress, Asian Division. My thanks to the staffs of all these institutions for their patient help and, in a few cases, flexibility about overdue fees.

　Two extended seminars have added vastly to my understanding of Xinjiang and the Qing dynasty. The first, a conference and field expedition in Xinjiang organized in 1992 by the Center for Research on Chinese Frontier History and Geography (Beijing) and the Sven Hedin Foundation (Sweden), gave me the chance to travel some of Altishahr's desert roads myself. The second, a month-long summer institute on the Qing palace at Chengde, sponsored by the National Endowment for the Humanities and held on the campus of the University of Michigan in Ann Arbor in 1994, first brought many of the issues discussed in this book into focus for me. I hope the organizers of both events will find in this book some sign that their efforts have paid off.

The financial support that I have received for this project includes tuition remission from the Inter-University Program in Yokohama for language study and research in Japan; a National Program Fellowship of the Committee for Scholarly Communication with the People's Republic of China and a Fulbright-Hays Grant for Doctoral Dissertation Research for my year in China; and a *China Times* Young Scholar's Fellowship, a Josephine de Karmine Fellowship, and a Foreign Language and Area Studies Fellowship for completion of the dissertation. A grant from the Pacific Cultural Foundation provided partial support during a year spent finishing the manuscript. The University of Arizona provided me with a summer stipend for Lü Hui-tz'u, my highly efficient research assistant, and the Department of History there further facilitated work on this project by graciously granting me leaves during my first years of teaching.

My warmest thanks go to my wife, Madhulika Sikka, who has supported me patiently in all possible ways over these years, despite separation by oceans, continents, and the chasm that sometimes divides the historian from the journalist. I complete this book on the eve of our anniversary, and though I am tempted simply to offer the manuscript to her in lieu of a present, I will not. She deserves much better.

J. M.

CONTENTS

MAPS, FIGURES, AND TABLES

"What do you want to study those frontier places for? All the history happened in China!" So a Chinese friend told me many years ago when I spoke of my growing interest in the Central Asian region known as Xinjiang—the Qing dynasty's "New Dominion," or the "Western Regions." My experience during my first years in graduate school seemed to bear him out. Although teachers and classmates encouraged my pursuits, nothing on our reading lists seemed to apply to the far west. This bothered me, but I carried on, motivated (and funded) to a great degree by virtue of the unconventionality and, perhaps, exoticism of my topic. Eventually, my efforts to link my peripheral interests with what seemed to be the central concerns of the field led me to start on a basic, material level, examining the physical exchanges connecting China proper to Xinjiang, and investigating the travelers—mostly merchants—who frequented the routes between China and the new Qing acquisition. Thus began what started as a study of commercial relations between China proper and Xinjiang in the Qing period.

In the course of my reading in the Qing archives, annals, and gazetteers, however, I realized that in the eyes of Qing policy makers, Chinese commerce in Xinjiang was inextricably linked to issues of control. Whenever the activities of commoners became objects of state scrutiny (and on the frontier, that was often), Qing sources almost invariably took care to distinguish the *type* of merchant—or farmer or herdsman—involved, whether they were Han Chinese, Muslim Han, local Muslim, Oirat, Andijani, Kazakh, Kirghiz, or members of another of the groups the Qing carefully distinguished. Thus, I could not consider commerce without reference to this aspect of the Qing government in Xinjiang, an aspect I have called, for lack of a better term, ethnic policy.

Somewhat farther along, I discovered that the two issues I had singled out, the economics of empire and the interactions of people in an imperial context, comprised core concerns of the Qing imperial enterprise and that what I was working to uncover was nothing less than the mechanics and ethos of Qing imperialism. Moreover, during the span of time I chose to study, policies changed and ideologies shifted as events encroached and the dynasty's circumstances worsened. My Chinese sources reflected a change in attitude toward Xinjiang: what was a Qing empire in the west at the beginning of my period began to sound more like a Chinese one by the end. And in pondering the differences between Qing and China, and why such a distinction seemed odd, I began to reflect again, this time with greater understanding, on why the empire in Xinjiang, a major preoccupation of the Qing court, has been of such little concern to historians in the twentieth century.

This is a study, then, of the workings and conception of Qing empire in Xinjiang during its first phase, from the initial conquest to the time of the mid-nineteenth-century Muslim uprisings that severed the region from control by Beijing for over a decade. Qing economic and ethnic policies in Xinjiang receive the most attention here, but in the course of examining these issues, I attempt also to shed light on a broader issue: the transition from a Qing dynastic empire to a Chinese nation-state.

The chapters below approach this subject according to the following plan. We begin at the Jiayu Guan, the western terminus of the Ming walled defense system, in the early nineteenth century. I consider the ambiguity and liminality of the Jiayu Guan (and Xinjiang) during the Qing and hazard some thoughts on why the historiography of early modern and modern China has paid so little attention to these issues. Chapter 1 then provides geographic and historical background to the region and introduces the discourse on Xinjiang's place in the empire that carried through the 1759–1864 period. In this discourse—the court and scholarly debates over imperial conception and implementation—the discussion of fiscal matters overlay deeper concerns about the proper limits and nature of the empire. In order to justify the conquest, the Qianlong emperor, who had pushed ahead with the conquest of Xinjiang in the face of domestic opposition from certain quarters in China, was concerned that imperial rule in Xinjiang be inexpensive to maintain. His court thus encouraged fiscal innovation in the new territory. Chapters 2 and 3 focus on the fiscal foundations, and limitations, of Qing rule in Xinjiang, outlining the means by which the military government was maintained without an agricultural tax base like that in China proper. Despite the emperor's hopes, the dynasty was forced to subsidize the Xinjiang garrisons in order to support its armies and officials there; these chapters quantify the extent of reliance on Chinese silver and examine the various means by which Xinjiang authorities attempted to reduce that reliance. Because many of these means involved the commercial economy, Chinese merchants in Xinjiang came to provide an increasingly important safety margin to the tight budgets under which Qing authorities in Xinjiang operated.

The subsequent chapters examine these private merchants and the policies adopted by the Qing toward their activities in Xinjiang, especially in the south, where the population of native Muslims was highest. Chapter 4 outlines the process of Chinese commercial penetration of Xinjiang, Qing control measures, Chinese settlement patterns, and the extension of Chinese urban culture to parts of the New Dominion. One central problem explored here is the degree to which Qing authorities attempted to segregate Chinese traders from the natives of southern Xinjiang; I examine the construction and inhabitation of walled citadels in southern cities in an attempt to illuminate this question. Chapter 5 describes the experiences of Han, Tungan (Chinese Muslim, today's Hui), and East Turkestani (today's Uyghur) merchants trading between China and Xinjiang. Case studies of two major articles of trade, tea and jade, further highlight these groups' activities and reveal that private commercial links between China proper and Xinjiang were segmented at gateway cities and functionally differentiated among distinct types of merchants plying different routes, including small-scale Chinese Muslim traders, representatives of Shanxi firms, and dealers in silk and jade from the Jiangnan region. Chapter 6 first considers ethnic policy in Xinjiang from a theoretical standpoint, contrasting the historiographical commonplace that the empire was Sinocentrically conceived with how the Qianlong emperor envisioned it. This chapter concludes with a case study of a grisly incident in Kashgar in 1830 that tested, and eventually led to the replacement of, the mid-Qing ethnic policy with one more favorable to Han Chinese. Analysis of this event suggests that part of the explanation to how a new, Greater China arose out of the Qing imperium lies in the convergence of Manchu and Chinese interests in Xinjiang. A concluding chapter traces the crumbling of Qing control in Xinjiang to the dual failure of silver stipends and the Xinjiang commercial economy and argues that the continuation of the debates over Xinjiang by statecraft writers in the first half of the nineteenth century—again, framed in economic terms—anticipated a more assimilationist Chinese model of empire that was to be implemented in the late nineteenth and twentieth centuries.

Chinese terms and names below are given in *Hanyu pinyin* and Manchu ones according to the Möllendorff system. For Mongolian terms, I use Antoine Mostaert's scheme as adapted by Francis W. Cleaves, except that γ is here written "ğ" and "j" printed without the haček. However, for Mongol names I have sacrificed technical accuracy for recognizability and readers' ease, and thus have Torghut, Khoshuut, and Chinggis Khan instead of Torğut, Qošuut, and Činggis Qa'an. For romanization of Uyghur (Eastern Turki) I follow the system used by Reinhard Hahn in his *Spoken Uyghur*, which is generally recognizable to Turkologists. For practical reasons, "ng" is substituted for Hahn's ŋ (the eng). Foreign terms in the text are generally given in Chinese, unless otherwise noted. Where versions are given in more than one language or where confusion might be possible, the language is identified as follows: Ch. = Chinese; Ma. = Manchu; Mo. = Mongol; Tu. = Eastern Turki, that is, Uyghur.

Researchers working on Qing Inner Asia often encounter non-Chinese personal names for which only the Chinese, and not the spelling in the original language, is available. It is inappropriate to write these as if they were Chinese names (that is, as "Fu Heng" or "Na Yancheng," for example). For such names, I adopt the following convention: the Chinese characters are transliterated in *pinyin* and linked by hyphens. Another method, now common among scholars who use *pinyin* in preference to the Wade-Giles system, is to run the Chinese characters of transliterated non-Chinese (especially Manchu) names together. However, I believe Gen-chu-ke-ze-bang to be somewhat more manageable than Genchukezebang. This convention also instantly distinguishes non-Han from Han personages, while preventing confusion in those occasional cases where a spelling might be a transliteration from either Chinese or an Altaic language (as with Fukanggan or Nayanceng, for example). Of course, the best course of all is to provide both non-Chinese and Chinese spellings; unfortunately, this is not always feasible.

Where possible, names of major East Turkestani and Kokandi historical figures and some terms have been given in Arabic transcription, to conform to the precedents established by Joseph Fletcher and Saguchi Tōru. There are no universally accepted spellings for non-Chinese Xinjiang place-names, and, indeed, many of those names have been changed frequently over the past two centuries. After an analysis of the spellings in the *Xiyu tongwen zhi* and modern Uyghur-language maps of Xinjiang, I have determined that there is no strong linguistic or historical basis to adopt either of these sources as a standard for place-name spellings; today's official Chinese versions (Kashi for Kashgar, Shache for Yarkand) are unfamiliar and not in popular use even in Xinjiang; some, like "Urumqi" for Urumchi, are based on a P.R.C. system for romanizing Uyghur that has now been abandoned. Thus, again for continuity, I follow Fletcher's spellings in the *Cambridge History of China*, volume 10. It is hoped that these will in any case be the forms most familiar to readers.

I refer to Qing emperors primarily as the Qianlong emperor, the Jiaqing emperor, the Daoguang emperor, and so on. When stylistic concerns require another name in order to avoid cumbersome repetition, I follow many Chinese scholars in employing the temple names Gaozong (for Qianlong), Renzong (for Jiaqing), and Xuanzong (for Daoguang).

Finally, a word on the terms "Inner Asia," "Central Asia," and "Xinjiang." Once, Europeans referred to a geographic and cultural entity known as Tartary. Though few agreed on where Tartary began and ended, or whether it included Cathay or not, everyone knew where it was. Our terminology today is hardly more concrete; thus it is with a certain arbitrariness that I adopt the following usages. In this book, "Inner Asia" is used for those northern and western territories that the Qing dynasty, in building its empire, added to the lands of former Ming China. Thus, Inner Asia comprises Manchuria, Mongolia, Xinjiang, and Tibet. I use the term "Central Asia" here to indicate the geographically central regions of the Eurasian continent, especially the Islamic lands once known by such names as Trans-Oxiana or Turkestan, including the former Soviet Central Asian republics of Kazakhstan, Kyrgyzstan, Tajikistan, Turkmenistan, and Uzbekistan, as well as Afghanistan. In the nineteenth and early twentieth century, the region known in Chinese as Xinjiang was commonly called Eastern Turkestan or Chinese Central Asia, and I therefore also include it within my definition of Central Asia. Xinjiang thus falls within a zone of overlap between Inner and Central Asia. I refer to Xinjiang in my title as "Central Asia" for the benefit of browsers or readers who are not China specialists; I intend no political message by this or any other terminological usages in this book.

CZGS   Caizheng guanshui (finance and customs). Subject category of archival holdings in the Number One Historical Archives of China.

GPSYYSA   "Gao Pu si yu yushi an" (The case of Gao Pu's illegal private jade sales). *Shiliao xunkan* (Historical materials trimonthly) nos. 19–28 (Feb. 1930 to March 1931).

GZSL   *Da Qing lichao Gaozong shilu* (Veritable records of the successive reigns of the Qing dynasty—Qianlong reign).

GZZZ   *Gongzhong dang Qianlong chao zouzhe* (Palace memorials of the Qianlong Period). Compiled by the Palace Museum, Documents Section. Taipei: Guoli gugong bowuyuan, 1983.

HJTZ   He-ning, ed. *Huijiang tongzhi* (Comprehensive gazetteer of Altishahr). 1804.

HYXYTZ   Fuheng et al., comp. *(Qinding) huangyu Xiyu tuzhi* (Imperially commissioned gazetteer of the Western Regions of the imperial domain). 1782.

LFZZ   Junjichu lufu zouzhe. Reference copy of palace memorial stored in the Grand Council; a class of document held in the Number One Historical Archives of China.

MZSW   Minzu shiwu (Nationality affairs). Subject category of archival holdings in the Number One Historical Archives of China.

NWFLW   Neiwufu laiwen (Communications to the Imperial Household Agency). A class of document stored in the Number One Historical Archives of China.

NWYGZY   Nayanceng (Na-yan-cheng). *Nawen yigong zouyi* (Memorials of Nayanceng). Rong'an, ed. 1830.

PDZGEFL   Fu-heng, et al., comp. *(Qinding) pingding Zhunga'er fanglue* (Imperially commissioned military history of the pacification of the Zunghars). 3 vols. *(qian, zheng, xu)*. 1768.

QDDA   Zhongguo diyi lishi dang'an guan (Number One Historical

Archives of China), ed. "Qianlong chao neidi yu Xinjiang sichou maoyi shiliao" (Materials on silk trade between China proper and Xinjiang in the Qianlong reign). In *Qingdai dang'an shiliao congbian* 12:44–214. Beijing: Zhonghua Shuju, 1987.

RZSL   *Da Qing lichao Renzong shilu* (Veritable records of the successive reigns of the Qing dynasty—Jiaqing reign).

SYMY   Shangye maoyi (Trade and commerce). Subject category of archival holdings in the Number One Historical Archives of China.

SZJL   He-ning, ed. *Sanzhou jilue* (Cursory record of three prefectures: Hami, Turfan, and Urumchi), Preface 1805.

WZSL   *Da Qing lichao Wenzong shilu* (Veritable records of the successive reigns of the Qing dynasty—Xianfeng reign).

XCYL   Qi Yunshi, comp. *Xichui yaolue* (Survey of the Western borders). 1807.

XJZL   Song-yun et al. *(Qinding) Xinjiang zhilue* (Imperially commissioned gazetteer of Xinjiang), Preface 1821.

XYWJL   Qi-shi-yi (Chunyuan). *Xiyu wenjian lu* (Record of things heard and seen in the Western Regions). 1777.

XZSL   *Da Qing lichao Xuanzong shilu.* (Veritable records of the successive reigns of the Qing dynasty—Daoguang reign).

YJHL   Ge Beng'e. *Yijiang huilan* (Survey of the Yili River region). 1775.

YJJZ   *Yijiang jizai* (Record of the Yili River area). C. 1862.

ZPZZ   Gongzhong zhupi zouzhe. Rescripted palace memorial; a class of document stored in the Number One Historical Archives of China.

ZTYLSY   Yong-bao. *Zongtong Yili shiyi* (Comprehensive survey of affairs in Yili). C. 1795.

BEYOND THE PASS

Introduction

Early in July 1805, Qi Yunshi traveled northwestward through the sere, sparsely populated landscape of the Gansu corridor on his way to exile in northern Xinjiang. His appointment to the Baoquan Ju Coinage Office in the capital the year before had not worked out well. When Qi took up his job as overseer, he had been able to check only the books, not the mint's actual copper stocks, because audits of copper supplies were carried out only at fixed intervals. When the scheduled audit took place and a large shortfall left by his predecessor was discovered, the blame fell on Qi, and he was banished to Yili.

Not that this surprised Qi, particularly. In the uneasy years surrounding the death of the Qianlong emperor and the demise of the corrupt imperial favorite, Hešen (He-shen), it had been easy to make enemies in the bureaucracy, and Qi had not improved matters by publicly exposing malfeasance among officials administering the grain transport system. Now they were getting even.

Nor was Qi Yunshi completely unprepared for what lay before him. Before the Baoquan Ju appointment, as a Hanlin compiler he had assisted in a major study of the elite genealogies of Mongolia, Xinjiang, and Tibet, the *Waifan Menggu Huibu wanggong biaozhuan*, and this task had exposed him

1

to the history and geography of the Qing lands in Inner Asia.* The diary he kept of this journey into exile reflects the objective, empirical approach of an eighteenth-century scholar in imperial employ: "Went west thirty *li* to Scorched Gulch. The earth is red in many places, but there is no gulch." Another day, "Went west forty *li* to Red Axe Lake. It is not a lake." Despite his background, however, as Qi jounced along the stony post road in his high-wheeled cart, the last city in China seventy *li* behind him and the late afternoon shadow of the massive Jiayu Guan (Jiayu Pass) fortification drawing nearer over the yellow plain, his heart grew heavy with the significance of the passage he was soon to make.

Qi knew the Pass's official function: although technically it lay well within the jurisdiction of Gansu province, it was the gateway to Xinjiang, the Qing's New Dominion in the far west. Here his party's papers were to be presented and checked—people could not pass through the stone gate at will. But these formalities did not overly concern him. Instead, Qi was recalling literary descriptions of the brooding crags and wind-swept fortresses that defend the Western Regions frontier. He may, for example, have remembered Li Bo's famous lines,

> The bright moon rising over the Tianshan glides into a boundless sea of cloud.
> A ceaseless wind over myriad miles whistles through Yumen Pass.
> Men of Han descend the Baideng Road; Tartars scout the bay of Kokonor.
> From this ancient battlefield, no one has ever returned![1]

With such images fueling his imagination, it is not surprising that Qi found the real Jiayu Guan nothing like he expected. The surrounding mountains were far away, and, he wrote in his journal that evening, did "not seem at all high or imposing." The fort itself was "merely situated on a rise of earth; there is no treacherous defile." Still, he knew the passage from China proper (*neidi*) to beyond the Jiayu Pass (*guanwai*) had to be one of great moment, so, once through, he lingered on the western side.

> I stood there, alone, not a soul in sight. I was determined to move ahead, but at the same time strongly reluctant to leave behind all that I love.

* As mentioned in the Note on Transcription and Proper Names, definitions of Inner Asia vary somewhat. I follow the practice of Joseph Fletcher and the *Cambridge History of China* and take Inner Asia to comprise the regions generally known as Manchuria, Mongolia, Xinjiang (Sinkiang), and Tibet. (Xinjiang is also considered to lie within Central Asia.) Qing control over Manchuria, of course, had been mostly consolidated before the Manchu conquest of China. The eighteenth-century Qing expansion added Mongolia, Xinjiang, and Tibet to the Qing empire.

These feelings warred confusedly within me for a moment while I beheld the landscape. Then, suddenly, I saw it all in a new light.

Qi does not share with us the exact nature of his epiphany, though he hints at it with the following, apparently matter-of-fact, observation: "What the ancients called Yumen Guan and Yang Guan are still several hundred *li* to the west, on the border of today's Dunhuang County. So Jiayu Guan is in fact not really remote."[2]

Not really remote—its distance diminishes as Qi decides the Jiayu Guan is not one of those dangerous passes into wilderness and barbarism that the Tang poets sang of so emotively. Those lie further west, he reminds himself, apparently resolving the incongruity between image and reality that had puzzled him. But in fact, by Qi's time, Yumen Guan and Yang Guan were no more than memories, ruins lost under the desert, and in any case, he knew he would not pass through them. He was already over the threshold; there would be no other, more definitive moment than this spasm of ambivalence to mark his entry to the Western Regions.

The idea of the boundary has recently been embraced by scholars in the humanities and social sciences as a powerful metaphor and hermeneutic device. At boundaries, differences are articulated and negotiated; decisions are made to include or exclude; categories are drawn up. Not only do boundaries distinguish two entities; they define the entities themselves: there can be no civilization without barbarism, no true religion without infidels, no Occident without the Orient, no Self without the Other. Yet boundaries are seldom rigid. Rather, they are porous surfaces where heterogeneous physical or conceptual zones come into contact and interpenetrate. Nor are they static, but change position, character, and meaning over time.[3]

Jiayu Guan in the eighteenth and nineteenth centuries was a boundary in all these senses, operating on both physical and symbolic levels. It was a fort and a gate in a defensive long wall, a military checkpoint that patently announced the border dividing the eighteen provinces of China proper, known in Qing sources as the "inner land," from the territory "beyond the Pass." (The paired terms, *neidi* and *guanwai*, remain in common use today, *guan* referring both to the Jiayu Guan and the Shanhai Guan, at the opposite end of the Ming wall, on the coast.) As suggested by Qi's ruminations, it was also, for both educated Qing subjects and the imperial court, a point of contact between the past and the present. Yumen Guan and Yang Guan, gates in the Han Dynasty mural defense system in the northwest, are prominent landmarks in a frontier literature populated with soldiers on lonely borderland duty, exiles banished beyond the pale, and princesses married off to coarse barbarian chieftains. Verses in this genre employ description of a hostile natural environment to stress the moral and cultural gulf that was seen to separate China from lands outside the walls. These resonances, familiar from Tang poetry or the fictional *Journey to the West* (*Xi you ji*) and easily triggered by the invocation of Han and Tang period Western Regions place-names, attached themselves to the later Jiayu Guan as well. In the period of cultural and strategic retraction that followed the reign of the Ming emperor Yongle (1403–24), this frontier fortress near the northwestern terminus of the wall aptly marked, in Chinese eyes, a boundary between civilization and chaos.

By the high Qing, however, Jiayu Guan was in many ways an incongruous relic. It was not of real strategic significance. No threat lay on the other side, nor was "beyond the Pass" the exclusive domain of non-Chinese; in fact, by this time, it was impermissible to apply the term *yi* (foreign, nonsubjects) to Xinjiang peoples.[4] Han Chinese* and Muslims from the west had been traveling back and forth in increasing numbers for decades, and Chinese colonies in Xinjiang were thriving. The Pass did not correspond to any climatic zone or particular feature of the natural landscape: where the wall and Jiayu Guan cut across Gansu, one side looks pretty much like the other, and, literalist that he was, Qi Yunshi was quick to note the discrepancy between the "Pass" here and the dramatic topography in the idealized literary images of frontier portals. Jiayu Guan simply divided one part of the empire from another—a purpose that, upon reflection, is not simple at all.

Boundaries and Modern Chinese History

Until quite recently, few Western historians of Qing or Republican China have taken their research beyond Jiayu Guan, and fewer still have done so for the period before the 1860s.[5] This is despite the fact that the Zunghar campaigns that ultimately resulted in the conquest of Xinjiang commanded the

---

* The term "Han," as generally used in the field of modern Chinese history, refers to the native Chinese-speaking inhabitants of the "eighteen provinces" of China proper, as well as migrants from China proper to places in Inner Asia. It is thus roughly synonymous with "Chinese" as commonly used, though not of course with today's inclusive political meaning of the word (which includes, as well as Han, members of any "minority nationality" with Chinese citizenship). Although as officially defined in the P.R.C. the Han nationality comprises the vast majority of today's Chinese population, this category in fact subsumes vast linguistic, cultural, and physical variety that in other contexts might be considered constitutive of "national" or "ethnic" difference. The Qing use of the term "Han" in Xinjiang differed slightly; see the discussion of Qing categories in Chapter 6.

attention and strained the treasuries of the Kangxi, Yongzheng, and Qian-long emperors; despite the fact that two major institutional innovations of the Qing, the Ministry for Governing the Outer Domains (Lifan Yuan) and the Grand Council (Junji Chu), were deeply engaged in the business of acquiring and maintaining the territory; despite the fact that the dynasty chose to re-conquer part or all of Xinjiang on several occasions in the nineteenth century, when most modern scholars believe (and many Qing ministers at the time agreed) that more critical problems required concentration of resources along the maritime frontier of China proper; and despite the fact that Mao Zedong and other leaders of the early Communist state likewise made reassertion of Beijing's control over Xinjiang an early priority. Why have so few historians in the twentieth century expended a similar proportion of their efforts on the region and the issues its conquest raises? Why has Qing imperial expansion in Inner Asia not been considered important? When one considers the prominent place occupied by "Western history" or "frontier history" in the historiography of the United States, the almost absolute neglect of China's eighteenth-century westward and northward expansion is all the more re-markable.

This elision of Qing Xinjiang and Inner Asia from the historiography of modern "China" is not accidental. To a great degree, it is the result of how the boundaries of modern Chinese history itself have been drawn by some of the field's most influential historians.

One of the scholars responsible for this phenomenon is none other than Owen Lattimore. This is ironic, of course, because Lattimore, a great friend of the nomad, journeyed personally through Manchuria, Mongolia, and Xin-jiang and left an important legacy of travel accounts and historical works focused on the people of these areas and their relations with China. But his best known and most read book, *Inner Asian Frontiers of China*, by the power of its highly original analysis and its stress on the Great Wall as the bound-ary par excellence defining the Chinese world, established a framework for understanding Inner Asia and China that few scholars have looked beyond.

In *Inner Asian Frontiers*, rather than survey Chinese–Inner Asian rela-tions chronologically, Lattimore's method was to seek "first principles" in ancient history and frontier geography itself. The bulk of his historical analy-sis thus concerns the interaction of Chinese and nomad states from before the Qin unification until the end of the Han dynasty in A.D. 220. Lattimore also devotes considerable space to the geographic, economic, and ecological differences between Inner Asian and Chinese areas. From these foundations, Lattimore draws a series of general conclusions: that the Great Wall line functioned to delimit the "geographic field" of Chinese history; that the marginal zone along that frontier served as a reservoir where societies sharing qualities of both the steppe and China proper developed and eventually moved on to conquer China; and that Chinese and nomad history were characterized by interrelated cycles. He casts these observations as laws of history.

> Hence for about two thousand years, from the time of the Earlier Han to the middle of the nineteenth century, the combined history of Inner Asia and China can be described in terms of two cycles, distinct from each other as patterns but always interacting on each other as historical processes—the cycle of tribal dispersion and unification in the steppe and the cycle of dynastic integration and collapse in China.

Lattimore's periodization here—the culmination in the nineteenth century—is significant. In his own travels he was struck by the effects of modern industrialism, particularly railroads, on Inner Asia, as well as the foreign presence in China in the 1920s and 1930s and imperialist incursions into China's frontier regions. He thus concluded that "it is the penetration of all Asia by the European and American industrialized order of society that is putting an end to the secular ebb and flow by making possible—indeed, imperative—a new general integration."[6]

Lattimore believed that it was the advent of the West in China in the mid-nineteenth century that brought an end to the pattern of historical interaction along the Great Wall frontier he had identified. Accordingly, he dealt with early and mid-Qing involvement in Inner Asia in surprisingly cursory fashion. He devotes no more than twenty pages to direct discussion of Qing Mongolia, Xinjiang, and Tibet; the century of Qing rule in Xinjiang before the Tungan (Hui) rebellions is covered in less than two paragraphs. *Inner Asian Frontiers of China* thus leaves readers with an impression of the absoluteness of the Great Wall frontier and its enduring role dividing historically antagonistic societies, the interactions of which follow a timeless pattern determined by the geological imperatives of climate and terrain. Only modernity (railways, firearms, Western and Japanese imperialism) could disrupt the age-old pattern and truly integrate China and Inner Asia. Such a view minimizes both the momentous changes in Inner Asia during the early and mid-Qing, and the changed significance of the Great Wall frontier in a *Qing* (not Chinese) empire that included both China and Inner Asia.[7]

The fundamental contributions of John King Fairbank have likewise served to deflect interest from Qing Inner Asia. Fairbank elaborated a complex of interconnected ideas that for a good part of the twentieth century have shaped understanding of China throughout, and often beyond, the English-speaking world. Some of these include the application of the tradition/modernity dyad to China; the Western impact/Chinese response paradigm; the notion of spontaneous sinicization through proximity to Chinese culture; and the use of the "tribute system" and "Chinese world order" as models of Chinese relations with non-Chinese. All have come under extensive reconsideration in recent years, and I will not reiterate these critiques.[8] However, it is worth noting how these key organizing concepts serve to marginalize the story of Qing activity outside of China proper and to heavily veil those aspects of the Qing imperial order that do not fit within a Sinocentric depiction of Chinese history.

None of these concepts was invented, held, or propagated exclusively by Fairbank, of course. These ideas are rooted variously in the early nineteenth century writings of Western China hands and in late nineteenth and early twentieth century nationalistic Chinese interpretations of imperial history. However, it was Fairbank's influential survey textbooks and graduate pedagogy that amplified and entrenched these ideas within our understanding of modern China. Moreover, Fairbank assembled these concepts for a purpose: to explain what has generally been seen as the Chinese failure to respond adequately to the West in the nineteenth century.

Perhaps the most basic of these interdependent ideas is the tendency to view "traditional China" as essentially changeless, or at least incapable of meaningful "transformation." Paul Cohen has examined this approach and remarked upon its origins in the self-congratulatory outlook of the nineteenth-century industrializing West. Cohen did not note, however, how this view underpins one of Fairbank's major interpretive models, the tributary system. The paradigmatic expression of the tributary system model appeared as a chapter in Fairbank's *Trade and Diplomacy on the China Coast* and, in more detailed form, as one of his and Ssu-yü Teng's three studies of Qing administration. Later, Fairbank developed the thesis further in "A Preliminary Framework" in the introduction to *The Chinese World Order*. There are slight differences of emphasis in these versions, but essential points of the theory remain consistent.[9]

Briefly put, Fairbank argues that through centuries of interaction with non-Chinese "barbarians," especially nomadic tribes to the north, China developed and by Ming times institutionalized a "diplomatic medium" that enshrined Chinese cultural superiority over surrounding peoples and the myth of the Chinese emperor's sovereignty over all humankind. Diplomatic ritual and rhetoric expressed an ideology that recognized no boundedness to the Chinese state, only varying degrees of accommodation to Chinese custom as one moved outward from the Sinic center. The hierarchical conception of domestic political and social relationships, so highly stressed in neo-Confucian thought, was thus extended to include foreign lands within a similar hierarchy that culminated in the Chinese Son of Heaven. In "the Chinese view . . . the imperial government's foreign relations were merely an outward extension of its administration of China proper."[10] Foreign peoples who approached China seeking commercial or other relationships were perceived by the Chinese court—or at least described in court records—as "coming to be civilized." The formal presentation of "tribute" by these peoples, along with such ritual acts as the kowtow, comprised in Chinese eyes a foreign acknowledgment of the supreme virtue of the Son of Heaven, and the foreigners' own subordinate position in the hierarchy. Foreigners were required to go through these rituals, even if they sought only commerce; trade thus assumed the guise of tribute. Diplomatic and commercial partners with a military advantage could be accommodated as well, as long as China's appeasing payoffs could be treated as "gifts in return." As Fairbank described it, this idealized imperial cosmology as laid out in the Chinese classics more or less determined the form of Chinese relations with foreign peoples continuously until the late nineteenth century; the tribute rituals remained the sine qua non of diplomatic practice over that same period—this possible, of course, because of the essential changelessness of China prior to contact with the West ("change within tradition"). Moreover, Fairbank suggests, this Sinocentric worldview remained in force even when the ruling dynasty was not Chinese. This had to be so, otherwise the tribute system model would not explain the Qing dynasty's incompetence at diplomacy with the West in the nineteenth century. Thus the notion of "sinification" also plays a crucial role: because China spontaneously absorbed and culturally converted its conquerors, according to Fairbank, the Manchus, too, internalized the conceits of the tribute system and thus were unable to respond adequately to the arrival of European traders and emissaries on Chinese shores.

In this way, the master narrative of modern Chinese history precludes all possibility that the Qing might deviate from the worldview or the diplomatic and strategic practices of its predecessors. Because there is no real distinction in this account between "Qing" and "China," the Qing expansion into Inner Asia—an approach radically different from that of the later Ming—was a somewhat problematic issue for Fairbank, who at first tended to treat the Inner Asian subjects of the Qing as foreign. Following a bibliographic note in "On the Ch'ing Tribute System," for example, he and Ssu-yü Teng write: "This cursory survey reveals many lacunae in our knowledge of *Ch'ing foreign relations: Manchu administration in Central Asia;* Sino-Dutch relations in the seventeenth century; tributary relations with Siam, Laos, and Liu-ch'iu; the Chinese side of foreign trade in general" (my emphasis).[11]

Later, in the introduction to *The Chinese World Order*, Fairbank leaves the status of Qing Inner Asia ambiguous. Manchus, Mongols, Turkic peoples, and Tibetans do not appear on a table of "Ch'ing Tributaries as of 1818," although Fairbank's list of the practices that "constituted the tribute system" (granting of patents of appointment, official seals and noble ranks, use of the Ch'ing calendar, presentation of tribute memorials and local products, escort of envoys by official post, performance of the kowtow, receipt of imperial gifts in return, trade privileges at the frontier and in the capital) applies to the dynasty's Turkic officials in Xinjiang as well as it does to foreign rulers—indeed, even Han officials engaged in many of these practices. Fairbank does, however, include Inner Asians two pages later on a second table of "Aims and Means in China's Foreign Relations," where they are relegated to an "Inner Asian Zone"—*outside* the "Chinese Culture Area" occupied by Korea, Vietnam, the Ryukyu Islands, and Japan. This suggests, paradoxically, that the Inner Asians with whom the Qing imperial clan intermarried, worshiped, and hunted (among other interactions) were culturally more distant from the "center" than countries that merely sent embassies, or even than Japan, with whom the Qing had no official relations at all until the latter half of the nineteenth century.[12]

Fairbank recognizes a difficulty here when he points out that the "Sinocentric world order . . . was not coterminous with the Chinese culture area." Even though they were culturally non-Chinese, Inner Asians had to be included in the Chinese world order because of their military superiority. Moreover, in his "Aims and Means" table he indirectly acknowledges that Qing relations with Inner Asia involved something other than the tribute system; the table indicates that Qing foreign relations with Mongolia, Tibet, and Central Asia were conducted through some combination of military control, administrative control, cultural-ideological attraction, Tibetan Buddhist religious attraction, diplomatic manipulation, and/or pursuit of material interest. Of these types of relationships, only cultural and ideological attraction (which Fairbank glosses as *wen* and *de*) seems to fit within the tribute system model.[13]

Therefore, "A Preliminary Framework" leaves Qing Inner Asian areas in limbo: Though part of the Chinese world order, they are not tributaries; though not Chinese, they are not foreign either. Fairbank did not himself pursue the contradictions inherent in the attempt to fit Qing Inner Asia into his "comprehensive" model, despite the challenges raised in the same volume by David Farquhar's article on the influence of Mongol political culture on the

Qing regime and Joseph Fletcher's revelations of decidedly nontribute system style Ming and Qing relations with Central Asian states. Fairbank's interests, and those of many of his students, for the time being at least lay elsewhere: with the nineteenth-century impact of the West and "China's" response.

Paul Cohen's 1984 reflection on the state of American scholarship of China's recent past identified and celebrated what was then a relatively new trend away from research driven by the paradigms of impact/response and tradition/modernity. This trend, Cohen writes, is characterized by an attempt to move beyond exclusive focus on the advent of the West and, instead, to "center Chinese history in China." Among the scholars Cohen singles out for praise in this regard is G. William Skinner, whose regional systems approach, by substituting geographically and economically determined marketing systems for political units of analysis (counties, provinces), literally redrew the boundaries of modern Chinese history for many scholars.[14]

Without questioning the utility of Skinner's approach to much of China proper, it is worth noting another of Skinner's boundaries that has generally gone unremarked. In laying out his central-place theory and defining China's eight physiographic macroregions, Skinner restricts his field of inquiry to a unit he calls "agrarian China minus Manchuria," deliberately excluding Inner Asia. Skinner posits a ninth macroregion in Manchuria for the later nineteenth century, but excludes this region from his analysis of the relationship between urbanization and field administration because of the lateness of Han settlement in the northeast. Similarly, although Skinner's *Modern Chinese Society: An Analytical Bibliography* defines "modern China" as "the territory of the present People's Republic of China plus Taiwan, Hong Kong, and Macau, from 1644 to the present," thus including Inner Asian lands, by design it excludes works concerning "non-Han peoples, whether natives of China or aliens."[15]

These calculated omissions of territory and people should give us pause. Why are they made, and why are they so readily accepted? It is not so much that the millions of people labeled "minority nationalities" living in the P.R.C. ought to be represented in works purporting to encompass "Chinese society," although that is perhaps a legitimate claim. (If not in some sense "Chinese," what are such people?) Of greater concern is the way in which these boundary markers preclude inquiry into a range of important topics. For example, others have noted how Skinner's scheme leaves little room for consideration of interregional trade. This is doubly true of trade between China proper and Mongolia, Xinjiang, and Tibet, regions completely ignored by Skinner, although this commerce was of great cultural, political, and economic significance on frontier areas, as well as on communities in China proper that produced commodities, such as tea, silk, or rhubarb, destined for frontier markets or that specialized in moving goods and capital between Inner Asia and the Chinese heartland.

Another topic occluded by Skinner's model is that of ethnic interaction. In applying central-place theory to China, Skinner takes as his point of departure "an isotropic plain on which resources of all kinds are uniformly distributed."[16] He then suggests how the irregularities of actual geography modify this ideal case. Less explicit in the model, however, is his working assumption that the regional systems are populated by "Han" sharing a single "Chinese" culture (albeit one characterized by class and occupational cleavages, differential distribution across the hierarchy of central places, and considerable variation among "little-local traditions").[17] Yet variations in local cultural or ethnic makeup, just like deviations from uniform topography, might dictate modifications of the central-place model. For example, what happens to the periodicity of market days (which Skinner suggests fit within a ten-day cycle in "traditional Chinese society") where Han and Hui (Muslim) villages lay closely interspersed? Friday worship at mosques brought (and still brings) practicing Muslims to central places in large numbers once every *seven* days. One could well ask similar questions for regions where the agrarian was juxtaposed with pastoral or slash-and-burn economies and the ebb and flow of trade followed other rhythms.

Skinner's answer to ethnic difference is to point out that it lay primarily at the peripheries of regional systems and "the frontiers of the empire" (by which he means the internal borders of China proper with Qing Inner Asian territories as well as the southwestern and maritime frontiers). "Tribes of non-Han aborigines and pockets of incompletely sinicized groups" occupied such places along with "heterodox sodalities . . . religious sects . . . seditious secret societies . . . bands of bandits . . . [as well as] smugglers, outcasts, political exiles, sorcerers and other deviants."[18] Skinner here has adopted the perspective of the mandarinate, of course, and this suits his purposes in "Cities and the Hierarchy of Local Systems," which include demonstrating that Qing field administration categories in China proper took account of special strategic needs in such frontier regions. But when calling on Skinner's work in teaching or writing, it is important to remember that the frontier situation can be interpreted somewhat differently. Rather than argue that non-Han peoples, like "other deviants," are concentrated in regional peripheries and leave it at that, might we not consider that it is precisely the occupancy of core areas and adherence to state-sanctioned ecological, economic, and political forms that *defines* what is meant by "Chinese?"* Such a view allows for a more complex consideration of interactions on frontiers, what exactly distinguished political or religious deviancy from the ethnic difference implied by the phrase "incompletely sinicized groups"; and, indeed, what "sinicization" might entail and to what extent it was a reversable process.[19]

There is a more concrete problem with Skinner's analysis of Qing territorial administration: he discusses only one of several Qing systems, that employed in China proper. In fact, the Qing developed other means of administering areas where non-Han population predominated. These included the *tusi* in southern and western China, as well as the *jasak* and *beg* systems in Inner Asia (more about these systems below). Civilization did not taper off into chaos and lawlessness on all these frontiers, as Skinner implies; rather, in many areas, Chinese *junxian* administration (with the familiar territorial units of *xian, fu, zhou, ting,* and so forth, administered by magistrates) simply gave way to one of the other systems.

It is noteworthy, too, that Skinner defines "China" in different ways for different purposes. While he chooses "agrarian China" with or without Manchuria for studies of marketing, social structure, and urbanization, his bibliography of Chinese society requires a definition inclusive of Inner Asia, even while it excludes non-Han peoples. While it is easy to accept this inconsistency as arising from the different practical concerns of each project, it nonetheless illustrates a common tendency of post-war American scholarship to alternate unwittingly between a definition of "China" based on Ming territorial and ethnic boundaries and one based on those of the Qing empire (eventually recreated by the P.R.C.), without acknowledging that two very different quantities are involved and ignoring the process that led from one "China" to the other, along with all the ramifications of that change.

For all their importance, then, perspectives shaping the foundational work of Lattimore, Fairbank, and Skinner have contributed to a collective blindspot in the field of modern Chinese history not only toward Inner Asia, but toward the differences between Qing and China and the process by which one became the other. Similar tendencies could no doubt be traced in the work of other historians. As recent work by Pamela Crossley and Prasenjit Duara suggests, the source of these tendencies lies in the project of modern Chinese nationalism, which from its inception was plagued by contradictions inher-

---

* In Qing sources, the term used for such people seems more often to be the generic *min* ("populace") than the culturally and ethnically flavored *han.*

ent in the process of constructing a postimperial "Chinese" nation from the ruins of a non-Han dynastic polity. On the one hand, the cultural and territorial parameters of the late Ming, as defined by such figures as Gu Yanwu and Wang Fuzhi, inspired nineteenth- and twentieth-century Han activists opposing the Qing dynasty. On the other hand, the legacy of the Qing conquests was an empire of great geographical and ethnic diversity, twice the size of Ming China, whose Inner Asian territories, if not people, remained highly desirable additions to a new Chinese nation-state. Efforts to articulate an image of the postimperial nation were further complicated by the fact that early Han nationalists, including Sun Yat-sen and Liang Qichao, had like the Taipings before them exploited anti-Manchu racial animosity to stir up popular support for their cause. Although there were some, such as Zhang Binglin, who advocated abandonment of Inner Asian lands and the creation of a racially pure China within the old Ming boundaries, the leaders of the Republic and People's Republic have generally sought to retain—and justify retention of—the Manchu empire while renouncing the Manchus.[20] Besides recurrent military operations, this task has often involved ideological contortion and historical legerdemain—Chiang Kai-shek's assertion that Manchus, Mongols, Tibetans, and Muslims are descended from the same original stock as the Han and are thus true "Chinese" and the current P.R.C. contention that Xinjiang and Tibet have been "Chinese" since ancient times are just two examples.[21] These rationalizations are strained, perhaps, but have nevertheless been highly successful: for most Chinese today, the former Qing frontiers, and not the narrower boundaries of the Ming, make up the "natural" extent, or sacred space, of the Chinese nation.[22] Historians, too, in our readiness to neglect what was non-Chinese about the Qing, have followed the ideological contours of Chinese nationalism. We have uncritically mimicked the nationalist tendency to treat the Qing dynasty as Chinese in its successes and alien in its failures.

Toward a Qing-Centered History of the Qing

In his state-of-the-field essays, Paul Cohen noted that in addition to de-emphasizing Western impact and directing their attention away from maritime regions to the Chinese hinterland, growing numbers of American scholars were turning to the eighteenth century in search of the indigenous underpinnings of nineteenth-century history. This tendency has continued, aided in part by the increased accessibility of Qing archival records in both Beijing and Taiwan collections. Delving into the eighteenth century leaves a very different impression than preoccupation with the disaster-ridden nine-teenth: the high Qing was a confident, expansive, and, in many ways, well-run imperial power. Official documents illuminate in much greater detail than previously possible the quotidian concerns of the Kangxi, Yongzheng, and Qianlong courts and reveal a Manchu dynasty that had eliminated inter-nal challenges to its supremacy; successfully coopted Han elites to help run the government apparatus in China proper; established a swift and effective network of imperial communications and intelligence; implemented systems of tax collection, local control, and famine relief on a vast scale, sponsored monumental works of scholarship; eliminated nomadic military threats; and doubled the size of the empire. This is a far cry from Lord Macartney's rudderless man-of-war or Karl Marx's crumbling mummy.[23]

And yet, although recent studies have followed the trends that Cohen hoped would lead to "a China-centered history of China," scholars of the last dynasty are talking about "China," or even "the Chinese empire," less than they used to, preferring to discuss "the Qing" instead. Similarly, the old usage of "Chinese" as a primordial, fixed ethnic category has been shaken by new anthropological approaches that treat ethnicity not as an inherent trait but as a relational identity constructed in opposition to other groups, or in re-sponse to state policies.[24] Once modern Han-ness (itself not a monolithic or static category) is taken to be a quality defined even partially in relation to non-Han peoples and the Manchu state, it becomes impossible to continue entirely ignoring those non-Han peoples, or the Manchu-ness of the Qing.*

---

* There has been some debate over the concept of ethnicity and its utility (or lack thereof) in the field of early modern Chinese history. Most notably, Crossley has attempted to head off confusion by arguing that both the term's original sense (applying exclusively to politically marginialized groups) and its current "overstretched" popular and scholarly usage limit its applicability to China ("Thinking about Ethnicity"; see also "*Manzhou yuanliu kao*," p. 762, n. 2). However, unlike those scholars for whom the nature of ethnic identity itself is a main focus (see works by Crossley, Elliott, Gladney, and Lipman in the bibliography), for the most part in this book I am not as concerned with the content of ethnic identity—whether it is cultural or linguistic or racial or national and so on—as with the recognition and manipulation of different groups of subjects, however constituted, by the Qing empire in its efforts to control Xinjiang. In other words, I devote more attention to external, state-imposed categories than to the dynamics of individual identity. In de-scribing these categories in general terms, it is extremely convenient to have a single word for this sort of distinction. The term "ethnicity" in its most general sense, then, though it obscures the multifaceted and dynamic nature of identity formation as understood by anthropologists, is precisely what I need, stretchmarks and all.

In steering clear of debates over the nature of ethnicity in early modern China, how-ever, I do not mean to embrace the primordialist approach of current P.R.C. "nationalities"

Thus it is simply too imprecise to conflate Qing and China, as has so often been the practice. Most writers on the eighteenth century (in China as well as the United States) now carefully distinguish the Qing dynasty and empire (including Inner Asia), from China proper (*neidi*). In referring to historical personages, they often specify Han, Manchu, Mongol, and so forth where "Chinese" might have sufficed in the past. It could even be said that a new, Qing-centered history is emerging, an approach more sensitive to ethnic considerations and the Altaic origins of the Qing. This trend is suggested, to give just three prominent examples, by Beatrice Bartlett's *Monarchs and Ministers*, Philip Kuhn's *Soulstealers*, and James Polachek's *Inner Opium War*, all of which identify lines of Qing domestic political competition that approximate, if not exactly follow, Manchu-Han ethnic divisions. In so doing, these books transcend earlier assumptions of a monolithic "China." This new approach is represented most strongly, however, in the recent and forthcoming work of scholars who in one way or another take the nature of Qing imperium itself as their focus and address issues raised by the Inner Asian connections of the Qing. Many, following the lead of Joseph Fletcher, seek greater understanding of the dynasty in Inner Asian history and traditions and consult sources in Inner Asian languages. Most make ethnic or cultural difference an important concern of their work. All attempt to move beyond the Sinocentric model and other paradigms discussed above in order to refigure the historian's approach to the Qing and, by implication, to modern China.[25]

These new perspectives, then, provide the context for this study of Qing empire in Xinjiang. The themes of Qing-centered history will recur occasionally throughout this book, with, I hope, the lilt of a catchy melody rather than the whine of a grinding axe.

Qing Imperialism

China's recent past can be read as a palimpsest of imperialisms. The familiar history of Western and Japanese encroachment in China during the nineteenth and twentieth centuries forms the clearest, uppermost text. Below

---

policy, or to imply that Qing dynasts viewed "ethnicity" from perspectives at all similar to those of today's Western social and political discourse. The interplay of political, racial, cultural, national, caste, and other elements in Chinese and Inner Asian thinking about social difference is a fascinating and lively subject with an important and growing literature, to which readers are referred frequently in the notes below.

that, obscured by overwriting and erasures, is the story of Qing imperialism. When viewed in the right light, however, this story too is legible.

"Qing imperialism" is not a familiar formulation; the very application of the term "imperialist" to the Qing is controversial. Chinese scholars and lay-persons alike will be perturbed by it, since China's victimization by imperial-ist powers is a central tenet of historical accounts and nationalist ideology embraced by Chinese across the political spectrum. Non-Chinese scholars, too, may question the accuracy of the term with regard to the eighteenth- and nineteenth-century Qing, or doubt the utility of invoking such an in-flammatory concept.

The controversy arises mostly because we tend to associate imperialism exclusively with the rapid European expansion in the late nineteenth cen-tury. Most fully elaborated theories of imperialism, beginning with Hobson's in 1902, were developed to explain this particular historical episode. Most famously, Lenin argued that imperialism represented competition among the advanced capitalist countries of the West to divide the undeveloped world into spheres of influence for the export of capital in search of greater profits.[26] In this view, or its many variants, China emerges as *victim* of imperialism.

The exact extent and nature of imperialism in China, as thus defined, has sparked much debate,[27] but I do not deny that China suffered from it. Never-theless, the Qing was also itself an empire, and it is with Qing expansion that I am concerned here. While the modern Chinese term *diguozhuyi* seems en-tirely restricted, in Chinese understanding, to the Leninist sense, there are alternative meanings of "imperialism" available in English. Historians refer to "Roman imperialism," for example, although attempts to explain the Roman expansion in Marxist-Leninist terms have not been widely embraced.[28] Like-wise, "Mongol imperialism" is occasionally used. Imperialisms of these earlier epochs are generally referred to as "old," in contrast to the "new imperialism" practiced by Europe, the United States, and Japan in the formation of their overseas, economically oriented empires during the late nineteenth and early twentieth centuries.

Since the late 1970s, cultural historians and critics have begun reexamin-ing Western imperialism, focusing less on economic, political, and military aspects and more on the language and cultural productions used to "repre-sent" and control colonial societies. Edward Said's influential book *Oriental-ism* launched this trend, but, more recently, scholars (including Said himself) no longer view imperialism (or, "colonialism," the term now more widely used) from the Western side exclusively, but instead consider it a dialogue in which the voice of the colonized joins that of the colonizer. Lately, the "post-colonial" condition, too, has come under scrutiny.[29]

The student of Qing imperialism thus faces a terminological thicket here. "Old" and "new" imperialisms, theories by Hobson, Lenin, Schumpeter, Arendt, Eisenstadt, and others, not to mention analyses of colonialist, subaltern, and postcolonialist discourse—all compete for attention. One might sift through old social science and new cultural studies literatures for applicable models and parallels; however, there exists no consensus on which model best fits nineteenth-century European expansion, let alone other imperialisms at other times. Moreover, we still know relatively little about the actual workings of Qing empire in Inner Asia, and to embrace an existing theoretical model or become preoccupied with parallels from the West may well be premature, if not ultimately misleading.[30]

More seriously, there is a basic dissonance when applying all such concepts to the Qing case: though they differ greatly from each other and employ competing terminology, all involve an opposition between the European West and its colonial territories. To apply these concepts to seventeenth- through nineteenth-century China and Inner Asia, they would have to be radically refigured to include multiple players and two-way colonialist relationships. Manchus were the physical conquerors of China, to be sure, but were also themselves the objects of a cultural assault; moreover, Manchu ancestral lands were eventually colonized by Han Chinese. Mongols were simultaneously members of the Qing conquest elite ruling over China and victims of economic exploitation at the hands of Chinese merchants. Han Chinese were among the first to suffer from Qing imperialism, but later became its most vehement publicists and proud beneficiaries. Existing bilateral models are inadequate to encompass the Qing situation, which might be charted like this: An entity called Qing is in imperial command at the beginning of the story. Gradually, however, a cultural and political unit we call China usurps the controls and, after some near mishaps, by the mid–twentieth century sits securely in the driver's seat of what was formerly a Qing vehicle. No simplistic approach to "Chinese imperialism in Central Asia" could capture this dynamic.

Thus, though readers will note in the following chapters some resonances with the concerns of old imperialism, new imperialism, and postcolonial studies, my main goal is to comprehend the evolving Qing imperialism in Xinjiang on its own terms. I will therefore proceed to examine "Qing imperialism" without further apology or reference to existing definitions, confident in the belief that where there is an empire,[31] there must be imperialism—the dynamic set of motivations, ideologies, policies, and practices by which that empire is gained, maintained, and conceived. I will use "colonialism" in a more specific sense to refer to the actual establishment of Han migrant settlements in Xinjiang, both agricultural and commercial. Regretfully, my sources in this project—or at least my abilities in working with them—do not allow the Xinjiang subalterns much room to speak. This is thus a study from the perspective of the Manchu, Mongol, and Han imperialists of the Qing who wrote the documents and books on which the research is primarily based.

I have chosen to focus on two central aspects of the Qing enterprise in the far west: economic policy and ethnic policy. The fiscal demands of empire building and the commercial penetration of Turkic Xinjiang by Chinese merchants were complexly interrelated problems that underlay the entire course of Qing expansion in Xinjiang. How was empire in Xinjiang to be financed? How "Chinese" was that empire to be? Together, these questions (and their changing answers) informed the Qing discourse on empire in Xinjiang, and in the analysis and narrative that follows, I attempt to consider them together.

From Qing to China

A few pages above, I discussed how both the work of seminal historians of modern China and the tenets of Chinese nationalism itself conspire to obscure the significance of the Inner Asian elements of the Qing and the process by which a new notion of China arose from the ruins of that Inner Asian empire. My point is that we cannot take the meaning of "China" for granted. Like any modern nation-state, China has assumed its current sense and shape only after a process of invention, a process Benedict Anderson has memorably called "stretching the short, tight, skin of the nation over the gigantic body of the empire."[32] In China, this process was an extended one, the onset of which predates by decades, if not longer, the revolution that toppled the last imperial dynasty. To see this clearly, think of the different answers a scholar in the late Ming and an educated Chinese at the end of the twentieth century would give to the questions, "Where is China?" and "Who are the Chinese?" We can readily guess how each would respond: The Ming scholar would most likely exclude the lands and peoples of Inner Asia, and today's Chinese include them (along with Taiwan, Hong Kong, and perhaps even overseas Chinese communities). These replies mark either end of the process that has created the ethnically and geographically diverse China of today.

But how would Qi Yunshi have responded to these questions in 1805? Did not his bemusement and ambivalence at passing through the Jiayu Guan arise from precisely these same concerns, from his difficulty in reconciling the sense of "China" bequeathed him by his knowledge of history and poetry with the expansive Qing reality spread out before him? Standing there outside the Pass, Qi Yunshi confronted a world reshaped by Qing imperialism.

This study argues that the notion of China pertaining today did not arise in 1912, or even in the late nineteenth century, but was invented in the course of a gradual accommodation by Han Chinese since the mid-Qing to the idea of a Greater China with the physical and ethnic contours of the Qing Empire. This accommodation was possible because Han Chinese were not only the objects of Qing imperialism. They were also, increasingly through the late eighteenth and nineteenth centuries, complicit in it as traders, homesteaders, farmers, prospectors, jade carvers, soldiers, militia, policemen, spies, historians, geographers, statecraft pundits, and eventually generals, administrators, and governors. Thus, as we investigate the workings of Qing imperialism in the Western Regions, we also learn something of how Qing became China.

CHAPTER 1

Landmarks

The region lies beyond Suzhou and Jiayu Guan, and borders to the
southeast on Suzhou, to the northeast with Khalkha, to the west with
the Congling Mountains, to the north with Russia, and to the south
with Tibet. It is 20,000 *li* in circumference. Zunghars live to the north
of the Tianshan. . . . To the south of the Tianshan reside the Muslim
tribes. . . . The Thirty-six Kingdoms referred to in the *Han shu* were all
west of the Xiongnu and south of the Wusun. To the north and south of
the Thirty-six Kingdoms were great mountains; between them, a river.
To the east, the kingdoms bordered Han, communicating via narrow
passes at Yumen and Yangguan. To the west, they extended up to the
Congling Mountains. Today, the Tianshan range extends unbroken
from Zhenxi prefecture westward to Yili, over 3,000 *li*. These are the
"North Mountains" of the *Han shu*. . . . The mountains to the west of
Kashgar and Yarkand are the old "Congling" range. From beyond the
Jiayu Guan, extending west to the Congling, lie the so-called "South
Mountains." And the central river is Lop Nor. . . . The various cities
of today's Muslim Region are thus those same cities of the Thirty-
six Kingdoms in the ancient Western Regions. This is certain without
doubt. And the Zunghar barbarians lived north of the Tianshan, in the
land of the Wusun. Their eastern frontier was Xiongnu territory.

(Qinding) huangyu Xiyu tuzhi 1 (tukao): 9b-11a

The "Western Regions" (*Xiyu*) is an ancient term for what came to be known
increasingly after the Qing conquest in 1759 as the New Dominion (Ch. Xinjiang; Ma. ice toktobuha jecen).[1] The scholars who wrote the first Qing imperial gazetteer of this newly conquered territory preferred the older term,
because for them the Western Regions landscape was strewn with historical as well as geographical landmarks. In fact, in passages like the one above,
the history and geography are virtually indistinguishable, as the writers shift
seamlessly from physical description of the land in their own time into a
"rectification" of Qing names with those of the illustrious past. The Han and

Tang dynasty points of reference loomed as large for these practitioners of evidential scholarship (*kaozheng*) as did mere topography.

Still, there would be no empire without territory, and imperial maintenance requires concrete climatological, orological, and hydrological knowledge. What was the Qing faced with in its New Dominion?

The Lay of the Land

The Western Regions that Qing Gaozong, the Qianlong emperor, added to his empire consist of two vast basins surrounded and divided by towering mountain chains and comprise an area of 1,646,800 square kilometers. (Despite some encroachment by Russia in the nineteenth century, Xinjiang today remains larger than Alaska and over three times the size of France.) The basin and range structure of the area, which is duplicated by the Himalayas, Tibetan plateau, and Kunlun range to the south, is the product of tectonic activity that has turned regions periodically covered by ocean during Paleozoic times (600–230 million years ago) into landlocked deserts. Most recently, the uplift of the Tibetan plateau and penetration of the Indian continental mass into Asia ongoing since the Tertiary (65 to 2 million years ago) has cast a rain shadow that is responsible for the extreme aridity of Xinjiang today. The same geological processes that resulted in China's southeastward incline and determined the drainages of the Yellow, Yangzi, Mekong, and other great Asian rivers thus left Xinjiang, for the most part, high and dry.[2]

Zungharia, the triangular, northern part of Xinjiang, known to the Qing as the Zunghar region (*zhunbu*) or Northern March (*Tianshan beilu*), is separated from Mongolia on the east by the Altai mountains and from southern Xinjiang by the Tianshan range. To the west, communications with what was in mid-Qing times the Kazakh transhumance (now the Republic of Kazakhstan) were relatively unimpeded. Chinese scholars today claim that Qing territory in Zungharia extended westward along the fertile Yili River valley as far as Lake Balkash; however, these frontiers, while periodically patrolled in the eighteenth century, were never precisely demarcated.[3] (The border with Kazakhstan now lies not far west of the city of Huocheng, formerly Huiyuan, the headquarters of Xinjiang's military government before 1884.)

Although at its center the Zungharian Basin contains large tracts of semifixed dunes and scrubland good only as winter pasture for animals, agriculture can be very successful in river valleys and along the foot of the mountain ranges, where mountain run-off is available.[4] The Zunghar khanate exploited

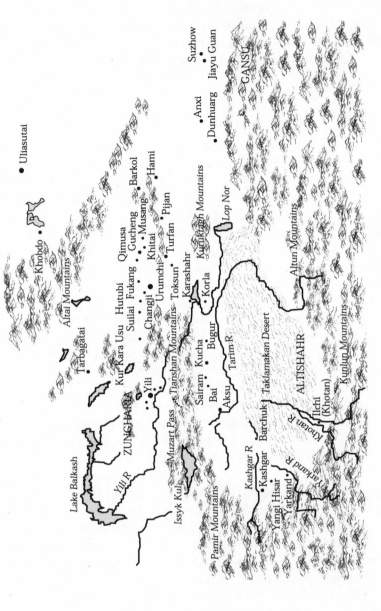

Map 1. Xinjiang in the Qing period (c. 1820).

this potential by means of forced resettlement of farmers from the south, and the Qing likewise made development of Zungharian agriculture a key element in its imperial strategy. Zungharia's prime agricultural lands, where the dynasty established its most fruitful colonies in the first years after the conquest, lay along the valley of the westward-flowing Yili river. Grain grown here by Han Green Standard soldiers and resettled East Turkestanis supported the Manchu garrisons and nomadic troops stationed in the Yili area.

Southern Xinjiang is an inland basin of still greater dimensions, defined by the Tianshan on the north, the Pamirs to the west, Kunlun and Altun mountains to the south, and the (somewhat lower) Kuruktagh range to the east. This region is referred to in Qing sources generally as *Huibu* (Muslim tribes or region), *Huijiang* (Muslim frontier), or the Southern March (*Tianshan nanlu*). It is also known variously in European and Central Asian sources as the Tarim Basin (for the river that encircles and empties into it), Chinese Turkestan, Bukharia, Little Bukharia, Kashgaria, and East Turkestan. Another term is "Altishahr," a Turki (Uyghur) word meaning "six cities," although the Qing identified eight principal cities and further subdivided the region into "the four western cities" (Khotan, Yarkand, Yangi Hisar, Kashgar) and "the four eastern cities" (Aksu, Ush [Ush Turfan in some sources], Kucha, Karashahr).

The Taklamakan Desert, at the center of the Tarim Basin, is one of the most forbidding places on earth. The surrounding mountains, in many places over 5,000 meters high, block moisture-bearing air currents and allow little rain to reach the interior. (Mean annual precipitation is less than 17 mm.) Irrigated agriculture is possible, however, in Altishahr's river valleys and piedmont zones. Poplar groves, hearty grasses, and tamarisk mounds colonize the desert out to several miles around oases and river beds; further into the Taklamakan, however, where no vegetation stabilizes the sand, loose dunes of 100 to 300 meters in height shift across the desert. In spring and summer, the severe heat is accompanied by frequent sandstorms, known in Turki as *qara boran*, "black winds." It was while trying to cross such deep desert terrain north of Khotan that the Swedish adventurer Sven Hedin nearly died in the spring of 1895, and all but one of his East Turkestani companions perished. Marco Polo reports that travelers in the Lop Desert, at the eastern end of the Tarim Basin, were often lured astray by ghostly voices and would erect signs before going to sleep at night to remind them which direction to travel in the morning.[5]

The Tarim is an entirely inland drainage. The waters of the Aksu and Kongque (Kongqi) Rivers flow south from the Tianshan highlands; the Kashgar (Kizil) and Yarkand Rivers run northeastward; and the Khotan, Keriya, and Cherchen Rivers flow northward from the Pamir and Kunlun ranges into the Taklamakan. In spring flood, some of these rivers may join the Tarim system, which historically emptied into the eastern corner of the basin. Between the first century B.C. and the early fourth century A.D., the Tarim and Kongque river system fed the terminal lake known as Lop Nor. Around A.D. 330, these rivers shifted their channels southeastward and created a new lake, Qara Qoshun, contributing to the disappearance of the Loulan city-state and posing an intriguing problem for such nineteenth- and twentieth-century explorers and geographers as N. M. Przhevalskii, Sven Hedin, and Ellsworth Huntington, who speculated on Lop Nor's "wandering." In 1921, human intervention caused the Tarim-Kongque system to flow once more into Lop Nor, creating a salt lake and marsh of 2,400 square kilometers. Isolated communities of farmers and fishermen still lived by the lake up to the mid–twentieth century, but in recent decades these Lopliks have been dislocated, not only by Chinese nuclear testing in the area but by increasing desertification. The continuous diversion of the Tarim Basin's waters since the Qing initiated large-scale agricultural development of southern Xinjiang in the nineteenth century has shortened river courses; dramatically increased water use since the 1950s resulted in the total desiccation of Lop Nor and other desert lakes, with the concomitant regional extinction of tigers, wolves, boars, and other fauna. (The Lop Region remains the last refuge of the wild camel.) Since 1972, the Tarim has flowed no further than the artificial Daxihaizi Reservoir, which lies 120 kilometers south of Korla and twice that distance from the now dry bed of Lop Nor.[6] The Qing imperial geographers' conflation of the Tarim River with Lop Nor, evident in the quotation at the head of this chapter, would not be possible today.

The Eastern March (*Tianshan donglu*), vaguely defined as the region east of Urumchi and west of Jiayu Guan, is itself bisected by the Tianshan, and some sources treat the cities of Urumchi, Gucheng, Khitai, and Barkol as part of the Northern March; indeed, geographically they lie in Zungharia. Turfan, Pijan, and Hami, on the other hand, lie in the Turfan depression, a stark stretch of cobble desert and rocky passes. This easternmost region, locally known before the Qing conquest as Uyghuristan, is 500 feet below sea level at its lowest point. Hot weather and a long growing season make raising fruit and long-staple cotton here a particularly productive enterprise, though intensive irrigation is essential (accomplished around Turfan with underground aqueducts called *karez*).[7] Melons, fruit jams, and raisins were among the "local products" regularly dispatched from the Eastern march to the Qing capital as tribute. Today, Turfan produces sweet wines, and Hami's eponymous melons are so famous as to have disrupted truck traffic throughout northwest

China when shipped by the ton to Beijing for the Asian Games in the autumn of 1990.

During the Qing, Zungharia communicated with China proper via the city of Gucheng and Inner Mongolia, and with southern Xinjiang via two principal passes. The city of Urumchi lies in the largest of these, a wide gap in the Tianshan range just west of the Boghda peak. Farther west, the high Muzart Pass through the Tianshan north of Bai linked the Yili region with Aksu and the Tarim Basin. It was through this pass that Manchu and Mongol troops, or bannermen, marched on campaigns to relieve besieged cities in southern Xinjiang. Travelers from China to Altishahr likewise came from Mongolia via Gucheng or along the Gansu corridor, passing through the Jiayu Guan, which the Qing maintained as a checkpoint. Central Asians reached Altishahr from passes in the Pamirs and the Kunlun Mountains above Kashgar and Yarkand. Because the Taklamakan was nearly impassible, in Qing times most official, military, and commercial traffic followed the "road system that ran around the rim of the Taklamakan like a loop of string, on which the oases hung like beads."[8]

The Historical Terrain

The efforts of the Han and Tang dynasties to extend Chinese power into Central Asia were the historical milestones against which the Manchu Qianlong emperor measured his own progress. From his point of view, his conquests compared favorably with the expensive, ultimately frustrated endeavors of both earlier dynasties.

Despite Zhang Qian's two famous journeys in search of Central Asian allies against the Xiongnu (c. 138–126 and c. 115 B.C.), and Han Wudi's spectacular victory in Ferghana (Dayuan) in 101 B.C., the Han dynasty's primary efforts in the Western Regions were focused closer to home, in what is now the western end of the Gansu Panhandle (which the Han colonized with Chinese settlers and defended with walls out to Yumen Guan and Yang Guan) and in the area around Hami (Yiwu) and Turfan (Jiaohe), which commanded Xiongnu access to the Tarim Basin. It was believed that establishing control over the Turfan depression and projecting influence further west could "break the right arm of the Xiongnu." By around 60 B.C. the Han had accomplished this, with agricultural garrisons in Bugur (Luntai), Korla (Juli), Turfan (Cheshi), and at Miran and Loulan in the southeastern Tarim Basin. The western Tarim Basin city-states, too, had by this time entered into diplomatic relations with the Han, based on exchange of gifts, dispatch of hostages to the Han court, support of Han outposts, and acceptance of the authority of the protector-general, the Han military official based near modern Korla. In return, they received trade privileges, financial aid, credentials of rule, and protection against the Xiongnu. Han soldiers established military agricultural colonies in the Hami and Turfan regions, near modern Karashahr and Bugur, as well as in Miran in the southern Tarim. The Han position in the Western Regions was tenuous, however, and during the Wang Mang interregnum (A.D. 8–23), the Xiongnu retook Turfan and reasserted their influence in the area.

Monarchs of the Later (Eastern) Han balked at the great costs of administering, defending, and colonizing territory so far from China proper, and at the financial aid (almost 75 million strings of cash after A.D. 73) demanded by the Tarim city-states. They thus fell into a pattern of advance followed by retreat from the Western Regions. Although the Han recaptured Turfan from the Xiongnu in 74, reestablishing military colonies and the protectorate-general, the dynasty withdrew again three years later following a Xiongnu attack. Ban Chao consolidated Han rule in the region during his tenure as protector-general (91–101) but the court again abolished the protector-generalship in 107 and once more relinquished its forward position in Central Asia. Although Han relations with the states of the Western Regions were reestablished in 123, the office of protector-general was not restored, and the Han court thereafter maintained only limited influence in the west.[9]

The Tang presence in Central Asia surpassed that of the Han insofar as it extended direct colonial rule over the Tarim Basin states and Zungharia and projected military influence more widely, into the area of modern Afghanistan, the Pamirs, and Ferghana. The stage for this expansion was set by Emperor Taizong's destruction of the khanate of the Eastern Turks (630) and the break-up of the Western Turk confederation. In the year 640, Karakhoja (Gaochang), a city-state in the Turfan area ruled for a century and a half by a Chinese or a Chinese-influenced house, was incorporated within the Tang empire as Xizhou. By 648, Tang armies under command of a Turkic general had subdued Karashahr and Kucha; the other Tarim cities submitted at this time and by 649 the local rulers of the "Pacified West" (Anxi) were all under the jurisdiction of a Tang protector-general based in Kucha. Although Tang control over Central Asia was frequently challenged and even interrupted by Tibet[10] and the Western Turks during the next few decades, generals serving the Tang emperor Gaozong (649–83) established further protectorates in Zungharia and beyond the Pamirs to Ferghana and the valley of the Oxus, extending Tang influence up to the borders of Persia. By the 680s, the dynasty maintained permanent border garrison armies in its Central Asian territories, and by the 730s the Tang further consolidated its control over the Tarim Basin and Zungharia with the creation of military governorships and garrison forces of 20,000 in each region. These armies grew grain in agricultural colonies and were financed by transit taxes levied on the merchants who plied the trade routes between China and Central Asia. In 750 the Tang general Gao Xianzhi (a Korean) was poised for further conquests in the west from a base in the Yili River valley, but a defeat by the Arabs near Talas the following year marked the watershed of Tang fortunes in Central Asia. Emperor Xuanzong's withdrawal of the main garrison forces from the northwest during the An Lushan rebellion (755–63) marked the end of Tang influence in the Tarim Basin and Zungharia.[11]

MANCHUS AND ZUNGHARS

As the Han had their Xiongnu and the Tang their Turks, the early Qing frontiers were troubled by the Zunghars. The Qing conquest of Zungharia and Altishahr arose from the dynasty's response to that threat. The Zunghars were a confederation of Oirat (Ch. Wala, Weilate, Elute)* tribal groups; "Oirat" is a general term for the non-Chinggisid (their leaders not descended from Chinggis Khan), western Mongol groups who generally pastured west of the Altai Mountains. From late Ming times, the Oirat are conventionally understood to have comprised four principal tribes: the Choros, Torghut, Dörböt, and Khoshuut. The ruling clans of the Choros and Dörböt tribes traced their descent from Esen, the self-proclaimed Mongol Khan who had threatened China and taken the Ming Zhengtong emperor captive in 1449. As the Choros became stronger in the early seventeenth century, it absorbed many of the Dörböt as well as another group, the Khoit; the resulting confederation came to be called the Zunghar, or "left hand," Khanate. Other Oirats were forced to relocate: from the early 1600s through the 1630s, the Torghuts and some Dörböts migrated through Kazakh country to the Volga river, where they became known as Kalmuks.[12] Around the same time, the Khoshuut moved to Kokonor (Ch. Qinghai; Amdo in Tibetan) and Kham (eastern Tibet). Meanwhile, back in Zungharia, by the 1630s the Zunghars had built a capital city; they enjoyed the services of craftsmen and settled

---

* In English, the name is often spelled Eleuth, Ölöd, Oelot, and so forth. Zunghar appears as Junghar, Dzunghar, Jegün Ḡar, and other variations.

farmers; they recorded religious and secular literature in a script modified from Mongolian to suit the Oirat phonetic system; and they had begun to assert themselves geopolitically, extracting tribute from Central Asian cities, concluding agreements with Russia, and rendering assistance to the Dalai Lama in Tibet. In 1640, the Zunghar Khan Ba'atur Khongtaiji convened a great assembly of western and eastern Mongols that composed a legal code and temporarily united the Oirat tribes with the Khalkhas of Outer Mongolia and the Kalmuks of the Volga under the banner of the dGe-lugs-pa (the so-called "yellow") school of Tibetan Buddhism. This early act epitomizes the dangers the Zunghars would pose to the Qing for more than a century: the Oirat confederation might have united peoples and lands in Tibet, Qinghai, Zungharia, and northern Mongolia into a pan-Buddhist, pan-Mongol front against a Manchu dynasty in China. The Qing was also concerned about the potential for a Zunghar-Russian alliance. The course of Inner Asian war and politics until the mid–eighteenth century was shaped by these threats and the Qing response to them.

The fate of Eastern Turkestan, too, hung on the Qing-Zunghar rivalry. In the oases of the Tarim Basin, the influence of the Moghul rulers, descendants of Chinggis (Genghis) Khan's son Chaghadai, had been waning since the late sixteenth century. In their place, rival branches of a Central Asian Naqshbandī Sufi brotherhood descended from Makhdūm-i A'zam (whence their epithet, Makhdūmzāda) enjoyed great prestige in Altishahr's religious affairs and increasingly in secular matters as well. Until the middle of the seventeenth century the Isḥāqiyya (also known as "Black Mountain" or "Black Hat") branch of this lineage was supreme; thereafter, however, a branch under the leadership of Khoja Āfāq (the Āfāqiyya, "White Mountain," or "White Hat") arose to challenge their supremacy. When driven into exile in Tibet by the Isḥāqiyya, Khoja Āfāq appealed to the Fifth Dalai Lama for help. The Dalai Lama called on the Zunghar khan, Galdan, who as a youth had trained in Lhasa to be a lama. In 1678 the Zunghars invaded Altishahr, and by the following year had seized control of Turfan, Hami, and the Tarim oases. Serving the Zunghars as local governors, the Āfāqī Makhdūmzādas extracted tax revenues for their nomadic overlords.[13]

Galdan moved aggressively in the east as well. Taking advantage of a feud between the Khalkha Jasaghtu and Tüshiyetü khans, and with political backing from Lhasa, in 1687–88 he invaded northern Mongolia, pressing as far as the Kerulen River and driving the Khalkhas to seek refuge with the Qing. A series of steppe campaigns between 1690 and 1697, however, including two in which the Kangxi emperor personally participated, resulted in the death of Galdan and a setback for Zunghar aspirations in Mongolia. Not least of the

Qing accomplishments during this period was the attachment of the Khal-khas, and northern Mongolia, to the empire.

The establishment of Qing bases in Hami and Khobdo seemingly confined the Zunghars beyond the Altai; however, a disastrous Qing foray in 1731, during the Yongzheng reign, allowed the Zunghars once again to overrun Mongolia temporarily before being pushed back by Qing and Khalkha forces. The two powers reached a truce in 1739, the fourth year of the Qianlong reign.

Qing interaction with the Zunghars over the next decade was primarily commercial, not military, but even this proved exasperating to the Manchu court. The dynasty allowed periodic Zunghar trade missions to Beijing and Suzhou (modern Jiuquan, Gansu).* The Zunghars violated virtually every restriction by which the Qing attempted to regulate this trade, arriving in off-years, bringing too many merchants (including Central Asians) in their delegations, and exceeding quotas on permitted quantities of goods. When the private merchants from Gansu and Shaanxi whom the Qing had ordered to handle the trade were bankrupted by these mandated exchanges of their silks, tea, and rhubarb for Zunghar livestock, hides, raisins, sal ammoniac, and antelope horn, the government was forced to step in to subsidize the trade and warehouse the Zunghar products for which the market was glutted. The Zunghars also demanded that the Qing finance "tea-brewing" (*aocha*) pilgrimages to Tibet in 1741, 1743, and 1746, thinly disguised trading trips for which the dynasty was forced to provide military escort, livestock, rafts for river crossings, and up to 300,000 taels to handle exigencies along the way.[14]

THE CONQUEST OF ZUNGHARIA

Internecine strife following the death of the khan Galdan Tseren in 1745 re-sulted in the emergence of Dawachi as khan, but in the process fractured the Zunghar confederation. When the Qianlong emperor prepared a new cam-paign against the Zunghars in 1754, many Zunghar groups defected to the Qing, including Amursana, a Khoit chieftain and former ally of Dawachi. The Qianlong emperor, Gaozong, put these Oirat defectors in the vanguard of an army of 20,000 Manchu, Solon, Chahar, Khalkha, other Mongol, and Han troops. Under command of Bandi and Amursana, they marched easily into Zungharia the following year, taking Kulja (Yili) without a fight. Dawachi was captured alive after escaping to Altishahr and was sent back to Beijing for a lavish ceremony in which he was presented to the emperor. Gaozong, in a show of indulgence to a steppe noble, made him a prince and installed him

---

* To avoid confusion, I will refer to the Gansu city as "Suzhou" and the city in Jiangsu province by the old postal name, "Soochow."

in a mansion in the capital. Flushed with this easy success, the emperor then gloated publicly, "It was truly the time to seize the opportunity, so I ordered the attack on two fronts. But [some] people have grown overly accustomed to peace, and while I faced many fearful naysayers, upright men eager to step forward amounted to hardly one or two in a hundred." Despite the misgivings of skeptics, he pointed out, in the end "the military expenses were only 10 to 20 percent what they have been in the past!"[15] Then, in a pattern of retrenchment following victory that the dynasty would repeat later, Gaozong withdrew most of the Qing forces from Zungharia, leaving only five hundred Chahar and Khalkha troops under Bandi's command in Yili.

Gaozong planned to reestablish the four Oirat tribes in the region, each under its own khan. Amursana would thus have become khan of the Khoits; however, he communicated to Beijing his desire to be recognized as khan of all the Oirats, and even began using an old chop of the Zunghar khan Dawachi's instead of Beijing's formal seal that identified him as a Qing general. Gaozong was furious, and on Bandi's suggestion ordered Amursana to Rehe (Jehol, today's Chengde) for an audience in the ninth month of 1755. Amursana eluded his escort, however, and soon thereafter his followers attacked the small Qing force in Zungharia. Yong-chang, in command of over 5,000 men in the Urumchi area, was afraid to advance to Bandi's aid and instead retreated to Barkol. Bandi and the Yili garrison force were killed.

In 1756 Qing armies again moved on Zungharia, but the campaign was ill-coordinated and plagued by poor intelligence. Amursana escaped to the Kazakhs, who hid him from Qing search parties. Later in the year, when the four tribes of the Oirats rose en masse, Amursana returned and, as the new Zunghar khan, retook Yili and forced the Qing general Zhao-hui and 1,500 Qing soldiers to flee southward; after a series of engagements and a twelve-day siege at Urumchi, Zhao-hui and his 500 surviving soldiers escaped to safety at Barkol. The Qing organized more forces, and Gaozong authorized mass slaughter of the Oirats. This Qing retaliation in 1757, combined with a smallpox epidemic, brought about the near extermination of those Oirats (primarily the Khoits and Choros) who had sided with Amursana. Amursana himself died of the disease in Siberia.[16]

THE BATTLE OF BLACKWATER CAMP

The collapse of the Zunghar khanate left a power vacuum in Altishahr. In 1755, Bandi had freed the brothers Khoja Jihān and Burhān ad-Dīn, Āfāqī Khoja brothers whom the Zunghars had held hostage in Yili. The two returned to East Turkestan, where the Qing hoped they would rule as loyal tributaries. Calculating that the Qing had neither the resources nor the will for another distant campaign so soon after the Zungharian wars, however, the Khojas defied Qing authority and killed a Qing envoy. Gaozong then ordered the conquest of Altishahr, though in this theater, too, the Qing campaign suffered from incompetence in the field and the emperor's anxiousness to declare victory and retreat.

In 1758, a Qing army under Yarhašan besieged Kucha, but allowed the "elder and younger Khojas" (as the brothers were known) to slip out of the city. Zhao-hui then advanced with his men from Barkol in pursuit of Khoja Jihān and Burhān ad-Dīn. Neither Aksu nor Ush would take in the Khojas, who next retreated to Yarkand and Kashgar to prepare a defense. Aksu, Khotan, and Ush surrendered peacefully to the Qing, and a Kirghiz chief in the latter city reported to the Qing forces that Khoja Jihān had only 3,000 bedraggled followers left, who were abandoning their weapons and slaughtering their horses and camels as they fled. On this news, the emperor decided that Altishahr could be easily (and cheaply) pacified, and after dispatching a small number of Chahar and Solon reinforcements to join Zhao-hui in Aksu, he instructed Fu-de (then in Zungharia) to camp with the main force in Pijan and Turfan and await word from Zhao-hui. Gaozong also informed Che-bu-deng-zha-bu, who had been charged with transferring grain from Urumchi to Kucha to support a lengthy Qing campaign, that he could cancel that operation and take his Chahar troops off to pasture their animals and rest. As Zhao-hui advanced toward Yarkand in the fall of 1758, therefore, his rear guard and supply lines were hundreds of kilometers behind him. After losing some men in a landslide and leaving others to guard the key crossroads at Barchuk, Zhao-hui approached Yarkand with just over 4,000 infantry and cavalry, their horses exhausted after the long desert journey. Since this number was insufficient to besiege the large city of Yarkand, he memorialized for reinforcements. Only on receipt of this dispatch did the emperor command Fu-de's main force to proceed immediately to Yarkand.

Zhao-hui's small army made camp in the tenth month on a forested knoll on the south side of the Yarkand river (locally known as the Blackwater, or Qarasu). Zhao-hui did not know it yet, but together Burhān ad-Dīn and Khoja Jihān still commanded 20,000 men-at-arms, both cavalry and foot soldiers, and this force was lying in wait in the mountains south of the city. The Khojas sprung their trap just as Zhao-hui led a detachment across the river to search for food. Ambushed in midstream, the Qing force was thrown into confusion and only succeeded in retreating to the Blackwater Camp after nightfall; there they were besieged.

Though his predicament had been avoidable and he must have recalled Bandi's fate more than once, Zhao-hui was at least lucky in his choice of the

Figure 1.   The raising of the siege at Blackwater Camp (*Heishuiying zhi zhan*).
Copperplate engraving after a drawing by Giuseppe Castiglione; part of a series of
sixteen engravings on scenes of the Qianlong emperor's conquests commissioned by
Gaozong and executed in France. Photograph courtesy of Compagnie de la Chine et
des Indes, Paris.

Blackwater campsite: while digging earthworks, Qing troops came upon the
Khojas' caches of grain; water was available from the river and from wells;
and as they cut trees for fuel and defense works, we are told, they added to
their supply of ammunition—so heavy was the rain of projectiles from the
East Turkestanis that the trees were full of shot (see Figure 1).[17]

After more than three months, Qing generals Fu-de and Šuhede relieved
Zhao-hui. East Turkestani resistance crumbled soon thereafter, and the Qing
took Kashgar in early 1759. The Khoja brothers fled to Badakhshan (north-
eastern Afghanistan) but were betrayed and executed by the Badakhshani
sultan, who sent their heads to Fu-de. Other Makhdūmzāda descendants received asylum in Kokand, across the Pamirs from Kashgar.[18]

High Qing Xinjiang

The Qing put Altishahr and Zungharia under a single military governor
(*jiangjun*), based in Yili, who was in charge of the garrison forces stationed in
Xinjiang cities and of the Mongol and Manchu tribal peoples raising livestock
on Zungharian pastures. The cities of the Tarim were administered by superintendents (*banshi dachen*) who answered to a councillor (*canzan dachen*) in

Kashgar or Yarkand as well as to the military governor. Other councillors served in Yili and Tarbagatai. These high officials (Ch. *dachen*; Ma. *amban*) were primarily concerned with banner affairs and defense in their jurisdictions, and during the first century of Qing rule in Xinjiang these positions were filled almost exclusively by Manchu or Mongol bannermen, and in a very few cases by a *Hanjun* (Han martial) or an East Turkestani. A separate, lower-ranked, military chain of command handled affairs of the Han Green Standard troops stationed in Xinjiang cities and also governed any Chinese* civilians in the Northern and Southern Marches, where no civil government for Chinese existed. The tasks of civil government for the Muslim and Turki-speaking natives of Altishahr fell to East Turkestani officials called *begs*, whom the Qing appointed to administer the Turki-speaking population.† In each city a panoply of beg officials handled such matters as grain tax collection, corvée supervision, and adjudication of civil disputes. Chief among these native functionaries were the hakim begs, classified as third rank in the larger cities and fourth rank elsewhere, who received cash stipends from the Qing in addition to revenues from lands granted them by the dynasty.[19]

The administration of the Eastern March was somewhat different. A vice banner commander-in-chief (*fu dutong*; later upgraded to banner commander-in-chief, *dutong*) commanded the garrison forces in Urumchi, but as the local Han population increased, districts (*xian*) and sub-prefectures (*zhou*) were created, and magistrates like those in China proper were appointed to handle civil affairs.[20] For some purposes these officials fell under the jurisdiction of the Shaanxi-Gansu governor-general. The *jasak* system pertained in Hami and Turfan, as well as among the Torghut and Khoshuut peoples settled near Karashahr. Jasaks, hereditary rulers with princely titles granted by the Qing, ruled over their peoples in these regions, subject to inspection by Qing military officials.[21]

For the most part, the Qing administrative system in Xinjiang retained its original form until the loss of Qing control over the territory in 1864. What changes there were the Qing implemented in response to incidents of unrest or invasion, with which Xinjiang's history abounds.

---

* I use the term "Chinese" below to indicate both Han and Chinese-speaking Muslims (Tungans or Hanhui, now known as Hui). See the discussion of Qing ethnic terminology in Chapter 6.

† A Qing census published in 1818 gives the following numbers of East Turkestani households in Xinjiang cities: Kashgar, 15,700; Yarkand, 18,341; Khotan area, 15,931; Ush, 810; Aksu City, 8,424; Sairam, 1,049; Bai, 593; Korla, 670; Bugur, 770; Kucha, 946; Shaya'er, 473; Yili, 60; total, 63,767 (Tuo-jin et al. [*Qinding*] *Da Qing huidan shili*, Jiaqing edition, 742: 11a–12a).

After the initial conquest (1757–59) and the Ush uprising (1765; discussed in Chapter 4), Xinjiang enjoyed the relative tranquility of *pax Manjurica* for about 60 years. In the 1810s, however, problems arose on the western frontier. By this time, many Muslims of Altishahr had become disaffected due to the excesses of rule by begs backed with Qing authority; opportunistic Kirghiz nomad groups made themselves available to support anti-Qing actions; and the khanate of Kokand began to assert itself in hopes of gaining special trade privileges in western Altishahr. Non-Chinese sources attest that the Qing agreed to pay Kokand an annual tribute to hold in check the khoja descendents, especially Jahāngīr (1790–1828), grandson of Burhān ad-Dīn. Despite this, Jahāngīr either escaped or was released and declared holy war on the Qing occupiers in East Turkestan, staging raids in 1820 and 1824–25 with the aid of Āfāqī Kirghiz tribesmen from the Pamirs.[22] In a 1826 attack, Jahāngīr also enlisted Kokandi merchants in Xinjiang and succeeded in fomenting an uprising of Āfāqīs in Altishahr, which allowed his force to occupy the four western cities. Although a Qing army dispatched from Zungharia and parts further east succeeded at great expense in reconquering the territory, some officials questioned the very viability of Qing rule in this region and suggested pulling back the Qing military forces and devolving control over these four cities to "native chiefs" (*tusi*)—in effect, abandoning western Altishahr by granting all-but-complete autonomy to the begs. The Daoguang emperor rejected this proposal and instead dispatched Nayanceng to Kashgar to oversee the reconstruction (*shanhou*) of Altishahr.

Nayanceng (Na-yan-cheng; 1764–1833), a Manchu of the Janggiya clan, was the grandson of Agüi, who had led forces in the original conquest of Xinjiang, and the father of Rong-an, who served as Yili councillor between 1827 and 1830. A Manchu wunderkind (*xiucai* by the age of 15, *juren* at 24, and *jinshi* at 25), Nayanceng's rapid rise through officialdom began with a series of appointments within the imperial academic establishment. When the Jiaqing emperor assumed real power in 1798, Nayanceng was made president of the Board of Works. By the time he was dispatched to Altishahr, he had already gained considerable experience in frontier affairs (in Guangdong and Kokonor) and in rebel pacification (the White Lotus and Tianli sects). From Kashgar in 1827 he supervised the withdrawal of the main pacification force and the reconstruction of Qing citadels and implemented reforms of Xinjiang's trade, taxation, troop deployment, currency, fiscal, and foreign policies that completely revamped Qing administration in the Southern March. His memorials (collected and published by his son) provide one of our best sources on Qing imperial government in Xinjiang.[23]

The keystone of Nayanceng's foreign policy initiatives was a retaliatory embargo of Kokand. This measure backfired, however, when the khanate staged an attack on Altishahr in 1830, ostensibly commanded by Jahāngīr's brother, Muhammad Yūsuf, to redress the grievances of Kokandi merchants deported by Nayanceng. Once again, after laborious and costly preparations, an army marched from Aksu to restore Qing rule in western Altishahr. Although the invaders fled, the Qing court was nonetheless forced to conclude with Kokand in 1835 what Joseph Fletcher has called "China's first 'unequal treaty' settlement": Kokand's representatives, the *aqsaqals*, henceforth enjoyed the right to collect customs duties on foreign imports and to exercise jurisdiction over foreigners in Khotan, Yarkand, Kashgar, Aksu, and Ush.[24]

By the 1830s, it was clear to both the court and officials in the field that without some fundamental change in Qing policy and defensive posture, the four western cities of Altishahr would remain vulnerable and continue to require costly rescue expeditions. Again, some suggested a strategic retrenchment to a more defensible line farther east. But a detailed survey of the topography of the Altishahr cities and of Xinjiang's revenues, expenditures, and tax base led an official to conclude convincingly that retrenchment would realize no real fiscal or security benefits.[25] From the 1820s, too, statecraft scholars began suggesting a different approach to pacifying troublesome Altishahr: colonization by Han Chinese and permanent settlement of a larger military force. This was the direction in which the dynasty moved (discussed in Chapter 6 and Conclusion).

The Khoja jihad flared up repeatedly after this, first in 1847 with an invasion known as the War of the Seven Khojas, backed by Kokand, followed by similar attacks on Kashgar, Yarkand, and Yangi Hisar in 1852 (led by Walī Khan, Katta Khan, Kichik Khan, and Tawakkul Khoja), 1854 (led by Shāh Mu'min, Husayn Khwāja Īshān, Walī Khan, and Tawakkul Khoja), and 1857 (the Kucha Uprising and the invasion by Walī Khan and Tawakkul Khoja). Meanwhile, the Russian commercial presence in Zungharia, growing since the 1840s, was finally legalized by the Kulja (Yili) Agreement of 1851, which allowed Russian merchants to trade at seasonal official markets in Yili and Tarbagatai and granted the Tsarist government permanent consulates in these cities. In the 1860 Treaty of Peking, Russia managed to extract consular and trade rights for Kashgar as well, setting the stage for the celebrated Russo-British rivalry in the Pamirs and Altishahr that would develop later in the century.

However, it was neither the Makhdūmzādas nor Russia, but the almost simultaneous eruption of rebellions by Tungans (Muslim Chinese) throughout Xinjiang in 1864, following hard on the Tungan rebellions in Gansu of 1862, that wiped out the last vestiges of Qing control in the region. Plagued by rebellion in China and chronic fiscal shortages, Qing imperial control over Xinjiang crumbled. The way was clear for a Kokandi army led by Yaʿqūb Beg to invade Altishahr and for Russia to occupy the Yili Valley.[26]

The Jiayu Guan, Qing Expansion, and "China"

The philosopher Wang Fuzhi (1619–92) is entered in Qing period biographies, but he was intellectually a man of the wall-building late Ming. He is noted, among other things, for the sharp categorizations he drew between *hua* and *yi*, Chinese and barbarian:

> The Chinese in their bone structure, sense organs, gregariousness and exclusiveness, are no different from the barbarians, and yet they must be distinguished absolutely from the barbarians. Why is this so? Because if man does not mark himself off from things, then the principle of Heaven is violated. If the Chinese do not mark themselves off from the barbarians, then the principle of earth is violated. And since Heaven and earth regulate mankind by marking men off from each other, if men do not mark themselves off and preserve an absolute distinction between societies, then the principle of man is violated.[27]

The fundamental distinction between Chinese and barbarians arises, according to Wang, not from biology, but from environment, which determines in turn the different "atmospheres," "customs," "understanding," and "behavior" of *hua* and *yi*. As Frank Dikötter has summarized Wang's thought on this question, "the purity of categories (*qinglei*) had to be preserved by strict boundaries (*juezhen*) and a specific *Lebensraum* (*dingwei*). The territory of the Chinese race was the 'middle region' (*zhongqu*) or 'divine region' (*shenqu*): 'North of the deserts, west of the Yellow River, south of Annam, east of the sea, the ether is different, people have a different essence, nature produces different things.'"[28]

The late Ming court chose to build walls as a military policy, but, as Arthur Waldron has shown us, the decisions that led to that choice were reached in a political climate that increasingly viewed the purity of categories and the strictness of boundaries as a litmus test of dynastic loyalty. To wall, or not to wall, involved "questions of Ming, and Chinese, national and cultural definition" as much or more than strategic considerations.[29]

To what extent did later Chinese scholars subject to the Manchu dynasts continue to map their moral and cultural world onto the physical one? Did they maintain the Ming sense of boundedness, of the moral imperative to distinguish *hua* from *yi* and center from outer, even while politically forbidden from voicing such sentiments? This, of course, is one of the great questions of Qing history, in part because the Qing dynasty consciously stifled such discussion and censored the record, leaving later historians with little to go on. Wang Fuzhi's writings could not be published until near the end of the dynasty and were little known in his own time; other writings on barbarians or frontier issues were suppressed during the censorship campaign of the 1770s and 1780s. But the *hua/yi* dyad and the sense that China (*Zhongguo*), as both civilization and state, is a naturally bounded entity centered on the Central Plain, has deep roots in Chinese thought. To be sure, Confucius could exhort the superior man to remain superior while living *amidst* barbarians and proposed going to live among them himself; likewise, Zhu Xi's philosophy is considered cosmopolitan and universalistic, and indeed it spread readily from China to other East Asian countries.[30] Nevertheless, a tradition that highlighted the spatial distinction between *hua* (or *xia*) and *yi* would have informed the worldviews of the well-read even in Qing times.

There is a famous description, at the conclusion of the "Tribute of Yu" in the *Shang shu*, of how Yu constituted the series of concentric and hierarchically arranged domains, each physically removed by a distance of five hundred *li* from its inward neighbor and each occupied by a politically and culturally inferior class of people. This idealized depiction and another, similar one in the *Rites of Zhou*,[31] as well as the "Chinese world order" model, are often cited to argue that clear boundaries were not an important part of the traditional Chinese worldview, which envisioned instead radiating zones of diminishing cultural and political affinity to China.[32] But the very next sentence following the account of Yu's great work reads: "On the east reaching to the sea; on the west extending to the moving sands; to the utmost limits of the north and south:—[Yu's] fame and influence filled up all within the four seas." Although the northern and southern limits are vague, the eastern and western boundaries of the realm are here defined quite clearly indeed.

In later Chinese writings, it is not hard to find other indications of a territorial definition of Chineseness and China (or the Middle States) coexisting with the universalistic cultural one. The Southern Song poet Chen Liang believed that only in the Central Plain was the immanent spatial energy (*qi*) of sufficient quality to support China's superior culture and maintain the Chinese ruler's Mandate of Heaven. The energy of Zhejiang and Sichuan, for example, was "peripheral," and that of distant nomadic lands "perverse and inferior."[33] There is, moreover, a tradition extending from the Han to the Ming that views features of China's natural landscape (mountains, passes, rivers) as boundaries created by Heaven. Such ideas were only reinforced by the debates over wall building during the Ming.[34]

Thus the concept that the places beyond the Ming boundaries were not

"China," and even that environmental factors could determine the difference between those living outside and the Chinese within, could not have been un-known to Qing literati. As we have seen, Qi Yunshi, when he passed through the Jiayu Guan in 1805, half-expected the new environment to work sudden changes on his being and was not entirely disappointed.

The Jiayu Guan, a relic of the Ming mural defense system, retained an official function into the Qing period: following the Qianlong conquests, travelers from China proper still had to present their laissez-passer before proceeding through its massive gate. But for those steeped in the Chinese literary tradition, the Pass represented a symbolic, psychological boundary as well: for many in the mid–eighteenth century, as for the author of the "Tribute of Yu," those shifting sands marked the end of China. Moreover, the Qianlong emperor's endeavors beyond the Pass, perhaps for the reasons just outlined, did not meet with complete approval from his ministers, but rather with considerable and surprisingly direct resistance.

Literati Dissent, Imperial Response

Liu Tongxun, a Shandongese grand councillor much trusted by the mon-arch, had been coordinating logistics as governor-general of Shaanxi-Gansu in 1755 when Amursana slipped free of his escort to Rehe and asserted his command over the tribes of the former Zunghar federation. Upon learning that the Manchu general Yong-chang had retreated from Urumchi to Barkol in response to this news, Liu suggested that a defensive perimeter be estab-lished in Hami, the Western Regions city closest to Gansu, and that the lands to the west be abandoned. In his memorial Liu included the almost admon-ishing phrase (reminiscent of the strict categories of Wang Fuzhi), "The inner and outer boundaries must be demarcated (*nei wai zhi jie, bu ke bu fen*)." Gao-zong, after expressing surprise that Liu had panicked so easily over Amur-sana, singled out this sentence for special censure. "Just think: ever since the [Zungharian] tribes came over to us of their own accord, all have been part of our territory (*bantu*). Yili is our border (*jiangjie*)! What's this about 'inner and outer' being divisible?"[35]

Liu Tongxun was a highly loyal, famously incorruptible official who had earlier risked his own career to openly criticize an imperial favorite and had thus won the Qianlong emperor's respect. Now, in 1755, he again spoke bluntly, expressing his belief that the natural boundary of the "inner" lay at Hami and that what lay outside could be justifiably left to the Zunghar nomads. This time, however, he went too far. Gaozong could not tolerate

such opinions and sentenced his minister to cautionary punishment. For the
Qianlong emperor, the natural limits of the realm were coterminous with
the limits of his military power and included steppe as well as farm land. He
found this reference to Zungharia as "outer" offensive.*

Two years later, during the imperial southern tour in the spring of 1757,
more Han officials questioned the wisdom of the northwestern campaigns and
the policy of courting Kazakh allegiance and trade. For the glimpse it gives of
his thoughts about the imperial enterprise in Central Asia, literati resistance
to it, and the consciousness of history on both sides, Gaozong's edict is worth
quoting at length.

> Amursana is now a wandering soul in a cauldron. Can he escape dis-
> memberment for long? That the rebels were able to pretend to power,
> stirring up the Oirats and the Muslims, was solely due to their reliance
> on the Kazakhs. Now, Ablai [the Kazakh sultan] has already surrendered
> and promised, should Amursana enter his territory, to capture him for
> the Qing. . . . I am gratified by this. Never, since ancient times, have the
> Kazakhs, that is, Dayuan, been in contact with the central states (*zhong-
> guo*). In former times, Emperor Wu of the Han Dynasty expended all his
> military strength, but he merely obtained horses and then returned. . . .
> Now we finally preside over the entire Kazakh horde, and they incline
> their hearts our way. . . . Nevertheless, know-nothing outsiders . . . say
> the Kazakhs are not to be trusted and raise the example of Amursana
> and Bayar, who became our ministers and then repeatedly rebelled, ex-
> hausting our troops and expending our treasure. There is no end to the
> complaints of these people. They do not know that the Kazakhs dwell
> more than 10,000 *li* away . . . and that up till now they have never sent an
> emissary, nor have we summoned them. Now [the Kazakhs] call them-
> selves "minister" (*chen*), receive our commands, and present horses in
> tribute of their own accord! Nevertheless, during the southern tour this
> spring, that National University student (*jiansheng*) from the south,
> Zhang Rulin, and that Confucian-school instructor from Zhejiang, Zhang
> Zhiye, submitted a memorial in which they rashly requested to enlist in
> the army. In this memorial they talked about how our troops and gen-
> erals were suffering! Worthless commoners who give currency to false
> rumors are not worth talking about. But fools like these two—have they
> ever been loyal to their ruler or loved their country? They just go ahead
> and predict disaster, without understanding the greatness of Tianxia![36]

---

* As governor of Shaanxi in late 1754, Chen Hongmou, too, had urged caution in the
campaign against Dawachi, as William Rowe will discuss in his upcoming work on Chen.

It is hard to interpret this extraordinary document as other than an imperial defense of the Zungharian and East Turkestani adventure in the face of criticism emanating from the Jiangnan. We do not have their original memorial, but one wonders if the two literati mentioned the Han dynasty precedents directly. Any scholar of the time would have known the story of the Han expedition to Dayuan (Ferghana) to obtain "blood-sweating" horses and would have readily recalled Sima Qian's critique of Emperor Wu's ruinous foreign campaigns: the Xiongnu wars of the second century B.C., along with expensive domestic projects, exhausted Han dynastic reserves of grain and cash. The same chapter of the *Shiji* (the *"Balanced Standard"*) tells the story of the upright official (and former shepherd) Bu Shi, who in 112 B.C. volunteered to leave his post as prime minister of Qi and "die in battle" against the Southern Yue.[37] The Zhangs' own enlistment request seems disingenuous and may itself have been an allusion to the *Shiji* critique.

In any case, the emperor picks up the historical thread in his response but hastens to distinguish himself from Han Wudi, depicting his forerunner's efforts in the far west as ephemeral in contrast to his own lasting ones. Gaozong scoffs at attempts by Han Chinese literati to understand frontier matters, and, later in the edict, the emperor further justifies the campaigns by asserting (not quite truthfully) that the conquest had been rapid and what casualties there had been were to Solon or Manchu bannermen—the dynasty had not dispatched Han Chinese border forces or conscripted peasants. Finally, Gaozong argues that his military budget amounted to only 30 to 40 percent of that during Yongzheng times (note the increase from the "10 to 20 percent" he had claimed in 1755) and that domestic allocations for disaster relief, river works, tax relief, and so on had actually increased, despite the military expenditure in Zungharia.

In 1760, the Qianlong emperor once again encountered domestic resistance to the Qing presence in Xinjiang, when he personally tested the successful *jinshi* candidates following the metropolitan examinations of that year. By this time, the dynasty had launched a large-scale agricultural reclamation program (*tuntian*) in Zungharia, and Xinjiang officials were busily creating the infrastructure to allow the military, penal, and civilian colonies to grow the grain needed to support the Qing garrisons in Xinjiang (see Chapter 2). One of the questions on the exam concerned *tuntian* policy, and at least one candidate suggested in his answer that such efforts "belabored the people" (*laomin*). Hua Li has pointed out that the airing of such an opinion in this exalted venue was not a casual matter; it indicates a considerable level of resistance in literati circles to Gaozong's policies in the far west, and in particular to the issue of Han migration to new farms in Xinjiang. Gaozong thus cast his response with a broad audience in mind: after denying that *tuntian* was in any way injurious to his subjects, he used the occasion to compose a long defense of agricultural development in Xinjiang in terms of economic benefits and lebensraum and had the edict distributed broadly to officials in the empire.[38]

Justifying Empire at Home

These exchanges (of which the published Qing historical record has preserved only the emperor's side) raise issues that will be with us throughout our consideration of the mid-Qing empire in Xinjiang. Since the Dawachi campaign, Gaozong faced criticism that the military expeditions in the northwest were too expensive, criticism that bore with it the weight of historical precedent. It is probably for this reason that he repeatedly withdrew the main Qing armies at the first indication of victory in the Zunghar wars—thus leading to the death of Bandi and his men in Yili and the near loss of Zhao-hui's force at Blackwater Camp. During the initial stages of postconquest consolidation, the same criticisms about cost—in lives, labor, and treasure—arose often, and the emperor responded as a modern politician might, quoting percentages saved over the policies of his predecessor and arguing that the imperial expansion into Xinjiang caused no economic hardship but rather brought conditions of prosperity to the northwest.

The emperor would repeat these arguments to unnamed critics in edicts over the next several years. In 1761, for example, Gaozong commissioned and announced the results of a study by Šuhede to the effect that after the Xinjiang conquest, the dynasty saved more in Shaanxi and Gansu than it paid to occupy Altishahr—and thus the "simple and stupid know-nothings given to frivolous discussions" were wrong.[39] In similar fashion, when in 1772 governor-general Wen-shou of Sichuan suggested opening a subscription list to raise revenue, Gaozong responded with a denial that revenue was necessary: by reducing the numbers of troops assigned to guard the borders within China proper and by cutting the food and horse allowances of Han-martial (*Hanjun*) garrisoned in the provinces, the emperor pointed out, he had already freed enough funds to finance Xinjiang and even save an additional 900,000 taels annually. He added that at the beginning of his reign, the Board of Revenue treasury contained only 34 million taels; by his 37th year of rule (1772), a surplus of more than 78 million had accumulated—further indirect evidence that the implementation of a forward policy in the far northwest produced savings for the empire.[40] Within a few years, the literary inquisition reached a high point, with Song- through Ming-period geographic works on the northern and northwestern frontiers comprising a principal category of books destroyed.[41] The Qianlong emperor thus rejected the criticism of his frontier policy in general and of Xinjiang finance in particular, especially that voiced by Han Chinese. The official line had been laid down.

Five decades later, this "forward defense dividend" argument was codified as historical fact in the *Qinding Xinjiang zhilue* (Imperially commissioned survey of Xinjiang), compiled by exiled scholars under the supervision of the Mongol high official, Song-yun, and dedicated by the Daoguang emperor in the first year of his reign (1821). The authors of this gazetteer draw an explicit contrast between what they describe as the Han dynasty's expensive and inconclusive forays into the Western Regions and the Qing's economical and decisive victories. "Our Dynasty has, in accordance with the will of Heaven above and the affairs of men below, taken [Xinjiang] without excessive use of troops, and holds it without wasteful expenditure of treasure."[42] How was this possible? The Manchu forces posted to defend Yili and Urumchi were transferred, the editors explain, from Rehe, Xi'an, Liangzhou, and Zhuanglang; the Green Standard Han troops came from Yansui, Ningxia, Xinghan, Xining, Guyuan, Suzhou, Hezhou, and Anxi. Because these troops had simply been reassigned to duty in Xinjiang, with no new soldiers mustered to replace them at their former postings, the provinces in China proper were spared the cost of these troops' salaries, grain, fodder, and so on. Even after the salaries and operating expenses of Xinjiang cities were paid, the gazetteer claims, China proper could still boast an annual savings of over 200,000 taels! "Not only has the acquisition of Xinjiang not wasted funds, it has saved the provincial treasuries money. And considering Xinjiang's flourishing state farms, newly established schools, mutual surveillance and protection by the common people, network of roads and surplus grain, [it is clear that] those who since olden times have advocated fortifying the passes [on the borders of China proper] as a means of pacifying the frontier could not come close to achieving this."[43]

Thus, in language similar to Gaozong's earlier, the authors justify a forward frontier policy and continued Qing administration of Xinjiang on the basis of savings made possible by reducing troop strength within China proper. The statecraft scholar Wei Yuan would reiterate this line of reasoning in 1842.[44] In fact, the debate over the economics of empire echoes and reechoes, in evolving form, throughout the era of Qing rule in Xinjiang, from the early warnings about the advisability of the Zunghar campaigns, to Daoguang period consideration of a retrenchment from western Altishahr, to the famous 1874 debate between Li Hongzhang and Zuo Zongtang over maritime and frontier defense, to the discussions surrounding the creation of Xinjiang province a decade later.[45]

Certainly, this discourse involves strategic and fiscal issues. But couched within it as well is the concern reflected in Liu Tongxun's call to demarcate the boundaries of inner and outer. What, exactly, was "China" under a Manchu regime? Could it extend beyond the Jiayu Guan, or was it limited to those natural, presumedly primordial frontiers butressed with masonry by the late Ming and taken as absolute by Wang Fuzhi? Should an emperor in Beijing concern himself with pastoral lands and peoples? The Qianlong emperor knew he should; some of his officials—mostly Han—still wondered.

Later, the undercurrent of these long-running debates over Xinjiang policy would shift direction and turn to question not *whether* the Western Regions belonged in the Qing empire, but on what—and whose—terms it was to be integrated with China. But in the mid–eighteenth century, fiscal problems were more immediate. Although Gaozong could deal with Han upstarts, he and his ministers in Xinjiang nonetheless faced political pressure to keep the imperial enterprise in the west from becoming too great a burden on the imperial fisc in China proper. And it is to these efforts that we now turn.

CHAPTER 2

Financing New Dominion

The august Qing is at the height of its military power, and the taxes
and rents of Altishahr, the harvests of agricultural reclamation as well
as commerce along [Xinjiang's] roads have filled our granaries and
storehouses, accumulating into a great surplus. Not only is China proper
not troubled by having to dispatch supplies in haste, but because of
continuous tax relief, the common people in the provinces of Shaanxi
and Gansu at first did not even know of the military campaigns. How
can the Han, Tang, Song or Ming dynasties, which exhausted China's
(*zhongguo*) wealth and power without gaining so much as an inch of
land, be compared with Us?

Da Qing lichao Gaozong shilu *597:33b–37a, QL24.9* ding chou

Gaozong's grandiloquence on this occasion, upon receiving the news that
Khoja Jihān and Burhān ad-Dīn had been captured in Badakhshan, reveals
his hopes but not the reality of Qing empire in the Western Regions. Despite
repeated claims of a fiscal windfall, the hard budgetary fact was that throughout the century between Qing conquest and the Tungan rebellions, the Qing
military government in Xinjiang remained dependent on China proper. And
because the cost of empire in Central Asia was a politically charged issue, not
only did the court continue to advance its argument about a forward defense
dividend, but it also urged officials in the field to strive toward the elusive goal
of "using the Western Regions to rule the Western Regions, and not provide
for [Xinjiang] expenditure from the central lands (*zhongtu*)."[1] These efforts to
reduce Xinjiang's dependence on the provinces included official trade of textiles for Kazakh livestock; agricultural reclamation; traditional Central Asian
as well as new forms of taxation; garrison commissaries; and such measures
as manipulation of exchange rates, renting out of government property, and
investment of government funds with private merchants. Many of these programs raised or freed up significant amounts of funds or provided in other
ways for the needs of the Qing frontier garrisons. Nonetheless, they never
sufficed to render the imperial government in Xinjiang independent of sub-

44

sidies from China, let alone realize a profit for the metropole. This fact highlights the fiscal vulnerability of Qing empire in Central Asia.

More positively, these forays into commerce reveal the creativity and activism of Qing authorities in Xinjiang and a state engagement with the market economy that at times transcended what was legally permitted in China proper. This difference between fiscal regulations and techniques in Xinjiang and China proper provides another reminder that we should think of the high Qing not so much as a "Chinese empire" or "Chinese dynasty," but as an empire, ruled by a Manchu house, that encompassed China proper as but one—albeit the principal one—of its extensive territorial holdings.

This chapter and the next examine the fiscal underpinnings of Qing dominion in Xinjiang, beginning with a discussion of the Xinjiang administration's basic needs for livestock, grain, and silver; how these needs were met; and how Qing officials used local monetary policy to stretch their stipends of silk and silver.

The Kazakh Trade

One of the most pressing challenges that the Qing faced during the Zunghar campaigns was the provision of livestock for war, portage, and food. This demand declined only gradually following the end of the war in 1759, as the work of city construction and agricultural reclamation in Zungharia required draft animals and the garrisons needed a supply of chargers to stock stud farms. Animals bred in China proper did not fare well on the long journey to Zungharia: out of 60,000 head of sheep driven from Barkol in 1758, for example, over 27,000 died en route. Horses, though more apt to survive the journey, were half-starved when they arrived in Zungharia and had to be fattened up again before battle or work. Others made it to Xinjiang only to fall victim to famished troops who ate them in lieu of delayed grain rations.[2]

Thus, when the Kazakhs who pastured near and within the former Oirat lands in northern Zungharia responded positively to an imperial overture in 1757, the news was welcome to Qing military planners. Not only did the Kazakhs promise intelligence regarding Amursana's whereabouts, but they also expressed a desire to engage in trade that could provide war horses and sheep to Qing bannermen. This frontier exchange of textiles for livestock, formally initiated in 1758, avoided for the most part the troubles that beset border tea-for-horse markets in the Song and Ming periods and became a keystone in the economic structure of Qing Xinjiang.[3]

After a few years of experimentation, the Qing-Kazakh trade was institutionalized along the following lines. Late in the year, officials in Xinjiang and the northwest remitted orders for certain varieties and colors of silk to the Imperial Silk Factories (*zhizao chu*) in Hangzhou, Soochow, and Jiangning (Nanjing).[4] With funds from local *diding* land taxes, the factories produced the fabrics in about a year's time. The factory commissioners then oversaw the inspection and packing of the fabric into special crates, each containing 45 bolts of silk, sheathed in paper and bamboo matting, bound with hemp cord, and clamped between boards. The crates were covered with oiled cloth to repel rain and shipped in a caravan under military escort to Suzhou, where they arrived in spring or summer, around eighteen months after the orders had been put in. After inspection for fading or mold, good silks were sent on to the Camel and Horse Offices (*tuoma chu*) in Yili and Tarbagatai in readiness for the trade season. After 1762, the Qing authorities in Xinjiang began collecting cotton cloth woven in Altishahr in lieu of the grain tax; thereafter, almost 100,000 bolts of this "Muslim cloth" (*huibu*) were shipped annually to the north to supply troops and to supplement the silk for trade with the Kazakhs.

Between summer and autumn, the Kazakhs began to arrive at the frontier outposts (*karun*)* en route to Yili or Tarbagatai. Qing guards escorted them to a site outside the city wall, where the nomads pitched camp. The trade fair was convened in a special "trade pavilion" (*maoyi ting*), a suburban walled stockade with Qing guards at the gates. In hopes of keeping Kazakh prices down, Qing trade delegation members (often Green Standard troops or exiled officials) attempted to conceal the "official" aspect of the trade fair by disguising themselves as merchants before transacting business. Oirats helped out as interpreters.

The Qing departed from Ming precedent by not attempting to fix horse prices by rigid fiat. Officials did make sure that prices charged for textiles in Tarbagatai were somewhat higher than those in Yili, in order to entice nomads to travel the extra distance to the latter city, which was more convenient for the Qing. Nevertheless, for the most part Kazakhs haggled with

---

* The term is Manchu; compare Mongolian *qarağul*, "sentry." In Chinese the word becomes *kalun*. Xinjiang's *karun* were enclosed forts built in frontier zones between territory under close Qing supervision and the pastures of independent nomads not enrolled in the banners. Although often represented on maps, the *karun* lines did not define borders and ran along the slopes of the Tianshan within Xinjiang as well as near the external periphery of Zungharia and Altishahr. (See, for example, the *karun* line north of Ush—below the city toward the bottom of Map 5—on the southern foothills of the Tianshan.) Patrols were mounted from *karun* into nomad territory under Qing jurisdiction; some *karun* lay along common travelers' and merchants' routes.

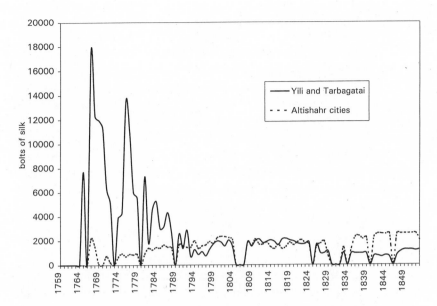

Figure 2. Official silk shipments to Zungharia and Altishahr, 1765–1853. Source: Millward, "The Qing-Kazakh Trade," Table B.

Qing "merchants" to determine prices on the basis of categories of animal and textile. (For example, around 1775, one five-color four-clawed dragon robe or a bolt of four-span two-color gilt satin could be exchanged for 4 horses or 32 sheep. On the lower end of the scale, a bolt of cotton cloth could be traded for 1 large sheep or 2 small goats.) The Qianlong emperor himself established this operating principle in 1758: "We are certainly not employing this trade as a 'loose rein' tactic, nor to profit at the Kazakhs' expense, but, rather, *we hope to obtain horses at a low price.* When you trade you should not be overly mean, nor need you be too compromising, but *operate on the principle that both parties get a fair deal*" (my emphasis).[5]

After the official trading was completed, private merchants were allowed into the trade pavilion to exchange tea or sundry goods for any livestock or pastoral products the Kazakhs had left over. Once all exchanges were completed, bannermen would escort the Kazakhs back beyond the *karun,* and officials would submit new silk orders to the Jiangnan factories, based on the nomads' demonstrated preferences.

In the annals of Chinese frontier horse markets, the trade with the Kazakhs is remarkable for its relatively trouble-free longevity. Livestock obtained from the Kazakhs not only supported the Qing military during the crucial first

years of consolidation, but the resale of sheep provided a source of revenue
for the Yili and Tarbagatai administrations. Moreover, horses were even sent
from Yili to supply the military in Xi'an and elsewhere in China proper.[6]
Although by the late 1790s the nomads no longer wanted as many bolts
of the expensive satins and dragon robes (*duan, jin,* and *mangbao*), and the
overall volume of silks shipped to Yili and Tarbagatai dropped from a high of
almost 18,000 bolts in 1767 to 1,000–2,000, the trade continued at a steady,
low level until the 1850s, when the Taiping Rebellion cut off production by
the Imperial Factories (see Figure 2). As the trade volume declined, Xinjiang
garrisons compensated with livestock from official ranches and the pastoral
operations of nomadic Mongol bannermen on the slopes of the Tianshan.[7]

The Kazakhs and the "Tribute System"

Much postwar historiography of China casts discussions of China's economic
relations with its nomad neighbors in terms of the "tribute system," which
is generally summarized in simple form: nomads from the west and north
traditionally presented horses and other pastoral products as "tribute" to the
court in return for lavish "gifts in return." Although these gifts were often
more valuable than the horses themselves, the Chinese court subsidized the
exchange in return for the political capital it gained from the "submission"
of foreign peoples in the tribute-presentation ceremonies. According to the
"tribute system" and "Chinese world order" model, all of China's foreign
trade before the advent of the West was similarly suffused with Sinocentric
ideological content—from the Chinese court's point of view, ceremonial win-
dow dressing was of primary importance, while the true economic content of
these exchanges remained an embarrassing secret.

  The Qing dynasty's foreign trade has been similarly treated,[8] and if one ac-
cepts that China's "traditional foreign relations" were determined by such an
enduring paradigm, then evidence may be found for such a view. Among the
most famous of the works by the Jesuit painter Giuseppe Castiglione are his
studies of "tribute horses." One painting particularly well known among students of Qing history is *Kazakh Tribute Horses*, which portrays a kowtowing
Kazakh presenting horses to the Qianlong emperor amid rustic furnishings
at the Chengde imperial summer retreat.[9] If the Kazakhs were tributaries, as
Castiglione's Kazakhs seem to be, was the exchange of silk for horses in Yili
not encompassed by the "tribute system"? Was it not "tributary trade"? The
Qianlong emperor himself did not think so. When, after trading in 1758, the
Kazakh sultan requested that his men be provisioned and horsed for their re-

turn trip—as would be done for members of a tribute mission—the emperor replied that "traders cannot be compared to those paying respects and presenting tribute. In the past we have never given them grain or horses. Just send them home."[10] Remember, too, the imperially mandated principles "that both parties get a fair deal." To be sure, the documentary traffic on Kazakh trade in these years is scattered with patronizing references to their "submission" and to the "special beneficence" bestowed upon them, and Kazakh headmen did sometimes meet with Qing *ambans* for tea, cakes, and the exchange of "tribute" for "gifts."* But the importance of ritual gift exchange in early modern Asian foreign relations notwithstanding (and James Hevia has recently enhanced our understanding of such exchanges in the context of Qing guest ritual[11]), the emperor's 1758 edict clearly distinguishes trade from tribute.[12]

The distinction is important, given the great influence of John King Fairbank's "Chinese world order" model on historians of the Qing and modern China. Fairbank argued that the Chinese were unprepared for the West in the nineteenth century because they had no framework with which to deal with foreigners except the "institutions and preconceptions developed over three thousand years of contact with pastoral nomads."[13] From this belief about "traditional Chinese" dealings with northern neighbors, Fairbank, following T. F. Tsiang, developed his theory to explain China's failure to respond adequately to the West. There is a great irony here, for as we have seen and will see further below, the Sinocentric notions that underlie the "tribute system" paradigm bear very little relation to Qing policy vis-à-vis the pastoral nomads or other peoples in or bordering on Xinjiang (or Mongolia or Tibet for that matter) during the period immediately antecedent to that of Fairbank's concern. Trade at frontier markets like Yili and Tarbagatai (or Canton, for that matter) could be carried out very pragmatically indeed. Once we have seen how the Qing traded with the Kazakhs, therefore, we can no longer accept such statements as, "all foreign relations in the Chinese view were ipso facto tributary relations."[14]

---

* Before the year's trade session came to a close, some of the Kazakhs might petition for an audience with the military governor, Xinjiang's highest official. The select nomad party would be escorted into the military governor's headquarters within the walled city and there be treated to tea and sugar cakes. If they chose to present a few horses, the governor would calculate the horses' value and give silk worth the same amount in return. This is the sole explicitly ceremonial component of the Kazakh trade, and it does not seem to have been either perennially practiced or considered essential. Significantly, the documentary discussion regarding the establishment of trade procedures in its first years makes no mention of these meetings between nomads and the military governor. (This information derives from gazetteer sources: YJHL, "maoyi," pp. 100–102; Sa-ying-a, *Qingdai chouban yiwu shimo*, XF1.2b–3b, DG30.3 *guichou*.) See also n. 12.

Planting the Frontier

The settlement of soldiers and civilians on reclaimed land to grow their own food has long been a staple element of Chinese frontier strategy. The Qing also adopted the policy and made development and colonization of "wasteland" a focus of its Xinjiang enterprise, particularly in the Eastern and Northern Marches, where the land was sparsely settled. The dynasty's massive efforts at land reclamation in Xinjiang left a legacy still important to agriculture in the Xinjiang Uygur Autonomous Region today and warrants monographic treatment on its own. Because this subject has been treated in much new Chinese research, however, I will discuss it only briefly here.[15]

Beginning with the first Qing campaigns against the Zunghars in Mongolia and the northwest during the Kangxi and Yongzheng reigns, grain supply was a key logistical problem. Military agricultural colonies (*juntun, bingtun*) in what is now the eastern part of Xinjiang provided a partial solution. From 1716, Green Standard troops farmed sites in Hami, Musang, Barkol, Turfan, and Altai, thus providing some of the grain needed in operations against the Zunghars. All these military colonies except Hami were abandoned in 1725, however, when the Qing relinquished control of these areas as part of the truce agreement concluded with Tsewang Araptan, the Zunghar khan. The Qing reestablished military farming on these sites after 1729, but by 1735 had again withdrawn to Hami.[16]

In 1757, the Qianlong emperor ordered that East Turkestanis and Green Standard forces be assigned to cultivate lands in the Yili region to supplement military grain supplies shipped from China proper.[17] Three years later Agūi brought 300 East Turkestanis from Aksu to Yili. This group, known as Taranchis,[18] became the Qing's first agricultural colony of East Turkestanis (*huitun*) in Zungharia. At the same time the dynasty reestablished Green Standard military colonies in the east of the territory and expanded these efforts northward and westward, organizing a cluster of important military farms around Urumchi. In addition to *huitun* and *bingtun*, the dynasty created several other types of agricultural colonies in Xinjiang over the next 40 years. These included penal colonies (*fantun* or *qiantun*), Chinese civilian colonies (*hutun* or *mintun**), and even banner colonies (*qitun*). (These Yili region banner lands were generally rented out to be worked by others.) Meanwhile, military authorities in the south oversaw the organization of East Turkestani households into state farms in Kucha, Aksu, Ush, Kashgar, Yarkand, and Khotan.[19]

---

* In Qing sources on Xinjiang, the character *min* indicates Chinese (both Han and Chinese Muslim, or Tungan) civilians, unless specifically modified with the character *Hui* (Muslim). The term *Huimin* indicates East Turkestanis. See Chapter 6.

During the Jiaqing (1796–1820) and Daoguang (1821–50) reigns, the military government in Xinjiang withdrew many of the *bingtun* soldiers from agricultural work. The land area and numbers of households devoted to civilian colonies continued to increase, however, stimulated by poor peasants and traders migrating from Gansu, Shaanxi, and elsewhere inside the Jiayu Guan. Gaozong had conceived of Xinjiang as an outlet for surplus Chinese population as early as 1760, recommending migration to Urumchi and Pijan as a solution to population pressure in Sichuan and China proper as a whole. The courts of subsequent emperors continued to support this policy, though most migrants originated in Gansu and Shaanxi, not Sichuan (see Chapter 4).[20]

As an incentive to potential migrants, the Qing offered settlers a grant of at least 30 *mu* (about 4.5 acres), a set of tools, twelve pecks of seed, and a loan of two silver taels and a horse valued at eight taels. This measure sufficed to create a population of around 155,000 Han and Tungan homesteaders in northern Xinjiang by the turn of the nineteenth century. This figure seems quite significant when compared to the Qing census figures of 63,707 East Turkestani households (at five per household, under 320,000 individuals) in southern Xinjiang, and only another 60 in Yili at the same time.[21]

After repulsing the Kokandi-sponsored invasion in 1830, the Qing established the first military and Chinese civilian colonies in the environs of Kashgar and other cities of Altishahr in the hope of strengthening control over this peripheral area. While agricultural reclamation by Chinese in Altishahr was carried out only on a small scale, the introduction of *bingtun* and *mintun* to the south was a departure from the earlier restriction on permanent Han and Tungan settlement of the Tarim Basin oases. Lin Zexu's field studies of irrigation and agricultural conditions (conducted during his Xinjiang exile in the 1840s), resulted in a further expansion of farmed land in the south (see Chapter 6).[22] Despite this burst of development, however, the *tuntian* on the fertile Zungharian plains continued to be the primary source of grain for the Qing garrisons in Xinjiang.

In land area brought under cultivation (over 3,000,000 *mu* by 1840, according to one estimate, with an additional 600,000 *mu* in the south by 1850), the Qing surpassed all previous Chinese dynasties that had established agricultural colonies in Xinjiang.[23] Scholars in China today proudly point out how the Qing agricultural enterprise and the associated creation on a large scale of hydraulic and communications infrastructure laid the social and economic foundations of modern Xinjiang. Though nationalistic, these claims are not without historical basis.

Nevertheless, for the Qing government in the eighteenth century, the primary goals of agricultural development in Xinjiang were more immediately strategic and fiscal: to provide a secure grain source for the soldiers garrisoned in Xinjiang and to spare the crushing expense of shipping grain from China proper. The Qing agricultural development efforts, then, must be evaluated on these terms, and indeed, by these terms the agricultural colonies had for the most part succeeded by the end of the Qianlong reign. The historian Fang Yingkai asserts that Xinjiang *tuntian* "completely solved the problem of military grain and lightened the burden on dynastic finances." Likewise, Wang Xilong concludes that "the military government [in Xinjiang] was established on the foundation of agricultural colonies (*tuntian*) and the armies stationed in Xinjiang relied for the most part on grain supplied by the agricultural colonies."[24] The sources contain many instances of officials announcing—even complaining of—grain surpluses. For example, in 1800 the imperial agent of Tarbagatai memorialized that "an excess of grain stored in the granaries accumulates over the years, not without waste."[25] In Yili, where around this time official and military personnel and their dependents consumed a yearly quota of about 160,000 piculs, the official granaries contained 540,000 piculs; Urumchi's granaries held 800,000 piculs.[26] Whether the grain was collected as tax or purchased on local markets, the state farms created an agricultural base sufficient to meet the needs of the Xinjiang military.

Local Sources of Revenue

Xinjiang's livestock and grain needs could be met locally, as could those for such strategic commodities as saltpeter and sulphur (used to manufacture gunpowder), lead (for shot), iron, copper, coal, and salt. Because the Qing authorities collected many of these items as tax payments, they required no monetary outlay. The government payroll, however, the largest item on Xinjiang's budget, was another matter. In addition to the grain allowance, Manchu and Mongol officials as well as the higher-ranked East Turkestani begs received both a primary salary (*feng*) and a "supplement for nourishing honesty" (*yanglian*). Rank-and-file soldiers, too, were paid a "salt and vegetable" stipend (*yancai*) in money, with which they purchased food and other necessities to supplement their grain allotments. These outlays all required cash.

Immediately following the conquest of Zungharia and Altishahr, and undaunted by the 23,160,000 tael cost of those campaigns,[27] the Qing court still entertained the notion that Xinjiang could eventually produce enough revenue to support the occupying banner and Green Standard forces. A court letter of mid-1760 ordered Šuhede (Shu-he-de), imperial agent at Aksu and concurrent president of the Board of Works, to conduct a survey of revenue and expenditure in each city of the newly conquered territory. In his edict, the Qianlong emperor asked explicitly about *tuntian* harvests and tax payments from East Turkestani households: "Are they sufficient for the officials' and soldiers' pay?"[28]

Gaozong hoped a direct economic benefit could be reaped from the conquest of Xinjiang, but his concept of a Xinjiang that could pay for its own occupation with local land and head taxes was far from the mark. Maintenance of the territory, even in peacetime, required annual shipments of Chinese silver. To ascertain the extent to which the administration of Xinjiang relied on the provinces of China proper, we must first understand Xinjiang's local sources of revenue and their limitations.

Xinjiang's tax system had no *diding*, the combination land tax and commuted corvée assessment that had been collected in most districts of China proper as a single tax, paid in money, since the end of the Yongzheng reign.[29] Local authorities in Xinjiang cities collected the grain tax (*tianfu*) according to a variety of schedules that varied with the locality, classification of land, and ethnic classification of the peasant. In much of the Eastern March, the land tax was collected at a grain-per-*mu* rate identical to that in Gansu, whence most of the Han settlers farming these lands had come. The Urumchi and Yili areas collected grain at a different rate per *mu*. Chinese peasant households who had borrowed oxen, tools, seed, and provisions from the government upon migrating to Yili paid 0.05 taels (5 *fen*) per *mu*, as did so-called merchants (those who migrated at their own expense and reclaimed land outside of state farms) who grew grain on private land reclaimed near Yili.

The Taranchis in Yili were assessed sixteen piculs of grain per household per year. Altishahri peasants were in theory assessed at a rate of one-tenth of the crop, the traditional Islamic *kharāj* tithe that had been in force under the Makhdūmzādas and Zunghars and indeed throughout Muslim Central Asia. Actual practice in Xinjiang varied, however, with officials in some of the southern oases collecting somewhat less than one-tenth, and in others collecting a flat per-*mu* rate. East Turkestani peasants farming official land (*guandi*) in Altishahr paid half their crop to the Qing government, except in Aksu, where the proportion was one-fifth. In Kashgar, Yarkand, and Khotan, much of the grain tax was payable in cotton cloth, which was then shipped north to Yili and Tarbagatai for trade with the Kazakhs and sale to bannermen and their families. There were other local variations and changes in the grain tax rates over time.[30]

In addition to the tithe (paid in grain or cotton), adult East Turkestanis also paid a head tax (Ch. *zhengfu*; Tu. *alban*), which, according to calculations based on 1782 tax quotas, amounted to six to eight *pul* (Altishahr's copper cash) per person. After the start of the Jiaqing period, residents of Aksu, Sailimu, and Bai no longer paid the *alban*. Other towns may have been relieved of the head tax obligation as well by late Qianlong times; a gazetteer of 1797 lists head tax payments only from the southwesternmost cities of the region: Kashgar, Yangi Hisar, Yarkand, and Khotan.[31]

The Qing modeled its tax system in Altishahr after that employed by the Zunghars, although initially the Manchus lowered tax rates from their Zunghar-period levels in a display of imperial munificence to the newly subjected Eastern Turkestanis. In 1759, General Zhao-hui submitted a report on Zunghar taxation levels in Kashgar and Yarkand, together with his own proposal to lower the land and head tax rates. In Kashgar, he would collect only 4,000 *patman* of grain and 6,000 *tänggä** of cash, as opposed to the 67,000 *patman* and 40,898 *tänggä* that Kashgarliks had owed annually to the Zunghars. Other taxes, such as collections of cotton and saffron or the tax on foreign commerce, Zhao-hui left unchanged.[32] Eventually, the military government collected a variety of other commodities as well, either as substitutes for or in addition to the grain tax and *alban*. These included levies payable in copper, gunpowder, sulphur, lead, raw cotton, grapes, gold, and fodder.[33]

The Qing adoption of the preexisting local tax structure is an example of the modus operandi of Manchu authorities in postconquest Xinjiang: they did not apply Chinese models to a non-Chinese setting. Moreover, although the Qing later raised Altishahr's *alban* tax quotas from their low levels of the first years after the conquest,[34] the quotas remained lower than or equal to Zunghar tax levels. This may have been because the Qing authorities saw low tax rates—lower at least than those levied by their predecessors and rivals—as a means of legitimizing their rule in East Turkestan. Because in Qianlong and Jiaqing times the Qing attempted to rule Altishahr through local elites (the beg officials), with only minimum military presence, the dynasty hoped to avoid excessive taxation of the East Turkestani population. Although native Altishahris cannot be said to have enjoyed low taxes (they were subject also to surcharges and illegal taxes charged by local begs), the tithe was light compared to what the Xinjiang government collected in the more fertile north.

---

* The *patman* (Ch. *bateman* or *patema*) was an East Turkestani dry measure, originally fixed in the Qianlong period at four piculs (*shi*) five pecks (*dou*), later changed to five piculs three pecks; in fact, there was considerable variation from this nominal value. See "bateman," in *Xinjiang lishi yanjiu* 1985. On East Turkestani units of measure in general, see Hōri, "18–20 seiki Uiguru no doryōkō."

The *tänggä* (Ch. *tengge'er*), traditionally equivalent to 50 *pul*, likewise underwent redefinitions during the Qing. See the section "Two Metals, Three Currencies," in this chapter.

Green Standard troops assigned to the Yili region agricultural colonies were taxed 18 to 20 percent of the crop.[35]

Another striking difference between Qing fiscal administration in Xinjiang and in China proper was Xinjiang's lack of a salt gabelle. The main reason for this was the ample supply of easily extractible salt throughout Xinjiang and particularly in the Tarim Basin, where saline lakes and surface salt crusts are common. In such geographical conditions, monopoly production of salt must have been deemed impossible, if indeed the Qing considered it at all. The government did briefly attempt to control the sale of salt to the Yili garrisons in 1772, after authorities discovered that Torghuts* were transporting salt to Yili to sell. But the Salt Bureau established to supply salt to the Yili military populace earned little revenue. Gross takings amounted to only 5.03 taels on sales of over 5,000 catties—after the bureau paid its operating costs it had cleared only 0.7 taels! It was not until 1909 that a full-scale salt administration was adopted throughout Xinjiang, and even then only in the north was it at all effective.[36]

Another important revenue source commonly drawn upon by the Qing state in China proper was merchant wealth, though this, too, was initially

---

* The Torghuts (Ch. *Tuerhute*) were a tribe of Western Mongols or Oirats, who in the late sixteenth and early seventeenth century were forced from Outer Mongolia into Zungharia by westward expansion of the Khalkha Mongols. In the first decades of the seventeenth century, under pressure from the Zunghar chief, Ba'atur Khongtaiji, groups of Torghuts migrated further west, settling eventually along the Emba, Yayik, and Volga Rivers. There they became known to Russians and surrounding tribes as Kalmuks. The Qing emissary Tulišen met with the Torghut khan, Ayuki, in 1714, in Siberia. By the latter half of the eighteenth century, the Volga Torghuts fell under increasing Russian pressure, especially in the form of military call-ups, and large numbers fled eastward in search of new lands. In 1770, under Khan Ubaši, the Torghuts began their epic return to Zungharia, harried by both Russians and nomads in Russian employ along the way. The Torghuts sought asylum in Yili in 1771. Gaozong, greatly pleased by their "return to allegiance," resettled them in Khobdo, Etsin Gol, and two sites in Xinjiang—east of Yili and north of Karashahr. The Torghuts continued to suffer from severe poverty, however, and appear most frequently in the Qing sources as smugglers, rustlers, prostitutes, and so on. Today a region much larger than the former Karashahr jurisdiction has been designated the Ba-yin-guo-leng Mongol Autonomous Prefecture, and some Torghuts and Khoshuuts (now classified simply as "Mongols") still live in Korla, Jinghe, and surrounding areas. There is a statue and a small museum commemorating Ubaši in the center of Jinghe (north of Korla) today. The prefectural government-run hotel in Korla features a yurt-shaped discotheque, with cement images of Mongol women dancing on the roof. See Khodarkovsky, *Where Two Worlds Met*; Ma Dazheng and Ma Ruheng, *Piaoluo yiyu de minzu*; Hummel et al., *Eminent Chinese*, pp. 660–61, 784–85 (Tulišen and Shu-ho-tê). De Quincey's famous essay "Revolt of the Tartars" and Hedin's chapter on the Torghuts in *Jehol* are amusing and vivid renditions of these same events.

available to the Xinjiang administration only in a limited fashion. For the first decades of Qing rule in Xinjiang there were few Han merchants or gentry of great financial stature; attempts to put tea sales on a monopoly footing repeatedly foundered on this fact. Chinese peddlers, small shopkeepers, and garden farmers were increasingly common, but there were no concentrations of commercial wealth in the newly conquered territory to compare with Lianghuai or Changlu, the main centers of official salt production in China proper. Rather, through the 1750s and 1760s, the most highly capitalized merchants in Xinjiang were natives of Yarkand, Khotan, and Kashgar, as well as foreign Central and South Asian traders resident in those areas. After defeating the Makhdūmzāda Khojas and while first establishing tax rates and other aspects of their administration in Altishahr, Manchu officials traded and solicited contributions from rich Muslim families eager to demonstrate loyalty to the new rulers. Thus, in early 1759, Šuhede was able to exchange rewards of silver, silk, and cloth for large gifts of grain, saving the expense of shipping the grain from Gansu to the Qing forces then campaigning farther west in Altishahr. Months later, the execution of Khoja Jihān unleashed a small flood of contributions from surrendering East Turkestani households, each rendering unto the Qing khan one ounce of gold. Ten wealthy Muslim trading families of Khotan, "Bode'erge and others," donated ten ounces of gold each.[37]

These were one-time windfalls, however. The Qing did not regularly exact funds from East Turkestani merchants on an official basis, perhaps out of concern that doing so would incur political repercussions undermining the primary Qing purpose of a stable Altishahr. In any case, the fortunes of the wealthiest East Turkestani merchant families declined under the Qing (see Chapter 5).

"Contributions"—in other words, exactions—from Han merchants in Zungharia were a second expedient, but they do not seem to have been common in Xinjiang until the Xianfeng reign (1851–61). Considerable numbers of merchant contributions appear in the sources between 1853 and 1855, the beginning of Xinjiang's fiscal crisis (see Conclusion). But even then, Yili authorities collected only 38,000 taels in merchants' contributions—less than 6 percent of the city's average annual silver allocation from the provinces. By contrast, it has been estimated that in China proper, money from contributions provided nearly 17, 54, 36, and 23 percent, respectively, of the Qianlong, Jiaqing, Daoguang, and Xianfeng period budgets.[38]

Merchant Loans and the Provisioning of the Qing Military

Merchant loans, on the other hand, were significant from Daoguang times or before. Especially in the 1820s and 1830s, local military officials in Xinjiang often resorted to loans or cash remittances from merchants to cover temporary shortfalls or the costs of urgent military perparations. For example, until Kucha was granted an increase in its allowance of Chinese silver, officials in this city were forced to borrow from local merchants every intercalary month because the budget provided for only twelve months in the year.[39]

Because of the distance from China proper, in times of military emergency it was primarily Chinese merchant capital and remittance services that financed the initial mobilization of Qing forces to defend Altishahr from Kokand and the Khojas. For example, as soon as he received the distress call from Kashgar in the fall of 1830, Urumchi commander-in-chief Cheng-ge arranged for a remittance (*huidui*) loan of 30,000 taels through merchants operating locally, with which he purchased flour, gunpowder, fuses, and other supplies for the upcoming campaign. The merchants were to be repaid in Lanzhou from an emergency shipment of 500,000 taels of official silver en route from China proper. But 30,000 taels was not enough for Cheng-ge's preparations, and because time was of the essence he obtained additional merchant advances totaling 200,000 taels by the following month (November). The government in Aksu, the staging area for the campaign, likewise found itself short of ready cash and faced severe inflation as the town filled up with Qing soldiers. Authorities there took out a remittance of 10,000 taels to supplement the contributions of hakim beg Aḥmad, some additional funds borrowed from prominent local Muslims, and 20,000 taels shipped from Yili.[40]

In addition to borrowing at least 210,000 taels of silver, the Qing turned to Xinjiang's Chinese merchants as a source of grain, carts, and draft animals needed for the campaign. Logistics had been a key problem in the initial conquest of Eastern Turkestan. By the early nineteenth century, the Qing relied heavily upon the Chinese merchant network to distribute and market foodstuffs in towns, where the army could then procure them en route. Evidence for this is found in an 1830 memorial by Sa-ying-a in which he complained that the scarcity of Chinese merchants in the Karashahr area exacerbated the problems of provisioning the army. Nor was 1830 the first time military requisitions had targeted the Chinese community in Xinjiang. Cheng-ge found that "in Urumchi the [Chinese] common people have not yet recovered after the last [requisition, in 1826–27], and commercial goods, carts, and camels are scarce." Similarly, because merchants were few in Aksu, in 1830 the army faced a camel shortage there; "since the last war," a report explained, the government had been forced to borrow from the native Muslims.[41] Thus in 1826, as in 1830, the Qing military appears to have relied extensively upon Chinese merchants for financial and material support.

Even with merchant credit rapidly available, it nonetheless took the Qing military months to respond to the Khoja and Kokandi invasions, during which time the four western cities were in enemy hands or under siege. Months more would have been required had Qing quartermasters in Xinjiang been forced to wait for silver to be carted from China proper before procuring necessary materiel. This situation reminds us just how tenuous was the fiscal basis of the Qing government in Xinjiang.

Xinjiang's Silver Lifeline

With the money revenues from head tax and merchant exactions limited, the salt monopoly impractical, and merchant loans feasible only as a last resort, the administration of Xinjiang depended almost entirely upon Chinese silver to pay military salaries, food stipends, routine operating expenses, and such special costs as repair of official buildings.[42] This annual budget of silver shipped from China proper to Xinjiang was transferred from prosperous provinces of China proper by a system of revenue sharing, hence the name, *xiexiang*, "shared pay"; other terms include *xiangyin*, *xieyin*, or simply *jingfei* (expenditure). In the early eighteenth century, the provinces of China proper were classified "surplus," "self-sufficient," or "deficit" according to whether their tax revenues (not including native customs or salt gabelle) were sufficient to meet the administrative needs of the province. "Surplus" provinces (Shanxi, Henan, Zhili, Shandong, Jiangxi, Hubei, Hunan, Zhejiang) were required to redirect to "deficit" provinces (Shaanxi, Gansu, Sichuan, Yunnan, Guizhou) and frontier territories such as Xinjiang a portion of their tax revenues.[43] Supplementing its share of provincial revenues, Xinjiang also received transfers of funds from salt commissioners, direct grants from the Board of Revenue, and merchant contributions.[44]

Xiexiang funds were transferred first to Gansu, then sent on to regional centers in Xinjiang: Yili, Tarbagatai, Urumchi, Kashgar (including Yangi Hisar), Yarkand (and Khotan), Aksu (and Ush), Kucha, Karashahr, Pijan, Hami, and Barkol. Officials in each of these cities memorialized in advance to the Board of Revenue and the governor-general of Shaanxi and Gansu, providing an itemized report of the previous year's expenses (*zouxiao*) and requesting *xiexiang* for the following year. Usually the transfers followed fixed quotas that changed in response to shifts in administrative status and the number of troops garrisoned in the various districts. The total amount of *xiexiang* funds allocated to Xinjiang rose over the period from 1758 to 1864; in particular, after the suppression of Jahāngīr's jihad in 1828, the upgrading of military preparedness in the south led to increased need for silver to pay the new troops and provide for their families (see Table 1; on troop strength, see Chapter 3).

How much *xiexiang* was sent to Xinjiang? There has been little study of this question, which is complicated by the fact that totals fluctuated from year to year and because a considerable amount of allocated *xiexiang* was offset in Xinjiang by official commercial activities and special taxes (see Chapter 3).

Despite the difficulties in estimating the exact totals of silver transferred from China proper, even approximate figures will help demonstrate why Qing officials in Yili, Urumchi, and elsewhere in Xinjiang strove to expand their local sources of revenue. Zeng Wenwu estimates that 3 million taels were shipped annually from China to pay military and official salaries. However, the source upon which Zeng relies for this figure is the *(Qinding) pingding Shaan Gan Xinjiang Huifei fanglue*, an 1896 text relating events of the 1870s.[45] It is inaccurate to assume, as Zeng does, that silver transfers to Xinjiang had remained unchanged for the one hundred years from mid-Qianlong to Tongzhi times. In fact, in the eighteenth century, *xiexiang* payments were considerably less than 3 million.[46]

From the gazetteer and other data assembled in Table 1, I estimate that by 1795 around 845,000 taels of silver were transferred to Xinjiang annually. Just after the increase in Altishahr troop levels in 1828, the sum was at least 905,000 taels,[47] probably higher.

A survey of Xinjiang's finances performed in 1838 by En-te-heng-e, the Yarkand councillor, corroborates these estimates and adds information for a later point in time. En-te-heng-e memorialized that "funds transferred to Yili amount to 670,000 taels per year [c. 1838], and the eight cities of Altishahr in total need no more than 250,000 taels." He adds that before 1826, Altishahr received 90,000 taels of *xiexiang*, in 1828 this was increased to 160,000 taels, and in 1830 this was increased again to 240,000 taels. Thus, according to En-te-heng-e, prior to 1826 Xinjiang (exclusive of Urumchi, Turfan, Hami, and other Eastern March cities) received 760,000 taels from China proper; after 1828 this amount increased first to 830,000 taels, and then to 910,000–920,000 (in the 1830s). If an estimate of Urumchi's stipend (90,000 taels)[48] is added to En-te-heng-e's figures, the results (850,000 taels before

TABLE 1

Xiexiang Silver Quotas and Shipments to Xinjiang

(in silver taels)

	1759–95	1796–1820	1821–27	1828–50	1851–62
Yili	610,000[a]	[610,000] 599,900[o] 630,000–640,000[b]	678,900[g]	—	610,000[h]
Tarbagatai		50,000–60,000[e]	—	—	—
Hami				50,000[n]	—
Urumchi	89,904 (1783)[f] 125,500 (1784)[f] [95,000–96,000] 60,000–70,000[c]		78,808[p]		
Karashahr		10,000[b,d]	—	—	—
Kucha		5,000[b,d]	—	—	—
Aksu		8,600[b,d]	—	—	—
Ush		12,000[b,d,l]	—	—	21,819[i]
Kashgar		8,000 (1795)[b] 18,000 (1802, 1803)[l] 12,000[d,l] 8,000 (1810)/(includes Yangi Hisar)		96,933[k] [91,251] 80,416 (1835)[m] [113,894] 95,116 (1841)[m] [97,895] 80,045 (1846)[m] [107,292] 89,476 (1847)[m] (includes Yangi Hisar) [97,460] 79,538	
Yangi Hisar				8,115[k]	—
Yarkand, Khotan		8,000[b,d]		[22,524] 19,884[m]	—

SOURCES: a. *XYWJL* (1777); b. *ZTYLSY* (c. 1795); c. Yong-bao et al., *Wulumuqi shiyi* (1796); d. *HJTZ* (1804); e. Yong-bao and Xing-zhao, *Ta'erbahatai shiyi* (1805); f. *SZJL* (1805); g. *XJZL* (1821); h. *YJJZ* (1856); i. Bao-da, *Wushi shiyi* (1857); j. *NWYGZY* (1830); k. *XZSL* 155:37b–38a, DG9.4 *jichou*; l. *ZPZZ MZSW* 75, JQ9–JQ16; m. *ZPZZ MZSW* 74, DG14–28; n. Zhong Fang, *Hami zhi* (1844); o. Qi Yunshi and Wang, *Xichui zongtong shilue*, 5:20 (1809); p. *XZSL* 290:4, DG16.10 *guichou*.

NOTE: Figures given in brackets represent quotas; actual amounts of *xiexiang* transferred follow without brackets. When noted in the table, years indicate the exact date to which a particular citation refers; otherwise, each figure indicates *xiexiang* for around the same time as the publication of the source from which it is derived.

1826, 920,000 c. 1828, and 1,000,000–1,010,000 between 1830 and 1838) are roughly in line with my estimates and demonstrate the rapid increase in *xiexiang* stipends after Jahāngīr launched the Khoja invasion.[49]

We have more precise figures for a later period. The 1844 *Hami zhi* lists Xinjiang's total silver outlay at 1,429,988.[50] But in the late 1840s, a flare-up of the Khoja troubles almost tripled the Xinjiang subsidy.[51] Xinjiang's *xiexiang* totals for various years from the period from 1759 to 1864 are summarized below.

1795	845,000
1826	850,000
1828	920,000
1838	1,010,000
1844	1,429,988
1846	4,186,036
1847	4,152,353
1848	4,045,430

Yambus for the Maharajah?

One question related to Xinjiang's *xiexiang* shipments is the extent to which silver transmitted to Zungharia and Altishahr remained there or was exported by foreign merchants and was as a result removed from circulation within China proper. This issue is particularly intriguing in light of the well-known theory that opium imports caused China to suffer a silver drain in the nineteenth century, with deleterious economic and social effects. It is impossible to determine with any precision how much of the silver shipped to Xinjiang between the 1750s and the 1860s was "lost" in this way. On the one hand, Chinese merchants must have brought some silver back—besides jade, there were few items that could be conveyed economically over the long road back to China proper (Chapter 5). And the mobile, upper-ranked military officials in Xinjiang may have brought silver savings with them when reassigned to China proper. On the other hand, the pay of lower-ranked officers, bannermen, and Green Standard soldiers (which comprised the bulk of *xiexiang*) would have been spent in Xinjiang by the men who received it.

Although there are insufficient data for even a rough quantitative estimate, it is apparent that a significant amount of *xiexiang* remained in Xinjiang or was exported. Silver sycee (*yuanbao*) and smaller pieces of silver circulated next to copper *pul* and cash (*zhiqian*) in Altishahr; the long-term tendency, moreover, was toward cheaper copper relative to silver. Under these conditions, Gresham's law predicts silver would have been hoarded in Xinjiang. Moreover, a Qing prohibition against export of Chinese bullion to South and Central Asia indicates that Kokandis and other foreign merchants were in fact exporting silver. Šuhede expressed concern over the drain of silver from Xinjiang as early as 1760, when he was serving in Aksu as assistant military governor, and Nayanceng made stanching the outflow of silver one goal of the new trade policies he introduced in 1828. Nayanceng accused local East Turkestani merchants of buying (imported?) goods with silver. Therefore, silver must have passed easily to local merchants from the hands of the Manchus and Han who might conceivably have brought it back to China proper.[52]

From the 1830s, and probably before, Chinese silver was continuously available on the market in Ladakh, and Punjabi traders eagerly purchased it. The hoof-shaped silver ingots, locally known as *yambu* (Ch. *yuanbao*), were greatly desired for their purity by the maharajahs of India and sold in the 1840s for 166 Company rupees apiece. This trade continued until the 1850s, when the supply of *yambus* dried up. Silver *yambus* were among the products exported to Kokand and Badakhshan as well.[53]

The possibility of a silver drain to Xinjiang and beyond is of interest to the monetary history of the Qing, in particular in light of debates over the effects of British and American opium sales on the Chinese economy. It has been argued that sales of foreign opium created a shortage of silver in China, with the result that silver's relative value rose vis-à-vis that of copper. This created severe economic and social side effects, particularly among the peasantry, who sold their crop for copper cash but had to pay taxes in silver.

One problem with this argument is the chronological discrepancy between the onset of the decline in market value of copper cash (noticeable as a secular trend beginning in the mid–eighteenth century) and that of the net outflow of silver due to opium purchases. Before 1827, the evidence indicates that Guangzhou enjoyed a net *inflow* of silver; thus opium alone could not have caused the inflation of silver values.

Exports of silver to Xinjiang may have contributed to the silver tael's rising market value in China proper; certainly *xiexiang* shipments, which began around 1760, correspond chronologically to the attested trend of declining copper cash value better than does the chronology of opium imports. Graphs of North China market exchange rates of copper cash for silver taels show the long-term trend of rising silver values beginning in the 1750s–1760s. What had been an extremely gradual increase in the relative value of silver to copper becomes more abrupt around 1760 and continues climbing until the end of the Qianlong reign (1795). This suggests that shipments of silver to Xinjiang may have affected silver values in China proper.[54]

There were, of course, other reasons for the changes in the copper cash–silver tael market exchange rate. Greater Qing extraction of copper from Yunnan and stepped-up minting of *zhiqian* from the 1730s began by midcentury to relieve the copper shortage caused by the growing Qing economy and the cessation of Japanese copper imports in 1715.[55] By the 1820s, large-scale counterfeiting of copper cash, along with opium sales, became sizeable factors.

With only sporadic figures on the yearly *xiexiang* allocation, then, and no way to determine how readily that silver could return to China proper, it is only possible to suggest that the transfer of silver bullion from the provinces of China proper to the military government of Xinjiang contributed to the long-term increase in silver value. Still, this case reminds us that however poorly integrated it was to the macroregions of China proper, Xinjiang was to some extent part of a pan-Qing economy and needs to be considered in investigations of the imperial fisc.

Two Metals, Three Currencies

Be it at an annual cost of 4 million taels or 850,000, silver drain or no, the maintenance of empire in the far northwest was a considerable financial proposition. Xinjiang's annual stipend throughout the eighteenth century was more, for example, than the annual *diding* tax quota of each of five poorer provinces in China proper (Gansu, Guangxi, Sichuan, Yunnan, and Guizhou). At the 1838 level, it would have required almost the entire *diding* tax revenues of either Fujian, Guangdong, Hubei, or Hunan to support Xinjiang's military government for a year. Military campaigns boosted costs still higher: defeating Jahāngīr cost 11,165,000 taels, at least 8 million of that coming from the Board of Revenue and the Chinese provinces.[56] Except for the *alban*, Xinjiang's major tax revenues were all collected in kind, not money. Therefore, the territory's administrators needed supplementary monetary income both to reduce the need for increased silver outlays from China proper and to fund local projects not allowed for in the *xiexiang* budgets, which provided little more than salaries and food stipends.

The impetus for local revenue enhancement began at the top. Gaozong, who as we have seen remained defensive about the costs of his imperial enterprise in Xinjiang, frequently encouraged his ministers and generals during and after the conquest to break free of administrative precedents set in China proper. In 1760 the emperor berated an official for memorializing on a petty matter regarding the Kazakh trade. Such ways, Gaozong complained, perpetuate "the bad habit of rigid formalism" (*juni zhi louxi*).[57] Officials on frontier postings apparently internalized this political culture of innovation, even to the point where one military governor felt he must explicitly justify employing in Yili an expedient with a Chinese precedent. In 1772 Šuhede memorialized,

> Yili is a newly opened area on the extreme frontier. All matters should be handled simply—it is not convenient to manage things in rigid accordance with the regulations of China proper (_zhao neidi zhangcheng juni banli_). But through the years [Yili] has grown increasingly crowded with all manner of officials, soldiers, and Chinese and Muslim farming households. Everywhere merchants are gathering like clouds, and although we cannot imitate the practices of inside the pass (_neidi_) in everything, no more can we fail to establish regulations in keeping with local circumstances in order to prevent foul play.[58]

Given the fiscal limits they faced in Xinjiang—the comparatively small agricultural tax base, the political need to keep tax rates low for East Turkestani Muslims, the impracticality of the salt monopoly, and the dearth of extortable merchants—administrators were forced to develop new techniques or expand upon old ones to raise money. And they were encouraged by the court to do so, since any money raised locally in the New Dominion meant less silver to be delivered there. Officials in Xinjiang thus devised a panoply of methods to enhance their revenue, including commercial taxes, official commissaries, even investment schemes. Central to this set of money-making techniques was Xinjiang's currency structure.

Even before the Qing conquest, Chinese cash (_zhiqian_) circulated in Hami and Turfan. In towns along the northern rim of the Tarim Basin, silver passed by weight; other forms of barter were also common. The south, however, had its own minted currency, the _pul_ (Ch. _hongqian_ or _pu'erqian_). The _pul_ was made entirely of red copper, unlike Qing "copper" cash, which was in fact cast from an alloy of copper, lead, and sometimes tin and/or zinc. The _pul_ was small and thick, with no central hole, and weighed between 0.14 and 0.2 Chinese ounces (_liang_). Originally, it bore on one face in Arabic script the name "Yarkand," where it was minted, and the name of the Zunghar khan (for example, "Galdan Tseren") in Oirat Mongolian on the other.

When Galdan Tseren succeeded Tsewang Araptan in 1727 he attempted to remint all the _pul_ in circulation in Kashgar, Yarkand, and Khotan by collecting the old currency from the East Turkestanis at the rate of two old coins for one of the new (bearing his name), melting down and reminting until all of the old coin had been replaced. As with other aspects of their administration in Xinjiang, the Qing followed this Zunghar practice. General Zhao-hui in

1759 proposed that half a million new Qing *pul* be minted from 7,000 catties of copper originally shipped to Xinjiang to cast cannon. Accordingly, a Han mintmaster named Zhi Kunyu was dispatched from China proper along with several other specialists. Zhi fired up the Yarkand furnace in the autumn of 1760, striking the first 2,500 strings of 1,000 *pul* each by the tenth month. The new *pul* was marked "*Qianlong tongbao*" (Qianlong currency) on one side and on the reverse bore the name of the minting city—in this case Yarkand— in Manchu and Arabic script. Although the new *pul* differed somewhat in design from the old—it had a central hole for stringing—it still consisted of un- alloyed copper and weighed the same as the Zunghar coin. Authorities called on local East Turkestanis to turn in their Zunghar *pul* at a rate of two for one of the new Qing *pul*, ensuring compliance by enlisting local elders to coordinate collection and by phasing in the requirement that the *alban* be paid in the new currency. Old coin was reminted into new, and after a year the Yarkand mint had minted over 4 million *pul*, of which almost 2.2 million had been returned to circulation in Kashgar, Yarkand, and Khotan; the remainder lay in the Qing treasury in Yarkand. Cash supplies were for the time being sufficient, and officials in Yarkand reported that while rich households could endure such ex- actions, the poor people could no longer afford to give up their old *pul* at the extractive two-for-one rate. Thereafter, by imperial grace, what Zunghar *pul* remained in circulation were exchangeable one-for-one with the new *pul*.[59]

By 1769 the Yarkand mint, having reminted virtually all the old *pul*, ceased operations. Still, the Qing continued to mint *pul* in other Altishahr cities. The Aksu mint, established on the Yarkand model in 1761, struck *pul* for Aksu, Kucha, Karashahr, Sairam, and Bai.[60] The operations of the Aksu mint were moved to Ush from 1766 to 1800, then returned to Aksu.

In 1775 a mint in Yili, the Baoyi (Ma. Booi), began producing Chinese- style cash of copper alloyed with lead or tin. This was in response to the severe shortage of currency for small transactions that accompanied the growth of Yili's commercial economy. Five of the Yili *zhiqian* were defined as equal to one *pul*, but the two forms of copper currency seem to have circulated sepa- rately, the *pul* in Altishahr and the Yili cash in the Northern and Eastern Marches.[61]

Copper required by the Aksu, Ush, and Yili mints was supplied by means of a tax assessed in Altishahr, the official sale of grain for copper, and official and private mining operations. According to the 1782 *Huangyu Xiyu tuzhi*, the Qing government in Xinjiang collected a yearly total of 13,716 catties of bulk copper in taxes from Karashahr, Kucha, Shaya'er, Aksu, Sairam, and Bai. In addition, sales of grain in Aksu, Ush, Kashgar, and Karashahr made avail- able a further 6,000 or so catties for use by the Yili mint. Such rates of copper collection proved unsustainable, however, and by 1804 tax payments of copper amounted to only about 8,100 catties annually. Mining thus remained the most important source of copper for Xinjiang's mints; the largest mine, at On Bash (Ch. Wenbashi) outside Aksu, produced around 16,200 catties per year.[62]

Although the two copper currencies circulated freely in their respective regions, the silver tael remained the official unit of account in Xinjiang. The Qing set salaries and, for the most part, tax quotas in terms of silver. Chinese silver came to the new territory in 50-ounce (*liang*) ingots (*yuanbao*) and circulated locally in smaller pieces. But, as in China proper, copper money was necessary for small transactions, including those by which bannermen and Green Standard troops got much of their food. The authorities in Altishahr paid soldiers and officials a portion of their wages in *pul*, calculating the amount according to an official rate of exchange. As in the provinces of China proper, Qing officials were actively concerned with the relative market values of silver and copper—the buying power of their wages and those of their subordinates depended on these rates of exchange. The *pul*-tael exchange rate in Altishahr presented special challenges, since the military government had in effect taken control of an established currency and grafted the silver tael onto it at an arbitrary rate of exchange.

East Turkestanis traditionally referred to a unit of 50 *pul* as one *tängä*. In 1759, during the preparations to mint the first Qianlong *pul*, the Qing adopted the *tängä* unit and set it at parity with the silver tael. Convenient though it was, this exchange rate nonetheless underestimated by half the value of silver on local markets. The following year, Yang Yingju and Šuhede memorialized that, because a tael of silver fetched a market price of 100–110 *pul*, as opposed to the 50:1 official rate, officials and soldiers were being short-changed on the portion of their salaries paid in *pul*. The officials therefore suggested adjusting the official exchange rate by which East Turkestanis paid their taxes and by which portions of military salaries were converted for payment in *pul*. The Grand Council's opinion on the matter recognized that the official *pul*-tael rate must fluctuate, since it was impossible to regulate market exchanges among "the Muslim masses": "We have not yet succeeded in using law to restrain [market exchange rates] in China proper, let alone in the Muslim lands." The Grand Council, with imperial concurrence, suggested that Šuhede as councillor (and the highest official in Altishahr) periodically adjust the official exchange rate to bring it into accordance with the market value of the tael.[63] This was a great departure from the policy in China proper, where the official exchange rate of 1 *kuping* tael to 1,000 cash remained fixed, despite market fluctuations, from the conquest of China to the 1840s.

By early 1761 officials in Altishahr cities had reset the official *pul*-tael rate at 100:1, following the lead of Aksu, where both tax payments and military pay had been converted at this rate for some time. The actual Yarkand market rate in late 1760 was 120:1, so local tax payers benefitted while bannermen still suffered by the new rate. It seems that the idea was still to maintain aesthetic symmetry between the two units of exchange: at 50:1 one *tänggä* had equaled one tael; at the new official rate one *pul* was equivalent to one *fen*.

That the Qing saw broad symbolic implications in the Altishahr exchange rate may be seen in a comment from the imperially commissioned Xinjiang gazetteer completed in 1782.

> At the time of the Han dynasty eight taels of silver equaled 1,000 cash [in the Western Regions]. That is, at that time silver was cheap and copper cash expensive. Recently in Altishahr, 50 *pul*—one *tänggä*—equaled 1 tael, so that 1,000 cash was equivalent to 20 taels of silver. Clearly, compared to Han times, cash was two and one half times as expensive. But since this region entered our dominion the price of money has declined to the point where 100 cash equals a tael. This is how our Sacred Dynasty nurtures [the Western Regions]: treasure flows so that it is there in plenty.[64]

In fact, the change from 50:1 (1000:20) to 100:1 was purely administrative, as we have seen, a correction of the original mistaken equation of the tael with the *tänggä*. But chief editor Fuheng allowed the passage to read as another one-up for his master over Han Wudi.

Politically symbolic as it might be, the *pul*-tael exchange rate in Altishahr in the year this gazetteer was published actually functioned in quite a different manner altogether. Already by the 1760s the market tael value had exceeded 100:1 (see Table 2); more importantly, no longer did a single conversion rate govern both collection and disbursement of official funds. Rather, local officials had begun to develop ways to exploit the discrepancy between legal and market rates of exchange.

In China proper, manipulation of copper cash to silver tael conversion rates was one of the common forms of petty corruption or "customary fee" (*lougui*) by which hard-pressed local magistrates supplemented their inadequate operating budgets. By accepting copper cash as tax payment at a slight premium over the going rate of copper-silver exchange, officials could make a small profit when converting the copper to silver themselves before submitting the taxes to the capital. Magistrates used funds realized in this way for stationery, to pay the cost of delivering taxes to Beijing, or to make up for shortfalls in tax collection. While technically illegal, the practice was common, particularly after the Qianlong and Jiaqing periods, and generally overlooked.[65]

TABLE 2
Pul-*Tael Market Exchange Rates in Altishahr, 1760–1847*
(in *pul* per silver tael)

	Altishahr	Yarkand	Kashgar, Yangi Hisar	Aksu	Karashahr	Ush	Khotan	Kucha
1759	(50)	—	—	—	—	—	—	—
1760	110	120	—	100 [100]	—	—	—	—
1766	178 [160]	70–80 [90]	—	—	—	—	—	—
1800	—	—	220	240	—	—	—	—
1801	—	200	220	240	>250 [250]	>250 [250]	>250 [250]	>250 [250]
1826	80–90	—	—	—	—	—	—	—
early 1828	100	—	—	—	—	—	—	—
late 1828	200	—	—	—	—	—	—	—
1845	400	—	—	—	—	—	—	—
1847	180–190 [110]	—	—	—	—	—	—	—
1857	—	—	—	—	—	(400)	—	—
1861	—	—	—	—	—	—	(720)	—

SOURCES: *HYXYTZ* 34:2b; *GZSL* 612:22a–23b, QL25.5 *renzi*; Tuo-jin et al., *(Qinding) Huijiang zeli*, 6:8a; *GZSL* 625:14b–15b, QL25.11 *guihai*, 757:1b–2a, QL31.3 *yiyou*, 1282:10b–11b, QL52.6 *jiachen*; Fu-jun, Fu-ming-a, ZPZZ MZSW 0075-3, JQ6.4.19; LFZZ MZSW 1217 *pian*, DG8; *NWYGZY* 76:43a–45b, DG8.3.25, 76:52a–b, DG8.11.22; Yi-shan, *Yi-shan Xinjiang zougao* 1:9b–10a, DG27.8.26; Bao-da, *Wushi shiyi*, p. 6a; Chang-liang, ZPZZ CZGS, XF11.12.16, microfilm pp. 22–27; *XZSL* 919:19b, DG25.7 *dingchou*.

NOTE: The "Altishahr" column contains figures given in the sources for the entire region rather than a specified city. Figures in parentheses are rates charged by the Qing for receipt of *alban*, grain tax, etc.; figures in brackets are exchange rates for payment of wages to rank-and-file soldiers. Note that these pay-out rates are close to the market rates themselves.

Authorities in Xinjiang likewise manipulated currency exchange rates, but with two major differences: in Xinjiang, such practices were a legal and imperially sanctioned means of relieving strain on the territory's *xiexiang* budget, and officials employed them on a much broader scale, implementing a variety of rates for local government disbursement, purchases, and sales, as well as for tax collection. Adding to the complexity, the rates charged for various purposes differed in each Altishahr city. The use of multiple *pul*-tael exchange rates began around 1765. In that year Yarkand collected 25,150 *tänggä* in head tax; this seems only slightly higher than the 24,000 *tänggä* taken six years previously, the first year in which the Qing formally collected the *alban* in Yarkand. But to keep up with the declining value of the *pul* relative to silver, local authorities had redefined the *tänggä* to equal 200 *pul* and thus collected over 5 million *pul* in 1765 (as opposed to 1.2 million *pul* in 1759). Later in the year, however, by buying *pul*, merchants forced up the coin's market value, with the result that the exchange rate dropped from 100:1 to 70:1 or 80:1. In an attempt to stabilize the *pul*, the Yarkand treasury thereupon sold its supply of the copper coin to soldiers and officials at 90:1. Having collected *pul* at 200:1 only a few months earlier, the treasury could afford such measures.[67]

Table 3 provides further examples of multiple official exchange rates at work in the cities ringing the Tarim Basin. As the figures for Yarkand in 1804 show particularly well, the *pul* value of high officials' salaries was calculated at one rate (100:1), which was also the rate employed for government purchase of grain and other expenditures. The rate for the food stipends of middle-level officials and military personnel (*yancai*) was higher (160:1), and that of rank-and-file soldiers and clerical staff higher still (220:1). This system assured that the rank-and-file, who received a considerable portion of their wages in *pul*, enjoyed the most favorable rate of exchange. After 1801, in fact, exchange rates for the rank-and-file payroll were adjusted quarterly to match the previous quarter's market rate, up to 250:1. The councillor, superintendents, and others who could afford it received fewer *pul* per tael.

Of course, another important variable was the percentage of a salary paid in silver versus that paid in *pul*. For example, in Karashahr in 1804 the superintendent received his *yanglian* ten months of the year in silver, and two months in *pul* exchanged at 160:1; his subordinates were paid 80 percent of their stipends in silver and 20 percent in copper, at exchange rates that varied with their rank. In Ush the proportions were 60 percent silver, 40 percent copper; in Aksu 70 percent and 30 percent. These percentages varied through time as well as from city to city.[68]

Other rates applied for government sale of silk or forced purchase of provisions, as well as for *alban* payments and rents on commercial and government land. The prices for forced purchase of grain or other official expenses in 1804, for example, were kept low by means of an exchange rate set at half the market rate. However, what evidence we have suggests that officials did not use exchange rates to disguise tax hikes. The *pul*-tael exchange rates that applied to East Turkestani households paying the *alban* and commercial taxes were in line with the current market rates.[69]

Manipulation of the *pul*-tael exchange rate and adjustment of the proportion of each currency used to pay salaries, food stipends, and other expenses gave Xinjiang officials a powerful tool for balancing their budgets. The ability to juggle the two currencies could provide considerable savings, especially because *pul* was locally minted from local copper and was thus readily available to Qing authorities in Altishahr. Between 1814 and 1815, for example, Tuo-yan-tai realized such a savings by paying the food stipend of Aksu's officials and troops entirely from accumulated *pul* savings (70 percent converted at 220:1 and 30 percent at 160:1). He saved China proper 11,000 silver taels in this way. Even on a routine basis, payment in *pul* resulted in sub-

TABLE 3

Official Pul-Tael Exchange Rates in Altishahr

(in *pul* per silver tael)

	Altishahr	Yarkand	Kashgar	Yangi Hisar	Aksu	Karashahr	Ush	Khotan	Kucha
1759	50 b	—	—	—	—	—	—	—	—
1760	70 b	—	—	—	—	—	—	—	—
1761	100 b	—	—	—	—	—	—	—	—
1765	—	200 t	—	—	—	—	—	—	—
1766	90 s	90 s	—	—	—	—	—	—	—
1787	160 yc, sk	—	—	—	—	160 yc, sk	—	—	—
1801	220 syc / 200 sk / 160 oyc / 100 yl	200 s	220 s	220 s	240 s	250 s	250 s	250 s	250 s
1804	160 o	100 o, gn, ex / 160 oyc / 220 syc		100 o / 160 oyc / 220 syc	200 sk / 220 r / 160 o / 220 s	200 sk / 220 r / 160 oyc	160 oyc / 220 s / 100 gn, ex	160 oyc	100 ex / 160 oyc / 120 s / 220 gn
1814	—	—	—	—	70% at 220 o / 30% at 160 o	—	—	—	—
1828	—	100 oyc / 160 o, yl	100 oyc / 160 o, yl	100 oyc / 160 o, yl	160 o, yl / 220 s	100 oyc / 160 o, yl	160 o, yl	160 o, yl / 100 oyc	—
1847	220 s	—	—	—	—	—	400 t	—	—
1857	—	—	—	—	—	—	—	—	—
1861	—	—	—	—	—	—	—	720 t	—

SOURCES: *GZSL* 625:14b–15b, QL25:11 *guihai*, 757:1b–2a, QL31:3 *yiyou*, 1282:10b–11b, QL52:6 *jiachen*; *RZSL* 87:28b–29a, JQ6.9 *renyin*, 287:9a–10a, JQ19.3 *jihai*; *HJTZ* 7:6a, 9a–b, 29a–b; 8:6a–b, 11b; 9:4a–b, 12b–13a; 10:3b–4a, 10b–11a; *HYXYTZ* 34:24b: Nayanceng, *NWYGZY* 76:43a–45b, 51b–52b; Yi-shan, *Yi-shan Xinjiang zouguo*, 1:9b–10a; Fu-jun, Fu-ming-a, ZPZZ MZSW 75-3, JQ6.4.19; Chang-liang, ZPZZ CZZS, XF11.12.16, microfilm pp. 22–27; Bao-da, *Wushi shiyi*, p. 6a.

NOTE: Abbreviations are as follows: b = rate for converting both revenue and expenditure; ex = rate for paying official expenses (*gongfei*); gn = rate for forced purchase of grain and sheep; o = rate for high officials' and officers' salaries; oyc = rate for officers' *yancai*; r = rate for receiving rent (commercial tax); s = rate for wages of rank-and-file soldiers, secretaries, workmen, interpreters; sk = rate for silk sales; syc = rate for soldiers' *yancai*; t = rate for collecting tax; yc = rate for *yancai* food allowance; yl = rate for *yanglian*.

stantial savings. Around 1804 Yarkand received in *xiexiang* and interest from Shaanxi investments (see Chapter 3) a total of 11,450 silver taels annually. If paid in silver, *yanglian* for the superintendent and his assistant, public expenses, grain purchases, as well as food stipends for imperial guards, Manchu and Han officials, soldiers, and East Turkestani interpreters would have cost 19,330 taels. In fact, Aksu paid out only 7,678 taels of silver; the remaining 11,652 taels worth were paid in *pul*, calculated by several apportioning formulae.[70] Such procedures, a normal part of Altishahr administration, were openly reported to the court.

Pul-Tael Exchange Rates and Cotton Cloth

The cloth woven by East Turkestanis in the area of Khotan, Yarkand, and Kashgar from cotton grown in the southern Tarim oases was one of the principal products the Qing traded for Kazakh livestock in Yili and Tarbagatai. Through manipulation of the *pul*-tael exchange rate in Altishahr, officials assured that garrisons in Yili could obtain sheep on favorable terms.

Early in 1762, Commander Xin-zhu and the prince Amīn Khwāja[71] proposed that excess grain in Yarkand and Khotan storehouses as well as that year's tax grain be sold to buy cotton cloth. Up to 60,000 bolts could be obtained in this way, they reported, and shipped to Yili to be exchanged with the Kazakhs for sheep. A few weeks later Xin-zhu suggested further that 2 million newly minted Qianlong *pul* in the Yarkand treasury likewise be used to purchase cloth. This would get the new money into circulation faster, he argued, than waiting for East Turkestanis to turn in their remaining Zunghar *pul* at a loss. This approach would "not only save the expense of shipping cloth from China proper, but the [new] currency will circulate freely and supplement the Muslims' livelihood." Xin-zhu added that the Yarkandi begs, too, were enthusiastic about the plan, particularly since it meant that the extractive forced exchange of old *pul* for new was coming to an end. With more cotton growing and diligent weaving, Xin-zhu predicted, the region's economy would in a few years be restored from the ravages of Zunghar rule and war.[72]

Meanwhile, the military government itself prospered by buying cloth cheap in Yarkand, Khotan, and Kashgar or, later, collecting it in lieu of tax grain and selling it dear in Yili and Tarbagatai. From Manchu documents, Wang Xi and Lin Yongkuang have compiled a list of cotton cloth prices in these cities.

	1762	1763	1764	1765	1766	1767	1783	1785
Yarkand	38	33	30	28	28	25	26	26
Khotan	48	33	30	25	25	28	24	24
Kashgar			28					

(Unit: *pul*/bolt)

After purchase at the above prices on the markets of the respective cities, the authorities had the cloth dyed for between eight and fourteen *pul* per bolt and shipped it north. We have no direct information on shipping costs, but sources quote the 1782, 1804, and 1827 prices of Altishahr cotton cloth in Yili and Tarbagatai at 0.4 taels; this was either the government's cost or the retail price charged Kazakhs and Qing personnel.[73] Comparing the *pul* cost with the tael price is hazardous, but if we assume (as Wang and Lin claim) that cloth prices remained steady after 1785, then at the 1801 exchange rate, one bolt of cloth, dyed, cost at most 26 + 14 = 40 *pul* at 200 *pul*/tael = 0.2 taels. This leaves a minimum of 0.2 tael per bolt for shipping and profit. But a simpler way to view the advantages of the official cotton cloth trade in Xinjiang is from Beijing's point of view: neither minting *pul*, nor purchasing, processing, and shipping cotton cloth cost the center any silver at all, yet the business kept mutton on the tables of the bannermen in Yili and Tarbagatai. Moreover, while market prices for cloth in Yarkand, Khotan, and Kashgar declined or held steady after the 1760s, *pul* values relative to silver declined greatly. Thus, as a proportion of taxes received, Altishahr's cloth grew less expensive over time.

Currency Troubles and Reform

The Altishahr mints reduced the weight of the *pul* from its original 0.2 Chinese ounces to 0.15 in 1771 and to 0.12 in 1774. After the Yarkand mint restruck almost all the old Zunghar *pul* and closed down, the Aksu and Ush mints continued to mint 1.6 million *pul* annually from raw copper taken as taxes and from On Bash and other mines.[74] The newly minted *pul* were distributed throughout Altishahr via official and military wages. One would expect *pul* inflation to have been severe given this continued increase in supply of the copper coin. A serious inflation would have undermined both the official cotton trade and the system of multiple *pul*-tael exchange rates. That *pul* values fell as gradually as they did is a puzzle; the most likely explanation is that in the 60 years of peace following the Qing conquest, during which time the Qing promoted agriculture and handicraft (particularly cotton cloth) production, Altishahr's economy grew at a rate sufficient to absorb a greater money supply. Just as important, the yearly influx of *xiexiang* shored up the value of the *pul*.

This effect of silver imports is especially noticeable during the Kokand-sponsored invasions after 1826. When Jahāngīr attacked Kashgar and Yarkand in that year and Manchu banners from Heilongjiang were dispatched to assist in the recovery of this territory, 8 million taels poured into Xinjiang to support the military effort. As Table 2 shows, *pul* values rose to 80:1 or 90:1 that year. Officials feared that at this exchange rate the Qing would be unable to provide the troops with sufficient clothes for the winter and contracted private merchants to mine additional copper in Aksu in an attempt to get more *pul* into circulation. One of the furnaces at the Yili Baoyi mint was assigned to mint additional *pul* for shipment south. Similarly, after the invasion of 1830, an official in Karashahr reported that fodder and similar items had to be procured with *pul*—with silver rapidly falling in value, merchants would not accept it as payment.[75]

The same phenomenon troubled Yi-shan and Zha-la-fen-tai in Aksu in 1847, as they coordinated the Qing response to the jihad led by Katta Khan and Walī Khan ("War of the Seven Khojas"). The market value of the silver tael had fallen from 400:1 to 180–190:1, yet because the treasury could afford to pay the troops at no more than 110:1, Yi-shan acknowledged that they would still be "left out in the cold."[76]

Earlier in the Daoguang period, officials in Altishahr had attempted to resolve this problem of periodic copper shortage with two attempts at currency reform, the first during Jahāngīr's jihad. In 1827 military governor Chang-ling ordered 50,000 taels of silver from China proper struck into silver *pul* coins. The coin never circulated freely, however, as Altishahris suspected the silver was adulterated with copper or lead, and the Qing withdrew it after a year.[77]

In the spring of the following year, Nayanceng, lately dispatched from his previous posting as governor-general of Zhili to supervise the postpacification work in Altishahr, proposed his own ad hoc currency reform. In order to stretch limited copper supplies (the On Bash mine had begun to play out), Nayanceng requested permission to mint a new, copper coin weighing 0.15 Chinese ounces and marked "worth ten" (*dangshi*). This new *pul* would be worth ten Yili copper cash (hence the markings) and two standard *pul*. Granted cautious imperial approval for a one- to two-year trial, Nayanceng used 30 percent of the Aksu mint's annual supply of copper to mint the ten-cash/two-*pul* coin and with it paid a portion of Aksu's (and the following autumn, Yarkand's and Kashgar's) military wages. Muslim merchants and the soldiers themselves reportedly found the new coin convenient, and it circulated at its marked value despite its disproportionately light weight. Encouraged by this favorable beginning, the imperial commissioner proceeded with the second stage of his plan earlier than promised, and in the spring of 1829 he began minting half of Aksu's available copper into "worth ten" coins, using the copper savings realized in this manner to mint still more *pul*, which he in turn distributed to the commands in the cities of Altishahr to pay their troops. In this way Nayanceng hoped to finance the increased numbers of troops stationed permanently in Altishahr after 1828.[78]

In theory, Nayanceng's reform would have allowed a reduction of Altishahr's *xiexiang* by 2,200 taels when 30 percent of the available copper was minted into ten-cash/two-*pul* coins, or by 3,500 taels when half the copper went for the new coin. But Nayanceng at the same time determined that all Altishahr officials should be paid only in silver—a decision that actually required a 3,000 tael *increase* in the region's stipend.[79] Nevertheless, Nayanceng's currency reform, though really little more than a monetary shell game, was a modest success. It brought the *pul* back down to its prewar levels (from 80:1 in early 1826 to 100:1 in the third month of 1828 to 200:1 in the eleventh month of 1828) without causing monetary chaos. It was, in fact, the most effective of his otherwise ill-starred economic and political programs in Altishahr and demonstrates the potential of Qing monetary policy in southern Xinjiang.

It is noteworthy that the idea of larger denomination copper coins as a response to monetary crisis became common in administrative circles in China proper by the middle of the Daoguang reign, not long after Nayanceng's reform in Xinjiang. Both members of the court and field officials, most notably, Guangxi governor Liang Zhangju (served 1836–41), proposed the minting of "large cash" (*daqian*) as a partial solution to the high silver price brought on, they believed, by purchases of opium from foreign traders. Although (or perhaps because) he had permitted the experiment for the opposite monetary conditions in Altishahr, the Daoguang emperor held off in China proper. It was not until the third year of the Xianfeng reign that the Board of Revenue ordered mints empire-wide to produce coins marked "worth ten," "worth fifty," "worth one hundred," and so on.[80]

This case illustrates again the willingness of Qing authorities to innovate in Xinjiang, going beyond what was legal or acceptable practice in China proper, but doing so with imperial sanction. This flexibility was to a great degree the product of both fiscal and political necessity. As shown in Chapter 1, the Qing conquest and consolidation of rule in Xinjiang took place in a climate of dissent or at least skepticism over the entire endeavor. While some of this criticism may have arisen from Han Chinese attitudes regarding the proper physical limits of China, it could only be expressed safely as concern over the costs of expansion. And indeed, those costs were sufficient cause for concern in and of themselves.

Sensitive to this criticism, the Qianlong court proclaimed the goal of self-sufficiency for Xinjiang and encouraged administrators in their efforts to achieve it. This proved possible in pastoral and agricultural sectors of the economy, but the occupying Qing force nonetheless remained heavily reliant on silver shipments from China proper. Xinjiang authorities thus went further, experimenting with the monetary system and exploiting Altishahr's comparative advantage in cotton cloth production in order to get as much from that limited silver budget as possible.

In the next chapter we will see further examples of this latitude in economic matters and examine in particular the Xinjiang government's engagement with the market.

CHAPTER 3

Official Commerce and
Commercial Taxation in the Far West

Our dynasty, too, has turned the energies of the realm to controlling
[the Western Regions], not unlike the age of Han with the Xiongnu and
Dayuan. As soon as we had surmounted climatic conditions, set right
the affairs of men, arrayed city defenses, and established civil administration, people began to think, "Was not this conquest exhausting to
the people? Is not maintenance too expensive? Have not the numbers of
soldiers been increased? Has not treasure been wasted?" In the Northern and Southern Routes, there are some 19,000 troops, with some
1,400 officials. There are permanent garrisons and rotating garrisons.
The soldiers and dependents of the permanent garrisons are Manchus,
Solons, Mongols, and Oirats, transferred from Shengjing, Heilongjiang,
Zhangjiakou, and Rehe. The Green Standard troops alternating on
frontier duty at the rotating garrisons are transferred from Shaanxi and
Gansu. The annual expenditure for their pay is some 678,900 taels—the
very sum China proper would have provided them [had they not been
transferred]. Where is this troop increase?

Wei Yuan, Sheng wu ji, 4:10a (1842)

Wei Yuan's claim that there were only 19,000 Qing troops in Xinjiang—
used to argue how cheaply the territory was taken and held—has been often
repeated in later Chinese sources. As will be shown below, this figure falls
far short of real Qing troop strength in the Western Regions. But it demonstrates how the concern over costs of empire in Xinjiang remained constant
throughout the era of Qing control in Xinjiang. This chapter continues the
examination, begun in Chapter 2, of how Qing officials in the Western Regions attempted to defray those costs and focuses in particular on the Xinjiang garrisons as economic actors and on attempts to tap the region's lucrative long-distance trade. Although the extraordinary methods of revenue
enhancement proposed—some implemented, some not—reveal considerable
inventiveness and at times a keen understanding of the special features of

76

the Xinjiang economy, they also demonstrate the political limits that circumscribed imperial administrators in a colonial setting. Moreover, as I will discuss in the final section, "The Fiscal Foundations of Empire," these measures failed to relieve the territory's dependence on silver from China.

Xinjiang Military Deployment

The part of Zungharia referred to by the Qing and by historians today as Yili was not a city, but rather a broad region bordered to the east and northeast by districts under the jurisdiction of Urumchi and Tarbagatai and to the northwest by lands within the Kazakh transhumance. Kirghiz nomads pastured flocks in the Tianshan range to the south. The governmental center of this district, and the central military command for Xinjiang as a whole, was a sprawling complex of nine walled cities spread over an area of approximately 3,750 square kilometers on the north bank of the Yili River. The Yili military governor's headquarters (*jiangjun fu*) and the quarters of some of Yili's Manchu bannermen were located in the central Manchu city, known as Yili or Huiyuan. About 25 kilometers to the east, Huining housed the remaining Manchu banners and their commanders, as well as the commandants of the Sibe, Solon, Chahar, and Oirat forces. These nomad bannermen themselves were camped in the pastures and mountainsides around Huiyuan and the eight cities, the Solons to the northwest, Chahar to the northeast, and the Oirat and Sibe south of the river in the area of today's Chabucha'er Sibe (Ch. Xibo) Autonomous County. Others were stationed at the *karun* guard posts surrounding Yili. West of the Manchu cities were five garrisons of Han Green Standard troops: Gongchen, Zhande, Ta'erqi, Guangren, and Suiding. These Han cities were surrounded by military farms on reclaimed land (*bingtun*). Southeast of Huining was Xichun, likewise a Green Standard fort. Ningyuan, at the easternmost corner of the complex, was inhabited by Taranchi Muslims transferred from Aksu and other East Turkestani cities to work the Muslim agricultural colonies (*huitun*) around Yili. More Muslims lived in outlying villages (see Map 2).[1]

The Qing occupation of Yili began in 1760 under the supervision of Agūi, who settled bannermen, Han soldiers, and Taranchis in the fertile Yili valley.[2] Through the 1760s and 1770s, Manchu, Chahar, Sibe, Solon, and Oirat banner troops, with their families, were transferred from Rehe, Liangzhou, Zhuanglang, Xi'an, Zhangjiakou, Heilongjiang, and Shengjing; some Oirat and Torghut troops were enlisted locally. Han Green Standard troops were transferred from Shaanxi and Gansu postings to garrison the new frontier in

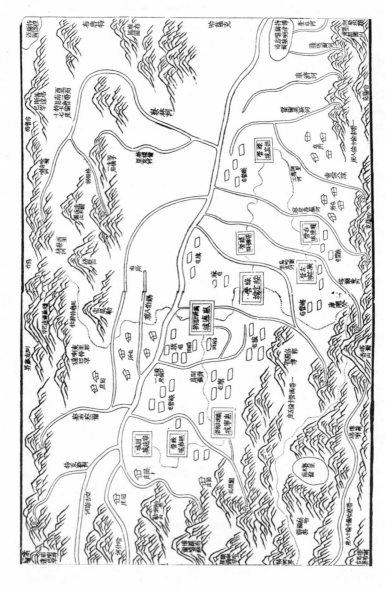

Map 2. The Yili military complex, c. 1809. Source: Qi Yunshi and Wang, *Xichui zongtong shilue* 2:5b–6a.

Yili. After 1778 the Han soldiers, too, were allowed to settle with dependents in the region. According to the 1807 *Xichui yaolue*, there were over 17,000 Qing troops, plus their dependents, in Yili by the late Qianlong period.

The Qing situated defense installations in other parts of northern and eastern Xinjiang in a similar pattern, with a series of walled garrison cities or forts to house Manchu and Han troops. In some places, such as Turfan, indigenous Muslim troops were billeted in like fashion. Although in Yili there were a few "banner farms" (*qitun*) worked by Solons, Chahars, and Sibes—not by Manchus—for the most part only Chinese and East Turkestanis worked the land.[3]

Wei Yuan's figure of 19,000 Qing troops in Xinjiang considerably underestimates real Qing troop strength in the Western Regions. Although there is some disagreement in the sources concerning the numbers of troops stationed in Xinjiang, before 1826 there seems to have been 35,000–37,000 soldiers, half of them Manchu or Mongol banner troops (*qibing*), posted in the Eastern and Northern Routes. Combined with another 4,000–5,000 in the Altishahr region, this amounted to a total of approximately 39,000–42,000 men for Xinjiang as a whole, around 18,500 of them Manchu or Mongol banner troops. Moreover, there were 1,200 Qing officials and large numbers of native begs (see Table 4).[*] In 1828 the Qing increased troop strength by 3,700 in Kashgar, 200 in Yangi Hisar, 600 in Yarkand, and 1,000 in Aksu.[4] (None of these figures includes family members, who would have been present in the Eastern and Northern Routes.)

As we saw in the last chapter, *xiexiang* silver provided only the basic wage (*fengxiang*) for these troops, plus a nonstaple food stipend for the Han sol-

---

[*] *XCYL*, j. 2. Figures from the imperially commissioned (*Qinding*) *huangyu Xiyu tuzhi* of 1782, corrected by Xie Zhining, likewise show total troop numbers of around 42,000. Xie provides a convincing argument why Wei Yuan's oft-quoted figure of 19,000 troops for Xinjiang's Northern and Southern Marches is mistaken. Zeng and other historians have followed Wei Yuan, but as we have seen in the last chapter, neither Wei's nor Zeng's figures are generally reliable (Xie, "Qianlong shiqi," pp. 9–12). Just a few pages later in the *Sheng wu ji* (4:11b–13a) the individual figures in Wei's city-by-city breakdown of Qianlong period troop strength in Xinjiang's three marches yield a total of 32,400; Wei's own subtotals here for the Northern and Southern Marches—themselves irreconcilable with the individual city numbers—add up to 21,090. It is easy to fault Wei Yuan's arithmetic; it is more important to understand that his figure of 19,000 troops appears in a tendentious passage justifying the conquest of Xinjiang in economic terms. His point is identical to that of Qianlong's 1772 edict to Wen-shou, which, indeed, Wei cites here as well: the control of Zungharia was possible with only 19,000 troops, all transferred from other parts of the empire. Hence, there has been no increase in numbers of men at arms in the empire, and no added cost to China proper.

TABLE 4
Qianlong-period Official and Military Personnel in Xinjiang

	Official	Military	Total
Yili	468	17,202	17,670
Tarbagatai	65	2,000	2,065
Urumchi*	408	17,707	18,115
Altishahr	259	4,721	4,980
Total personnel	1,200	41,630	42,830

SOURCE: XCYL, j. 2.
*Including Hami, Barkol, Turfan, and Kur Kara Usu.

diers (yancai) and "nourish integrity" (yanglian) stipends for higher-ranked officers and officials. This left few funds for the other costs of maintaining a garrison, especially one that included military families. Nomadic components of the Qing military in Xinjiang had their herds and some farmland; the Qing provided them with a small allowance, but otherwise expected them to fend for themselves.[5] However, the Manchus within Huiyuan and Huining, of whom there were over 6,000 households by 1771,[6] and those similarly garrisoned elsewhere in Xinjiang required and received additional assistance from the Xinjiang government, primarily for the maintenance of dependents and other family-related expenses. The authorities provided special aid to support Manchu bannermen with large families; for the orphaned, widowed, crippled, sick, and old; and to help with education, wedding, and funeral expenses. The Xinjiang government also guaranteed that such essential items as medicine, cloth, tea, and sundry manufactures were available to bannermen, Green Standard troops, and their families in Yili, Urumchi, and other Xinjiang garrison cities.

Given their limited silver budget, how could officials afford to provide such aid, goods, and services? They went into business.

Tea and the Beginnings of Official Commerce in Xinjiang

Qing officials had used commerce to supplement their budgets in Xinjiang from the first, when during the military campaigns against Amursana and the Makhdūmzāda Khojas they traded Chinese silk and cotton cloth for livestock and provisions. In addition to the border trade with the Kazakhs in the north, officials shipped cloth to Altishahr, where it found a ready market and allowed the army to procure grain more cheaply than by direct cash purchase. In the spring of 1759, for example, cotton cloth from Gansu and elsewhere in north China shipped via Suzhou to Kucha, Aksu, and Ush served as a hedge against rising grain prices in these Altishahr cities. Šuhede and Yung-gui (Yong-gui) could trade for grain and avoid alienating the local population with forced purchases.[7] The following year, Šuhede suggested that camels and mules being driven by the military from Hami to Aksu be loaded with trade goods (tea and tobacco) for the trip out. In this fashion, the considerable costs of driving livestock could be partially allayed by selling the goods in Altishahr. Besides tobacco and various kinds of tea, the Qing sold light silks and fine chinaware in the newly conquered city of Aksu.[8] In subsequent years the Qing continued to transport and sell goods from China proper in Xinjiang cities. Silk was of course a popular item; in 1765 Yang Yingju in Lanzhou received an order from the assistant military governor in Kashgar for 780 bolts of several varieties of silk for use as ceremonial gifts and for trade with the East Turkestanis and Kirghiz. Qing silk shipments to Yarkand, Kashgar, Ush, Aksu, and Karashahr started arriving two years later and continued steadily until the 1850s, interrupted only as a result of Jahāngīr's jihad. Other items included cotton cloth, hides, agricultural tools, clothing, shoes, and felt, as well as medicines and spices.[9]

But of the items the Qing government shipped to its garrisons in Xinjiang, tea was primary. In 1755, a large shipment ("100,000 catties") was forwarded to Hami to entice the Zunghars to come to terms. Several years later the dynasty instituted annual shipments to supply the new Yili and Urumchi area garrisons with tea that would in theory be less expensive than that which tea merchants had already begun to transport to Xinjiang. Yang Yingju reported that around 1762 the garrisons needed 103,500 catties annually. He proposed that troops en route to tours of duty in Xinjiang could transport the tea to depots in Hami and Barkol and then to points west. By the following year the Qing had begun to send 125,000 catties of brick tea annually through the Jiayu Guan to be infused and drunk by Manchu bannermen and their families, as well as any Oirats or Muslims (Taranchis) who wished to buy it. For a while, at least, it appears that official prices undercut those of the tea merchants already doing business in Yili.[10]

Although the officers and troops in Xinjiang paid for this tea—either through voluntary purchase or by direct deduction of part of their food stipend—Qing tea shipments to Xinjiang at this early stage were not a fully commercial enterprise, but were rather designed to resolve a quartermaster's predicament of massive proportions. The Qing managed tea production and sales with a licensing system derived from Ming precedents, themselves legacies of the more highly organized Song system. The Ming dynasty had used both tea and salt sales certificates (*yin*) as compensation for merchants who contracted to ship grain to the military camps along the northern border.[11]

During the Qing, merchants hoping to sell tea in the northwest were likewise required to buy licenses (chayin) entitling them to purchase tea at plantations (in Jiangsu, Anhui, Jiangxi, Zhejiang, Hubei, Hunan, Gansu, Sichuan, Yunnan, and Guizhou) and sell it in border areas. Throughout the Yongzheng reign, Qing authorities at four functioning Tea and Horse Agencies in the northwest collected as tax half of the tea shipped by merchants. The government then used this "official tea" (guancha) to trade for horses from Tibetans, Zunghars, and other nomad groups along the frontier. Merchants, meanwhile, were allowed to sell their "merchant tea" (shangcha or fucha) on local markets. A problem arose, however, because, unlike its predecessor, the Qing really did not need to engage in border horse trade as a long-term, large-scale measure. With Mongolia under control, the Tea and Horse Agencies became an anachronism.

From the last half of the Kangxi period until near the end of the Yongzheng reign, the Tea and Horse Agencies in the northwest conducted no tea-for-horse trading; nevertheless, they continued to collect tea license fees from merchants. In Kangxi times this posed no problems, for the Tea and Horse Agencies collected the fees in silver. But under Yongzheng these offices collected and stored 1.36 million catties of tea annually and, except for the four years from 1731 to 1735, exchanged none of it for horses. Furthermore, because merchants with licenses understandably turned over to the government only the poorer quality tea (much of it adulterated with grass and twigs), keeping the better product to sell themselves, "official tea" could not compete with "merchant tea" in Xining, Taozhou, Lanzhou, and other urban markets in the northwest. The fact that the governors-general and provincial governors, upon whom fell the responsibility for this tea, could not change prices in response to the market without first memorializing and receiving approval from Beijing virtually assured that little of the growing stock of tea could be sold off. At the beginning of the Qianlong reign in 1736, when the tea tax reverted to payment in silver, the northwestern Tea and Horse Agencies had over 2.6 million catties of tea on hand.[12] In 1755, when the Qing finally found a use for all that tea, over a million catties remained.[13] It was this surplus brick tea, passed up twenty years earlier for its poor quality by Tibetans in Xining, that the dynasty transported to Xinjiang for the banners, deducting the costs of tea and shipping from their wages. Moreover, the Tea and Horse Agency supplies apparently held out for almost another fifteen years: after 1767 Tarbagatai still received tea from Xining and Taomin, sites of two of the Tea and Horse Agencies.[14] In 1770, the Grand Council suggested supplying the Torghut Mongols (who had recently been resettled in Xinjiang after their calamitous return journey from the Volga region) with tea from Gansu's Tea and Horse Agency. This time, however, the reply came that because of the (early Qianlong) change to collection of tea license fees in silver, "there was not much tea left in Gansu." This legacy of the superannuated Tea and Horse Agencies had finally run out, although the offices continued to function as part of the general system of tea administration.

Formation of the Xinjiang Commissaries

There is no record of bannerman complaints about the quality of their tea. Perhaps this was because life in the new cities of Yili was spartan in all respects and must have seemed doubly so to those Manchus transferred from the more urban setting of Xi'an. Ming-rui, as Yili military governor from 1762 to 1766, was in charge of settling each wave of arriving troops into quarters and arranging for their provisions—all for the most part before the construction of the Yili garrison towns was complete. (Huiyuan, the first city built, was finished only in 1765). During this period Ming-rui memorialized the court with a suggestion that an endowment (*zisheng yinliang*) be established, presumably by imperial grant, the interest from which could be used to pay for weddings, funerals, rewards, and condolences for the Manchu banners. Gaozong replied, "The soldiers garrisoning Yili are all from Zhuanglang and similar places and are steeped in Han customs. They are good-for-nothing rubbish (*feiqi wuyong zhi ren*)! We specially ordered them to submit to hard labor and train their [military] skills. An endowment?! That would let them profit. Certainly not."[15]

Despite this rebuff, however, Ming-rui and other officials had by the mid-1760s created with local funds a network of investment and retail ventures that would provide extra money for just those social needs the emperor initially opposed. Central to these endeavors were various kinds of commissaries, or *guanpu*, that competed with local merchants to provide retail goods to bannermen and their families. In 1764 the bannermen garrisoning Yili contributed (or had deducted) fifteen taels each from their resettlement allowance to establish an official cloth shop (*guanbupu*). The cloth shop distributed profits to its investors. After some years, when the cloth shop had repaid the principal, the Yili government started dispatching officials with a small military escort to Lanzhou on alternate years. There they borrowed 60,000 taels (80,000 after 1790) from the provincial treasury and purchased stock for the store, which later sold these goods to Yili bannermen and their dependents, deducting the price directly from wages. The provincial treasury was repaid through a deduction from Yili's annual *xiexiang* allotment. Profits in the store

initially ran to 70 taels monthly—more than the monthly *yanglian* of a banner commandant.[16]

From these beginnings the commercial network grew. A series of official pawnshops further supplemented banner revenues. The Gracious Benefit
pawnshop (*Enyi Dang*) was established in 1766 with 10,000 taels from the
guanbupu. In 1773 it borrowed an additional 10,000 taels and later returned
the entire 20,000, having accumulated its own operating capital of 30,000
taels. It charged borrowers 2 percent monthly interest and remitted its profits
to the cloth shop. In 1787 a new branch opened, specifically to provide aid for
Yili's Manchu widows, widowers, and orphans. Because profits from the New
Gracious Benefit pawnshop proved insufficient for this purpose, three years
later the Gracious Relief pawnshop (*Enxu Dang*) was established, capitalized
initially at 10,000 and later 13,000 taels. The earnings of the New Gracious
Benefit and the Gracious Relief pawnshops were deposited in a special treasury dedicated to the Manchu bereaved.[17]

While the official cloth shop provided clothing and revenue and pawnshops brought in funds for eleemosynary use, other specialty shops opened
to cater to the garrisons' other needs while contributing their profits to the
growing administrative slush fund. In 1771 an apothecary (*yaopu*) opened
for business with stocks of drugs and 1,044 taels borrowed from the cloth
shop. The Yili apothecary henceforth purchased supplies on the same Lanzhou trips and delivered its profits into the same fund as the official cloth
shop.[18] Commissaries also sold the tea shipped from Gansu; cotton and cotton
cloth from Altishahr; and lumber, charcoal, stationery, agricultural tools, and
various products from the Kazakh trade, including hides, furs, and stomach
lining traded by the nomads in the trade pavilion after the conclusion of the
primary exchange of livestock with the Camel and Horse Office.[19]

All of this official commerce was legal, and the Beijing bureaucracy learned
every detail in volumes of reports flowing in from Yili. Expenditures and allocations of silver, copper cash, silk, grain, tea, cloth, livestock, and medicines,
along with military and agricultural equipment, were recorded in Manchu
and Chinese in reports often more than 50 pages long. These were sent first
to the governor-general of Shaanxi and Gansu for inspection and then forwarded to the Board of Revenue in the capital. One indication of the growing
scale of official economic activity in Yili (and later, other Xinjiang cities) is
the fact that the bureaucracy soon despaired of carefully reviewing Xinjiang's
economic reports. In 1773 the court dropped the requirement that these economic reports be submitted bilingually. After 1774 the reports were to be
sent directly to the board, bypassing the review in Lanzhou. Finally, around
1778, the forms were condensed into a single "four column list" (*sizhu qing-*

dan) for each city, thus greatly reducing the volume of data to be reviewed by the Board of Revenue.[20] By the same token, however, the switch to summary economic reports ceded greater autonomy in economic matters to the Yili military governor.

Following Yili's example, other cities in Zungharia and along the route between Hami and Urumchi established official shops; those in Urumchi developed particularly quickly. As in Yili, Urumchi began with an official cloth shop, capitalized with borrowed funds—in this case from the soldiers' clothing allowance. The store opened in 1772, selling goods purchased in Lanzhou and Xi'an, repaid the banners in three years, and at the same time made almost 20,000 taels profit, which allowed it to operate independently. Profits thereafter were stored in the Urumchi treasury to provide stipends for needy troops and official trips.

From as early as 1762, the increasing population of the Urumchi area had created a shortage of fuel. From 1772, when Urumchi's official cloth shop opened, the assistant commandant began mining coal to distribute to the soldiers and officials; repayment came through direct deduction of wages, and profits joined those from the official cloth shop in a charitable fund.

In 1774 the Gracious Attainment pawnshop (*Encheng Dang*) opened in Urumchi with 21,312 taels from a horse insurance fund (*majia*).* By 1785 the Gracious Attainment was operating in the black with over 30,000 taels of its own capital. After a further infusion of 10,000 taels from the official cloth shop in 1791, the pawnshop's yearly earnings of 6,000 taels were dedicated to the support of Manchu widows and orphans.[21] In 1775, Urumchi officials borrowed 1,000 taels from the official cloth shop to finance a labor agency (*jiangyi ju*), the exact functions of which are unclear; it was, however, a profitable enterprise, and by 1780 had repaid its loan and was worth 7,659 taels. Other projects included a lumber store, a mill to grind grain for the Manchu garrison, another pawnshop with a second-hand clothing shop next door, an official apothecary with four resident medics, and a shop that sold bureaus and chests.[22] All were run by the Manchu garrison.

In Tarbagatai, the government sold silk, tea, and cotton cloth to officials and troops at a profit from as early as 1765. The Tarbagatai *guanpu* were not formally established until 1802, however, when officials memorialized that the high prices for goods brought to the frontier by merchants, including clothing and weapons, amounted to a severe hardship for the banner forces.

---

* The *majia* fund was a pool into which each soldier, including the Green Standard troops, was required to deposit the price of a new horse. When invested, this horse insurance fund yielded interest that financed replacements for military mounts that sickened or died.

They requested and received Grand Council approval to follow Yili's example and open a garrison store with locally available funds. The explicit aims of this project were to undersell local merchants and to provide supplemental revenue for official travel expenses and maintenance of military horse herds. Tarbagatai's imperial agent, Xing-zhao, was authorized to dispatch an official to purchase goods in China proper. Green Standard laborers built ten *guanpu* buildings under the supervision of skilled carpenters and mudbrick masons. Xing-zhao personally contributed the paint and nails.[23]

The garrisons of Turfan, Barkol, and Gucheng also operated official shops and pawnshops. Officials in Turfan, for example, sent buyers at three-year intervals to Xi'an, Liangzhou, and Lanzhou to procure stocks of cloth and tea with 4,000 taels borrowed from the treasuries of Shaanxi and Gansu provinces. As elsewhere, the advance was repaid out of *xiexiang* silver before the stipend was shipped to Turfan. Barkol's was one of the most prosperous pawnshops: in 1806 it held clothing as collateral on 30,320 taels worth of loans and had cash reserves of 1,665 taels.[24]

Although Gaozong had rebuffed Ming-rui when the military general first broached the subject of an endowment for the welfare of the Manchu banners in Yili, by 1770 he relented, acknowledging that the Yili garrison forces, stationed there in perpetuity, were well trained and satisfactorily inured to hardship. Although we do not have Ming-rui's original memorial, it seems that he had hoped for a grant from the imperial household to establish the endowment. (Both Yongzheng and Qianlong emperors had made such grants—known as *shengxi yinliang*—to garrisons elsewhere.)[25] By 1770, however, over 30,000 taels of tax and rent revenue had accumulated in the Yili treasury, enough to establish the extra-budgetary endowment fund at no cost to Beijing. The emperor ruled: "Let favor be shown to the Yili soldiers through bonuses, condolences, weddings, and funerals [provided by the endowment]."[26] Investment at interest thus became another means by which garrison authorities in northern Xinjiang supplemented their budgets.

Presumably, one of the earliest instances of such investment in Xinjiang involved the 30,000 taels just mentioned, although we have no further information on this case. But in 1777 Huiyuan invested 50,000 taels of its *guanpu* profits. In 1789, the Yili military governor and imperial agent borrowed 27,000 taels from the horse insurance pool and invested it at 1 percent monthly interest with merchants from Shaanxi Province in China proper. The officials then used the interest income to supplement the widows and orphans fund, for which pawnshop revenues had proved insufficient. These and other examples of investment of Xinjiang's official funds, most of which were raised entirely by Xinjiang authorities themselves, are summarized in

TABLE 5
Official Qing Investments in Zungharia, 1770–1854
(in silver taels)

	Source	Amount	How Invested	Monthly Interest Earned	Recipient of Earnings
1770	Tax and rent income	30,000			
1777	*Guanbupu* profits	50,000			
1789	Horse insurance fund	27,000	Shaanxi merchants	1%	Yili widows and orphans
1793	Xi'an provincial treasury	64,800	Shaanxi merchants		Chahar banner aid
1799	Horse insurance fund	20,000	Local merchants	1%	Urumchi *guanpu* for military welfare
1834*	Yili surplus tax and rent incomes	10,000	Local shopkeepers	.9%	Supplement for Yili Manchu military and official food stipends
1850s	Horse insurance fund	40,000	Shaanxi merchants	1%	Yili garrison widows and widowers
	Rent income	10,000	Pawnbrokers	.9%	Food allowance for Yili-region border patrols
	Proceeds from sale of horses and sheep	15,000	Pawnbrokers	.9–1%	Chahar widows and widowers; Chahar river works and general maintenance
		10,000	Pawnbrokers	1%	Green Standard widows and widowers
		28,000	Pawnbrokers	.9%	Yili Sibe garrison
	Public funds (*gongxiang*) remaining in local treasury	10,000	Pawnbrokers	.9%	Yili Manchu garrisons
		8,000 6,000	Pawnbrokers	.9%	Yili Solon garrison

SOURCES: *GZSL* 854:1b–2a, QL35.3 *gengchen*; Yong-bao, *Zongtong Yili shiyi*, pp. 192–93, 202–3; *SZJL* p. 145; Te-yi-shun-bao, Su-qing-ke, ZPZZ MZSW 0094-3, DG14.11.28; *YJJZ* p. 25b.
*The 1834 item was a proposed investment; we have no record of whether it was approved.

Table 5. The sources we have suggest that such investment became an increasingly important supplement to garrison budgets, especially during the Xianfeng reign, when *xiexiang* shipments were no longer regularly available.

The emperor acquiesced to investment of official funds in Xinjiang and presumably knew, from their inception, about the activities of official stores. However, the Qianlong court was initially ambivalent about such active participation in commerce by its Manchu banners in Zungharia. In 1775, a few years after the first Yili *guanpu* set up shop, Gaozong reacted. "The Manchu officers and soldiers of Yili and Urumchi garrisons now have all established commissaries and appoint [personnel] to engage in trade. This is far from what is meant by 'defending the frontier!' Moreover, Manchu troops from childhood are trained at riding and shooting; they are not accustomed to commerce. In time, this will surely lead to trouble. It has a strong bearing on their character." The emperor asked the Grand Council to consider the question. In their answering memorial, these ministers echoed Gaozong's fears, but recognized the fiscal importance and established history of official commerce in Zungharia.

> Yili and the other cities have opened shops. Although this has profited the soldiers, we fear lest in the long term [the Manchu bannermen] will become like the Han, fond of leisure and treating work with contempt, so that their skills will deteriorate. [Preoccupation with commerce] should be strictly prohibited. But in these places the *guanpu* have already been in operation a long time and cannot be eliminated all at once. Let Iletu (Yi-le-tu) and Suo-ruo-mu-ze-ling summon rich merchant commoners from Urumchi, Barkol, and Hami to come manage the business. The annual profits can still be apportioned to support the soldiers.[27]

The rescript on this recommendation (*congzhi*) indicates that it was adopted, and this concern in 1775 may have had a temporary effect, for although I have found no other record of any interruption of business as usual, in 1789 the Yili military governor, Bao-ning, requested permission to establish official shops to prevent private merchants from hoarding and price gouging. Without explicitly mentioning any precedent, he echoed earlier arguments by pointing out how profits from *guanpu* could help fill two of the standard shortfalls of Xinjiang's military budget: replacement of horses and funds for official trips. The existence of such a proposal suggests that Yili's official shops had indeed been shut down for a period. When the emperor agreed to Bao-ning's proposal, authorizing Bao-ning to send buyers to China proper, he reestablished the Yili official shops.[28]

Despite this memorial, I have found no further information regarding implementation of the 1775 decree. On the contrary, the lengthy gazetteer accounts of official shops and investments dating from after that year make no reference to the decree or to enlisting Urumchi merchants to take over operations. It is unclear to what extent, if any, the mundane tasks of running these official enterprises in Zungharia as a whole were ever turned over to private Chinese merchants. In each city of northern Xinjiang, at least after

1789, if not from 1770, the *guanpu* remained the keystones of official invest-ment portfolios that linked retail stores with local and regional treasuries, the Gansu treasury, and *xiexiang* budgets, not to mention the debt, consump-tion, and welfare of the Manchu banners. Profits from official shops were integrated into Xinjiang's fiscal administration as a whole; for example, loans against *xiexiang* were used to purchase new stock, and purchases by banner-men were paid for by direct deductions from the payroll before disbursement of wages. In Xinjiang, where there were almost no ranking Han officials, it seems inconceivable that authorities would delegate such critical fiscal con-cerns to Han merchants, even if ones rich enough could be recruited.

Perhaps inevitably, given the opportunity to sully themselves through commerce, some Manchus chose to do so. Word reached Beijing in 1827 that soldiers sent from Yili, Urumchi, Barkol, and elsewhere to purchase uniforms in China proper used the trips as cover for a secret trade in women, gam-bling equipment, antiques, and curios. According to the censor Niu-jian, who broke the case, "There's nothing forbidden that they don't bring back." The commissioner argued that items needed by the Xinjiang garrison should as much as possible be purchased in Xinjiang. "In future, bows and arrows and the like can be bought in China proper, but cloth and tea are readily avail-able outside the Pass and should be obtained there to avoid shipping costs and abuses."[29] Again, we see that the capital viewed the established official com-merce in northern Xinjiang with some suspicion and would have preferred a system that relied more heavily on private merchants to supply the garrisons. Nonetheless, nothing changed.

From the perspective of Xinjiang officials, especially those responsible for banner and Green Standard garrisons, official shops and related investments were too useful to forgo. A survey of the benefits of the commissary system must begin of course with the goods and credit it made available, apparently at a fair price, to the populations of Huiyuan, Ningyuan, and other Manchu garrison cities. But as we have seen, private merchants could also provide cloth, medicine, sundries, and credit, albeit more expensively. More than simple PX stores, however, the *guanpu* were highly profitable operations (the cloth shop and apothecary, for example, realized an annual return of over 50 percent) and allowed Xinjiang's administrators to perform tasks for which the primary budget of *xiexiang* was insufficient. Tables 6 and 7 show the earnings from investments, official stores, and pawnshops in Urumchi and how these revenues were disbursed around the end of the Qianlong period.

In addition to such fixed annual expenditures, moreover, the *guanpu* reve-nues proved useful for special purposes. In 1769, for example, the official cloth shop provided students in Yili's new banner school with stipends for

TABLE 6
Capital and Annual Earnings of Urumchi Commissaries, c. 1796
(in silver taels)

Guanpu Type	Capital	Earnings
Cloth shop	19,640	10,000
Pawnshop	41,092*	6,250
Labor agency (*jiangyi ju*)	4,000	1,200
Lumber shop	3,000	1,550
Apothecary	1,000	500
Second pawnshop	—	1,030
Total	68,732	20,530

SOURCE: Yong-bao et al., *Wulumuqi shiyi*, pp. 33a–b.
*Includes 10,000 taels borrowed from the treasury's *majia* fund, repayable in five years.

TABLE 7
Annual expenditure of Urumchi Guanpu Revenues, c. 1796
(in silver taels)

Welfare for retired, crippled, aged, widows, orphans, and those with many dependents among banner population	12,000
Forgiving of payments to horse insurance fund	3,000
Stipend for soldiers on official business or when driving game on hunts	2,100
Per diems for soldiers on long trips; carriage, *karun*, and ranch workers' stipends	Individual daily amounts
Public expenses and coal stipend for infantry	1,500
Replastering commissary buildings	200
Repayment of treasury loan for barracks repair	1,400
Pawnshop repayments on treasury *majia* loan	2,000

SOURCE: Yong-bao et al., *Wulumuqi shiyi*, pp. 33a–b.

paper, brushes, and tea. The teachers in this school were Han, Manchu, and Mongol, but the shop also supported students at a Russian school, which operated from 1792 to 1795 (after which the Russian teacher was sent home). In 1796, *guanpu* meltage fees (presumably a surcharge levied on customers who paid in copper cash) funded the training of a squadron of soldiers in the use of scaling ladders.[30] One night in the summer of 1790 a flash flood on a river outside Urumchi destroyed the Manchu garrison mill along with the side buildings in which grain was stored. Urumchi officials drew on the horse insurance fund to make the necessary repairs to the mill, arranging to repay the sum from the following year's *guanpu* profits.[31] Similarly, Urumchi officials combined *majia* funds to rebuild the Urumchi barracks. The 11,409 taels from the horse insurance fund was repaid from the official shops' takings in only eight years.[32]

Another case demonstrates particularly well how official commerce allowed Xinjiang authorities flexibility in financial matters and the ability to provide relief for Manchu banners in emergencies. In 1813, when an epidemic broke out in Huiyuan, Manchu officials and soldiers bought almost 7,000 taels worth of medicine on credit—more than could reasonably be deducted from their salaries in a single year. The military governor and councillor instead temporarily cleared the deficit with profits from a sale of livestock to Manchus and Oirats and deducted the cost of the medicine from salaries over the next few years.[33]

Xinjiang's Official Commerce and China Proper

Official shops and government investment were not unique to Xinjiang's administration. In fact, from the second year of the Yongzheng reign (1724) the Imperial Household Agency provided loans (*shengxi yinliang*) to provincial yamens and Manchu garrisons in China proper and the northeast for investment in retail shops or pawnbroking. As in Xinjiang later, the profits were spent on the welfare of soldiers, including the Green Standard troops, and their families. The *shengxi yinliang* thus served as endowment funds, except that recipients of these imperial loans owed interest to the court; interest rates varied with locality from 8 to 15 percent, but usually were around 10 percent annually.

Although vigorously promoted by the Yongzheng emperor, this practice of making imperial credit available to local garrison officials became controversial under his son. Soon after Gaozong succeeded to the throne, Šuhede, then a young censor, memorialized against the imperial investments on the traditional grounds that commerce "is not the essence of the court," and in particular warned that the loans had come to be used in a manner contrary to their original purpose. As became increasingly clear through revelations that continued throughout the first half of the Qianlong reign, local officials put an ever larger proportion of their *shengxi yinliang* into usury, reloaning money at much higher interest and rolling the earned interest back into capital. As a result, officials neglected garrison retail commerce and, more importantly, the rank and file whom the imperial loans were designed to benefit in the first place. In some places, local civil or military authorities allocated the interest income to the main budget, where it paid their own "nourish integrity" (*yanglian*) stipends and other costs that should have come out of land tax revenues. Besides these quasi-legal subversions of imperial intent, outright embezzlement was not unheard of.[34]

By 1754 the Qianlong emperor decided to call in the remaining loans and end the system of imperial investment. However, the *shengxi yinliang* had become so thoroughly integrated into local fiscal administration that not until 1770 could all the provincial yamens find alternative sources of capital (including deductions from military pay and horse insurance funds) and completely phase out their reliance on imperial investments.[35]

Military governor Ming-rui, in trying to provide social services for the bannermen newly arrived in Huiyuan and Ningyuan, faced the problem common to garrison administrators elsewhere in China: while expenditures on bereavement, marriages, funerals, and similar assistance to Manchu military families were legitimate and necessary, no provision was made for these expenditures in Xinjiang's main budget. Ming-rui hoped to fill that budget gap with the interest from an imperial endowment, but his request came too late—by the 1760s Gaozong considered the *shengxi yinliang* program rife with abuse and was phasing it out. As a result, Ming-rui and his successors were forced to develop their system of official shops and investments without imperial capital, drawing on *xiexiang*, the horse insurance fund, military clothing and settlement stipends, commercial rents and taxes, and eventually the earnings of the official enterprises themselves for a source of working capital. Moreover, the *guanpu* and various official investments seem to have operated effectively and without deviating from their original design for almost a century. There is no evidence that large amounts of the shops' capital were siphoned off into high-interest loans, nor have I discovered any cases of serious abuse, though no doubt there were some.

It is a curious coincidence that the period of the Yili commissary system's development corresponds to the tenure of Šuhede as military governor in Yili (1771–73). Although first to note local abuse of imperial investments in China proper early in the Qianlong reign, Šuhede presided over the expansion of a similar official commercial network in Yili and, in 1775, was a member of the Grand Council that advised against eliminating the Yili official shops outright, suggesting instead (as shown above) that merchants be brought in to handle the business. Thus reprieved, Yili's official commercial network proved longer lived and of greater fiscal importance than similar official enterprises in China proper or the northeast.

The Southern Commissaries

From the time when its armies first occupied the oases rimming the Taklamakan Desert, the Qing had engaged in official commerce to help feed them and to relieve strain on extended supply lines and the imperial treasury. Qing officials in Altishahr oversaw the sales of silk, tea, and other products on local markets for *pul*, which they then entered for accounting purposes under primary revenues and used for soldiers' wages, food stipends, and so forth. This allowed a savings of the equivalent amount of *xiexiang* silver. Around 1804, for example, Qing officials in Ush sold between 200 and 300 bolts of silk and 3,250 catties of tea—the tea sales alone were worth over 500 silver taels.[36]

The cities of southern Xinjiang did not initially follow Yili, Tarbagatai, Urumchi, Barkol, Turfan, and Hami in establishing *guanpu*. The main reason for this was the relatively small number of troops stationed in the south: before 1828, there were only around 5,000, of whom only 825 were Manchu bannermen.[37] Moreover, the non-Manchu troops, primarily Han soldiers of the Green Standards, were not permanently stationed in southern cities but rather served there on rotational tours of duty. Thus they brought no dependents to Altishahr. The only military farm (*bingtun*) in the south in Qianlong times was in Ush, and this employed only 650 Han troops. Because *guanpu* and official investments were primarily designed to provide for the welfare of banners, particularly the Manchus, and their dependents, during the first decades of Qing rule there was little need for such institutions in Altishahr.

After Jahāngīr's invasion and the Altishahr rebellion in 1826, however, the court decided to station banner forces permanently in Kashgar, Yangi Hisar, Yarkand, and Aksu and to increase total troop strength in the south by 5,500 men. Furthermore, these soldiers were allowed to bring dependents.[38] Facing the problem of supplying necessities at war-inflated prices to the bannermen in these cities, Nayanceng decided to follow the example of Yili 60 years earlier and establish official shops in Kashgar and Yarkand.

Like Nayanceng's other economic programs in Altishahr, opening *guanpu* in the south was a major reform. However, his proposals in this regard were not entirely economic in scope, nor were they exclusively directed at succoring the banners. Rather, he intended them as weapons in a campaign to control foreign trade and traders in Altishahr, particularly Kashgar and Yarkand, cities astride the trade routes to Central and South Asia. After recapturing the southern cities from Jahāngīr, the Qing had placed an embargo on trade with Kokand, hoping to force the khanate to turn over the remaining Khoja descendants whom it was harboring. In mid-1828 Nayanceng deported all Kokandi merchants who had resided in Xinjiang less than ten years.[39] In order to prevent other foreign merchants from establishing an enclave in Kashgar or Yarkand, to interdict smuggling of tea and rhubarb to Kokand, and to staunch what he saw as a drain of silver from Xinjiang due to East Turkestani purchases of foreign goods with specie, Nayanceng proposed moving all foreign trade out of town. Under Nayanceng's plan, foreign merchants would be allowed to exchange goods only under close official supervision in

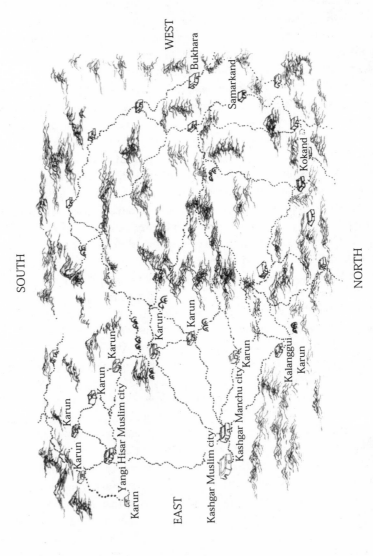

Map 3. The Kalanggui *karun* and the route to Kokand. Source: Based on LFZZ MZSW 1490.

trade pavilions (*maoyi ting*) in the mountains outside Kashgar and Yarkand. Nayanceng's proposal was based on the precedent of the trade pavilion outside Yili, which had been the venue for successful trade with the Kazakhs each autumn for almost 70 years.

In his memorials on the subject, Nayanceng explicitly links the institutions of the *maoyi ting* and *guanpu*. For example, he planned to erect the trade pavilion in a remote spot called Mingyol (Mingyueluo), 100 *li* from Kashgar beyond the Kalanggui *karun* on the main route to Andijan and Kokand (see Map 3). This, Nayanceng reported, was according to the "precedent of the Yili *guanpu*." All exchanges at the new trade pavilion were to be by barter, at officially fixed prices. After this trade enclosure in the mountains was established, "so that, externally, we may check up on barbarian merchants' whereabouts and [prevent] illegal domicile, and, internally, restrain those traitorous merchants who speculate and conspire," Nayanceng considered it also "necessary to open official shops in order to stamp [the papers of merchants] coming and going and to control what is ours."[40]

As in Yili, the main difficulty in setting up the southern *guanpu* was finding seed money. Nayanceng determined that he would not need to draw upon Altishahr's primary silver revenues, but could capitalize the new official shops with proceeds from the sale of property confiscated from the deported Kokandi households. Almost 69,000 catties of tea had been obtained through these confiscations. Nayanceng hoped to distribute it to the soldiers garrisoning Altishahr, deducting the tea's market value from their wages to realize 50,000 taels of savings from *xiexiang*. The Qing had also taken about 181,000 taels in cash and other property from the Kokandis and rebel Altishahri merchants. The bulk of this went to repair walls, military post stations (*juntai*), irrigation canals, and other infrastructure damaged during the war, as well as for construction of the trade compound and barracks at Mingyol and of the new commissaries in Kashgar and Yarkand. However, about 15,000 taels were left over after these projects, and Nayanceng also invested this in the official shops.[41]

The Daoguang emperor approved Nayanceng's proposal reluctantly, expressing the reservation that, although the plan to control border trade in southern Xinjiang according to the Yili model looked fine on paper, over time the strict regulations would exist in name only and Qing administration of the *guanpu* would become a farce (*wansheng*). In addition, some officials were concerned that, because the trade would be between "Muslims and barbarians," calling in Han merchants to handle the corrupting business matters would not be an option: Altishahri beg officials would have to be used.[42] Still, the Kashgar and Yarkand trade pavilions seemed to function smoothly enough at first. A party of merchants from Bukhara (Buga'er) applied for permission to trade in the autumn of 1828 and was accommodated at Mingyol, where under guard by 200 Qing troops they traded 40 percent of their goods for tea and textiles from the *guanpu* stocks and the remainder with private merchants, including perhaps some Han or Tungan from China proper in addition to Altishahri traders.[43]

Nayanceng proposed that the commissaries' profits be distributed to the Manchu and Han officials and soldiers in Kashgar and Yarkand, with a fixed portion reserved for yamen administrative expenses and maintenance of government buildings. He later suggested that these revenues could provide gifts to tributary Kirghiz whose transhumance included the mountains around Kashgar and Ush—this would mean a further savings to the treasury of 1,000 taels annually.[44]

Such uses of the revenues from official commerce followed the precedent set in northern Xinjiang. There was a major difference between southern and northern *guanpu*, however: in the south, they never turned a profit. Six months after the establishment of the Kashgar trade pavilion and official shop, Jalungga (Zha-long-a), who succeeded Nayanceng as councillor, reported that the *guanpu* had already faltered. "If this thing can work, then carry on," grumbled the emperor. "If not, then shut it down. I will not run it from this distance!"[45]

Jalungga, along with E-er-gu-lun and Isḥāq, the Kashgar hakim beg, told the story of the failing *guanpu* in their subsequent memorial. When Nayanceng first established his sytem to control foreign trade by channeling it through the trade pavilion and official shop, the Jahāngīr hostilities had only recently concluded. Prices were high and the shop set its tea prices even higher than the going market rate, at 0.8 taels per catty. Since the fourth month of 1829, however, market prices for tea had plummeted as a direct result of the embargo on Kokandi merchants, who had been the principal buyers of Chinese tea in Kashgar. Nayanceng had intended to sell off the confiscated stocks of tea through sales to Qing soldiers in Altishahr. In such a market, however, this was impractical and most of the 69,000 catties ended up as inventory in the official shop. Although the Bukhara merchants had traded for tea, Jalungga mentioned in this memorial that "it is forbidden for tea to be exported beyond the *karun*, and the local market for tea is limited," suggesting that in the zealous attempt to keep tea out of Kokandi hands, all foreign sales of tea had been suspended. "When goods are plentiful, their price is low," the three officials noted, displaying a sounder appreciation of supply and demand than their predecessor had. "Merchants ship and turn around [tea] quickly, without seeking extra profit, allowing them to sell cheap." The commissaries' stale, overpriced tea stocks, on the other hand, found no buyers.

The one somewhat profitable aspect of the business was the purchase of sheep from Kirghiz nomads for resale in Kashgar and Yarkand. But even this small success turned out to be short-lived. The Kirghiz found the Qing price for Yarkandi cotton cloth too high and brought progressively fewer sheep to the trade pavilion over the months. Whereas in its first five months of operation the *guanpu* earned over 10,000 taels from sheep sales, profits on this side of the business fell to 6,500 over the next ten months. The situation in Yarkand and Ush (where a third, embryonic *guanpu* had opened) was similar.[46]

Near the end of 1829, therefore, Jalungga and his colleagues sought and received approval to shut down the ill-fated Altishahr *guanpu* operation and allow local Muslims and "barbarians" to trade directly, under official supervision.

The debate over what to do with the sum of money salvaged from sheep sales and a steeply discounted liquidation of the tea stocks makes a revealing epilogue to the story of the failed Altishahr official shops. In it we see that officials in Kashgar, although relieved to be free of the unworkable *guanpu*, nonetheless wished to retain the measure of financial independence that the control of a capital fund could provide. In their memorial of late 1829, Jalungga and his colleagues proposed that, since 40,000 taels were left after the *guanpu* experiment, an equivalent sum could be deducted from the next *xiexiang* shipment (due in 1831) and invested for the Altishahr authorities in Gansu and Shaanxi at 1 percent monthly interest. This interest income could then be sent to Kashgar and Yarkand annually to subsidize administration and tributary gifts. The Board of Revenue, however, disagreed. After deliberation, the board responded that there were not many wealthy merchants in Gansu and, because Xinjiang's funds had long been entrusted with Shaanxi merchants, it was "inconvenient" to invest further amounts. The 40,000 taels should instead be spent *in lieu of* the equivalent amount of *xiexiang*—thus in effect passing a one-time savings on to the provinces that subsidized Xinjiang's military government. But despite the emperor's agreement with the board's plan, Jalungga memorialized again in late 1829 or early 1830, this time suggesting that "since the budget for 1831 has already been drawn up," he would prefer to put the money (by now, with the addition of some other miscellaneous revenues, a tidy 80,000 taels) in a special emergency fund designed to prevent Kashgar from being caught short of cash should the city be attacked again. We do not know the fate of this 80,000, but Kashgar did indeed get its emergency fund eventually.[47]

The troubles of the Kashgar and Yarkand *guanpu* stemmed from a problem with their initial conception: Nayanceng borrowed the example of two distinct institutions that had been successful in Yili, the trade pavilion and the official shop. In Yili and Tarbagatai the trade pavilion was simply an enclosure that served as venue for official and supervised private trade with the Kazakhs, trade that was aimed primarily at securing livestock and hence fell under the purview of the Camel and Horse Office of the Yili government. The *guanpu*, on the other hand, served as the cornerstone of a complex of official investments designed to raise revenue for Manchu banner welfare and miscellaneous projects that fell outside the *xiexiang* budget. While there were points of contact between the Kazakh trade and northern official shops (notably, the sale by the *guanpu* of livestock, pastoral products, and Altishahr cotton cloth), they were distinct in both management and purpose. In attempting to transplant these institutions to Altishahr, Nayanceng conflated them—a fact that is clear from his use of the terms *guanpu* and *maoyi ting* almost interchangeably in his early memorials on the subject. But rather than serving as banner retail outlets for goods from China proper, Nayanceng's *guanpu* were in theory simply clearinghouses for the confiscated goods of deported Kokandis and nomad products from the trade enclosure. In practice, they served as little more than warehouses for these goods. Unlike the northern commissaries, Nayanceng's shops did not attempt to undersell local merchants, nor did they procure goods from China proper (although the idea was proposed). Rather, they fixed tea prices unreasonably high, ensuring that none would sell domestically; at the same time, restrictions on tea export cut off the potential foreign market. Nayanceng had launched the Kashgar and Yarkand administrations into the tea business just when Qing sanctions against the Kokandis caused the local tea market to collapse.

The Qing and the "Silk Road"

To many, the "Silk Road" of the high Qing period—especially the various trade routes across the Tarim and Zungharian Basins, which the Manchus conquered and maintained—does not live up to the golden reputation of earlier eras. Scholars have suggested various reasons for this "decline," including competition from maritime trade routes, the loss of China's exclusive control over silk technology, and the political fragmentation of the Eurasian Steppe, east and west, that followed the demise of the Mongol empire. But much of this sense of decline may be more a matter of historical perception.*

---

* We have few quantitative measures of ancient Silk Road commerce. However, our modern fascination with the region's history seems to stem not so much from the volume or even value of ancient trade, per se, but from other concerns. For the Japanese, for example, the eastward transmission of Buddhism is of key importance. Han Chinese take

S. A. M. Adshead, while stressing the enduring cultural significance of this "avenue of contact" between China and elsewhere, has recently questioned "the picture of the silk road as a major Eurasian intercontinental link channelling silk in one direction and precious metals, stuccoes and glass in the other," suggesting that its "economic importance has been exaggerated."[48] On the other hand, the long-distance trade passing through Xinjiang in the eighteenth and early nineteenth centuries, while perhaps less glamorous insofar as it was based as much on tea and rhubarb as on silk, was probably no less lucrative than in earlier times, even if most consumers of these products lived considerably nearer than Rome.

In analyzing economic change in early modern Central Asia, Adshead draws a distinction between "the east-west trade, long distance, concerning luxuries, irregular and largely irrelevant to nomadism, though taxable by its empires" and "north-south trade, concerning necessities, regular, having a real impact on nomadic society, though less useful to [nomadic] empires." Adshead makes the distinction in regard to the views of Omeljan Pritsak and Joseph Fletcher on how changes in the world market in early modern times affected Central Asian empires. Pritsak has argued that the early modern decline in trans-Eurasian luxury trade weakened states such as the Uzbek and the Zunghar because it deprived them of tax revenues. Fletcher, on the other hand, stresses the deleterious effects of commerce on nomad societies ("consumerism, sedentarization and class division"). Adshead reconciles the apparent contradiction between these two views by pointing out that the two scholars are considering "fundamentally different kinds of trade in Central Asia."

Both types of trade existed in Qing Xinjiang. As I will discuss in detail in subsequent chapters, Chinese merchants eagerly engaged in the "north-south" trade (the directions are meant in their figurative, as well as literal, sense), purveying goods to economically and technologically less developed societies. The Qing state attempted to guard against such trade's "deleterious effects." Chinese merchants also carried the long-distance "east-west" trade goods, but it was primarily the khanate of Kokand that benefited, taxing this

---

satisfaction from and geopolitical justification in the knowledge that their eponymous Han dynasty progenitors explored and conquered Western Regions territory, as did the Tang (a dynasty that, unlike Yuan and Qing and despite an undeniable whiff of the barbarian, Han today claim as their own). And, for reasons not unlike those of the Chinese, Europeans and Americans take pleasure in the exploits of Western explorers, archaeologists, and treasure hunters who have unearthed *Indo-European* civilizations (not to mention Caucasian mummies) along the old Silk Route or devised cunning Great Game moves to determine whether Britain or Russia would dominate the pivot of Asia.

TABLE 8
Customs Tariffs in Qing Xinjiang as Paid on Imports
by Different Classes of Merchants

	East Turkestani	Foreign Tributaries (including Kokand)	Kashmir, Badakhshan, and the Pamir Countries	Muslims	Non-Muslims
Up to 1760	10%	5%	—		
1760–1807	5%	3.3%	2.5%		
(duty on silk, cotton cloth, hides)	10%	5%	—		
After 1807	—	Exempt—duty seldom collected	Exempt—duty seldom collected		
1829	5%	Trade embargo	2.5%		
1832	5%	Exempt	Exempt		
After 1835				2.5%	5%

SOURCES: *PDZGEFL zheng,* 83:21b–22a, QL24.12 *dingyou; HYXYTZ* 34:17b–18a; *HJTZ* 7:8b, 9:5a; Li Hongzhang et al., *(Qinding) Da Qing huidian shili,* j. 983, n.p., "Menggu minren maoyi"; *NWYGZY* 77:12b–14a, DG9.1.12; *XZSL* 209:18, DG12.4 *wuzi;* Wathen, "Memoir," p. 661; Naqshbandi, "Route from Kashmir, via Ladakh, to Yarkand," p. 382; Tuo-jin et al. *(Qinding) Huijiang zeli,* 6:10; Fletcher, "The Heyday," pp. 373, 379.

commerce from a position astride the trade route. The Qing conquest and development of Altishahr and Zungharia actually lifted many political and logistical barriers to travel and commerce, allowing a final floruit of "east-west" trade on which Kokand thrived, despite increasing competition from maritime routes. It is thus somewhat odd, then, that the Qing did not make a priority of tapping this considerable east-west transit trade.

Customs barriers at each oasis town in the Tarim had been a bane of itinerant merchants, and a boon for ruling powers, from ancient times. The Tang, for example, collected customs in its Western Regions holdings.[49] However, with the exception of Hami (see next paragraph), there were no internal customs in Qing Xinjiang from the time of the conquest until the 1850s. Customs were collected, at low rates, on the value of goods imported from abroad by East Turkestani merchants, Kirghiz nomads, foreign tributaries, and "other barbarians," with tax rates depending on the place of origin of the merchant involved. Until 1760, the Qing maintained the old Zunghar tariff rates, assessing 10 percent of the value of goods imported by local merchants and 5 percent on imports by foreigners. Early in 1760 the Qing lowered the duties to 5 percent for Qing subjects (East Turkestani merchants), 3.3 percent for foreign tributaries (*waifan,* including Kokandis and many Kirghiz groups), and 2.5 percent for other foreigners (Kashmiris, Badakhshanis, and others from the Pamir countries). The tariff on imported silk, cotton cloth, and hides was higher: East Turkestanis paid 10 percent ad valorem and tributaries paid 5 percent. In 1807 the Jiaqing emperor announced an exemption from customs for all foreigners, including the Kirghiz, who entered the *karun* to trade in Kashgar or Yarkand. Nonetheless, Nayanceng in 1829 fumed that foreign merchants should have been paying customs duty, but the intercession of hakim begs on merchants' behalf and "loose rein" impulses of Altishahr ambans resulted in general failure to enforce the law. After Nayanceng's disastrous attempt to block all trade with Kokand, however, the new Qing policy in 1832 granted a general tariff concession to Kokandi and all other foreign traders in Altishahr. This Xinjiang duty-free zone was short-lived; after another accord in 1835, Kokand took over Xinjiang's customs collection, and the khanate's representatives in Altishahr, the *aqsaqals*, levied a 2.5 percent duty on the value of imports by Muslim merchants and 5 percent on non-Muslims' goods. (The history of Xinjiang's foreign customs duty is summarized in Table 8.)[50]

There are two exceptions to the general Qing failure to tax Xinjiang transit trade. One was the road-pass system, discussed in Chapter 4. The other was a somewhat anomalous customs barrier in Hami. All commercial traffic entering Xinjiang from the Gansu corridor, whether ultimately bound for Zungharia or Altishahr, passed through this city. According to the Hami gazetteer, merchants coming and going from China proper paid a per-cart tariff and purchased road passes for at least some time during the 1759–1864 period:[51]

Carts exiting the *Guan* (Jiayu? Hami gate?) to sell goods	Yearly, per cart iron-rim wheels wooden-rim wheels	3 taels 2 taels	To defray costs of transporting exiles through Hami
Carts shipping goods toward Turfan or Barkol	Yearly, per cart	2 taels	To pay guards escorting exiles
Merchants entering the *Guan*	Yearly permit (per person)	0.4 taels	
Chinese traveling to Turfan or Barkol	Yearly permit (per person)	0.7 taels	
"West route" merchants shipping or selling jade pieces	Yearly license	Tax based on weight	

Tapping Private Commercial Wealth in Xinjiang

For the most part, however, the empire concerned itself with monitoring, and taxing, the sedentary commerce of Chinese merchants settled in Xinjiang cities. As Qing armies advanced into Zungharia in the 1750s, these Han and

Tungan (Chinese Muslim) merchants from China proper were close behind. Official documents note their presence almost immediately after the fighting ended. Developing garrison towns in Yili and Urumchi offered commercial opportunity, and the availability of land must have been still more attractive. Many of the "merchants" referred to in Qing sources were in fact simply commoners with means to immigrate and cultivate their 30 *mu* without financial assistance from the government. Some, too, were able to purchase additional land and hire laborers to work it. Because these cultivators were independent, unlike the commoners working state farms or soldiers on military farms, they were under no obligation to produce grain and could specialize instead in more lucrative fruits and vegetables. Truck farms (*caiyuan*) sprang up on the outskirts of Yili, Urumchi, and other cities in northern and eastern Xinjiang.

Qing authorities wasted no time in attempting to tax these commercial farmers and the private merchants who opened small shops or peddler's stands in Xinjiang cities, mostly on government land. (Although no explicit description of the distribution of government land [*guandi*] and private land has come to light, the general principle seems to have been that, because the new cities in Zungharia were founded by the Qing, virtually all land was state-owned.) Control, rather than revenue, seems to have been the initial goal—or at least the justification—of this commercial taxation: virtually all the Han and Tungan inhabitants of Xinjiang at this time were recent immigrants, and Qing officials expressed a need to monitor these Chinese merchants in the growing frontier towns.

In 1762 Urumchi Commander-in-Chief Jing-ge-li suggested categorizing the over 500 new shops in Urumchi into three classes for inspection and taxation; he proposed that commercial farmland, of which over 300 *mu* was by then under cultivation, should also be surveyed and taxed. The emperor not only agreed with the proposal but ordered its implementation in "Yili, Yarkand, Aksu, and other cities," in all of which merchants and commercial farmers occupied government land. "This [policy] will help us inspect [the merchants] and also be of benefit to public finances."[52]

Jing-ge-li proposed taxing Han and Tungan shops in Xinjiang 0.3, 0.2, or 0.1 taels per month, depending on the size of each establishment. Commercial fruit and vegetable farmers were to pay 0.1 taels per year on each *mu* of land they cultivated. Throughout Xinjiang, Qing authorities undertook the necessary surveys almost immediately. The same year, we learn, there were eight large, eleven medium, and fourteen small shops in Kashgar, mostly in the "new city," although a few Han merchants opened up shop among the Kashgarliks in the Muslim city. In Urumchi, where immigration from China proper was much greater, the merchant population was higher.[53]

Many local authorities embellished upon this system by building housing, shops, or bazaars on government land and renting this property out at per-*jian**** rates considerably higher than the standard commercial tax (which was assessed per merchant household). In Yili in 1768, for example, the Hui-yuan authorities constructed 80 shops outside the main gate of the city. Each Manchu banner received monthly rents from 10 of these shops, applying the takings toward stationery and other miscellaneous expenses. Around the same time, officials in Urumchi's Manchu garrison rented out 400 shops; likewise, government-owned structures surrounding the Urumchi drum tower were rented to private merchants. By 1784, competition from privately constructed housing and shops in Urumchi forced the authorities to lower rents on officially owned property in less central locations.[54]

The second important commercial tax in Xinjiang was the stamp tax on livestock exchanges; this was first instituted in Urumchi in 1764 and somewhat later in other cities. To collect this tax, the Xinjiang authorities required that an official license and seal accompany each transaction involving camels, horses, sheep, asses, mules, cattle, or pigs, for which a fee amounting to 3 or 4 percent ad valorem was paid by the buyer. Livestock rustling was a common crime in Xinjiang; documenting exchanges and channeling trade in animals through official brokerages was thus an important control as well as a revenue-raising measure.[55]

Qing sources refer to this livestock stamp tax variously as "tax at point-of-sale" (*luodishui*), "commercial tax" (*shangshui*), and other terms. Commercial taxes on shops and truck farms, along with revenues from official property, were all called "rents" (*fangzu*). These "rents," in combination with the stamp tax, appear in budget accounts as *zushui*, "rents and taxes." The combination and hence the nomenclature was unique to Xinjiang, and for this reason one gazetteer compiler took pains to explain the usage.[56]

For accounting purposes, "rents and taxes" were generally pooled with official shop revenues, and surplus *zushui* funds provided start-up capital for many official shops, as well as discretionary funds for government projects: temple support and maintenance of military post stations in Ush, a food sti-

---

* The *jian*, or "bay," a unit of spacial organization in Chinese architecture, is a rectangular room or space defined by walls or columns that separate it from adjoining spaces. Officials in Qing Xinjiang used it, apparently as a measure of area, for tax purposes. The classical bay was three by six meters in area, but these dimensions varied over time and from place to place (see Laurence G. Liu, *Chinese Architecture*, pp. 27–28).

Alternatively, the term could be used for "room" in a more vernacular sense; see the discussion of San-cheng's proposed tax reform below.

TABLE 9
Growth of Commercial Taxation in Urumchi, 1763–77
(in silver taels)

	Building Rents	Land Rents	Livestock Stamp Tax	Total
1763	1,082.5	144.1	—	1,226.6
1764	1,258.6	189.6	376.4	1,824.6
1765	1,377.3	218.1	419.9	2,015.3
1766	1,695.6	316.5	424.3	2,436.4
1767	2,701.9	358.2	528.1	3,588.2
1768	2,802	487.5	712.4	4,001.9
1769	2,925.6	596.3	712.5	4,234.4
1770	3,092.7	600.8	820.2	4,513.7
1771	2,856	606.8	779	4,241.8
1772	3,250.8	605.7	844.5	4,701
1773	6,103.2	652.3	920.9	7,676.4
1774	5,370.4	675.1	877.5	6,923
1775	5,767.9	713.7	931.2	7,412.8
1776	5,379.4	510	893.8	6,783.2
1777	5,801.3	556.5	966.8	7,324.6

SOURCE: Wulumuqi zhenglue, pp. 131–35.

TABLE 10
Commercial Taxes Collected in the Eastern and Southern Marches, c. 1804
(in silver taels)[*]

Yili[†]	Urumchi[‡]	Karashahr	Kucha	Aksu	Ush	Kashgar[§]	Yangi Hisar	Yarkand
17,600–18,700	24,803.6	986.4	135.9	886	675.41	177.6	2.5	170

SOURCES: HJTZ 7:8a, 30; 8:7a; 9:4b–5a, 12b–14a; 10:4, 10b–11a; SZJL p. 120; LFZZ MZSW 1447-2; XJZL 9:13.
*Some values have been converted from pul to taels at current local rates.
†Figure from c. 1821.
‡Includes Urumchi region (Changji, Suilai, Futong Counties) as well as Jimusa, Yihe, Gucheng, Turfan, Kur Kara Usu, and Jinghe, each of which remitted taxes to the Zhendi Circuit treasury.
§Figure from 1809.

pend for demobilized infantry in Yili, a gift of sheep to needy Chahar in Tarbagatai, or a special purchase of grain at harvest time in Urumchi.[57]

In Yili and especially Urumchi (where by the nineteenth century rents made up over a quarter of the local budget), "rents and taxes" provided significant supplementary funds to Xinjiang officials. In Altishahr, however, zushui did not realize a great deal of revenue. The fixed low rates, capped at 0.3 taels per month even for the largest businesses and at 3 (later 4) percent on livestock exchanges, were one reason for this; another was the fact that only merchants from China proper were subject to the rents and tax. Thus despite the importance of commerce in Altishahr, "rents and taxes" revenues remained relatively low. (See Tables 9 and 10.)

San-cheng Goes Too Far

One official in Altishahr attempted to secure a greater portion of local commercial wealth for his administration. San-cheng, who had been cashiered and demoted seven years earlier, took up the post of Yarkand assistant superintendent in 1810. After verifying a survey of local merchants carried out by the Manchu secretary, San-cheng memorialized with a plan to bring recently arrived small merchants onto the tax rolls. This particular proposal met with approval, but San-cheng had still grander schemes. To the three categories of shops established by Jing-ge-li's 1762 memorial, San-cheng planned to add an "upper" and an "upper upper" grade; these larger shops would owe 0.5 and 0.6 taels per month. Other cities had amended the Jing-ge-li proposal by adding additional tax brackets based on finer gradations. In Karashahr, for example, the rates were 0.16, 0.12, 0.08, 0.06, and 0.04. None, however, had exceeded the ceiling of 0.3 taels per month. Furthermore, in order to regulate small itinerant merchants, San-cheng proposed a tax on small shops and inns (where traveling merchants stayed and stored their wares) on a monthly 0.05 tael per *jian* basis—as opposed to the flat rate based on the land area occupied by the establishment. San-cheng claimed that this new rate, "half that charged the third grade shops," was concessionary; in fact, it comprised a steep *increase* over previous tax levels because of his change in the method of assessment. Established shops, too, would have faced higher burdens. An inn with ten to twenty *jian* would have faced an increase from the previous top rate (0.3 per month) to 0.5 to 1 tael at the new proportional rate. Finally, and most seriously, San-cheng wanted to classify Altishahri Muslim merchants and add them to the commercial tax rolls in Yarkand, a violation of the dynasty's policy of distinguishing Chinese and East Turkestanis.

San-cheng's thinking is hard to understand. Could he have confused the per-*jian* rent charged merchants who rented commercial and residential space in official buildings with the three-tier tax rate paid by merchants who built their own shops on government land? It seems unlikely: if we today with an incomplete documentary record can understand Xinjiang's commercial taxation, surely San-cheng could not have made such a blunder in a functioning yamen with the relevant precedent-setting memorials on file and a staff with local experience. Yet could San-cheng have deliberately planned to confuse his superiors in the capital with an ambiguous memorial, in hopes that the response would give him expanded authority to tax? He sent out a lateral communication on his proposal to Tie-bao, the Kashgar councillor, only after dispatching his memorial to Beijing—in itself a violation of standard practice (he should have consulted with his colleagues and superiors in Xinjiang first on such an important matter). Alarmed, Tie-bao wrote a sternly worded criticism of San-cheng's attempted reform and sent it off to Beijing "in order to avoid creating chaos." In this memorial, Tie-bao clarified the distinction between officially built structures rented out by the *jian* and private shops on government land taxed by size on the three-tier system. He added that almost all merchants who had conducted business in Altishahr for some time had subdivided their land and constructed side buildings and warehouses. If, as San-cheng had proposed, every merchant who added on a shed was subjected to a tax increase, "that would cause a great disturbance." The Jiaqing emperor and the court had in fact noted San-cheng's radical departure from precedent. "I knew long ago this man was unsatisfactory!" the Jiaqing emperor wrote in his rescript to Tie-bao. As a result of his misconceived plan, San-cheng was recalled to Beijing for an investigation after less than three months in Yarkand. ("Unbearably muddleheaded!" fumed the imperial rescript on San-cheng's later self-criticism.) Tie-bao and an aide had to travel to Yarkand to make sure San-cheng had not already implemented the plan.[58]

San-cheng's reasoning may escape us, but his intentions are self-evident. While venality is not out of the question, San-cheng could have found less conspicuous ways to line his own pockets. Rather, he most likely sought to expand the legitimate fiscal base of his administration in Yarkand by tapping more efficiently the region's growing commercial economy. Regardless of whether his proposals were disingenuous or simply incompetent, he believed that Xinjiang's commercial tax levels, set 50 years earlier in the wake of a war and as merchants from China proper were just beginning to migrate and do business in Xinjiang, had become inadequate by the Jiaqing period. Nor was San-cheng alone in trying to secure a greater portion of Altishahr's commercial wealth for the benefit of Qing administration in Xinjiang.

Nayanceng's Tea-Tax Plan

As part of his post-Jahāngīr reform program, Nayanceng hoped to implement a comprehensive system to inspect and tax the large quantities of tea sold in Xinjiang. While in Gansu en route to take up his post in Kashgar in the winter of 1827–28, he heard reports of huge quantities of tea being sold in Xinjiang's Northern and Southern Marches without proper license. In addition to tea brought in by Qing authorities for sale to officials and the military, 400,000–500,000 cases (*feng*) of tea were sold by merchants throughout Xinjiang. The Qing licensed merchants to sell only 200,000 cases of tea in the northwest through the vestigial Tea and Horse Agencies in Gansu and Qinghai; this tea could legally be resold by itinerant merchants who purchased it from large tea merchants in Gansu. Still, this left 200,000 to 300,000 cases of the tea sold in Xinjiang unaccounted for, and Nayanceng concluded that it was being sold under false license or without license at all. The high prices Nayanceng found upon his arrival in Xinjiang also disturbed him. Tea within the Jiayu Guan cost only 1.1 to 1.2 taels per case; he viewed prices of 7 to 10 taels in Altishahr to be a clear sign of abuse.

Nayanceng drew more evidence of mercantile malfeasance from the fact that at some of the military post stations near Yarkand, local Muslims had attacked merchants from China proper at the time of the Jahāngīr troubles. Since Jihāngīr's forces had not reached these post stations and thus could not have incited local Muslims to rebellion, Nayanceng reasoned, then Chinese merchants must have brought these attacks upon themselves by inflating prices during wartime. Nayanceng thus found the Han and Tungan merchants from China proper as much to blame for the recent disturbances as Kokandi traders and the invaders themselves: "Traitorous merchants trade [tea] privately and plot with foreign barbarians to exploit the Muslim masses.... The situation worsens with each passing day. Something must be done."[59]

In the summer of 1828, Nayanceng decided to crack down on illegal tea trading and traders by fixing the price of tea and establishing a series of tax barriers to inspect and tax tea shipped from China proper. The model for this plan was the system of inspection stations regulating the export of tea via Mongolia to Kiakhta for trade with Russia. Nayanceng requested authorization to set up an inspection and taxation station at Jiayu Guan similar to those at Shahukou, Guihua, and Zhangjiakou (all north of Beijing).[60] In its final form, Nayanceng's tea taxation network would also have included inspection stations in Gucheng, Urumchi, and Aksu, a tax barrier at a key bridge at Kuitun north of Kur Kara Usu on the route from Urumchi to Yili and Tarbagatai, as well as stations to collect tax at points of sale in Yili, Tarbagatai, Kashgar, and Yarkand. Special *karun* were to be built at communications nodes and on alternate routes to interdict smugglers. Merchants entering Xinjiang via the Gansu corridor would obtain licenses at the Liangzhou Circuit yamen; on these would be recorded their names and the amount and type of tea they had to sell. At the Jiayu Guan and at each subsequent station the merchants would pay the tax and receive a new pass that listed their destination in Xinjiang along with the other information. The process would have been identical for merchants who came to Xinjiang via Mongolia and Gucheng, except that they were to be issued the first license in Zhangjiakou (Kalgan), Guihua (Köke Khota), or Dolonnor.[61] The particulars of each merchant's tea shipment were to be reported to officials at their destination and to Yili as a check on both smuggling and on the officials collecting the tax. This tea tax would be cumulative, based on a three-level division of Xinjiang by distance from China proper; thus a merchant bound for Kashgar would be liable to pay tax three times: at Jiayu Guan, Aksu, and Kashgar, while one bound for Yili would pay at Gucheng, Urumchi, and Yili.[62] Despite the addition of a tax on the already high price of tea in Altishahr, Nayanceng calculated that his policies would ultimately benefit Altishahr consumers, including the military, since he planned simultaneously to fix retail prices at 4 taels per case of brick tea in Aksu and at 5 taels in Kashgar. He argued that based on the wholesale price of 1.1–1.2 taels in China proper and his own estimates of shipping costs (1.2–1.3 taels as far as Aksu), merchants could sell at the fixed price and still clear 1.5–1.6 taels profit on each case of tea they sold in Aksu, 2 taels for sales in Kashgar. Curiously, Nayanceng neglected to include the tax itself in this calculation. In fact, even if merchants could buy wholesale and ship at the costs Nayanceng suggested, after taxes they would have cleared only 1 tael per case in Aksu, 1.2 in Kashgar.[63]

Nayanceng's memorials present the tea tax and fixed tea price principally as a means of regulating merchants from China proper, whose high prices and dealings with Kokandi traders he considered threatening to Xinjiang's stability after Jahāngīr. But he also promised that the tax would create considerable revenue for Xinjiang's administration and, in particular, finance the increased numbers of troops and their dependents now permanently stationed in the south without requiring an increase in Xinjiang's primary budget of silver shipments from the provinces. Echoing a familiar theme, he wrote, "It is my ignorant opinion that the needs of the Muslim Territory be met from the Muslim Territory's revenues; it is not worthwhile to draw on *xiexiang* from the main [imperial] budget to support frontier wilderness."[64] Assuming Chinese merchants would import an annual 200,000 cases of brick tea to Kashgar and Yarkand, Nayanceng projected tax revenues for Xinjiang of "over 100,000 taels." This estimate did not even include tax on loose tea (*zacha*), for which Nayanceng had no sales figures. Had the Qing tax collectors truly been able to collect it, this potential tax revenue alone could have financed Qing administration in Kashgar and Yarkand after 1828 with 60,000 taels to spare (compare Table 1).[65]

As was the case with the Altishahr official shops, however, Nayanceng's scheme was founded upon a gross contradiction: even given a high rate of merchant compliance and successful collection of the tea tax, the Qing could not have profited by taxing the tea trade while prohibiting the export of tea to Kokand. As long as the tea embargo cut off much of the market for Chinese tea in Central Asia, little tea could flow through Xinjiang and Qing revenues would have been limited.

Asked to advise the throne on this plan early in 1829, the grand secretaries Tuo-jin, Chang-ling, and Fu-jun rejected it on the grounds that it would give merchants an excuse to raise prices and that military personnel would as a result have to draw *more* heavily on silver stipends to buy their tea. In their judgment, the unsettled frontier region needed soothing after Jahāngīr, not an inflationary tax that would in any case be difficult to collect.[66]

The Fiscal Foundations of Empire

The preceding chapters have surveyed the fiscal structure of the Qing empire in Xinjiang. Trade with the Kazakhs and agricultural reclamation supplied the Qing military with livestock and grain, but for geographical, historical, and political reasons, local land and head tax revenues were limited. The Xinjiang government thus depended upon shipments of silver from China proper to pay the Qing soldiers and officials—an uncomfortable fact that the Qianlong emperor both attempted to explain away and encouraged his officials to alleviate. To reduce this reliance on *xiexiang* and to raise revenue for administrative, maintenance, and welfare costs not included in the main budget, authorities in Zungharia and Altishahr turned to that sector of the region's economy left open to them—commerce—and both taxed it and engaged in it their official capacity. Through currency manipulation, sales of silk and tea, commissaries, pawnbroking, investments, and "rents and taxes" on commercial property and livestock exchanges, the Manchu and Mongol officials who governed Xinjiang attempted to secure a greater proportion of Xinjiang's wealth for the purposes of military rule.

The Qing fiscal policies in Xinjiang fit into a broader pattern noted by students of Qing economic history, namely, the growing importance of commercial taxes relative to that of the land tax as a proportion of government revenues. This phenomenon, illuminated in the work of Wang Yeh-chien,[67] was particularly pronounced after the mid–nineteenth century, when fiscally strapped imperial and provincial governments attempted to penetrate more deeply into the booming economies of local marketing systems through a variety of "other" taxes, most of them commercial. Susan Mann has argued that it was the crises of the mid–nineteenth century that forced the dynasty to abandon the primary reliance on agriculture and the land tax (the *ben*) dictated by the norms of Confucian statecraft and turn increasingly toward commercial taxation (the *mo*). Nevertheless, according to Mann, this shift toward greater revenue-gathering from the commercial sector should be seen not as a symptom of dynastic decline, but as part of a process of nation building.[68]

In Xinjiang during the Qianlong period, we witness the same process at work—with a difference. There was no tradition of Chinese peasant land tenure in the Western Region, no *diding* tax rolls, no precedents concerning Han Chinese whatsoever. For Altishahri Muslims, the new Manchu overlords did follow tradition—Central Asian tradition—in implementing a taxation system. But with regard to Chinese immigrants to the Eastern and Northern Marches, Xinjiang was a tabula rasa. Qing authorities thus turned readily, mostly without ideological inhibitions, to the commercial economy. With agriculture for the most part devoted to providing grain, Xinjiang authorities were forced by circumstances, and encouraged by the emperor, to rely more heavily than their colleagues in China proper upon commercial taxation and the related technique of currency manipulation as sources of revenue.

We might take this line of thinking even further: It may not be entirely co-incidental that some policies conceived in Xinjiang by officials under pressure to limit *xiexiang* shipments were later employed in times of stress in China proper: the "worth ten" coin, Nayanceng's tea tariff—which, as an internal customs, anticipates the likin tax—and, after 1835, the Altishahr "treaty port" system in which the Qing conceded extraterritoriality, an indemnity, and control over customs to a foreign power in hope of avoiding costly border wars.[69] Xinjiang was a laboratory of sorts.

Finally, how successful were these measures at relieving Xinjiang's reliance on the silver stipends?

Although we lack the annual itemizations (*qingdan*) that would answer this question diachronically for each of Xinjiang's cities, we have in gazetteers "snapshots" of Xinjiang's finances for given years. Table 11 displays *xiexiang*, revenue from commercial enterprises, and commercial taxes as well as the head tax (*alban*) for major Xinjiang cities around 1795. Except for Kucha, where revenue from government sales, interest, rents, and commercial taxes amounted to only 3 percent of the value of *xiexiang*, in all the remaining cities the proportion is sizeable; in absolute terms, the amounts for Yili and Urumchi are especially impressive. We lack this type of data for the period following the watershed of 1828, but a comparison of Kashgar's assigned *xiexiang* quotas (from Table 1) with the *xiexiang* amounts offset by locally raised commercial revenues gives an indication of the importance of these sources of official revenue during the later period:

TABLE 11

Sources of Official Monetary Revenue in Xinjiang, c. 1795

(in silver taels)*

City	Xiexiang	Head-tax (alban)	Revenue from Commercial Activities	Commercial Revenue as Percentage of Xiexiang
Yili	610,000		79,560	13%
Kashgar	8,000	13,245	3,623	45% (includes Yangi Hisar)
Yangi Hisar	Included in Kashgar budget	2,677	—	—
Yarkand	8,000	12,575	5,600	70% (includes Khotan)
Khotan	Included in Yarkand budget	4,800	800	—
Ush	12,000		1,400	12%
Aksu	8,600		2,483	29%
Kucha	5,000		144	3%
Karashahr	10,000		980	10%
Urumchi	95,500		44,740†	47%

SOURCES: ZTYLSL 128–75; Yong-bao et al., Wulumuqi shiyi, 28a–29, 33a–b; Table 6.

NOTE: Figures do not include internal transfers of cash or of copper cash minted and distributed in Xinjiang.
*Values of rents and taxes converted from pul to taels at soldiers' pay exchange rate for 1801.
†Includes entire Zhendi Circuit and Kur Kara Usu.

	1835	1841	1846	1847	1849
Xiexiang quota requested	91,251	113,894	97,895	107,292	97,460
Xiexiang shipped	80,416	95,116	80,045	89,476	79,538
Xiexiang savings	10,835	18,778	17,850	17,816	17,922

Significant as these savings were in relative terms, however, overall, revenue from these commercial sources, other taxes, and savings from the manipulation of currency exchange rates were still insufficient to achieve the official goal of "using the Western Regions to govern the Western Regions." The revenue from all commercial sources in 1795, for example, was equivalent to less than 17 percent of the total silver stipend shipped to Xinjiang to meet that year's budget. Even under the innovative fiscal policies implemented in the territory in the Qianlong period, Xinjiang could not pay for itself.

In hindsight, then, there is a logic to San-cheng and Nayanceng's tax plans, for both attempted to tap Xinjiang commerce more effectively, the former by raising commercial tax rates and extending them to Muslim merchants, and the latter by taxing the high-volume, "east-west" trade in tea. There were specific reasons behind the court's rejection of both proposals; but the fact that the dynasty made no further attempts to widen the scope of Qing commercial taxation to include Central Asian Muslims suggests that stability and control were just as important as revenue enhancement in determining Qing tax policy in the Western Regions. And in the first decades of Qing rule there, the primary objects of Qing concern were the Han and Tungan migrants drawn to Zungharia and Altishahr almost before the smoke and dust of 1759 had cleared.

CHAPTER 4

"Gathering Like Clouds": Chinese Mercantile Penetration of Xinjiang

Duty took men of old to such frontier towns:
In court today, those prized horses may still be found.
The long road through mountains and passes—when will it end?
All through our hall, the strings and flute weep for you, my friend.

Zhang Wei, "Seeing Off Lu Ju on Embassy to Heyuan," Tang Dynasty

The shops lie packed like fish scales left and right.
State-planted willows wave out front, a verdant brume.
Once everyone's gone home through lamplit night,
Lute-song rises here and there beneath the moon.

(Wealthy traders and merchants of substance reside north and south of the old city gates. Even after the night market has closed, there is always fluting of the bamboo and strumming of silken strings. They say this local custom relieves the hardship of a day's work.)

Ji Yun, Random Verses of Urumchi, 1771[1]

The Manchus brought the Western Regions into China; merchants and a few sophisticated exiles like Ji Yun brought China to the Western Regions. The process was uneven and much evidence of it disappeared in the conflagrations of 1864, but from 1759 until that time the influx of merchants from China proper to the cities of Xinjiang created outposts of Chinese urban culture and commercial life throughout the New Dominion.

In the winter and spring of 1759–60, Shaanxi-Gansu Governor-General Yang Yingju spent several months surveying the newly conquered Muslim territories. Yang (whom we have met as Lanzhou supervisor of the Kazakh silk trade) was among the first Qing civil officials to visit Altishahr. When he arrived, he found Chinese—that is, Han and Tungan—merchants already there.

According to one source, by 1759 Chinese merchants in "Pijan, Aksu, Ush,

Khotan, Yarkand, Kashgar, and so on [had] all established markets where they cluster together . . . to trade." This date may be a year or so too early for the western Altishahr cities mentioned; however, in that same year Yang noted the presence of forty merchant households from China proper living as far west as Toksun, where they had opened shops outside the Qing fort.[2]

The penetration of the New Dominion by Chinese merchants was indeed rapid, and this raises several issues regarding Qing policy. How were these Chinese migrants controlled and their impact on East Turkestani society managed? Given that the Qing already recognized the Chinese as a destabilizing factor in Mongolia, would Chinese merchants be allowed to mix freely among the East Turkestani Muslims, or would they be segregated in walled compounds like the bannermen and Green Standard soldiers? What effect would the Chinese influx have on urbanization and urban life in Xinjiang? The material in this chapter suggests some answers to these questions.

Go West Young Han: The Open-Guan Policy

Wherever Qing armies ventured in Inner Asia, Chinese merchants were seldom far behind. This was true during the Kangxi, Yongzheng, and early Qianlong campaigns against the Zunghars in Mongolia and in the Hami region, where Han merchants from north China "chased the camps" (*gan daying*) to supply the armies and trade with nomad groups; it was equally the case in Xinjiang during the conquest of Zungharia. In the autumn of 1755 with the Qing advance westward and initial pacification of the Zunghars, before Amursana's rebellion, Chinese merchants were permitted to continue the periodic Zunghar border trade under military supervision in Barkol.[3] Later, when these customers were all but wiped out, the Qing forces in Zungharia still required supplies. At first, merchants could only haul goods to Barkol via Suzhou and Anxi in Gansu—a route that required over 300 *li* (150 km) of travel through bleak cobble desert and ensured that prices in the north would be high. This detour had become institutionalized in 1734 when, following Yongzheng's disastrous sortie against the Zunghars and the Qing withdrawal, merchants had been forbidden to travel beyond the line of frontier *karun* in western Mongolia. In the summer of 1756 Huang Tinggui memorialized to have this restriction lifted, since the area as far west as Yili had by then been all but secured by the Qing. The proposal was approved, and from the spring of this year the "northern route" via Khalkha and Uliasutai was once again opened to supplement the Gansu corridor (or "western route") to Xinjiang.

Guards in the *karun* were instructed to allow properly documented merchants traveling toward Barkol and Hami, and later Yili, to pass freely after inspection.[4]

In those days, the Qing military was particularly interested in the "cattle, sheep, and goods" that merchants drove from China proper to bases in Zungharia, thus reducing official expense. But the Qing court's decision to allow free commerce between Xinjiang and China proper proved to be more than a temporary military expedient. Repeated pronouncements on the subject reveal that the Qianlong court viewed the "free flow" (*liutong*) of people and commerce to Xinjiang as necessary, in an almost nutritional sense, to the sustenance of the population and the consolidation of Qing control over the region. When, over time, those merchants crossing Mongolia (and trading on the way) caused "incidents of competitive strife," frontier officials in 1759 suggested closing the northern route to merchant transit. In his return edict, the Qianlong emperor scoffed at such thinking as "displaying extreme ignorance of commerce," tantamount to "giving up food for fear of choking." With sufficient inspection to root out crooked merchants (*jianshang*), "the goods of each people may be exchanged, to the benefit of the economy."[5]

The Qianlong court's thinking about the role commerce and Chinese merchants would play in the New Dominion became fully clear early in the following year. Zhou Renji, governor of Guizhou, memorialized on the large numbers of people pouring into Sichuan from other provinces and requested that a law prohibiting such migration be enacted. Again, the return edict employed the aphorism about food and choking to dismiss the governor's concerns. Why fret needlessly over the presence of a few "disreputable types" among an otherwise peaceable migrant population? Recognizing that interprovincial migration was due to population pressure, Gaozong proposed Inner Asia as an outlet for crowded Han masses and a fertile field for mercantile endeavor.

These days the population increases daily, but agricultural lands are limited to their present size. We should think of how the flow [of population] may succor the homeless impoverished. For instance, now outside Gubeikou [a pass north of Beijing] there are several hundred thousand households of Chinese (*neidi minren*) going to farm. . . . And for those farming outside the pass, clothing and food are more abundant each day. . . . The Western Realm is pacified; our territories are vast. Places like Pijan and Urumchi are continually putting more land under cultivation in state farms, and the numbers of itinerant merchants (*kemin*) applying themselves diligently to commerce grow with each passing day.[6]

Other edicts over the next few years further encouraged and smoothed the way for merchants from China proper to travel to the northwest. Of special concern were those traders, primarily from Shanxi and Beijing, who plied the northern route across the steppe to Zungharia or this route's southern variant via the Ordos and Alashan. From the time of the reopening of the northern route in 1756, both Mongols and Chinese wishing to cross the border to Barkol, Hami, or Pijan to trade with the military garrisons and growing state farm population had first been required to obtain permits from the Uliasutai general, a detour that added hundreds of kilometers to what would otherwise be a relatively direct westward journey from Zhangjiakou or Guihua (Hohhot). In mid-1760 this regulation was revised: henceforth Mongols with their livestock and Han merchants with livestock and other goods could obtain passes from their local jasaks or officials in charge of the areas through which they passed. Merchants who departed from Zhangjiakou or Guihua could now travel directly to Xinjiang, thus cutting over 40 days from the journey. Underlying this reform was the reasoning that "merchants must congregate [in the newly conquered areas]; this will be more beneficial to Xinjiang."[7]

In order to accelerate Xinjiang's commercial development, especially in the eastern and northern areas, where most of the civilian and military state farms were located, the dynasty encouraged and even sponsored merchants to migrate along with the peasants relocated for agricultural reclamation work. These "merchants" were not all engaged solely in commerce; many came to take up offers of free land, on which they grew cash crops. They were classified (and, as described in Chapter 3, taxed) differently from peasant homesteaders, however, probably because in China proper they had not been registered on the *diding* tax rolls but were engaged in private trades or working unregistered land. Whatever their origins, in 1762 the settlement at government expense of these "merchants" (*shangmin*) or "householders" (*humin*) and their dependents began. In 1772, 32 households were brought out to the Urumchi area to open new farmland, and 123 to engage in commerce. The next year the authorities resettled 4 more merchant families to Urumchi, and in 1776 35 merchant households were moved from Pijan. In 1778, 1,136 merchant households migrated with government help, either from China proper or the city of Urumchi to *tuntian* farms in Dihua (Urumchi) prefecture and nearby counties of Jimusa, Fukang, Changji, Hutubi, and Manasi.[8]

Although government-financed resettlement took place only in the Eastern and Northern Marches, the invitation to Chinese merchants applied to Altishahr as well. For several years, Yang Yingju reported in 1763, merchants had been traveling freely to Altishahr, hindered by no official obstructions or coercion. Banner commander-in-chief Yunggui reported from Kashgar:

> Since the pacification of the Muslim Region, merchants from China proper coming via the post road, and the Muslim villagers, have been mutually amicable and free of criminality. Moreover, Muslims at the post stations (*taizhan*) irrigate and open farm land. Water and fodder are plentiful along the road, and there is no impediment to travelers. If this is made known to merchants, soon they will come to trade and in no time [this area] will be just the same as Hami and Turfan. This, moreover, will be of benefit to officials and troops.[9]

In an edict to the Grand Council, Gaozong ordered that this information be publicized, but that merchants merely be encouraged, not coerced, into going to Xinjiang. Passes should be issued to those wanting to go, and over time his goal of a "natural circulation" of merchants would come about of its own accord.[10]

This picture of the cities of Altishahr thrown open to Han merchants from China proper differs considerably from the impression left by the writings of Joseph Fletcher and others on Qing Xinjiang. "The Ch'ing government," Fletcher writes, "maintained a strict policy of segregating Altishahr from contact with the Han Chinese for fear that Han businessmen would take over Altishahr economically." Although, as we shall see below, Han merchants were not allowed to bring their families or marry and settle locally, and authorities made some attempts to segregate merchants from China proper from East Turkestanis *within* Altishahr cities, the general policy toward merchants from China proper trading in Altishahr was in fact just the opposite of that implied by Fletcher: they were encouraged to come.[11]

By 1764, officials in Shaanxi noted that merchant traffic in the counties of Jingyang and Sanyuan had increased "several times" since the opening of Xinjiang. As a result, they petitioned to have the character designations of these posts upgraded, as well as those of three other counties for which official business had increased for the same reason. The requested designations for the five Shaanxi counties were "trade center, busy, vexatious, strategically important, and shorthanded" (*chong, fan, nan, yao, que*).[12] By 1772, reported the Shaanxi-Gansu governor-general, Wen-shou, the flow of people westward was so great that there were long delays getting through the Jiayu Guan gate in Gansu. He suggested that the gate be left open during the day for all to pass out of; only those returning need be questioned.[13]

New Infrastructure and Systems of Control

The Qing improvement of Xinjiang's communications infrastructure, while primarily intended to facilitate military transport and transmission of official correspondence, greatly aided merchant travelers as well. One of the earliest concerns of the Qing military government in Zungharia and Altishahr was the quality and security of the main roads that linked cities within Xinjiang and connected Xinjiang to foreign countries and to China proper. Kashgar's roads to Kokand, and Yarkand's routes to Tibet, Kashmir, Leh, and Badakhshan were rugged and undefended against Kirghiz and other highwaymen until the system of Qing *karun* was completed and manned. Within Xinjiang, authorities saw to it that East Turkestani workers were established in perpetuity to maintain the road through the key Muzart Pass that linked Yili with Altishahr. Groups of laborers stationed every three miles along the glacier track kept it swept and marked with cairns, allowing caravans and troops to avoid crevasses and moraines.[14] Xinjiang's eastward desert routes, although generally more readily passable than those through the mountains, still required work. After inspecting the route between Gansu and Urumchi, Wenshou requested in 1772 that a military detachment be sent with stone workers to widen several sections of the road and facilitate cart traffic.[15] Development of wells, springs, and canals and construction of water tanks and inns along this route began as early as 1757, when Qing military personnel traveling between the Jiayu Guan and parts west noted that such improvements would help military and merchant alike. Work began with some success on the Gobi Desert section between Anxi and Hami by the following year, and by 1777 Qi-shi-yi[16] could report that beg officials in Altishahr had channeled water and built caravanserais at intervals along the highway, each staffed by several households of East Turkestanis to provide for travelers' needs. The Turki word for these hostels, *länggär*, entered Chinese as *lan'ganr* and is found in Altishahr place-names to this day.[17]

The most important Qing addition to Xinjiang's communications infrastructure was the establishment and manning of a variety of relay stations along Xinjiang routes. There were four different kinds of station: The *juntai* provided fresh horses and provisions for the express imperial communication service linking the territory with Beijing for the transmission of important official documents; the *yizhan* fulfilled the same functions for ordinary imperial and local document transmission; *yingtang* were water depots for military use; and the *karun* (Ch. *kalun*), in mountainous or border regions, were used for patrols and merchant travel. In fact, however, in Xinjiang the differences implied by these classifications were more administrative than practical, since all four types of station could share the same routes and most functions could be handled by a single type of post station. Between Urumchi and Yili, for example, along the 1,700-*li* (850-km) branch route traveled by official correspondence, there were 20 *juntai*, 21 *yizhan*, and 14 water depots, as well as *karun* and private caravanserais. From Turfan to Kashgar, on the other hand, 62 *juntai* handled all official functions. Because of their flexible nature, the post stations are often referred to in Qing sources by the omnibus term *taizhan*.

Besides provision of water, horses, food, and lodging for official messengers bearing urgent memorials, the *taizhan* put up traveling officials and exiles as well as beg officials and foreign tributaries en route to and from imperial audiences in the capital. Official consignments of *xiexiang* silver, silk, cotton cloth, tea, and other goods were shipped via post stations. Moreover, as in Qing Mongolia, Xinjiang's official post-station system protected merchant caravans. In return, merchants helped supply the often remote *taizhan* with goods.[18]

The *taizhan* as far west as Hami had been established during the Zunghar campaigns; those north and northwest of Urumchi were originally built around the time of the first victory over the Zunghars in 1755. With the second flare-up of hostilities the Qing lost control over these routes, but in 1758–59 restored the post-station system in Zungharia and constructed new *juntai* along the Southern March from Urumchi to Kashgar, Yarkand, and Khotan.[19] In Altishahr, the post-station duties fell as corvée service upon the East Turkestani population, as did the cost of providing post horses (Mo. *ulağ-a*; Tu. *ulaq*). (In this the situation was similar to that in Qing Mongolia.) Beg officials, Manchu secretaries (Ma. *bithesi*; Ch. *bitieshi*), and, at some post stations, small detachments of Green Standard soldiers supervised the *taizhan*. Merchants from China proper built shops at the *taizhan* as far west as Aksu, but not at those in the easternmost part of Altishahr. In 1831 it was proposed that merchants be invited to do so, in order to protect lines of communication in times of rebellion and invasion.[20]

A Tungan merchant, Ma Tianxi, journeyed from Turfan to Kashgar in the early nineteenth century. His account confirms the importance of the post stations to merchant travel in Altishahr. In approximately two months on the road between these two cities, a merchant would spend 46 nights at the Qing *taizhan* or in settlements near by. Food, lodging, and water were always available. Even at the smallest post station, East Turkestanis from the nearest village sold travelers water and bread for themselves and beans for their horses. Because in places the distance between *taizhan* was too great for a caravan to travel in one day, Ma reported that he was sometimes obliged to camp beside the road; however, even in sparsely populated areas such bivouacs were necessary only about one night out of five.[21] In the Eastern and Northern Marches of Xinjiang, where traffic was heavier and post stations more closely spaced, merchants could count on room and board at the end of each day and a steady supply of water along the route.

The Road-Pass System

The *taizhan* network was also the chief means by which the Qing monitored the movements of *neidi* merchants in Xinjiang. A pass system similar to that governing Han merchants in Mongolia applied to those merchants wishing to trade in Xinjiang.* Merchants applied for road passes (*lupiao*) with appropriate authorities in China proper: in Beijing, Zhangjiakou, or Guihua for those journeying along the steppe route, or in Suzhou for those reaching Xinjiang via the Gansu corridor. The passes recorded the number of merchants in a party, the merchants' names, registered place of origin, age, distinguishing physical features, goods, and itinerary. Cities in Xinjiang could issue passes for subsequent destinations upon a merchant's turning in the original pass and paying a fee of a few *pul* to cover administrative expenses. East Turkestani merchants exiting the *karun* line to trade and Kirghiz, Kokandi, Kashmiri, and other foreign merchants entering Altishahr and Zungharia were issued similar passes. All road passes were to be inspected and countersigned at various points en route to insure that merchants maintained their original itinerary and had not picked up unregistered or contraband goods and that the passes matched the man. Cities served as primary inspection points; in Aksu, the brigade commander (*youji*) in charge of pass inspection was the same officer responsible for the area's *taizhan*. In Kashgar, the commander of the city defense battalion (*chengshou ying*) supervised inspection of passes and reported to the seals office (*yinfang*), where clerical staff of the councillor's yamen prepared further submissions to Yili. Some Xinjiang city administrations had a passport office (*piaowu chu*) to handle such matters.[22]

---

* The pass system for Mongolia was established in 1720 by decree of the Kangxi emperor. Initially, only a limited number of trading permits were issued, but this rapidly increased to 174 in 1792 and 800 in 1798. Many merchants failed to comply with the pass laws, as with other restrictions on length of residence, trading in the camps of the Mongol banners (as opposed to designated towns), and so forth. See Sanjdorj, *Manchu Chinese Colonial Rule*, pp. 33–34.

Because passes were inspected at each point and were relinquished upon return to China proper and because the information they bore was shared between yamens in different cities, in theory the road-pass system allowed the authorities to generate a record of each merchant's travel, although in practice this probably was not possible.

One indication of the administrative importance placed on the pass system in Xinjiang is a memorial explicitly mentioning passes and registration documents for foreign Muslim merchants, along with tax records, as a main use of paper in Xinjiang's yamens and a reason why no yearly paper surplus could be realized.[23] Still, resourceful merchants could avoid checkpoints, and often did. Two coconspirators in the famous Gao Pu jade smuggling case did so in the following way: Zhang Luan and Li Fu set out from Yarkand with a pass to Aksu. There they exchanged this for one terminating in Ush. Somehow they kept this pass as far as Pijan, where they turned it in for a pass to Hami, but they failed to turn this one in at all, carrying it with them all the way to Fenyang county, Shanxi, where it was later seized as evidence against them.[24] Although the system seems easily circumvented in this case, the fact that the well-connected Zhang Luan went to such lengths to confuse his paper trail suggests that the passes were to an extent effective in governing merchant activities in Xinjiang.

Other Control Measures

There were also measures for the control of merchants residing permanently or sojourning for long periods of time in Xinjiang. Han and Tungan residents in Xinjiang's Eastern March were organized in *baojia* units and governed by local civil officials just as in China proper. Elsewhere, especially in Altishahr, a headman known as *xiangyue* was responsible for Han and Tungan settlers under his supervision. Whether he expounded the Sacred Edict (the maxims of the Kangxi emperor) is unclear; in sources on Xinjiang, *xiangyue* refers generally to the title and office of this unranked headman, an elder of the mosque or local community, and not the "village lectures" elsewhere associated with this term.[25]

Until early in 1760, Chinese merchants accused of crimes in Xinjiang were to be sent to Suzhou—back to China proper—for trial and punishment. This practice was of course unworkable in the long run: "If it were Yili or Yarkand, how could [the criminals] be sent to Suzhou?" the court wondered.[26] Thereafter, then, two legal systems operated in Xinjiang: (1) Qing law, administered by Manchu, Mongol, and Han military and (in the Urumchi area) civil officials, and (2) Muslim law (sharīʿa) of the Hanafite school, administered by the begs and ākhūnds (Ch. ahong)* of the native East Turkestani bureaucracy. Application of these legal systems was roughly divided along ethnic lines. Thus, even when in Altishahr, Han and Tungan merchants from China proper were subject to judgment and punishment according to the Qing code. In the Urumchi area (Zhendi Circuit) they were under the direct supervision of magistrates, and in Altishahr cities that of the commander of the city defense battalion. Serious legal matters (murders, robberies, and lawsuits) that involved people from China proper fell ultimately under the jurisdiction of the seals office of each city.

Under certain circumstances, however, this juridical division by ethnic category did not hold. While less serious crimes among East Turkestani subjects probably seldom reached the attention of Manchu authorities, murders and thefts were supposed to be reported to military officials. And although these officials were advised "not to adhere rigidly to the statutes and precedents of China proper," this meant only that Confucian-influenced sentencing for familial crimes was to be partially modified, not fully abandoned. If among the East Turkestani a nephew killed his uncle, or a younger brother murdered his older brother, then these cases "naturally must be decided according to the statutes and precedents of China proper (neidi)." Only murders involving more distantly related clan members were to be treated according to Islamic law.[27] Likewise, migrants or travelers from China proper were sometimes subject to Muslim law, particularly in cases that involved Han crimes against East Turkestanis. Horse thieves from China proper who stole Muslims' horses, for example, were to be dealt with according to the "old Muslim law"—decapitation followed by public display of the head. Other robberies were punished by chopping off perpetrators' fingers. To do otherwise, the court determined, would be "unfair." Fights between Chinese and East Turkestanis in Kashgar around 1850 seem to have fallen somewhere in between Qing law and sharīʿa: they were to be adjudicated by the secretary for Muslim affairs (Huiwu zhangjing). The hakim beg and Kashgar ākhūnd handled disputes between East Turkestani and foreign Muslims.[28]

In addition to these overlapping legal systems, there were statutes directed specifically at Chinese merchants in Xinjiang. For example, the traditional prohibition on the export of metal implements (steel, iron, copper, and tin)

---

* Ākhūnds were East Turkestani religious functionaries recognized by the Qing. Like begs, they were tax exempt and enjoyed official status. See Fletcher, "Ch'ing Inner Asia," pp. 73–74, 77.

to a border region remained in effect until 1793, after which the need for agricultural equipment on the state farms outweighed fears that plowshares would be beat into swords. Han merchants were not to force Muslims to sell their crop at cheap prices at harvest time for later resale at a profit; they were not to charge more than 3 percent monthly interest, assess compound interest, or to cheaply evaluate and acquire houses or land in lieu of debt repayment.[29] These statutes reflect the dynasty's fears that profiteering Han merchants would create resentment leading to rebellion in Altishahr. Significantly, however, for the first five years after the conquest, there were no formal limitations on contact between merchants from China proper and East Turkestani Muslims in Xinjiang.

Chinese merchants were prohibited from crossing Xinjiang's borders to do business with foreign peoples, although a small number seem to have done so anyway. As we saw in Chapter 2, private merchants could trade legally with the Kazakhs only under strictly controlled conditions. When the Han civilian Zhao Liangzai was apprehended in 1779 trying to sell livestock he had purchased privately from the Kazakhs with the help of a clerk at the *karun*, Gaozong decided to make an example of those involved and doubled cangue sentences all around. Private trade across Altishahr's borders was also forbidden. In 1790, a Chinese merchant named Zhang was apprehended in Kucha with over 20,000 furs. Superintendent Xiu-lin arrested him on suspicion of violating the temporary embargo on trade with Russia, but Gaozong saw a more grievous offense in the fact that Zhang must have obtained the pelts by traveling to Central Asia via passes at Ush, Kashgar, or Yarkand.[30] Early in the Jiaqing reign, the case of Gong E, a merchant from China proper who went to Uriyangkhai to trade, brought to light the numbers of Han venturing beyond the *karun* line in this northern sector of Mongolia, despite prohibitions. The court ordered generals and other ambans in Xinjiang as well as Mongolia to improve surveillance on the merchants in their territories, even itinerants bound somewhere else.[31] In the late 1820s, a considerable number of Chinese merchants were taken as prisoners to Kokand and elsewhere following the Khoja invasions; upon their return they were always closely interrogated by suspicious officials.[32]

Xinjiang authorities did not prevent East Turkestani subjects from traveling to areas outside direct Qing jurisdiction. The court decided in 1794 to issue passes permitting groups of East Turkestanis, led by headmen responsible to the Qing, to trade among the "Burut" (Kirghiz) tribes in the Pamir and Kunlun mountains. Trading farther afield was technically illegal, but enforcement of this limitation must have been difficult. Implicitly recognizing this, the court simply ruled that it would not attempt to seek redress for robberies of its subjects who traveled too far, or for those who exited the *karun* without proper documentation.[33]

The Ush Rebellion and Segregation Policies in Xinjiang

Five years after their conquest of Altishahr, Qing authorities were startled by an uprising in Ush that required over half a year to repress. Particularly worrisome was evidence that prior to taking up arms, the East Turkestani inhabitants of Ush had appealed for aid from Central Asian rulers sympathetic to the Makhdūmzāda Khoja cause.

Severe misrule and exploitation of the Ush Muslim population lay behind this revolt: as the story comes down to us, hakim beg ʿAbd Allāh, a member of a Hami family ennobled by the Qing, gave his retainers (Ch. *alebatu*, from Mo. *albatu*) free rein and he himself engaged in extortion of the Ush populace. The Qing superintendent, Su-cheng, was no better: with his son he took East Turkestani women into the yamen and "displayed licentiousness," then allowed them to be gang-raped by the servants.

The incident that ignited the Ush uprising seems to have been the impressment of 240 East Turkestani men in March of 1765 to transport oleaster seedlings (*shazao shu*, often translated "jujubes").[34] The porters mutinied not far from the city, fashioning clubs from the saplings to attack their military escort. Upon returning to Ush, the porters, joined by much of the city populace, slaughtered ʿAbd Allāh, Su-cheng, the garrisoning force, and several other officials. The violence of their rebellion was matched by the severity of the Qing response: when the city finally fell after a prolonged siege, Ush was almost totally depopulated, and those women, children, and elderly left alive were relocated to farms in the Yili region.[35]

After the retaking of Ush, Xinjiang military governor Ming-rui suggested several reforms aimed at preventing similar situations from occurring. Primary among these were measures putting the hakim begs of Altishahr's cities under closer supervision by Qing military authorities to prevent nepotism, usurpation of functions assigned to lower beg officials, and other abuses. Another reform codified the protocol for meetings between beg and Qing military officials, while additional suggestions dealt with taxation and cadastral surveying. Somewhat curious, given that none of the accounts mention any Han role whatsoever in the uprising, was one item concerning Chinese merchants in Xinjiang. Ming-rui proposed:

The places where Chinese dwell (*minren juchu*) should be segregated. [The numbers of] traders from China proper will in future gradually increase. If they live close to the officials and soldiers they can still be controlled and not allowed to foment incidents. [But] if they are permitted to follow their inclination and settle in among the Muslims (*Huiren*), this will easily cause trouble. I request that the relevant ambans be ordered to thoroughly investigate [merchants from China proper] and have them all move to areas of military residence to do their business. If they continue to live mixed among the Muslims, they are to be punished.[36]

According to this rule, approved by the court, merchants from China proper who journeyed to Altishahr for short or long stays were to reside in proximity to the Qing garrison in each city, segregated from the native East Turkestani population. There is no evidence that Chinese merchants were involved in the Ush uprising; perhaps it was simply nervousness at this early example of Altishahri unrest that led Qing officials to move to tighten the relatively lax rules that had governed Chinese merchants up to that point. More likely, however, it was the recent example of the 1755–58 uprisings in Mongolia that underlay the segregation policy. These loosely linked rebellions arose from noble and popular Mongol dissent over onerous corvée duties at the post stations and *karun* posts, and even greater fury at Chinese merchants and moneylenders.[37] Han and Tungan traders in Xinjiang served an important purpose in supplying the military garrisons, and resident Chinese merchants provided a significant amount of commercial tax revenue, but Ming-rui and others now sought to minimize Han contact with the Muslim population lest the traumas caused by the commercial penetration of Mongolia be repeated in yet another Qing Inner Asian territory.

Historians in the twentieth century have made much of this policy of segregation in Xinjiang, and it has even been credited with assuring the peace for the six decades between the Ush uprising and the Jihāngīr war.[38] Yet as we shall see, when merchants from China proper accepted the imperial invitation to ply their trade in Xinjiang, the segregation order was seldom rigidly enforced, and what segregated Chinese and East Turkestani communities did exist did not develop until after the troubles of 1826.

The Chineseness of Xinjiang Cities

"Diverse goods converge like the spokes on a wheel, trade doubles, livestock and vehicles are gathered; all is just as in China proper"—so Hešen (He-shen) imagined Xinjiang from his seat on the Grand Council in 1784.[39]

The expanding Chinese role in Xinjiang's commercial development inspired Qing exiles and officials to record descriptions of a densely vital urban landscape, the teeming marketplaces overflowing with goods. The language used to describe Xinjiang's growing towns ("just as in China proper") is in sharp contrast to the bleak images of vast, lonely wastes traditionally found in Chinese poetry depicting the Western Regions. Consider, for example, Zhang Wei's poem quoted at the head of this chapter, or Hong Liangji's despairing lament, *Exiting the Pass*, written of his journey into exile in 1799–1800:

> For half a lifetime, never one idle stride.
> Scaling the Five Peaks left my temples hoary white.
> But now, outside the Wall, for ten thousand *li*,
> East, west, north, south—Heaven's Mountains all I see.[40]

Qi-shi-yi's 1777 *Record of Things Heard and Seen in the Western Regions* evokes a very different atmosphere in his description of the markets of Yarkand: "The bazaar street is ten *li* long. On every bazaar day the goods are gathered like clouds and the people cluster like bees. All manner of miraculous items and treasures may be found. The livestock and fruits in particular are beyond compare. People here are respectful to people from China (*zhongguo zhi ren*) and love and honor the magistrates."[41]

Such bustle and bounty was of course due not only to the presence of merchants from China proper. Altishahr cities, particularly Yarkand and Kashgar, had been important commercial centers before the Qing conquest, and after 1759 South and Central Asian merchants contributed greatly to this picture of plenitude and vigorous commercial activity in Altishahr. But in eastern Xinjiang and Zungharia, it was the Han and Tungan merchants who replicated the Chinese commercial scene just as peasants, exiles, and soldiers on the state farms were creating an agricultural landscape reminiscent of China proper.

The Eastern March

Since well before 1759, merchants from China proper had frequented Hami, Turfan, Barkol, and other cities on the *Tianshan donglu*, or Eastern March. East Turkestani residents in this area, moreover, had maintained close contacts with China, even in Ming times.[42] But it was later, after the Qing conquest, that the Eastern March (which also included Gucheng, Kur Kara Usu, Pijan, and Urumchi itself) received the nickname "Little Soochow-Hangzhou" (*xiao Su Hang*) for its concentration of merchants and abundance of grain and other goods.[43]

HAMI

The crossroads of trade and post-station routes to Zungharia, Altishahr, and Gansu, Hami was, as we have seen, an important center for Qing trade with the Zunghars and, later, a base for merchants supplying Qing armies in Barkol and Zungharia. With its military garrisons, merchant quarters, and old "Muslim city" (*Huicheng*), Hami may have been partially segregated, though apparently not in the manner Ming-rui suggested. In any case, separation of merchants from the local population was not a serious concern to the Qing in the Eastern March, and the sources thus do not distinguish clearly the ethnicity of merchants populating cities in this region, or the neighborhoods of these cities. Most notable here, rather, is the expansion of commercial activity and Han presence over time. As Qi-shi-yi described the city in 1777, there were large numbers of well-stocked merchants gathered primarily outside the west gate of the new city, which contained the yamens of the Qing administration. The Hami prince (*junwang*) and his establishment lived in a citadel five *li* to the west; poor East Turkestani villages dotted the surrounding area. By 1804, we know, there were also markets and traders both inside and outside the prince's old "Muslim city." Forty years later, each city had a large, well-defined commercial sector. In the Qing compound, an inner wall contained the administrative buildings, principal state temples—including those to the Gods of War (Wu Miao) and Literature (Kuixing Lou)—as well as the military citadel (*bingcheng*); a broad avenue ran between this inner wall and the eastern outer wall, across which the temple to the God of Medicine and a mosque faced each other. On the northern end of this avenue, a prosperous area lined with shops straddled a sentry gate in the northeast corner of the outer wall. Further off in the northeast suburbs lay an East Turkestani neighborhood.

West of this main city, a new, smaller cantonment had been built adjacent to the Hami prince's walled palace. The inner compound consisted of housing for Qing military personnel and dependents, but between the inner and outer walls to the west was another commercial avenue where "soldiers and people (*min*) lived together." Shops and civilian residences were concentrated around the northwest sentry gate; to the southwest was a mosque, and just outside the southwestern gate the Hami *junwang*'s residence. By 1846 there were three Han ancestral halls and temples in the immediate outskirts of Hami city, the Luo (1773), the Sun (1813), and the Lü (1846), as well as a temple to the God of Wealth (*caishen*) dating from 1845—all indications of the growing numbers and economic clout of Han merchants.

The illustrations of the Hami cantonment printed in the 1846 *Gazetteer of*

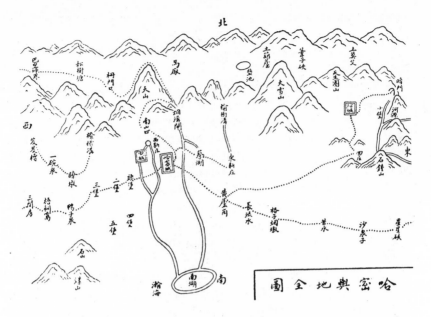

Map 4. Hami and environs (Muslim city to left). The dotted lines indicate roads, and parallel lines rivers. Source: Zhong Fang, *Hami zhi*, 1846.

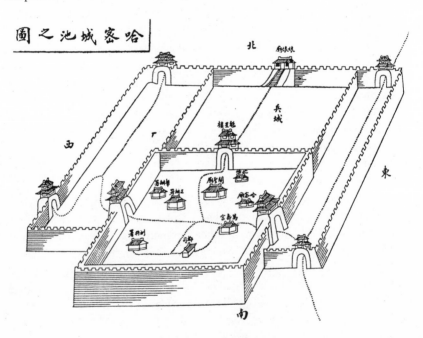

Figure 3. The Hami cantonment. Source: Zhong Fang, *Hami zhi*, 1846.

Hami ignore new settlement and commercial development described in the gazetteer's own text, but indicate locations of some official structures as well as city walls (see Map 4 and Figure 3).[44]

TURFAN

At Hami the road to Urumchi split, one fork leading north of the Boghda Mountains to Barkol and Gucheng, and another south through Pijan (in 1782: "densely populated; merchants converge"[45]) to Turfan. The layout of Turfan was similar to Hami's, with a Manchu cantonment enclosing barracks, yamens, and official temples, and the East Turkestani population under the control of the Turfan *jasak* prince (Ch. *zhasake junwang*)* growing fruit and cotton on *karez*-watered farmland surrounding the city. Besides the Manchu bannermen, the population of the garrison city itself was mostly Han and Tungan, who were not permitted to farm land privately, and thus may be assumed to have been primarily tradesmen.[46] East Turkestani merchants from Altishahr traded here as well, and even some Andijani merchants.[47] The town was an emporium for silks and teas from China proper, which along with local grapes and melons were shipped westward to Urumchi; Turfani cotton was shipped eastward to China proper.[48]

There seems to have been considerable interaction between the merchants from China proper and Turfani Muslims, although the Qing sources tend to enlighten us only when that interaction turned ugly. In 1803, for example, during the lunar year-end festivities, a Han, Zhang Liang'er, was observing a parade of Turfanis dancing in the streets when some youths insulted him in Turki. Zhang understood the language, however, so he gave chase. When A-bu-du-lu-pu, a bystander, intervened, Zhang turned to confront him instead of the escaping youths. Picking up some dried feces from the ground, Zhang thrust it in A-bu-du-lu-pu's face. Enraged, A-bu-du-lu-pu shoved Zhang, who fell awkwardly on some rocks and sustained injuries to his side and arm. A-bu-du-lu-pu and a friend of Zhang's named Li Quan then helped Zhang home, but he died nine days later.[49]

This story is interesting in that it suggests a fairly complex relationship between Han and native Muslims in Turfan. On the one hand, it reveals a degree of ethnic tension, but on the other, there is evidence of communal interaction as well. Zhang knew some Turki, at least, and Li Quan and A-bu-du-lu-pu were likewise able to communicate. It is hard to say how common such linguistic ability was among the Chinese and Turkestanis in Turfan or

---

* *Jasak*, the term used by the Qing for the hereditary heads of the eight Mongol banners and other nomad chiefs, was also applied to the prince of Turfan.

Xinjiang in general (although there are other such cases), but even this suggests that Chinese merchants in Turfan had a basic familiarity with the culture around them, despite Ming-rui's 1765 proposal to limit Chinese contact with East Turkestanis.

BARKOL AND GUCHENG

These cities had been important staging centers for the Zunghar campaigns, and their settlements of Chinese merchants had taken root at that time. In particular, the lifting of restrictions on merchant travel across the steppe route in 1756 made Barkol and Gucheng termini of a busy highway frequented by Shanxi traders. There were few if any East Turkestanis here, but Khalkhas brought livestock to sell—preferably to Chinese merchants, who paid a better price than official Qing quartermasters. Manchu citadels (*Mancheng*) were built adjoining the Han settlements after the conquest of Xinjiang (Barkol's in 1773 and Gucheng's in 1775). Wen-shou came to Barkol at harvest time in 1772 and was impressed by the abundance of inexpensive grain from local state farms. He commented on the large number of Shanxi merchants in the area: those with sufficient capital had already reclaimed land for their own farms. He also noted that the official practice of shipping in goods at state expense to provide for the needs of the bannermen was not very successful in Barkol. Because of the city's proximity to Anxi and Hami, "merchants circulate, goods gather like clouds, and it is truly difficult [for the government] to sell such things as silk gauze or satin." Merchants thus competed easily with official livestock purchasers and commissaries in this part of the Eastern March, and it was in Gucheng, a major transshipment point for tea, that official stores in Yili and Tarbagatai procured their tea supplies. In Daoguang times, Barkol was noted for its concentration of pawnshops, money shops, and dry-goods stores.[50]

In 1769 Gaozong was puzzled by a report he received listing prices for various goods in all the cities of Xinjiang. "Xinjiang is a vast area. The prices of all things naturally cannot be the same as within the pass . . . and Hami's and Barkol's circumstances cannot be as one with Urumchi's," he mused. "But recently, commercial communications and mercantile comings and goings are uninterrupted—how can the prices differ by several hundred to a thousand percent? What's especially hard to understand is that the prices for iron goods, oil, and sesame recorded in Yarkand and Kashgar on the remote frontier are far less expensive than for places like Hami and Barkol that border on China proper."[51] The emperor suspected fallacious reporting by Xinjiang officials, but another explanation might be that, even at this early date, the rapid influx of Han homesteaders and merchants drove up prices for these items in "Little Soochow-Hangzhou," despite the area's relative proximity to China proper. In Altishahr, where there were no Chinese homesteaders and Han and Tungan merchants entered more slowly and never in such great numbers as in the Eastern March, demand for such mundane Chinese products remained relatively low.*

URUMCHI

Although Yili remained Xinjiang's political and military capital until after the 1864 Tungan rebellions, Urumchi became the region's commercial and financial center soon after the conquest, thanks to large numbers of troops, exiles, and peasants working state farms in the area, most of whom were permitted to settle permanently and bring out dependents. Many "merchants"— including private farmers and laborers as well as tradesmen—likewise took advantage of Urumchi's rich potential in the first decades after the conquest.

The rough military camp and earthworks built in 1755 (in Jiujiawan, northeast of the modern city) were replaced in 1758 by a proper walled enclosure about 500 meters in circumference and 3 meters high, with four gates. This was situated south of Hong Shan, in the area known today as Nanguan (along Jiefang Road, south of Renmin Road), and housed the superintendent's offices, military barracks, and so on. The area's growing garrison force and increased duties occasioned by the flourishing *tuntian* land reclamation required that the city be rebuilt and expanded to twice its original size in 1763. This walled city, named Dihua, initially housed the entire Urumchi garrison; in 1765, however, ground was broken just to the north for New Dihua, and two years later the military government moved into these new quarters consisting of 2,000 barracks rooms and 617 "bays" (*jian*) for yamens, storehouses, granaries, and temples. (Today's "Nanmen," "Beimen," and "Daximen" place-names recall features of New Dihua.) In 1772 the Manchu banner

---

* Sesame was at any rate difficult to come by in Xinjiang in the late eighteenth century, as Ji Yun discovered (*Wulumuqi za shi*, p. 15, stanza 88 [*wuchan*]):

> Oh, the shine of fresh-pressed sesame paste!
> What a shame the north-route merchants can't have a taste.
> Because the "Heavenly Woman" you think you look upon,
> Turns out to be just "peach blossom rice" of that man from Ruan.

(The "huma" [sesame] is "zhima," which Su Dongpo has discussed so discriminatingly. But Westerners [i.e., local Urumchi residents] use hemp seeds for sesame, and the oil has a horrible taste. Unless you're a local, you can't eat it.)

troops and officials moved a few *li* northwest of Dihua (to a site at the western end of today's Nanchang Road, near the August First Agricultural Institute), to a new cantonment eight *li* in circumference, its four gates each signed in Manchu, Mongol, Chinese, and Arabic scripts. Officially called Gongning Cheng, this site later came to be popularly known as "the old Manchu city" (*lao Mancheng*). Dihua thereafter served as the Green Standard base. In 1825 a second Manchu city (*xin Mancheng*) was built just east of New Dihua (in the area of today's Jianguo Road) to house overflow Manchu bannermen and their dependents.[52]

Some historians have discussed the existence of separate Han and Manchu cities (such as Dihua and Gongning) in Urumchi, Barkol, and Gucheng as examples of the "segregation policy" in effect in Xinjiang.[53] This is misleading, for in fact Manchu garrisons (often including Mongol bannermen) were walled off from surrounding Han populations in China proper as well—most dramatically in Beijing, where on Dorgon's order in 1648 Han and Tungan were expelled from the entire walled city. This is indeed a segregation policy, but it has nothing to do with the regulation promulgated after the Ush rebellion. In fact, as will be discussed below, the special conditions in Altishahr often led to Green Standard troops and Manchu and Mongol bannermen sharing a walled citadel, with only East Turkestanis excluded; groups segregated in China proper could thus be integrated in Altishahr.

The official gazetteers of Urumchi tell the heights, thicknesses, and circumferences of all these walls, and, read on their own, leave an impression of a grim frontier outpost, dominated by one, then two, then three fortresses. They neglect to mention the merchant community and commercial structures that threatened to engulf these compounds almost before their completion. From less formal sources we discover that what met the eye of an observer gazing south from the slopes of Hong Shan around 1770 was the Temple to Guandi, the theater, and the market.[54]

The presence of Guandi temples in Xinjiang cities is quite intriguing. According to Hong Liangji, exiled briefly to Xinjiang in 1800, they were ubiquitous outside the Pass, with even villages of only two to three households boasting a small temple to this God of War. Guandi temples commemorated Guan Yu (A.D. 162–220), the famous hero of the Three Kingdoms period and a deity of complex cultural and political importance. Starting in the early eighteenth century, the Qing brought the Guandi temples under official control, enlisting the popular god for the official cult. That the Qing constructed Guandi Miao in the garrisons or Han areas of most Xinjiang cities, often with merchant "contributions," suggests the enlistment of architecture and cult to the purpose of empire building—a practice that resembles the Roman construction of state temples, fora, baths, and amphitheaters in frontier cities in Spain, Gaul, and Britain.[55]

But to return to Urumchi. To a traveler in 1777, the city was "the most prosperous and populated place outside the Pass." Further, "Because [Urumchi] is easily approached from all four directions, the name-brand stores (*zihao dianpu*) crowd together like fish scales; the marketplaces and thoroughfares are broad. People come from all over to the teahouses and wineshops. There are thespians, singers, and skilled craftsmen—nothing is lacking."[56] Han and Tungan merchants had moved into and reshaped the old Dihua city; there was now a "South China Lane" (*Jiangnan xiang*), where people from the affluent south-central provinces congregated. There were busy markets both north and south of the old city as well.[57]

We have some more precise indications of the pace of Urumchi's commercial development. As early as 1762, merchants from China proper had opened 500 shops or stalls in Urumchi's markets and were growing cash crops on over 300 *mu* of land in surrounding areas. It was this that led banner Commander-in-Chief Jing-ge-li to develop a plan to tax Chinese merchants in Xinjiang; as tax rates remained constant, the commercial tax takings for 1763–77 reveal the rapidly growing numbers of merchants in the Urumchi area (see Figure 4).[58] By 1784 there were so many privately owned shops and dwellings in central parts of the city that Manchu garrison officials were forced to reduce rents on the buildings they rented out in more remote locations. A *baojia* survey undertaken in the last year of the Qianlong reign (1795) revealed that out of a total of 20,662 civilian households (129,642 individual men, women, and children) in the Urumchi region, 11,545 households (43,791 individuals) were registered as merchants; 355 of these "merchant" households* were engaged in commercial agriculture, paying tax in silver, working a total of 27,090 *mu* of land—the rest, presumably, were engaged in business. There were 143 additional merchant households working land in Turfan, Kur Kara Usu, and Jinghe, outside the Urumchi administrative region.[59]

Foreign tourists in Urumchi today sometimes complain that the city is "too Chinese" in comparison with the Central Asian atmosphere of southern Xinjiang; many believe Urumchi's East Turkestani culture has been erased by Han immigration and architecture. In fact, the Uyghur population and cul-

---

* As discussed in Chapter 3, Chinese migrants to Xinjiang who were not established on state farms (*tuntian*) were classified as merchants (*shangmin*), even if engaged in agriculture. This was perhaps because they had not been registered peasants in China proper to begin with.

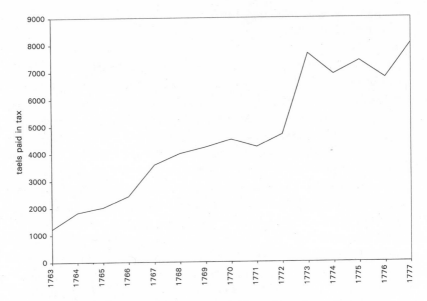

Figure 4.   Growth of commercial tax revenue in Urumchi, 1763–77. Source:
Wulumuqi zhenglue, pp. 131–35.

ture in the city today is a relatively recent feature, for Urumchi in its first decades in most respects resembled a north Chinese town, populated primarily
by Tungans from Gansu and Shaanxi and Han from many Chinese provinces,
in addition to the bannermen. In Ji Yun's day, a little more than a decade after
the city's founding, Urumchi could already provide most of the foodstuffs
and entertainments a metropolitan sophisticate demanded. There was good
bean curd to be had, and a serviceable local vinegar. Shaoxing-style wine was
produced locally by the Xia family, originally of Guizhou, but liquor import-
ers did an annual 20,000 to 30,000 taels worth of trade as well. Tobacco, too,
was good business: locals were in the habit of offering a smoke to whomever
they encountered, and tobacco merchants could afford to donate over 1,000
taels one year to the temple of their patron, the Fire God (*huoshen*). Seafood,
including even shrimp (no doubt dried), was shipped in from Beijing and Guihua by northern-route merchants. The fruit from Turfan was marvelous, but
people in Urumchi preferred expensive specialties from further east: hazelnuts, chestnuts, hawthorn berries, and pears — even mandarin oranges could
be obtained in season. When Ji first arrived in Urumchi in 1769 there were no
booksellers, although some merchants occasionally sold copies of novels and
mystery tales. But after Urumchi was granted a quota of examination candi-

dates and opened an academy in 1771, specialist book retailers set up shop, and "the sound of recitations could be heard."

Even without books, there was plenty to do. The several wineshops in the city offered music and performances nightly, "reminiscent of Beijing." One could get a seat for several cash. Women as well as men came great distances to attend these shows. The players included professional boy singers and many skilled amateurs, often exiles. One group of convicts organized a troop to perform *kunqu* opera. Lao Liu, the carpenter, "was best at female roles. Though over 30, he had not lost his looks." There were bordellos, too, on the back streets. Ji Yun provides a guide to these districts:

Topsy-turvy clothing, at night no screen over the door,
lovely flowers lent to men to gaze upon as they wish.
If people coming west ask where the gay (*fengliu*) places are,
Look for a pole a *zhang* high, at the end of a yellow earthen wall.

(Where there is a pole erected in the house, these are the women's lanes. This is also called 'sacrificing to the god's ear.')[60]

Merchants were a flamboyant and powerful presence in the city. Recent arrivals were often confused by the local style that wealthy merchants affected, with their long coats of yak's hair serge dyed such colors as "pine" and "rose"—considered women's colors by northern Chinese. The merchants organized native-place associations, each with a temple and festivals to its own city god. "As soon as the Liangzhou festival is over, it's time for the Ganzhou one. Pipes and drums greet the god, not stopping all day long." As elsewhere in the empire, these organizations exercised great influence in Urumchi, commanding the allegiance of sojourners from their respective native cities. Ji Yun's barber was required to go to the temple for four or five days running during his native-place festival and dared not open for business even when an eminent customer needed a shave and a trim.[61]

The Northern March

Yili and Tarbagatai were more remote than Urumchi, with greater populations of bannermen (including Chahar, Oirat, Sibe, and Solon as well as Manchu troops); many of these nomad soldiers were actively engaged in animal husbandry in the mountains. The massive land reclamation efforts relied primarily on state farms, and there was less private homesteading of land than in the Eastern March. The annual Kazakh trade required government shipments of silk from China proper and cotton cloth from Altishahr; official limitation of this trade to the trade pavilions seems to have assured that, for the first half-century at least, private trade remained a sideshow to the main attraction of textiles-for-livestock. Official business in the Northern March, then, played a relatively larger role, and private commerce a smaller one, than in the eastern or southern region of Xinjiang.

YILI

Although of less economic importance than Urumchi, Yili was nevertheless home-away-from-home for growing numbers of Chinese merchants from the latter half of the eighteenth century on. And despite the fact that Han Green Standard troops and Manchu bannermen were stationed in separate garrisons of the Yili complex (see Chapter 3), Chinese merchants clearly moved among all nine cities. For the most part, however, we are aware of their arrival only because special officials were posted to handle them. In 1764, Military Governor Ming-rui predicted that lawsuits would inevitably arise as a result of the large number of merchants living among the bannermen and their families. Ming-rui requested that a special civil commissioner (*lishi tongzhi*) be established in Yili to handle cases involving Chinese and bannermen, as well as certain other civil affairs. The court approved the request, stipulating that only officials fluent in Mongolian and Manchu as well as Chinese could hold the position.[62] Significantly, here in Yili the dynasty did not respond to this evidence of potentially troublesome ethnic interaction by tightening segregationist policies.

The next military governor, Agüi, pointed out in 1767 that Yili now boasted a population of over 20,000 bannermen and Taranchis, several thousand Green Standard troops and exiles, and a constantly growing number of Chinese merchants congregating in the cities of Huiyuan (the military governor's headquarters) and Suiding (a Green Standard garrison). Among these traders, "few were good," and a single magistrate was not enough to handle all the trouble that arose. Deputy magistrates (*xunjian*) were therefore selected from among worthy officials in Shaanxi and Gansu for posting to Huiyuan and Suiding, where they governed the merchants, adjudicated legal matters, looked after granaries, and supervised the jails. Five years later, Šuhede established a tax and inspection system on transactions of livestock, despite imperial instructions that Yili not rigidly adopt the institutions of China proper (where such sales were officially supervised). But, Šuhede reasoned, merchants from all over, many of them disreputable, had been "gathering like clouds," and it was necessary to crack down on a wave of rustling incidents.[63]

As Yili's population continued to swell with soldiers, military dependents,

merchants, and Muslims,[64] the court approved further administrative changes
to accommodate an expanding agenda of civil duties. In 1780 the current civil
commissioner was retitled "commissioner for civil pacification" (*fumin tongzhi*) and assigned to handle criminal cases. Two additional deputy magistrates
were appointed at the same time, bringing the total number of these officials
to four.[65]

By the early nineteenth century, Yili could boast at least one of the diversions of urban Chinese living. In 1808, there were two opera troupes in
the Yili region. Dramatic pursuits were not, of course, what Gaozong or his
son had in mind for the homesteaders and bannermen defending the frontier,
and to prevent farmers and bannermen youths (*zidi*) from falling into low-
class (*xialiu*) ways, Military Governor Song-yun simply forbade the troupes
from recruiting any new members. The Jiaqing emperor found this response
wanting in severity, however, and, reminding Song-yun that Yili was a military camp where the banners should dedicate themselves to martial drilling,
he ordered that the troupes be driven back to China proper.[66]

TARBAGATAI

Tarbagatai's administration underwent much the same expansion, with gradual appointments of civil officials outside the banner system to accommodate
the influx of merchants, whose number was thought to include many un-
desirables. In 1766 Shaanxi and Gansu dispatched a civil commissioner to
Tarbagatai to inspect and guard against cases of banditry among the "increasing numbers of merchants coming and going since the autumn of 1765,"
and to look after grain supplies. By 1819 the merchant population was large
enough to require the posting of secretaries literate in Chinese. In the past,
Tarbagatai's affairs had mostly involved "barbarians," so only the Manchu and
Mongolian written languages were used in the transaction of official business.
But with the numbers of Han and Tungan merchants in the city increasing
daily and the "surprising frequency" of brawls, theft, and murder, the need
arose for personnel able to record testimony in the original Chinese. Thus
an unfortunate exile, Li Tong, originally of the Board of Punishments in the
capital, was kept on for an additional three years to handle such business after
the completion of his three-year sentence. (Apparently it was difficult to get
qualified Han officials for Tarbagatai service otherwise, for in 1829 another
exile was similarly retained after doing his time.)[67]

Despite the need for such officials, however, Tarbagatai never seemed to
attract merchants from China proper in such numbers as other Xinjiang cities,
perhaps because of its severe northern climate and the fact that official trade
took priority in dealings with the Kazakhs. Whatever the reason, a memorialist later complained that the paucity of Han in Tarbagatai had inhibited his

land reclamation efforts. There were only 141 Han households resident in the city circa 1834, and 47 of these "households" consisted of a single man each.[68]

The Southern March

The Qing did not open state farms in Altishahr for subjects from China proper until after the 1830 Kokandi invasion. For the first 70 years of Qing rule in the region, then, except for Green Standard soldiers and a small number of Chinese enslaved to begs, all other Han and Tungan in southern Xinjiang were officially classed as "merchants." Indeed, most were in fact engaged in commerce, with only a small number raising crops on government land or land rented from begs. Merchants from China proper settled in Altishahr somewhat more slowly and in smaller numbers than they did in the Eastern and Northern Marches. Although they could travel, trade, and live indefinitely in Altishahr cities, they were not allowed to bring out families or marry locally until the 1830s. Whereas in Urumchi and other places in the Eastern March cities resembling those in China proper were created in the first few decades after 1759, in Altishahr the Qing occupation produced a pattern of Qing walled garrisons constructed within or beside older East Turkestani cities. Before 1828, Chinese merchants dwelt within these Qing citadels, near them, or among the East Turkestani population; no general rule defines their residence patterns.[69] After Jihāngīr's invasion, a more segregated pattern did emerge in Kashgar, Yangi Hisar, and Yarkand, the cities most threatened by Kokand and the Makhdūmzādas.

KARASHAHR

For a traveler proceeding southwest along the post-station route from Turfan, the first large city encountered was Karashahr. It consisted, in fact, of three discrete settlements and the pastureland in the Tianshan to the north. Karashahr itself was an old fortress in the valley of the Yulduz (Ch. Kaidu) River, first occupied by the Manchus in 1757, who placed it under the command of a superintendent with a small force. The walls were rebuilt in 1778, 1787, and 1794. The East Turkestani towns of Korla (to the southwest), and Bugur (west of Korla) fell under Karashahr's jurisdiction, and at the time of the Qing conquest were populated by only a few hundred households each of Dolans.* The

---

* Dolan (Ch. *duolan* or *duolun*) was a Turki name for the mountain people who pastured Khoja Jihān's horses on the southern slopes of the Tianshan. The Qing considered them a variety of East Turkestanis (*Huizi*). Qi Yunshi, comp., *Xichui yaolue*, 2:10.

Qing gave lands in this part of the Tianshan to a group of Khoshuuts, and after the return of the Torghuts from the Volga region in 1771, a large portion of this Oirat tribe were resettled in the Karashahr region and encouraged to farm as well as pasture animals.[70] When Qi-shi-yi passed through in the 1770s he was not much impressed by the Torghuts, finding the men larcenous and the women meretricious. Torghut children were often sold into slavery among the East Turkestanis, and some were resold in Badakhshan and Hindustan. Of course the refugees had only recently settled in Karashahr after an odyssey during which many of their number had perished; despite Qing aid, they remained extremely poor. Qi-shi-yi's account must be read circumspectly.[71]

Qi-shi-yi wrote that Torghuts and East Turkestanis lived in the small city of Karashahr. (He did not mention any merchants present, and where he encountered Chinese tradesmen and busy markets elsewhere in Xinjiang he usually described them.) By the first decade of the nineteenth century, however, there was a sizeable community of Han and Tungan merchants in the Karashahr region. We first learn of this in a case involving allegations of extortion and other abuses on the part of Karashahr's superintendent, Yu-qing, in 1807. Yu-qing was accused of using capricious arrest and strong-arm tactics to extort payments from merchants running a still and pawnshops in Karashahr. Investigations revealed that the still had opened only recently; the bootleggers had formerly run a mill. Because merchants in town needed liquor for New Year celebrations and processions of temple gods, the pair diversified, probably during the tenure of Yu-qing's predecessor (Lai-wu, served 1804–6), and began distilling some of the grain ground in their mill into spirits. Similarly, the pawnshops were not exclusively engaged in pawn-broking. Rather, they were dry-goods stores, none highly capitalized, whose managers occasionally took goods in pawn at 3 percent monthly interest.[72]

Of note here are the hints about the rate at which merchants from China proper arrived in Karashahr. If we assume that Chinese trading communities had to achieve a certain population before such secondary industries as distilling or financial services like pawnbroking could be locally profitable, then Karashahr reached that stage probably in the decade prior to 1807. (An official investigating Yu-qing reported that there were no formal pawnshops [*diandang*] in Altishahr, only Karashahr's dry-goods stores with their side-line pawnbroking operations.)[73]

Another indication that the numbers of Chinese merchants in Karashahr increased around this time is a request in 1810 by the Karashahr superintendent, Ha-ban-a, to station a detachment of troops in Korla and Bugur, because "in the two Muslim towns under Karashahr's jurisdiction . . . Han merchants (*maoyi Hanmin*) have been gradually increasing," and owing to the distance from the Karashahr garrison to these towns, special precautions were necessary. Clearly, Han residence in Muslim cities was not considered illegal, though it was a source of concern. The next year, the authorities tallied the Chinese merchants in Karashahr for tax purposes. They discovered 1,417 shops in Karashahr and 446 shops at the post stations (perhaps including Korla and Bugur).[74]

KUCHA

The next major city along the *taizhan* route stood behind an old city wall of willow staves reinforced with earth and sand. The Qing moved into Kucha in 1758 and set soldiers to work building yamens and temples. The outer wall was rebuilt in 1793. In 1811 there were 169 businesses in town managed by Han or Tungan merchants. For Kucha we do have some evidence of segregation, but only for a later period: a traveler in 1873, describing the city as it had been before the Qing loss of Altishahr to Tungan rebels and Ya'qūb Beg, mentions a wall dividing the town into two sections, one for the "Chinese" garrison and traders, as well as the "Kalmak" (i.e., Manchus and Mongols of the banners), and the other for the Muslims.[75]

AKSU

Qi-shi-yi noted Aksu's large size, the volume and variety of its grains, fruits, and other produce, as well as the many camels, horses, cattle, and sheep to be found in the city. Good local artisans excelled in jade carving and saddlery; the people were rich and litigious. "Merchants from China proper and traders from foreign tributary countries crowd in like fish scales or clusters of stars; the streets and markets are in commotion. Whenever you happen upon bazaar time, [you are packed in] shoulder-to-shoulder, your sweat falls like rain and you are enveloped in a cloud of wares."[76]

Aksu's fortifications were more elaborate than Kucha's or Karashahr's, with both inner and outer walls, the *su däwaza*—water gate—where the Aksu River entered the city, and towers at the corners and gates. The neighborhood of one of the towers, the Guanyin Ge, was a particularly busy market frequented by Han and foreign merchants. Along the dense web of lanes and alleys within the walls were teahouses, shops, and inns; the official buildings and barracks for Manchu and Green Standard troops also lay within the cantonment. The bazaar, five *li* (2.5 km) in length, extended between the Qing cantonment and the Muslim city below. This was a crossroads for all Altishahr and a major jade entrepôt. Affairs of the private merchants in Aksu initially fell under the purview of officials in Ush, but after the revelation of Gao Pu's jade smuggling scheme in 1778, officials were posted to Aksu to inspect merchant road passes.

Residence in the Aksu area seems to have been only roughly divided along ethnic lines. Chinese merchants inhabited the cantonment along with Qing military personnel. Whether East Turkestani and foreign merchants were excluded from residence there is unknown; they could enter to transact daily business. In 1828, while searching for a site on which to quarter 2000 soldiers newly posted to the city, Nayanceng noted in a memorial that the East Turkestani mosque lay outside the city to the northeast, while just southeast of the city were "shops and houses of traders" (*maoyi puhu*). It is unclear from Nayanceng's reference whether or not this commercial district was exclusively or primarily Han and Tungan; however, the 130 shops and 859 residences of Chinese merchants recorded in the 1811 survey may have been in this area. The outlying towns of Bai and Sairam were under Aksu's jurisdiction and were primarily East Turkestani.[77]

USH

After the repression of the rebellion in Ush, the Qing rebuilt and repopulated this city almost from scratch. A new fortress, called "Yongning" ("eternal peace"), was erected abutting a steep hillside at a remove from the remains of the old town (see Map 5). Nayanceng later renamed this citadel "Fuhua" (roughly, "confident transformation"). The authorities located the garrison barracks and government offices within the citadel, and official temples, including the Imperial Hall (Wanshou Gong), were built on the heights, with the altars to land and grain behind them. The Guandi temple bore an inscription on copper from the Qianlong emperor, commemorating the Qing victory over the Muslims who rebelled in Ush in 1765.[78]

After the rebellion, the Qing moved hundreds of households of East Turkestanis from Aksu, Kashgar, Yarkand, and Khotan to repopulate the area and revive its agriculture; 810 East Turkestani families farmed and paid grain tax by 1780, and 38 additional families worked farmland allotted to the city's beg officials. By 1857, there were 2,958 registered East Turkestani households under the jurisdiction of Ush. Most townspeople lived in mudbrick structures in an unwalled area below and southeast of the Qing citadel.

Despite the small numbers of Han and Tungan in Ush in the 1780s, by 1811 Ush registered 746 large and small shops and domiciles of merchants from China proper. The Chinese traders were governed by officials in the yamen of the city defense battalion, which handled civilian litigation, interrogated vagrants, arrested miscreants, and set market prices on commodities. Two squad leaders (*bazong*) patrolled the bazaar, reporting major cases to the amban.

There were many foreigners—primarily Central Asians—in both Aksu and Ush; in the latter city in 1828 there were 120 households of Andijanis, of whom 50 had resided there for over ten years and were primarily engaged

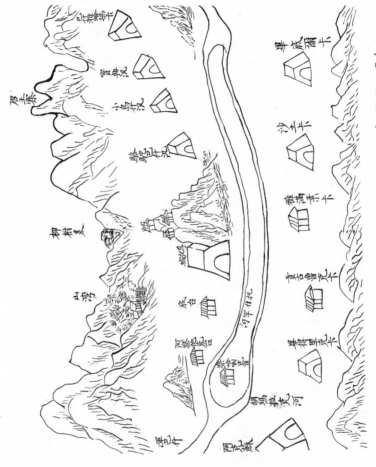

Map 5. The Ush citadel (*Fuhua cheng*) and environs. Source: Bao-da, *Xinjiang Fuhua zhilue* 1:12.

in agriculture. The other 70 households consisted of traders who frequently crossed the *karun* to return to Kokand, and of whom many were apprehended with stocks of rhubarb and tea. Interestingly, the Han and Tungan merchants seem to have outnumbered the Andijanis in Ush, insofar as we may compare figures for Chinese shops in 1811 with those for Andijani households in 1828.[79]

KASHGAR

Yang Yingju arrived in the westernmost city of Xinjiang in April 1760, and in his reports mentioned no Han merchants. Two years later, having found the old city of Kashgar too congested, the Qing authorities constructed a new walled compound to contain the barracks, treasuries, granaries, yamens, armory, Imperial Hall (Wanshou Gong), and Guandi Temple. They built this city two *li* (1 km) to the northwest on a riverbank, the former site of Burhān ad-Dīn's orchard estate. This cantonment, called in Chinese "new city" (*xincheng*) or by the official name Laining Cheng, came to be known by Turkestanis as Gülbağ, "rose garden." Not long after the new city's completion, it was already home to 28 establishments run by merchants from China proper selling food, drink, and small sundries; there were five more, including one large shop, in the old city. Five years after that, in 1767, there were a total of 50 shops, stalls, and restaurants in both old and new sections of Kashgar; many were situated in a dense quarter outside Laining Cheng. The influx of Chinese merchants was clearly quite rapid. Moreover, although none was highly capitalized and most of the new shops added between 1762 and 1810 were ranked "small" or "medium," during the first few years at least the businesses expanded over time: in 1762 their average size was 2.75 rooms or "bays" (*jian*); by 1767 that had increased to 3.4 *jian* each.[80]

By Qi-shi-yi's time, the old and new cities "adjoined closely"—probably through development of the land originally separating them. The Manchu traveler describes the city's luxurious style in the 1770s, the wealth of its inhabitants, and the skill of its goldsmiths, jade carvers, singers, and dancers. Qi-shi-yi found the East Turkestanis here better tempered than in Kucha and parts east, where "the Muslims are violent and the villages uncivilized." A later visitor tells us of the Friday bazaars held in the old city and horse markets outside the wall. Although Kirghiz brought a great number of horses for sale here, apparently the Chinese preferred mules.[81]

In 1794, councillor Yong-bao had an extramural commercial quarter of 150 *jian* erected outside Laining's south gate, to be rented to merchants from China proper who "previously lived in the Muslim city." This looks like an attempt—albeit 30 years after the promulgation of the edict mandating such procedures—to segregate the Han and Tungan population from the native Kashgarliks.[82] To be sure, control over these sojourning, single male merchants must have been one reason for building these shops and accommodations, but the official need for rent revenue was surely equally important. As we have seen, revenue from Kashgar's official commercial activities, primarily rents and sale of silk, amounted to almost half the value of Kashgar's annual *xiexiang* allotment (see Table 11). Moreover, if it was a segregation measure, segregation per se was not strictly enforced. Merchants from China proper continued to live in the Kashgar Muslim city well after this date: in 1810, there were "in the new and old city" a total of 96 Chinese merchant establishments not on government property (hence owing tax, not rent). Furthermore, we know that somewhat later Han and/or Tungans even resided and traded in the East Turkestani villages of Kashgar's hinterland.[83]

During the invasion led by Jahāngīr, Chinese merchants joined with the Manchu bannermen and Green Standard forces to defend Laining citadel. This merchant militia included traders from Zhili, Shaanxi, Gansu, Sichuan, Shanxi, and the Jiangnan, and almost 900 died fighting the Khoja supporters. As it did for the East Turkestani begs who died in the line of duty, the Qing government arranged for relief funds to be sent to the families of the deceased merchants and honored them with temple sacrifices according to the same protocol followed for dead footsoldiers.[84]

The Makhdūmzāda followers destroyed Laining Cheng, and the Qing rebuilt the city, as it did Manchu cantonments in Yangi Hisar and Yarkand. Fortunately for the dynasty, Kashgar authorities were able to recover a remarkable amount of money by confiscating the property of East Turkestanis who had joined the Khojas and by selling off Andijani merchants' stocks of tea and rhubarb. With 107,089 taels thus obtained from "rebels" ʿAbd Allāh and Mi-la-sa Sulaymān, the Qing built (among other things) a strong new fort about twenty *li* (10 km) southeast of the Kashgar Muslim city, furnished with barracks, yamens, storehouses, temples, and 4,318 commercial units to be rented out. Qing officials referred to this new city at the time of its construction as the "Manchu city" (Mancheng), as opposed to "Muslim city" (Huicheng) or "old city" (Jiucheng) for old Kashgar. Locally the fort was "Chinese city" (Shaihr-i-Khatai) or "new city" (Yängi Šähär). Not until somewhat later did this Qing cantonment come to be known as the "Han city" (Hancheng).[85]

With the construction of a new cantonment, including merchant quarters, after the great watershed of the Jahāngīr invasion, something resembling true segregation for Chinese merchants and East Turkestanis had arisen in Kashgar. Although they still attended the Friday bazaars, which Qing officials supervised in a cursory fashion,[86] the merchants from China proper now lived a good distance from Muslim Kashgar.

YANGI HISAR

Eastern Turkestan is itself walled in by mountain ranges to the north, west, and south. From Kashgar, foreign trade routes continued west past the *karun* line and through the Pamir passes to Kokand and elsewhere in Central Asia. The main *taizhan* route turned back southeast, however, continuing along the string of oases between the mountains (the Kunlun) and the desert (the Taklamakan). Yangi Hisar lay two days' journey along this road from Kashgar, in open country at the base of a barren ridge. The town conducted much trade with the Kirghiz and was famous for its dancing girls and musicians.

After taking the city in 1759, the Qing divided the existing mud-walled town into two sections with a wall running east to west through the center and quartered the troops and officers in the northern half. In 1775, with a donation from the hakim beg, Sultan Khoja, the Manchus built a new extension for the garrison, abutting the northern wall of the old city, which they left entirely to the East Turkestanis. A single gate through the three-meter-high wall afforded communication between Muslim and Manchu quarters of Yangi Hisar.[87]

There were no Chinese merchant shops recorded in Yangi Hisar until 1794, when five small enterprises were registered; these were first taxed in 1806. In 1811, there were 33 shops. Nineteen years later, however, authorities in Yangi Hisar mustered a militia of almost 500 Chinese "merchants and exiles" to help defend the city against the Kokandi invasion. Chinese homesteading was not yet permitted in Altishahr, and as there were no large exile colonies and those few exiles present were generally enslaved to begs, it seems likely that the bulk of this force was composed of merchants. (At that time, the soldiers stationed in Yangi Hisar and nearby *taizhan* amounted to only 360 men.)[88]

As in Kashgar and Yarkand, the Qing rebuilt its Yangi Hisar cantonment after Jahāngīr's attack. Mobilizing confiscated rebel funds, authorities constructed new yamens, barracks, temples, and storehouses some distance away from the Muslim city behind crenelated battlements seven meters high and a surrounding ditch seven meters deep. Also in the new settlement were 503 units to be rented to merchants from China proper. This cantonment was called "Manchu city" by officials in charge and known as "new city" (Yāngi Šähär) in Turki.[89]

YARKAND

Two or three days' journey further southeast took a traveler to Yarkand, a city reportedly more opulent even than Kashgar, and a major entrepôt for Xinjiang's foreign trade with the Himalayan countries and South Asia. The old city, which had served as Khoja Jihān's stronghold, was contained within a sturdy earth wall over five kilometers in circumference and ten meters high, entered by five gates. On taking the city in 1759, the Qing chose not to construct new fortifications, but simply added gatehouses and guardhouses, built new official buildings where necessary, and where possible converted existing structures to government use. The contributions of officials, soldiers, and Chinese merchants paid for the erection of a Guandi Temple. Most Qing offices were situated in a corner of the western section of the city, separated from East Turkestani dwellings by only a thin earthen wall.[90]

During the Jihāngīr war, the yamen, barracks, and treasury in Yarkand were all destroyed. Nayanceng, dispatched to the region to oversee postwar reconstruction, was concerned about the close proximity of Qing personnel and the East Turkestanis under the old arrangement. He thus proposed that a new cantonment be built on higher ground a little over a kilometer west of old Yarkand. Funds realized from the sale of rebel property sufficed to build this "Mancheng," and new walls, temples, yamens, and barracks, as well as 1,132 *jian* for rental to Chinese merchants were erected on the new site within a compound about 1.5 kilometers in circumference. In addition to occupying official rental space, merchants from China proper built outside the new city and in the direction of old Yarkand, so that eventually a bazaar extended from the Mancheng all the way to Yarkand's east gate.[91]

In 1830, a Kokand-sponsored army torched these extramural houses and businesses as the infuriated Chinese merchants watched from the ramparts of the new city (see Chapter 6). Partially as a result of this event, the final reshaping of Yarkand's urban structure under the Manchus was the erection of an outer wall in 1835. This new, rectangular rampart surrounding the Manchu city was over two kilometers in circumference and allowed those merchants who had formerly lived outside to reside within a defensive perimeter.[92]

Qi-shi-yi described the density, activity, and prosperity of Yarkand with his accustomed metaphors ("clouds," "bees," "the teeth of a comb"). Already in 1777 he noted the presence of merchants "from Shanxi, Shaanxi, Jiangsu, and Zhejiang [who], balking at neither distance nor danger, sell their goods here." There were also Andijanis, Kashmiris, and other foreign merchants. The old city's main bazaar extended the length of the town between the eastern and western gates, with a circular marketplace in the center of town. These were the venues of the Friday bazaar, but the many "Chinese shops" along this road, "some exceedingly well built," did a busy trade all through the week. The street running from the east gate to the Manchu city was "a lively scene of activity and trade," lined with restaurants and stalls, with "the cattle market and gallows on one side, and the horse market on the other."[93]

Despite its many *madrasa* colleges and mosques, Yarkand under the Qing impressed visitors with its free-spirited ways: Qi-shi-yi describes dancing girls, actors, and "sodomy in the style of Fujian and Guangdong." Women were generally not veiled, regardless of social standing, and horseflesh—not a meat permitted within Islam's dietary restrictions—was openly sold and commonly consumed, a practice not to be found in contemporary Western Turkestan.[94] One East Turkestani's complaint to a British agent in the 1870s, during the reign of Ya'qūb Beg, is particularly revealing about life in Yarkand under Qing rule.

> What you see on market day now . . . is nothing to the life and activity there was in the time of the *Khitay* [i.e., Chinese]. Today the peasantry come in with their fowls and eggs, with their cotton and yarn, or with their sheep and cattle and horses for sale; and they go back with printed cottons, or fur caps, or city made boots, or whatever domestic necessaries they may require, and always with a good dinner inside them, and then we shut up our shops and stow away our goods till next week's market day brings back our customers. Some of us go out with a small venture in the interim to the rural markets around, but our great day is market day in town. It was very different in the Khitay time. People then bought and sold every day, and market day was a much jollier time. There was no Kazi Rais with his six *muhtasib* armed with the *dira* to flog people off to prayers, and drive the women out of the streets, and nobody was bastinadoed for drinking spirits and eating forbidden meats. There were musicians and acrobats, and fortune-tellers and story-tellers, who moved about amongst the crowds and diverted the people. There were flags and banners and all sorts of pictures floating at the shop fronts, and there was the *jallab*, who painted her face and decked herself in silks and laces to please her customers. . . . Yes, there were many rogues and gamblers too, and people did get drunk, and have their pockets picked. So they do now, though not so publicly, because we are now under Islam, and the *Shariat* is strictly enforced.[95]

This positive impression of the commercial conditions pertaining in Yarkand under Qing rule was echoed by a "Mussulman merchant" in conversation with an explorer in the employ of Britain's Great Game rival, Russia. The merchant believed that "thanks to Chinese rule there was a safety in the country that was favorable to the development of trade such as had never existed before in consequence of the ceaseless robberies and internecine wars." He pointed to the Chinese shops and caravanserais for the accommodation of itinerant merchants as examples of Yarkand's advantages.[96]

Chinese merchants arrived in Yarkand around the same time as they came

TABLE 12

Chinese Shops and Merchants in Xinjiang Cities

(in number of shops, except as otherwise noted)

	1762–63	1767	1794–95	1810–11	1828–30	1834–35	1861
Aksu	—	—	—	130 shops, 859 houses	—	—	—
Karashahr	—	—	—	1,863	—	—	—
Kashgar	33	50	—	96	>888*	—	c. 2,000
Khotan	—	—	—	0	—	—	—
Kucha	—	—	—	169	—	—	—
Tarbagatai	—	—	—	—	—	141	—
Urumchi	500	11,190 "house-holds"	—	—	—	—	—
Ush	—	—	—	746 (includes houses)	—	—	—
Yangi Hisar	—	—	5	33	c. 500*	—	—
Yarkand	19	—	—	184	c. 400*	c. 200 "Han merchants"†	c. 5,000 "merchants and family members"

SOURCES: *GZSL* 647:17, QL27.11 *wuchen*; Yong-bao et al., *Wulumuqi shiyi*, pp. 23a–24a; Tie-bao, ZPZZ MZSW 0080-6, JQ16.1.10; 0080-7, JQ16.4.5; LFZZ MZSW 1447-1, JQ16.1.10, 1447-2, n.d. (c. JQ14–15), 1447–49 n.d. (c. JQ16), 1447–49 *qingdan*, n.d. (ca. JQ16); Na-yan-bao, LFZZ MZSW 1447-5, JQ16.2.24; Na-yan-bao, LFZZ, JQ16.3.28, and Tie-bao, LFZZ, JQ16.5.9, cited in Hua Li, "Qing zhongye Xinjiang yu neidi de maoyi wanglai," p. 290; Jalungga (Zha-long-a), LFZZ MZSW 1222-6 (new no. 8053-59) *pian* (rescript DG9.6.27); Bi-chang, Chang-li, et al., ZPZZ MZSW 0555-1, DG10.11.17; Ha-lang-a, ZPZZ MZSW 0544-8, DG10.12.13; Gen-chu-ke-ze-bang (?), ZPZZ MZSW 0085-4, c. 1834–35; Davies, *Report*, Appendix 29a, pp. cccxxiii–xxv; Wathen, "Memoir," p. 654; Forsyth, *Report*, p. 36.
*Sources cite figures in number of "merchants."
†Excludes Tungans, artisans, and itinerant traders.

to Kashgar: within a few years after the Manchu conquest of Altishahr. In 1763, Yarkand superintendent Xin-zhu taxed nineteen merchants who occupied 44 *jian* (an average shop size of about 2.3 "bays" or rooms). By 1811 there were 141 shops liable for commercial tax and three merchants farming government land. In addition, 43 businesses operated in buildings rented from East Turkestanis, including the hakim beg. The average shop size at this time was 2.9 *jian*, but in fact size seems to have been unevenly distributed, with a small number of large stores and many tiny stalls. We have no more commercial tax figures for Yarkand after this time, but there are some indications of the numbers of individual merchants: 118 merchants from Zhili, Shaanxi, Gansu, and Sichuan, led by a Tungan, Jin Zhongpu, died while defending Yarkand from Jahāngīr's followers in 1826. As in Kashgar, these men were honored with official sacrifices and their relatives compensated. In 1830, a fifth-rank beg named Duo-lie-su-pi said that there were over 400 Chinese traders in Yarkand.[97] Finally, we have the estimates from British agents: 200 resident Han merchants in the early 1830s (excluding Tungans, Han artisans, and itinerants); 5,000 "Chinese and Tungan traders, shop-keepers, and followers" in the new city circa 1861; and, "during the Chinese occupation," a "floating population of nearly 10,000 followers, suttlers, artificers, pedlars, and merchants whose activity brought life, wealth and prosperity to the city." A new policy, enacted in 1831, allowed Han settlers and merchant and Green Standard dependents to move permanently to Altishahr (see Chapter 6). Although these later figures of 5,000 and 10,000 are impressionistic, they indicate a sizeable increase in the numbers of Han and Tungan in Yarkand, an increase probably brought about by this policy change.[98] (Available figures for the numbers of Chinese shops and merchants in Xinjiang cities are summarized in Table 12.)

KHOTAN

The easternmost city in southern Altishahr, Khotan, was actually a group of six small towns. The Qing occupied the largest of these, Yiliqi (Tu. Elichi), walling off the southeast corner of the existing earthen compound for the headquarters of the commandant and military personnel and leaving the rest of the city to the East Turkestanis. Yiliqi came to be known as Hetian Cheng (Khotan City).[99]

Although jade and gold brought some traders and adventurers to Khotan from China proper, perhaps because of their small numbers or Khotan's relative remoteness, they were never officially taxed, nor were government rental units constructed to house them. Instead, the few resident merchants, who dealt in jade, gold, carpets, and local silk, wool, and gold filigree fabrics, rented space from East Turkestanis and lived among them. They included merchants from Shaanxi, Shanxi, and Gansu, organized under a *xiangyue* headman. The city walls, official buildings, and regional post stations were repaired after Jihāngīr, but as the threat of invasion was never so great here as in Kashgar, Yangi Hisar, and Yarkand, no new city was constructed until 1884 (when Xinjiang's new provincial authorities implemented *junxian*-style administration throughout Altishahr and at the same time built a separate military compound in Khotan).[100]

"Manchu Cities" or "Chinese Cities"? Rectifying the Names

Zeng Wenwu and Lin Enxian, when discussing divided cities and removed cantonments in Xinjiang, use the term "Hancheng" ("Han city," or "Chinese city") for the Qing citadels, regardless of the time period in question.[101] This is highly misleading, for, as shown above, these city sections or fortresses were referred to as "Mancheng" (Manchu city) or "Xincheng" (new city) when first completed.

Once again, it is instructive to see what Wei Yuan, that early Chinese nationalist, had to say on the matter. On reconstruction in Altishahr after Jihāngīr, he wrote, "According to the original Muslim custom, [Altishahr] had no walled cities. When Xinjiang was first pacified in the Qianlong period, beside the Muslim villages shoulder-high walls (*qiang*) were erected; these were called "Hancheng." They contained only the official yamens, barracks, granaries, and treasuries; the merchant (*shangmin*) market streets were all outside the Hanchengs, or mixed among the Muslim houses. Therefore in the uprisings of 1826, the four cities [of western Altishahr] were easily lost."[102]

Wei Yuan is wrong on three counts here. As shown in this chapter, some places in Altishahr did in fact have fortified cities before the Qing conquest, the Qing did not in all cases construct cantonments in Qianlong times, and such cantonments as were built were not at the time called "Hancheng"— at least not in Qing sources available today. Why, in any case, would the cantonments be called "Han cities" if the Han merchants lived outside? This absurdity, inherent in Wei's argument and in the terminology employed by Zeng, Lin, and others, is most patent in a sentence from the *Xinjiang jianshi*, the official line on Xinjiang's past, published in 1980 in the People's Republic: "The Qing dynasty prohibited people of the Han nationality from going to southern Xinjiang, and even if there were [Han] merchants there to trade, they were only allowed to live near the Hancheng."[103]

The distinction between "Mancheng," or "Xincheng," on the one hand, and "Hancheng," on the other, is not a trivial or pedantic one. Though these nineteenth- and twentieth-century historians may not even have been aware of the terminological shift they were executing, in doing so they have contributed to the historiographical erasure of the Manchu role in the creation of the empire and the conflation of "Qing" and "China" by turning Qing cities in Xinjiang into Chinese ones retroactively. The proposal by Gong Zizhen (Wei's contemporary and colleague) to sinicize Xinjiang's population, economy, and environment (see Conclusion) is analogous, as are attempts in the early Republic to redefine "Chinese" in politically expedient ways.

Qing Xinjiang was not yet China. Han Chinese coexisted there with other peoples, and the Qing employed a variety of institutions and techniques to govern them. Distinct administrative systems—military, beg, *junxian*, jasak —functioned in different parts of the territory; two different legal codes and sets of judicial personnel were juxtaposed in Altishahr in a complex overlap wherein a criminal's origin and ethnicity partially determined the selection of tribunal and means of punishment. Special restrictions applied to Han and Tungan in Xinjiang during the first decades of Qing rule there: they needed passes to travel, they paid commercial taxes to which East Turkestanis were not subject, they could not marry locally or bring dependents to live in Altishahr, they could not reclaim and cultivate land in Altishahr, and they were not allowed to venture abroad.

Despite these constraints, however, from soon after the conquest until well into the nineteenth century, Chinese merchants entered Xinjiang, including Altishahr, in significant numbers. Moreover, Ming-rui's 1765 proposal to segregate them from East Turkestanis notwithstanding, there is no evidence that strict segregation was ever actually implemented as official policy—no such law was printed in the 1842 collection of the substatutes of Altishahr (*Huijiang zeli*). The construction of shops and residences for Chinese merchants, such as those built in the shadow of Laining Cheng in Kashgar in 1794, can best be understood as a means to extract rent revenue from the traders and to accommodate them near the refuge of the Qing cantonment and not as a government plan to segregate them from the local population. Merchants dwelt and did business in the old Muslim cities of Kashgar, Yarkand, and Khotan up to and after 1826; they were taxed normally by officials who knew their whereabouts and seemingly did not mind. Should we view the erection of new fortresses removed from the old cities in Kashgar, Yangi Hisar, and Yarkand as belated implementation of a 60-year-old edict regarding merchants from China proper, as some scholars have done? Or was this rather primarily a military response to the increasingly unstable situation vis-à-vis Kokand and the Khojas? The latter explanation best fits the data we have.

Nevertheless, despite their freedom of movement within Altishahr, Chinese merchants in Altishahr cities did tend to segregate themselves from East Turkestani areas and gravitate toward Qing citadels, or to the space between the cantonments and Muslim old cities. This was especially the case in the western cities after the Jahāngīr invasion, and the reasons for it may be easily surmised. As we have seen, Chinese merchants and the commercial economy they stimulated were an important source of supplies and supplemental revenue for Qing imperial outposts in Xinjiang. Thus in some cities the Qing government actively encouraged such a settlement pattern by making housing and commercial property available to Chinese merchants inside or in the immediate extramural area. And for their part, Han merchants most likely felt more comfortable near the Qing forts, in the company of their Chinese compatriots, close to native-place societies, and in the shadow of the Guandi and other temples, than out among the bazaars and mosques of Central Asian Xinjiang. (For Tungans, who were Muslims, the situation was somewhat different, as we shall see in the next chapter.)

Though named "Manchu cities" initially, the new citadels that Chinese merchants in Altishahr eventually cohabited with Qing garrison forces did come to be called "Hancheng" by the 1840s. This change is an important historical fact that should not be obscured by anachronistic application of the term "Hancheng" to the cities in Qianlong times. By the early nineteenth century, the remarkable advance of Chinese merchants into Qing Central Asia resulted in major shifts of Qing ethnic policy, with implications for the imperial conception as a whole. Before we consider that shift, however, we will take a closer look at some of the merchants themselves.

CHAPTER 5

The Merchants and Articles of Trade

Qalmaqqa böz, Xitayğa söz.
To the Kalmak, cloth; to the Chinese, words.

Nineteenth-century East Turkestani proverb[1]

As with the terms "Manchu city" and "Han city," words employed in Qing sources can indicate where conceptual boundaries were drawn and how the various human and territorial pieces of the Qing realm fit together. Although the Qing permitted commercial intercourse between China proper and Xinjiang, throughout the Qianlong reign and into the nineteenth century these regions remained distinct. This distinction is clearly illustrated by the terminology used in official sources to refer to both regions. When official Qing materials discussed Xinjiang in juxtaposition to China proper, the latter was occasionally *Zhongguo* (central country) or *zhongyuan* (central plain), and most commonly *neidi* (inner land). Xinjiang appears often as *guanwai* ("beyond the pass" or "frontier portal").[2]

Qing official terminology likewise distinguished different groups of people, though not always with the terms one might expect. In Xinjiang's Chinese-language official correspondence and in gazetteers, the generic word *min* ("people," "person," "subject") and compounds containing this character (*shangmin, jumin, minren*) occur far more frequently than the term *Han*. Often, such words appear in conjunction with the term *neidi*, which makes their meaning unambiguous. *Minren* and similar terms were almost never applied to East Turkestanis, and in fact were often used in contrast to such words as *Huizi* or *Huimin* (Muslims), by which the East Turkestanis were known. For example, Qing officials divided the lists of militia men who died during the defense of Altishahr cities into two categories, *boke Huizi* and *shangmin*; when these persons' names and places of origin are listed, we see that the former category contains Turkic names of begs and East Turkestanis, while the latter is made up exclusively of the names of Han and/or Tungan from the provinces of China proper.[3]

Qing materials commonly include Tungans with the Han in such terms as *shangmin, neidi shangren, min,* or *jumin.* Where the Tungans' religion was at issue, however, they were distinguished more precisely as a variety of Han, the "Han Muslims" (*Hanhui*) or "Muslims from within the pass" (*neidi Huimin*). Thus Nayanceng fulminated against the "*Hanhui* who have been squatting in each city of Altishahr, cheating East Turkestanis out of their money, and teaching them to break the law."[4]

East Turkestanis were called "Muslims" (*Huimin, Huizi*; Ma. *Hoise*). The term *chantou*, "wrapped head," for the East Turkestanis—a reference to the turbans worn by some East Turkestani men—came into official use only in the Guangxu period, around the time the Qing placed Xinjiang under provincial administration with primarily Han officials; this usage continued into the Republican Era. The term was known at least as early as the mid-Qing, however. The 1809 *Xichui zongtong shilue* explains the origin of the term *Huijiang* ("Muslim frontier," i.e., Altishahr) in the following way: "From Hami and Turfan to the eight big cities of the west, the wrapped-head Muslim masses (*chantou Huizhong*) live together in their clans. Therefore [this region] is called *Huijiang*." Kokandis or others from western Turkestan were generally subsumed under the name *An-ji-yan* (Andijanis), or referred to as *yihui* (foreign or barbarian Muslims), *Huishang* (Muslim merchants), or a similar compound.[5] And there were of course names for the other peoples in Xinjiang: *Ha-sa-ke* (Kazakh), *Bu-lu-te* (Burut, Kirghiz), *Ka-shi-mi-er* (Kashmiri), and so forth.

Because Qing officials in Xinjiang carefully maintained these terminological distinctions—more carefully, in fact, than they did the physical segregation of Chinese from East Turkestani—the historical record left by government dispatches makes it clear that there were distinct classes of merchants, divided on ethnic, regional, and professional lines, carrying on the trade between Xinjiang and China proper.

East Turkestani Merchants

> When I said, "Kiss me once!" she said, "Bring me silk-stuff!" When I said, "I am no dealer in silk-stuff! . . . What shall I do my friend?" She said, "If you want me, oh, boy, bring me some silk-stuff!" Having gone forwards and returned and come home and opened the box and taken out the bank-notes and taken the copper coins and put them into the saddle-bag and put a lock on and entered the stable and saddled the horse and put on the saddle-bag and mounted the horse and gone to Peking and taken to a pigtail and become a rich Chinaman and opened a shop and bought silk-stuff and stuffed it into a sack and loaded it on

an ass and also pulled the saddle-girth in, when I came to my friend she
said, "Come here my beloved! . . . Where is your crepe de Chine?"

From an East Turkestani verse[6]

Compared to the rich Kokandi merchants who controlled the tea and rhubarb markets to the west, or the Chinese traders with access to the fortresses
and the Manchu overlords, East Turkestani merchants lacked economic and
political influence in Qing Xinjiang. This had not always been the case. In
the seventeenth century, merchants from the Tarim Basin cities and Turfan
participated in a trading network that linked the Middle East, India, Trans-
oxiana, Russia, Siberia, Gansu, and Qinghai. Membership in Naqshbandī
religious brotherhoods afforded these "Bukharans" (as Turkestani merchants
were known in Central Asia) a measure of independence from local rulers and
allowed freedom of movement despite the political fragmentation of Central Asia in the seventeenth century. After the Zunghar occupation of the
Tarim Basin cities late in the century, East Turkestani merchants allied themselves with these western Mongols, trading with the Qing at Suzhou and
even traveling to Beijing as "envoys" of the Zunghar khan.[7] After the Manchu conquest, however, East Turkestani merchant guilds lost their influence
and merchants their mobility. Qing administrative structures left Altishahr
natives at the mercy of beg officials imported from Hami and Turfan, and the
pass system legally limited the distances and duration of foreign and domestic trading trips. West Turkestani merchants, on the other hand, could continue to work the powerful Naqshbandī networks; they enjoyed the support
of the Kokand khanate, and Xinjiang's structure of import duties was skewed
in their favor. East Turkestani merchants may have been forced to ally with
Kokandi and other foreign merchants to be successful.[8]

Nonetheless, although Qing sources are largely silent about their activities, East Turkestani merchants seem to have played a considerable commercial role in the late eighteenth and nineteenth centuries. They traded with
Kazakhs and Kirghiz in the mountainous regions surrounding the Tarim
Basin. Some ventured to Ladakh, to which Yarkandis could travel legally.
And if the pass system proved inconvenient, the "*ortung*" (Turki for the
karun guard posts) "could be easily avoided." (Nayanceng railed against the
loose enforcement of pass laws for East Turkestanis exiting Xinjiang; fairly
porous borders had been customary before his arrival in Altishahr—and became common again after his departure.)[9] Moreover, while traveling between
Xinjiang cities or even to China proper and Beijing, although native East
Turkestanis were in theory required to obtain passes from the Qing ambans
through their hakim begs, in practice they could pass check points unin-

spected. Ji Yun noticed the ease with which East Turkestanis moved between
Turfan and Urumchi around 1770:

> The Turfan tribe of old has had close relations [with China],
> Selling fruit, they come all the time to the inner city gate [i.e., inside the
>   city walls],
> Just like swallows in high spring upon a bridge,
> They come and go as they please, paying no attention to anybody.
>
> *(Turfan has for a long time belonged to the empire [nei shu]. No different from locals
> [tu ren, i.e., Chinese in Urumchi], [Turfanis] come to trade and are not inspected.)*

In 1803 a case arose in which a Kashgari named Se-pa-er traveled without
a pass through Hami, Turfan, and Karashahr on his return from Beijing. (A
Tungan who was handling Se-pa-er's luggage had to apply for passes and was
detained by the authorities.) Somewhat later, around 1835, an East Turkestani
reported that no passport was necessary for him to go from Yarkand to Beijing, and nothing prevented him from staying as long as he wished in China
proper. Foreign merchants, too, could travel as far as Beijing with a pass obtained for a few *tänggä* from the amban in Yarkand.[10]

Tribute Trade

Many East Turkestani traders visited China proper on the occasion of begs'
imperial audiences. After Zhao-hui's successful conclusion of the Altishahr
campaign in 1759, on his "triumphal return" he escorted the first wave of
newly appointed beg officials, together with East Turkestani nobles whom
the dynasty was relocating to Beijing. Subsequent contingents followed over
the next three years until all begs above fourth rank had been granted an
audience and an all-expenses-paid trip to the capital. In 1774 the system was
revised, and the court then entertained delegations led by hakim begs of Khotan, Yarkand, Yangi Hisar, Kashgar, Aksu, and Kucha on a six-year rotating
schedule. After 1811 the schedule was again changed, this time to a nine-year
cycle. All begs above the fourth rank thereafter visited the capital once every
nine years; newly appointed begs fifth rank and below were granted audiences in the year following their appointments.[11]

As often when such junkets were provided at court expense, the retinues
multiplied and their luggage swelled year by year. The beg missions became
markets on the move across north China, creating difficulties for the person-

nel of the post stations along the route, who were responsible for providing horses and carts for the begs and baggage. Gaozong was not particularly anxious about this problem ("Begs from Altishahr coming for an imperial audience in their proper year bring a few things with them to sell—what is wrong with that?"), but the volume and weight of goods to be carted was considerable. Around the end of the Qianlong era, begs of various ranks and ennobled rulers in Xinjiang were permitted to bring the following amounts of luggage (given in catties) with them to Beijing.

third ranked:	4,000
fourth ranked:	3,000
fifth ranked:	2,000
sixth ranked:	1,500
male relative:	600
wang:	8,000
beile:	6,000
beizi:	4,000
gong:	3,000

A memorialist who drew attention to the problems caused by such large caravans pointed out that even allowing for sufficient clothing for the journey and a certain amount of "local products" as gifts to the emperor, the current quotas were excessive and could reasonably be reduced without compromising the dynastic principle of largess to "outer vassals" (*waifan*).[12]

The court approved this proposal, but permanent solutions were never possible to the problem of quasi-covert trading by tributary missions. In 1816 the Lifan Yuan issued a notice that Xinjiang begs routinely exceeded their luggage quotas, to the extent that the excess baggage delayed the delegations' arrival in Beijing by weeks. The "three kneelings and nine kowtows" of the imperial audience ritual were scheduled for the first day of the new lunar year (*yuandan*), but in some years the Xinjiang delegation did not reach the capital until the 27th of the 12th lunar month—just three or four days before the ceremony. After a policy review, the court decided that all begs whose turn it was for an audience should assemble well ahead of departure time in Hami, where the Hami superintendent would inspect and weigh all items except "local products" (melons, raisins, fruit preserves, small knives, and so on, to be presented to the emperor) and limit them to the stipulated weight. If begs brought extra servants, their baggage allowance would be reduced as a penalty. After the missions' departure, each official through whose jurisdiction the caravan passed, from governor-general down to county-level officials, was to repeat this procedure and would be held responsible for escorting the begs and their baggage train within quota from his bailiwick. "Criminal merchants" and carriers of "private goods" discovered on the way were subject to severe punishment—which indicates that trading on the audience missions was not a sideline the begs engaged in on their own, but probably involved commercial specialists as well.[13]

These beg visits to the imperial capital, when carefully considered, pose another interpretative challenge to the "tribute system" model by which "China's traditional foreign relations" have been understood. Consider the word *fan*, for example, as in *waifan*. The term has been variously translated "vassal," "dependency," "tributary," or "colonial" in English and has generally been understood to refer to non-Chinese. John King Fairbank himself noted the greater complexity of the term and pointed out that it, like tribute, was applied to persons and matters domestic as well as foreign, noting that Ming Dynasty Princes of the Blood were known as *fanwang*.[14] Nevertheless, there is a tendency in all of Fairbank's work on tribute and the "Chinese world order," and among those influenced by it, to treat the Mongolian, East Turke-stani, and other *waifan* under Qing rule as foreign because they were not culturally Sinic and because they undertook "tribute missions" to the Qing court. It is, of course, a major argument of this book that this view obscures the real nature of the Qing empire.

One way to clear up the confusion is to abandon the idea of a mono-lithic, unchanging "Chinese world order" and look instead specifically at the Qing case. With regard to such uniquely Qing institutions as the Lifan Yuan (charged with handling the East Turkestani begs), a better understanding of the Qing outlook can be gained simply by examining, as Ning Chia has done,[15] the Manchu name for the agency: *tulergi golo be dasara jurgan*. The term is rendered as "ministry for ruling the outer *provinces.*" *Golo*—prov-ince—is the same term applied to Hubei or Fujian and was not used for Kokand or the Kazakhs. This is not to say that administratively Xinjiang was indistinguishable from the provinces of China proper (to which the term *golo* was principally applied); we have seen ample evidence of Xinjiang's special administrative status. But in the Manchu term translated as Lifan Yuan in Chinese, the accumulated semantic baggage of two millennia of usage, under which the term *fan* labors like begs en route to Beijing, is neatly avoided. Thus, while Altishahr and Zungharia were physically outlying (distinguished from *neidi*, "within the pass"), they were certainly not "foreign" following the Qianlong conquest.

In Chapter 2, I argued that knowledge of how the Qing traded with the Kazakhs allows us to refute Fairbank's statement "All foreign relations in the Chinese view were ipso facto tributary relations." Consideration of the Xinjiang begs' imperial audience trips (*rujin, chaojin*) presents us with the paradoxical case of "tribute missions," which seem to be precisely what Fairbank had in mind, but which have little to do with foreign relations. The begs' way to the capital was paid, they presented "local products" to the throne and received "gifts in return," and they were allowed to trade en route and in Beijing—a privilege they regularly abused. While seemingly embarked upon a classic "tribute mission," these men were not in fact ambassadors, nor were they troublesome nomads to be appeased with gifts and trade—to compare them, say, to a delegation from the Xiongnu to the Han court in the first century B.C. (as is implicit in the Fairbank model) obscures far more than it reveals.[16] Rather, the begs were Qing officials who held their offices and ranks at the pleasure of the emperor; the highest-ranked among them, the hakim begs, had the right to memorialize the throne directly. Thus not only were Qing foreign affairs not conducted entirely through the "tribute system," but "tribute missions" (or, more precisely, imperial audience trips) were not exclusively for foreigners.

East Turkestanis in Beijing

Little is known about the community of East Turkestanis resident in the capital. The Qing relocated to Beijing several members of eminent East Turkestani families who had aided in the conquest of Altishahr. These included members of the Khoja clan descended from Makhdūm-i Aʿzam via ʿInāyat Kirāmet, as well as Huo-ji-si from Ush and others, along with the household establishments of each. The East Turkestani nobles were entered into the Mongol Plain White Banner, under the supervision of the Lifan Yuan.[17] The dynasty also resettled a number of captured followers of Khoja Jihān and a troupe of artisans and entertainers. These East Turkestani musicians and dancers performed at court banquest on the emperor's birthday, new year's day, and other special occasions; with their families they numbered over 300 when first brought to Beijing, over 1,800 by Guangxu times. The prisoners and entertainers were organized under a banner captain (*zuoling*) and their stipends paid by the Imperial Household Agency.[18] Commoner East Turkestanis in Beijing—such as Mai-ma-di-min, who was held in Beijing pending trial for rhubarb smuggling in 1792—were placed under the supervision of this captain. Early in 1760, the Qing finished constructing quarters for the noble East Turkestanis southwest of the palace, just below West Chang'an Avenue on the site of today's East Anfu Hutong. Later, when mansions were built for these princes, the East Turkestani quarter, popularly known as the "Muslim Camp" (*Huizi Ying*), became home for the Altishahri goldsmiths, musicians, and dancers. According to a persistent folk tradition, Rong Fei (Xiang Fei), Gaozong's East Turkestani concubine, is said to have gazed wistfully over the wall from her residence on the south bank of Nanhai (the present Xinhua Men) at the activity in the bazaar and mosque of the Muslim Camp.[19]

We do not know how many East Turkestanis lived in Beijing, or what their occupations were. Presumably, in addition to prisoners, artisans, entertainers, and East Turkestani nobles, there was a small floating population of merchants and clerics that either joined this community from Xinjiang or developed out of the original group as its population expanded. One man, named Se-pa-er, although described in an 1803 official Imperial Household Agency document as a "vagrant unemployed barbarian Muslim of Kashgar," nonetheless had the wherewithal to accumulate so many trade goods that he needed to hire a roustabout for the journey home to Altishahr. His Tungan employee had been a bondservant of another East Turkestani resident in Beijing, Qi-mu-shi-ding, and as a result himself dressed as an East Turkestani, wore no queue, and had adopted Turkestani customs. Yet only when he tried to travel in Xinjiang was he found out. This suggests that East Turkestanis were not uncommon in Beijing in the late eighteenth and early nineteenth centuries.[20]

Chinese Merchants in Xinjiang

People in Xinjiang divided the Chinese merchants operating there into two groups: the north bend traders (*beitaoke*) and the west road traders (*xiluke*). The north bend group took their name from the great oxbow of the Yellow River; they came to Xinjiang via the northern route that passed through Inner Mongolia north of the oxbow, or they detoured south to cut across the Ordos. These merchants were primarily from Shanxi province or Beijing and operated out of bases there and in Zhangjiakou and Guihua, cities that were also the departure points for trade with Mongolia and with the Russians at Kiakhta. Because some Shaanxi merchant firms functioned in a manner similar to that of the Shanxi companies, I have included them in the discussion of north bend traders, although some followed different travel routes.

The west road traders came to Xinjiang via the Gansu corridor, Suzhou, and the Jiayu Guan—a "west" road from the perspective of China proper. Their origins were diverse, including Guangdong, Hunan, Jiangsu, Zhejiang, and Sichuan provinces, but primarily they came from Shaanxi and Gansu. This group also included many Tungans. (See Map 6.) For the purposes of this section, I will consider the *xiluke* as a whole and take up the special circumstances of the Tungans in a later section.

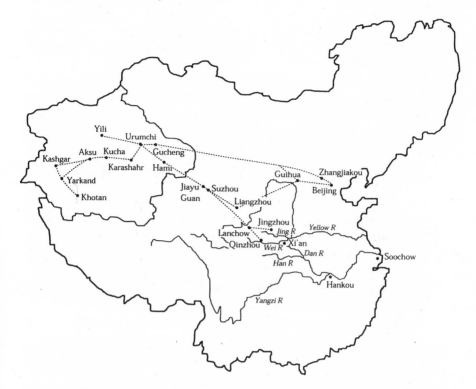

Map 6. Trade routes of north bend traders (*beitaoke*) and west road traders (*xiluke*).

THE NORTH BEND TRADERS

It was the north bend traders who brought Ji Yun his shrimp and hazelnuts. "Big merchants mostly come from the North Bend, saving 30 stages over the official route," Ji wrote, adding that the "rich merchants all originate in Guihua; the locals here call them the *beitaoke*. . . . From Guihua to Dihua takes only two months, but you must bring your own cooking pots and tents."[21] Most from Shanxi, some from Shaanxi (Xi'an) and Zhili (Beijing, Zhangjiakou), the north bend traders represented some of China's most powerful merchant houses. Of course, Chinese from the Shanxi area had always been adept at trade with nomads, and there are records from the Han dynasty of trade between the Xiongnu and Shanxi merchants. The Shanxi firms of Qing times began to take shape during the late Yuan and Ming, trading tea for horses on government contract, and they had established a unique structure that linked tea-growing concerns (production) in south and central China with trading on the borders (retail) in loose vertical conglomerates. This structure allowed the firms of the eighteenth and nineteenth centuries to purchase, process, and package tea according to the particular needs and tastes of various markets: jasmine-scented tea for north China, brick tea for Xinjiang and Mongolia, black tea for Russia.

Another characteristic of these companies, to become most pronounced during the Qing, was their close relationship to the imperial government, especially in financial operations. In the late Ming, several Shanxi merchant families began trading with the Manchus from bases in Zhangjiakou, procuring for them grain, horses, and weapons. After the Qing occupation of Beijing in 1644, these merchant houses were rewarded with the title "imperial merchants" (*huangshang*), and thereafter, like the merchants of Huizhou in Anhui province, Shanxi merchants were granted lucrative contracts to manage the dynasty's salt administration. One particularly prominent Shanxi merchant family, the Fans, in addition to management of the salt monopoly, was also responsible for supplying grain to the Qing armies during Kangxi's and Yongzheng's forays against the Zunghars. (As we have seen, scions of this house later served as consultants during the opening phases of the government trade with the Kazakhs in Zungharia.) The Qing pacification of Khalkha and reduction of the Zunghar threat opened Mongolia to Shanxi firms' steppe retail operations in an unprecedented fashion; the Treaty of Nerchinsk (1689) initiated direct tea trade with the Russians, which was likewise dominated by Shanxi concerns. Meanwhile, close connections with the wealthy Imperial Household Agency and government deposits in Shanxi remittance banks (*piaohao*) provided the firms with huge infusions of capital. Shanxi trading and financial operations ramified throughout the empire during early and mid-Qing, with remittance banking and pawn-broking particularly important in the south, and mobile and sedentary trade in tea, dry goods, and light manufactures, along with money-lending, comprising the basis of their commercial success in the northern and western border regions.[22]

Underlying this success beyond the passes was the Shanxi traders' training and discipline and an organizational structure that allowed them to fan out and do business widely throughout Mongolia, Xinjiang, and even Tibet. Apprentices, many from Datong and Shuoping prefectures in Shanxi and Xuanhua prefecture in Zhili, were brought into the firms at the age of fifteen or sixteen. During the apprenticeships, which could last from two to fifteen years, these boys worked for an experienced trader in the field; one large firm regularly sent young workers to Khobdo for training in Mongolian, Uyghur, Kazakh, or Russian languages, and their bilingual ability gave rise to the name "interpreter firms" (*tongshihang*) as a general term for these companies. By the conclusion of the apprenticeship, the young employees had accumulated experience and their own capital. Generally, then, they returned to Shanxi at company expense—the firm might even pay for presents for their relatives. After marrying, the new journeymen would set out again, returning home on leave only every few years. Once established in this way, some Shanxi merchants worked for a salary based on the quality of their salesmanship. The firm would not allow itself to lose money: if operations were unprofitable, the employees made up the loss from their own pay. Other Shanxi traders operated on a share partnership or quasi-independent basis, maintaining ties to the home firm, often purchasing wares from caravans dispatched by the home company and availing themselves of the firms' remittance network to transfer funds.[23]

Large Shanxi shops in outlying areas, including Xinjiang, often went by the same name or one similar to that of the home firm, thus I translate the general term for such large stores, *zihao*, as "name-brand." They are best thought of as branches or even franchises of a company back in Shanxi—or, in some cases, Zhili or Shaanxi.[24]

A typical name-brand store (*zihaopu*) was designed as a double compound with a smaller square compound in front consisting of a front sales area, two wing buildings, and the "counter" (*changgui*) or office, where the manager handled financial matters. Behind this a larger courtyard opened up, somewhat lower than the front buildings, but likewise enclosed by side and back rooms. These served as a hostel for guests of the firm, including caravan teamsters or nomads in town to trade. In this yard would be stored goods and coal; it was used also as a stable for livestock. (See Figure 5.)[25]

Xinjiang's best known north bend trader is the infamous Zhang Luan, who conspired with the Yarkand superintendent Gao Pu to smuggle thousands of catties of jade from Yarkand to Soochow in the late 1770s. But Zhang's career before his fateful involvement with that errant Qing bondservant and official provides a detailed case history of a Shanxi merchant in eighteenth-century Xinjiang.[26]

As a young man from Youyu County, Shuoping Prefecture, Shanxi, Zhang got a job in 1768 as a camel teamster for the San Yi Dian, a Guihua concern that traded Chinese cloth for hides in Mongolia and Xinjiang. A San Yi Dian manager, Jia Youyu, from the same county as Zhang, found the young man very able and the following year promoted him to partner and sent him to run the San Yi's Aksu branch. In 1773, Zhang used 10,000 taels of the shop's funds to buy jade, which he sold in Suzhou for 23,000 taels. However, he repaid only 9,000 taels (in cash and goods) of the San Yi Dian's capital, and Jia had to travel to Xinjiang to collect the remainder. Despite some hard feelings following this incident, Zhang maintained a relationship with the firm even

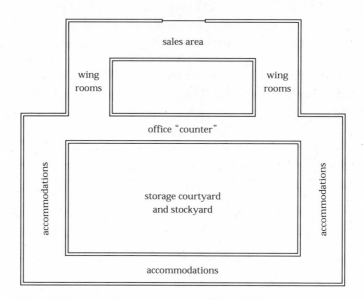

Figure 5.   Plan of a typical *zihao* store. (1) Sales area, (2) wing rooms, (3) office "counter," (4) storage courtyard and stockyard, (5) accommodations.

after resigning in 1776. When he left the San Yi Dian, Zhang returned to Shanxi, where he formed a partnership with three men from the south of the province. The four pooled 13,000 taels of capital to start their business. One of these men, a salaried partner, had worked for the San Yi at Shahukou, a pass in the Ming wall just north of Youyu. His job took him to Yarkand with goods caravans, and there he met Zhang Luan.

Zhang's new enterprise dealt in Soochow silk and Yarkand jade, as well as felts, hides, carpets, cotton cloth, and other items. At the time of his arrest in 1778, Zhang possessed fixed assets worth 4,583 taels in Soochow (a house evaluated at 4,000 taels and copper, tin, china, and draft animals worth 583 taels). He was owed 2,321 taels in debts in this southern city. Other current assets included 500 taels worth of tea bound for sale in the Suzhou branch of the San Yi, 500 taels worth of china en route to Gansu and Shaanxi, a shipment of silk and embroidery of unknown value likewise destined for the northwest, an investment in a consignment of goods from the Guihua San Yi Dian to Urumchi, and a Buddha head carved from "leadstone" already sold for 1,321 taels to a collector in Guangdong. Several begs in Yarkand, including the hakim beg Hudawī (E-dui), owed him a total of 10,126 taels for silks purchased on credit. Zhang held remittance slips for 11,790 taels, which he planned to redeem at the Shangwen Yinhao and other money-shops in the capital. His family holdings in Shanxi included a tiled house, a fifteen-room earthen building rented out to a dyer, a cloth shop, and a drygoods store as well as livestock and debts receivable. Zhang Luan had of course also invested heavily in jade.[27]

Most north bend merchants did not rub shoulders with imperial bondservants or wind up at the center of celebrated smuggling cases involving commodities monopolized by the Imperial Household Agency. Were not Zhang Luan exceptional, we would not know so much about him. Yet his story highlights general characteristics of the north bend traders and their businesses. Most striking is the extent of the San Yi *zihao* network: testimony in this case reveals that, besides the home office in Guihua, this firm had branches in Shahukou, Suzhou, Aksu, and probably Urumchi and routinely did business in Yarkand, where it may have had a base as well. The branches, while remaining affiliated to the home office and drawing on the firm for capital, could act with considerable autonomy—as Zhang did when he began speculating in jade with San Yi money. These firms sold on credit and relied on remittance services to finance business transactions across long distances. Indeed, their activities spanned the empire and linked the Jiangnan with Altishahr. Primary profits for richer merchants like Zhang Luan derived from exchange of Chinese luxuries for jade; more mundane manufactures (dry goods, hardware) and pastoral products served as the staple articles of trade.

Other individual north bend traders included the following:

- Li Dequan of Xin Prefecture, Shanxi, sold miscellaneous items in Aksu and around 1785 bought 34 pieces of scrap jade for 6,000 cash.

- Zhang Dakui of Wencheng County, Shanxi, ran a drygoods and hardware store in Aksu. He traded cloth and tea for 1,300 worth of low-quality jade stone in 1785.

- Li Shaokang, 51 years old, of Gan Prefecture, Shaanxi, opened and ran the Yuan Tai Quan name-brand store on North Avenue in Kashgar's new city sometime before 1830.

- Liu Shaojun, 66 years old, of Yongning Prefecture, Shanxi, ran the Tong Tai Xing name-brand store outside the Kashgar fort. During the Kokandi invasion of 1830 he moved into the walled new city, transporting some of his stock in four or five carts. He did not have time to save all his goods, however—an indication of the size of his business. Note also the location of his store, *outside* the new city.

- Mr. Xie, 60 years old, from Weinan County in Shaanxi, ran the Yu Qing Gong name-brand store outside Yili's north gate in the 1840s.
- Mr. Yuan, 77 years old, from Xi'an County, Shaanxi, sold silk, cotton cloth, and seafood from the Yong Shun Gong name-brand shop in Yili in the 1840s.
- Xi'an's Heng Sheng Shun silk and velvet shop had a branch in Urumchi as well as one outside the north gate of Yili, called the Heng Sheng Xing, managed by a man likewise surnamed Yuan.

Lin Zexu, during his banishment to Yili in the 1840s, wrote to his family in Xi'an to urge them to have an acquaintance bring them round to the house of the Heng Sheng Shun's manager in Xi'an to pay their respects. Lin hoped that having forged a personal connection in this way, they could then ask the company to deliver letters to him at the branch in Yili. (Lin found that letters coming from his family by official post often arrived torn or opened.)[28]

THE WEST ROAD TRADERS

Goods and merchants from south China mostly traveled to Xinjiang via the Yangzi River as far as Hankou, then northwest along the Han River past Xiangyang and into Shaanxi on the Dan River. From Xi'an they were conveyed northwest on the Jing River to Jingzhou, or, less commonly, via the Wei River into Gansu at Qinzhou (modern Tianshui). Jingzhou transshipped the bulk of southern goods, while Liangzhou served the same function for trade items arriving in Gansu from the capital and elsewhere in north China. Suzhou (today's Jiuquan) was the next bulking center, whence Xinjiang-bound traffic embarked for Hami.[29]

The Chinese merchants who traded in Xinjiang via the Gansu corridor were a diverse group, including Han and Tungan and, in addition to the majority who came from Gansu or Shaanxi, natives of several provinces of China proper. For the most part, west road traders' operations were smaller in scale than those of their north bend counterparts, often amounting to little more than long-distance peddling. Discussing merchants from Gansu and Shaanxi who did business in Altishahr, Tie-bao reported in 1811 that they were "sellers of snacks and foods, tiny, un-united hardware [dealers]. There are no large-scale merchants."[30] The individual cases about whom we know a few details tend to confirm Tie-bao's assessment.

- Lei Ying, of Heyang County in Shaanxi, was a partner around 1778 in the Zheng Heng store (pu) in Hami, which sold sundry goods. Sun Quande worked in a similar shop, also in Hami. Both men dealt in jade on the side and loaned money to local Tungans, including an ākhūnd surnamed Ma.

- Wei Zhongxiao, from Jin County in Gansu, ran a store selling miscellaneous items, including tea, in Kashgar around 1784.
- Wang Ming, of Ling Prefecture in Gansu, was dealing in cloth and tea from his shop in Aksu when he was caught smuggling jade in the bottom of his cart in 1784.
- Around 1785, many Gansu natives were illicitly mining gold in the Khotan area.
- Song Liangdi, of Zhangye County, Gansu, grew vegetables in Aksu until he was caught in 1785 in possession of 50 catties of scrap jadestone.
- Hu Kui, from He Prefecture, Gansu, worked as a laborer in Kucha around 1785.
- Cao Zhi, originally of Wuwei County, Gansu, was a butcher in Yarkand. He was arrested in Kucha in 1785 with nine ounces of jade sewn into his trousers.
- Zhang Bao came to Kashgar in 1816 at the age of 34 and opened a shop or inn outside the citadel.
- Xing Sheng, 33 years old, of Meng County, Henan, went to Kashgar in 1826 as a trader. Four years later he joined other Chinese merchants in the militia to defend the city against the Kokandi invasion.
- Liang Dashou, 26 years old in 1830, was a native of Xi'an who grew up in Yili and operated a small shop at the Jin Ding Temple. He loaned money to the Yili hakim beg, Isḥāq, and later followed him to Kashgar to seek repayment.
- Yan Lianggui, 34 years old, a native of Ning Prefecture in eastern Gansu, came to Kashgar in 1827, where he ran a small business away from the walled city. He sheltered in the garrison compound when he heard rumors of the Kokandi attack and was put in charge of a troop of 50 merchant militiamen.[31]

As is clear from the last few examples, Chinese merchants in Kashgar were swept up by military events during the Khoja and Kokandi invasions of the 1820s. One group captured by Jahāngīr included an exiled Catholic from Shanxi (Zhu Tianzhao) and six Tungan merchants (Li Shengzhao, Tian Guan, Ma Tianxi, Wu Erqi, Liu Qifeng, Nian Dengxi). They were taken prisoner and their queues cut off when the Kashgar citadel fell in September of 1826. Because they refused to fight with Jahāngīr's forces, they were enslaved: Nian was first given to a beg and after a failed escape was sold to Prince Batur Khan of Bukhara. Liu Qifeng and Wu Erqi had been given to Omar Khan of Bukhara, but were taken as booty in battle by Batur, who tried to give them away as dowry for a Muslim woman. When Liu and Wu refused, they were cursed, beaten, and tortured. Zhu, Tian, Li, and Ma were indentured to Andijani Muslims; Li was resold to a man named Sandeman in Tashkent but somehow managed to plan an escape with Zhu, Tian, and Ma. They had heard that the Kokandi border guards killed on sight any Chinese trying to recross the Pamirs to return to Altishahr, and the route via Badakhshan seemed no more promising, with little water and food available and widespread illness in the region. So the four fled westward, where "outer barbarians would not interrogate them closely." Dressed in robes and turbans they passed inattentive border guards into Bukharan territory. Begging their way through villages up the Amu Darya, they had reached "Wuluganqi" when they met up again with Nian Dengxi, in flight from Bukhara. The five learned from Central Asian merchants of a route from Russia to China and joined a caravan traveling farther northwest to get to Russia. In a place called "Mayijangaer," Liu Qifeng and Wu Erqi joined the party, and all seven pulled camels, hauled loads, and begged from the Central Asians until they arrived in Orenburg, probably sometime in 1831. There they appealed to the Russian border guards for travel papers.

Seeing that these men were Chinese, the guards detained them while seeking instructions from superiors. The seven merchants were then sent under escort to Irkutsk, where they were again delayed until winter, when the freezing of Lake Baikal opened the route to Kiakhta. Because by this time the rags they wore "hardly covered their bodies," the Russian authorities in Irkutsk provided them with clothing and small sums of money. At some point while in Russian care, the men were questioned about conditions in Xinjiang, and Ma Tianxi provided an account of the post-station trade route, which eventually found its way into a British publication (see Chapter 4). Finally, the Russians escorted the seven to Kiakhta for repatriation in 1832. Sensibly, in time for the inquest in Kulun (Urga, now Ulan Bataar), the men had already made a start on growing back their queues and could boast three to four inches of hair; Liu Qifeng had begun secretly while still in Bukhara—surely at some risk—and his hair was now a foot long.[32]

Tungan Merchants

Liu and the other Tungan merchants had their hair forcibly cut after being taken prisoner. Later, they were able to disguise their Chinese identity by adoption of the turban and other forms of Central Asian Muslim dress. As they neared home, however, once again they took their cues from the Qing.

This incident serves as an apt reminder of the Tungans' ambiguous status in Xinjiang. As reflected in the official Qing terms for them, *Hanhui* or *neidi Huimin*, they were, on the one hand, Chinese-speaking and considered Gansu and Shaanxi to be their homes; on the other hand, as Muslims, they shared the Islamic faith—if not the precise manner of practicing it—with the East Turkestanis. Educated, devout Tungans could read Arabic and perhaps some Persian as well, which gave them a lingua franca with similarly cultured natives of Altishahr. As might be expected, given that they shared cultural traits with both Han and East Turkestani, Tungan merchants in Xinjiang often mediated commercially between these two groups.

Many Gansu and Shaanxi Tungans, facing repression and relegation to marginal lands after periodic rebellions,[33] migrated to Qinghai, Tibet, and Xinjiang where they engaged in long-distance trade, specialized as transport workers, or set up small businesses as restaurateurs, butchers, or hide and wool dealers. In the northwest provinces of China proper, they also traded tea on government license, splitting the business with Shaanxi and Shanxi merchant groups.[34]

Like Han west road traders, Tungan merchants moved to Xinjiang soon after the Qing conquest and took their small-scale operations throughout Zungharia and Altishahr. One area where they held a particularly prominent position was in Urumchi, where the names of the Tungan mosques scattered throughout the old part of the city today record the origins of these Muslim Chinese traders: Lanzhou Si, Suzhou Si, Shaanxi Da Si, Hezhou Si, Ninggu Si (Ningxia and Guyuan), Balikun Si (Barkol), Sala Si (Salars), Qinghai Da Si, Dongfang Si (Suiyuan, Hohhot area). Although most of the presently existing mosques were established after the 1864 rebellions and have been rebuilt or relocated since their foundation, they follow the pattern of the older Shaanxi Da Si and Lanzhou Si. In the Lanzhou mosque, for example, Tungan merchants could stay temporarily in the large courtyard in simple accommodations or even tents. Outside was a stable and a lot to park carts. Although the mosque excluded no one, merchants from Lanzhou would naturally assemble in the Lanzhou Si for prayers, and the assembled worshipers included many business contacts. There was no accommodation within the compound of the Shaanxi Da Si, but rooms and storage were available in a hostel nearby. This mosque was first built before the Tungan rebellions with contributions from Tungan merchants, originally of Shaanxi, who resided in Urumchi.[35]

The Tungan mosques of Urumchi, then, in addition to their religious function, served much the same purpose as did native-place association halls (*huiguan*) for Han merchants: they provided an itinerant merchant with lodging, storage, and the company of others from his home town with whom he could trade, borrow funds, and exchange information.

The available data on individual Tungan merchants in Xinjiang suffer from the same systematic flaw as do those for Han, namely, that Qing officials tended to note only those Tungan merchants accused of crimes or involved in military events. The most egregious case is that of Zhao Junrui, Gao Pu's and Zhang Luan's coconspirator in the jade scandal. Zhao was a Tungan from Weinan, Shaanxi, who went west to seek his fortune in 1759 or 1760 and did not return to Weinan again until 1778 (when he was apprehended while on his way home with illegal jade). After a few years selling a variety of things in Yarkand, he had become one of the city's most eminent Chinese merchants and served there as a *xiangyue* headman. He socialized with Yarkand's beg and Manchu officials and (a gesture ironic in hindsight) had presented Gao Pu with the gift of a carved jade item upon the latter's assumption of the post of superintendent. In Aksu and Yarkand, Zhao owned 4 inns, a restaurant, a house, 15 asses and horses, and 160 camels. In Shaanxi he had a large house, a somewhat smaller store, 78 *mu* of land, livestock, clothing, jewelry, and furnishings. In 1778 Zhao went to Gao Pu's yamen for a road pass home to see his father in Weinan, and the superintendent entrusted him with 3,000 catties of jade to smuggle into China proper. Thereafter, the Qing authorities confiscated in Shaanxi 4 cartloads of hides and clothes and 71 cases of silks and embroidery from Soochow bound for sale in Xi'an.[36]

Although Zhao's story is not representative of the careers of most Tungan merchants in Xinjiang (like many rich Han traders he worked the lucrative Soochow-Altishahr route trading silks and jades), it is useful to note the extent to which he had invested in livestock, restaurants, and inns—enterprises in which less wealthy Tungan merchants were commonly engaged. Some examples of other Tungan merchants follow.

- Zhao Yongfu came to Turfan in the fifth lunar month of 1822 and worked as a hired laborer. In the eighth month of the following year he proceeded to Yarkand and opened a food stall. In 1826 he went to Kashgar to collect debts. He helped defend the city when Jahāngīr attacked in the sixth month but was captured; his queue was cut off, he saw Jahāngīr himself and then worked as a cook until the Qing army arrived. Zhao then turned himself in to the Manchus and again started work as a laborer.

- Ma Jianlin exited the Jiayu Guan in 1823 to make his living in Turfan. In 1827 he followed the Qing army to Yarkand, where he married an East Turkestani woman named A-bi-dai.

- Ma Delong drove a cart to Yarkand in 1824 and there sought to make a living. He married A-bi-bai but soon after went to Urumchi in search of sustenance. In 1827, working as a camel teamster, he accompanied the Qing army back to Yarkand.
- Chang Fengqing, in his early thirties in 1828, had done business in Yili until 1826, when he joined the Qing militia coming south to recapture Kashgar from Jahāngīr.

Several observations may be drawn from these examples. First, the poverty of these merchants is striking, compared with the Han merchants discussed above. Second, each of these Tungan merchants was involved in one way or another with the Qing defense and counterattack against Jahāngīr. We should not make too much of this, given that the sample is not representative of Tungan merchants as a whole. Nonetheless, it is noteworthy that the advance of the Qing army served as the mechanism that drew these merchants deeper into Altishahr. Third, being Muslim did not prevent Tungans from fighting alongside the Qing against Kokandis and followers of the Khojas. (In fact, a leader of the Kashgar merchant militia, Zhang Mingtang, who was killed in the 1826 invasion along with 886 other merchants, was a Tungan.) On the other hand, being Chinese did not prevent them from marrying East Turkestani women.[37]

The Tungans' double identity made some Qing officials in Altishahr nervous. Behind this anxiety lay the history of Tungan relations with the Qing dynasty. There had been a Tungan rebellion in northwest China from 1645 to 1649, soon after the Qing assumption of power in Beijing. The rebellion, with a Ming restorationist thrust, was also linked to the Muslim governor of Hami. By the time of the Qing conquest of Xinjiang, relations between Han and Tungan in Gansu and Shaanxi were generally deteriorating, and Qing officials viewed Tungans as a potentially disruptive influence in this area.

In 1761, a Tungan named Muḥammad Amin Ma Mingxin returned to China after years of study in Bukhara and Yemen. He built a mosque, gathered initiates, and began to teach a new branch of the Naqshbandiyya to Tungans in Gansu and Qinghai. His teachings, influenced by the reform movements then prevalent in Islamic centers of the Middle East, opposed the emphasis placed on saints and their tombs in Central Asian and northwest Chinese mystical sufism. More important than this, however, Ma allowed the use of the *jahr*, or vocal style, in the remembrance (*dhikr*),* hence his "path" came

---

* "Literally, 'remembrance,' 'recollection,' 'mention.'" In Sufi mystic ritual, "The word has acquired a technical sense of 'litany' in which the name of God, or formulae like 'God

to be known as the "Jahriyya." These teachings challenged those of the established Naqshbandī faction in the northwest, known as Āfāqiyya after the Makhdūmzāda Khoja Āfāq, who had preached and established a chain of initiates in Gansu and Qinghai in the 1670s. Struggles for power by these two branches of the Naqshbandiyya path (often inaccurately labeled "New Sect" and "Old Sect") led to violence, and the Qing arrested Ma Mingxin in 1781 after a rival accused him of "heterodoxy." In response to a subsequent uprising by his Jahriyya followers, the Qing put Ma Mingxin to death. More unrest followed. Through much of this, the "Old Teaching" Āfāqiyya sided with the Qing. In 1784 a major rebellion of "New Teaching" believers under Tian Wu took the Qing three months to repress, and the dynasty enacted a series of measures to proscribe the Jahriyya.[38]

The Āfāqiyya-Jahriyya disputes in Gansu, Qinghai, and Shaanxi corresponded to the migration of Tungans from these provinces to Xinjiang. After the Tian Wu uprising in particular, Qing officials became concerned that rebel followers were fleeing to Altishahr. As a result, itinerant Tungan merchants in Xinjiang were subjected to unusual scrutiny and harassment by Qing officials in the New Dominion.

In 1784, following the Tian Wu rebellion, Qing guards in Kucha searching for smuggled jade in the cart of a beg en route to an imperial audience discovered something still more worrisome: letters and texts in Arabic script. The beg was not implicated, but the authorities arrested the cart driver, a Tungan named Han De, originally from Xining. Han De had first exited the Jiayu Pass with his father and had been driving carts for a living for more than a decade. The Arabic books belonged to another Tungan, Ma Guoying, who worked in a salt and tea shop in Aksu. Guoying had asked Han De to deliver them to a relative, Ma Qijiao (a.k.a. Idil), an itinerant trader based in Kucha. Other Tungan merchants, including Qijiao's correspondent, "Ismaʿīl," were likewise caught up in the Qing investigation.

The Tungans involved in this case were all sent to Lanzhou for questioning, and the materials were presented to the Tungan *xiangyue* in that city to be screened for heterodoxy. The *xiangyue* pronounced them wholesome "Old Teaching" texts—simple Qurʿāns. Although found innocent, Han De and the others were nonetheless to be banished to insalubrious southern China, a sentence only later commuted to resettlement under probation in Urumchi. The emperor reprimanded Xinjiang officials for exceeding their brief in this

---

is Most Great' (*Allāhu Akbar*), are repeated over and over again in either a high or a low voice, often linked to bodily movement or breathing. The *dhikr* is often one of the most important activities of the sūfi." Netton, *A Popular Dictionary of Islam*, pp. 70–71.

case by searching the belongings of a beg. Gaozong did not intend seizure of scriptural texts and investigations of begs to be part of the imperial audience experience. "And except disciples [of the New Teaching] and those Muslims surnamed 'Ma' [whom the emperor presumed to be relatives of Ma Mingxin], do not go searching Muslims wildly like this again."[39]

Such imperial concern for the rights of good Muslims is admirable, perhaps, but Gaozong thus unwittingly exposed a sizeable proportion of the Tungans in Xinjiang ("Ma" is the most common Tungan surname) to arbitrary search and seizure. Over the next month the Qing dragnet hauled in Ma Tingxiang, Ma Wenlu, Ma Runeng, and Ma Cang in Kashgar, all "merchant Tungans" (*maoyi Huimin*) from Gansu; their names were not on the wanted list of the Tian Wu rebels from Jingyuan (Lanzhou Prefecture, Gansu), and Guo-dong memorialized for instructions on what to do with them. He received an admonishment from the emperor: "The good Muslims of Jingyuan trade everywhere. Where did you get the idea to arrest and investigate them all?" His edict ordered that the four Mas be released to remain in Kashgar or return home, as they wished.[40]

Besides revealing the anxiety of Xinjiang officials—for whom mixed imperial signals could have made life no easier—these cases illustrate the archetypical employments of the Tungan merchants in Xinjiang: cart driver, itinerant merchant, tea merchant. Moreover, the adoption of Islamic names by Ma Qijiao and his correspondent, and the three protagonists' concern with the conveyance of Qurʿāns suggest that there was a religious as well as commercial component to their relationship; they may have shared membership in a *menhuan* (a religious, social, political, and commercial organization formed by Tungan Sufi orders).

The Qing classification of Tungans as a subcategory of Han (*Hanhui*) led to a curious problem when Tungans assimilated with the native East Turkestani population. The first such instance we know of involved not a merchant but a Green Standard soldier, Hai Tanglu, rotated to Kashgar duty around 1824. In that year he began frequenting the Kashgar market to discuss scripture with Andijani Muslims. He then disguised himself as an Andijani merchant, got an Andijani saddle and horse and tried to escape west past the *karun* aided by an East Turkestani named Yūnus. His actions were considered a "great breach of the law" by field officials, and, while the court agreed, the Grand Council had to request the Board of Punishments and the Court of Colonial Affairs to deliberate and advise the court on exactly what law Hai had broken.[41]

Later, Nayanceng was greatly exercised by the instances of "desinification" he discovered among Tungans in Kashgar, Yangi Hisar, and Yarkand while directing postpacification reforms after the Jihāngīr invasion. The case focused

on Ma Delong and Ma Jianlin (described above), who married East Turkestani women, and two other Tungan merchants, Ma Fu and Zhao Yongfu,
who in addition to marrying locally were apprehended without their queues.
They claimed to have been captured in 1826 by Jihāngīr's followers and
forced into servitude until the arrival of the Qing army, but Nayanceng
found their behavior suspicious and recommended that they be "exiled and
flogged as traitors (*Hanjian*)."[42] And so they were, although a distinction
was drawn between those who "cut their queues and joined the foreigners"
(Ma Fu and Zhao Yongfu) and those whose only crime was to marry East
Turkestani women; for this, Ma Delong and Ma Jianlin received lighter sentences. Nayanceng urged that in the future Tungan movements in Xinjiang
be closely monitored through the pass system and that Tungan–East Turkestani intermarriage be explicitly prohibited. The Board of Punishments drew
up statutes from these precedents, which were later included in the *Collection
of the Substatutes of Muslim Xinjiang* (*Huijiang zeli*).[43]

Nayanceng attributed the East Turkestani support Jahāngīr received in
Altishahr in part to Tungan commercial and marital relations with East Turkestanis, which supposedly stirred up dissent against the Qing.[44] His analysis
was oversimplified inasmuch as it neglected the religiopolitical charisma enjoyed by the Makhdūmzāda Khoja clan among the Āfāqiyya in Altishahr,
but by his focus on Tungans Nayanceng suggests that it was indeed these
merchants who dealt most directly with the East Turkestanis. Bi-chang, in an
analysis of the Kokandi invasion staged two years later, indirectly makes a
similar point while more or less praising Tungans, not condemning them.

> Tungans (*Hanhui*) among the common people and in the army still
> keep the fast and chant the scripture. They are by no means the same
> as the East Turkestanis (*chantou*), but rather originate in China proper,
> where their parents, wives, and children remain. They find the food of the
> Western Dominion convenient and study and comprehend the Muslim
> language. . . . Moreover, the East Turkestanis suffer exploitation at the
> hands of the Tungans and detest them. In 1830, the Tungans defended the
> city of Yarkand and because they made fearless spies, the Qing army con-
> stantly employed them, benefiting much from their strength. Not a few
> Tungans were commended and received feathers and buttons of rank.[45]

Tungans seem to have made up a large percentage of the Chinese merchants in Altishahr and to have enjoyed the most contact with the native East
Turkestanis. This suggests a rough division of labor between the larger Han
firms, which arranged shipments of consignments of goods for sale in larger
stores in Xinjiang, and Tungan merchants, generally with less capital, who

occupied a niche depending on direct marketing among East Turkestani urban and village populations—a position that may have earned some the enmity of their customers.[46]

Further evidence of diversified commercial roles for Han, Tungan, and East Turkestani merchants in Xinjiang emerges from study of Xinjiang's main articles of trade.

Xinjiang's Tea and Rhubarb Trade

It's a long way from the Fujian sea.
What Xinjiangese knows *xiaolongtuan* tea?
They just always say that official tea's "heat"
Cuts the bone-chilling cold of mountain spring water.

(It's not easy to get good tea. Locals in Urumchi drink only the official brick tea [fucha]. They claim that the water in this place contains a cooling humor that harms the stomach, but that the warm character of brick tea can counteract this tendency.)[47]

There were various types of tea available in Xinjiang, just as there were various types of tea drinker. *Fucha*, or "supplementary tea" best suited the tastes, not only of longtime residents of Urumchi, but also those of the Mongol and Manchu peoples stationed in Xinjiang. These bannermen also bought "big tea" (*dacha*) and "catty tea" (*jincha*), which were somewhat cheaper brick teas. The Central Asians, on the other hand, especially the Kokandis who bought much tea in Xinjiang, preferred "mixed tea" (*zacha*), which came in large bundles, and "fine tea" (*xicha*)—leaf teas such as bohea (*wuyi*), jasmine (*xiangpian*), *baihao*, and *zhulan*.

Of these teas, only "supplementary tea" was regularly shipped into Xinjiang via the Gansu corridor. The term arose from the time when the Qing traded tea for horses in the Gansu and Qinghai border regions of China proper (see Chapter 3). Merchants who contracted to ship tea under license from south China to the Tea and Horse Offices in Gansu and Qinghai were allowed to sell an additional amount of tea themselves—hence the name "supplementary." By the early Qianlong period, although the Tea and Horse Offices in Xining, Taomin, Hezhou, Zhuanglang, and Ganzhou were no longer in the business of bartering tea for horses, merchants were still required to purchase licenses. The licensed merchants shipped tea as far as the northwest, but then for the most part resold it in Liangzhou and other Gansu cities to private west road traders, often Tungans, who carried it to Xinjiang under a system known as "substitute sale of accumulated licenses" (*daixiao zhiyin*).[48] The west road traders carried no licenses and were not officially contracted, but the tea remained recognizable as government tea—perhaps the packages bore special markings. About 600,000 catties of *fucha* were imported annually to Xinjiang in this fashion; the tea continued to be known there as *fucha* throughout the eighteenth and nineteenth centuries, although it had long since ceased to be supplementary to anything.[49]

The other types of teas reached Xinjiang primarily via the Mongolian steppe route in the caravans of north bend traders, who in theory paid a tax on it when exiting the passes at Guihua or Zhangjiakou. Tea was of course a specialty of Shanxi firms, whose tea trade at Kiakhta with the Russians was a primary source of income, and it was an obvious extension of this business to ship to Xinjiang as well. But just as *fucha* was transferred from rich merchants in official service to private traders in Gansu before continuing on to Xinjiang via the Gansu corridor, "mixed tea" and other brick and leaf teas seem to have changed hands on Xinjiang's borders before distribution in Xinjiang. North bend traders shipped it to Gucheng, where they traded it for grain and flour (produced in Zungharia), which they then carried north to sell to Mongol nomads and bannermen in Khobdo and Uliasutai for silver and pastoral products. From Gucheng, other merchants distributed these teas throughout Xinjiang. According to an 1828 estimate, between 100,000 and 300,000 catties of mixed and fine teas were exported from Yili and Tarbagatai in a year, which comprised "70 percent" of the tea brought north by Chinese merchants. Thus, at a minimum, north bend traders carried 150,000–450,000 catties of tea into Xinjiang annually in the early nineteenth century.[50]

PRIVATIZATION OF XINJIANG'S TEA TRADE

Chapter 3 discussed the official shipments of tea from the Tea and Horse Offices in Gansu and Qinghai to the military garrisons of Xinjiang cities in the first decade after the conquest. By the late 1770s, such official tea sales, paid for by deductions from military *yancai* stipends, had for the most part been replaced by private trading in tea. (The exceptions were Yili and Tarbagatai, which continued to procure for official sale approximately 100,000–115,000 catties of tea per year until the 1850s.) The privatization of tea sales to the Xinjiang garrisons happened first in Urumchi, where the superintendent requested the cessation of official tea shipments in 1768 on the grounds that the official price was higher than that charged by merchants. Surrounding counties stopped putting in requisitions for tea during the following few years.[51]

With a variety of privately traded teas available in Xinjiang, there was less demand for *fucha* and consequently fewer licenses were purchased to ship tea to the Gansu and Qinghai Tea and Horse Offices. The offices no longer needed tea, but the license fees were a source of revenue that one governor-general, at least, hated to see decline. Nayanceng, who served in Shaanxi-Gansu from 1822 to 1825, memorialized sometime before the summer of 1823 that private sales of tea in Xinjiang should be forbidden in order to improve the sales of Gansu tea licenses. The Board of Works approved this suggestion, but the negative results of the new policy soon became clear in Zungharia. Yili General Qing-xiang reported that tea shortages occasioned by the new policy were causing severe hardship to Han and Muslim alike in the territory under his command. Moreover, the interdiction of private tea sales in Xinjiang had redounded upon the Qing garrisons and the livelihood of the Mongols in Uliasutai and Khobdo, who had depended on the north bend traders' triangle trade with Gucheng for grain and flour. On hearing of these troubles, the court authorized the shipment of 7,000 cases of *zacha* to Gucheng annually, but still did not permit free sale of this mixed tea in Xinjiang; rather, it ordered Qing-xiang to study the possibility of enacting in Xinjiang a state tea monopoly like that of China proper, employing rich local merchants to distribute tea on government contract. While the general looked into this, the 7,000 cases sat in Gucheng. Qing-xiang reported back the following year (1824) that Xinjiang lacked merchants rich enough to take on the risks of managing a government monopoly and that Gucheng's garrison population of 2,000 military personnel plus "not many" civilians could not consume so much tea. Ultimately, the court reopened Xinjiang to private trade in mixed and other varieties of tea through Gucheng; *fucha*, however, as before could be shipped in only from Gansu. In addition, a customs station was established in Gucheng to tax incoming tea. The revenues thus realized were sent to Gansu to make up for lost tea license fees.[52]

In the 60 years following the conquest of Xinjiang, the activities of north bend traders had linked the economy of northwest Mongolia to the private tea trade in Xinjiang (and ultimately Kokandi demand); these merchants had, moreover, proven to be more efficient suppliers of the garrison and civilian population in Zungharia than Qing quartermasters. As for the Gansu corridor, the other main trade route into Xinjiang, state control over tea sales did not reach beyond the Jiayu Guan. West road traders, operating on low margins, handled the retail distribution of tea initially produced and shipped to the northwest by rich official merchants (*guanshang*) in China proper, who were unwilling to carry it further. Though the dynasty had not entirely deregulated the tea business in Xinjiang, it did permit its wholesale privatization. Abandoning monopoly as a revenue device, by the 1820s the Qing taxed tea sales in the New Dominion only at the customs house in Gucheng and via the "license" fees—now paid in specie—to the moribund Tea and Horse

Offices. Although the embargo of Kokand in 1828 led to the implementation of more stringent inspection procedures and Nayanceng's flirtation with more extensive tea taxes (see Chapter 3), by 1831 the tea trade in Altishahr and Zungharia returned to essentially the same pattern as earlier in the decade.

RHUBARB

The 1828–31 embargo cut off Kokand's supply of rhubarb as well as of tea. As the utility of this product, and hence the reasons behind Kokand's demand for it, are not immediately obvious to readers today, a word about the purgative root is in order.

Although best known in the twentieth century for its stalks, which, baked in pies or stewed with sugar and cream make a tart dessert, it was the medicinal value of the rhubarb root, particularly that of several strains grown in western China, that commanded the world's attention. Clifford Foust has presented evidence that Chinese "great yellow" (*dahuang*) began to reach Europe in quantity via the Middle East as early as the eighth or ninth century, where it was known from the classical pharmacopeia for its cathartic properties. Later, rhubarb became something of a panacea to Europeans. According to one source from the 1720s, rhubarb "possesses the double virtue of a carthitic and astringent. . . . It readily evacuates particularly the bilious humors, and strengthens the stomach walls. It is given with great success in all obstructions of the liver, in the jaundice, in diarrhoeas, and in the fluor albus and sometimes given as a purgative, sometimes as only an alterant; and which way ever it is taken it is an excellent medicine, agreeing with almost all ages and constitutions."[53]

In the sixteenth century, Central Asian merchants were the most active shippers of rhubarb. It became a major article of the Sino-Russian caravan trade even before the conclusion of the Treaty of Nerchinsk (1689) opened China's commercial relations with Russia. The Romanov empire thereafter managed Russian imports and exports of rhubarb under one form of monopoly or another until 1782, maintaining quality control and dominating sales of the drug in the Western European market until the mid–eighteenth century. Even so, significant amounts of rhubarb continued to move westward through Xinjiang, India, and Central Asia. The root was one of the major items desired by the Zunghars in their trade with the Qing at Suzhou. After the Qing conquest of Zungharia and East Turkestan, Qing officials in Xinjiang were very aware of the great demand for rhubarb to their west and south. Qi-shi-yi, for example, wrote rather fantastically of Hindustan, "Rhubarb is especially valued, and people will gladly exchange for it more than ten times its weight in gold. Thus to cure all ailments and sores in this place would require no less than a hundred [ounces of gold]. When honored guests come to a feast they are given rhubarb instead of tea. If in their youth people do not ingest this drug they will surely die, so no matter how poor, every little Muslim must have half an ounce hanging in a bag at his chest to lick and sniff at."[54]

All kinds of traders in Xinjiang dealt in rhubarb, so curtailment of the rhubarb trade affected Han, Tungan, East Turkestani, and foreign merchant alike. When for reasons of foreign policy or border defense the Qing embargoed trade with Russia or Kokand, mere possession of the root could get a merchant into trouble. The 1727 Treaty of Kiakhta demarcated the Mongolian-Siberian border and established normal trading relations between the Qing and Russia. After 1737, the bulk of that barter trade took place in Kiakhta (Maimaicheng) on this border. In 1764–68, 1779–80, and 1785–92, however, owing to border disputes, the Qing shut down the Kiakhta trade, and the court ordered officials in maritime and northern border regions to increase vigilance lest goods destined for Russia be exported by third parties. Rhubarb, of course, like tea, was a prime Russian import. Therefore, during the longest Kiakhta embargo (1785–92), memorials and edicts concerning rhubarb smugglers in Xinjiang sped back and forth across the post route. In Aksu, the emperor learned, Ma Chengxiao and four others sold rhubarb to an Andijani named La-ha-mo-te. Gaozong pointed out that, although Kiakhta was closed to Russian traders, Yili, Kashgar, and other Xinjiang cities could easily become conduits for the root through the offices of Kirghiz and Andijani merchants—indeed, the La-ha-mo-te case provided concrete evidence of such smuggling. "This is all due to traitorous merchants conspiring to profit by buying from inside the Pass and selling to Andijani Muslims, who turn around and sell to the Russians," rescripted the emperor. "If I enact a strict embargo but the Russians can still get rhubarb, what's the difference [between this] and not embargoing at all?"[55] Nor were East Turkestanis exempt from scrutiny. After a group of East Turkestani merchants from Hami were caught shipping 5,000 *jin* of rhubarb from Suzhou to Urumchi in 1789, the court promulgated an edict warning the Muslims of each city in Xinjiang that rhubarb traffickers would henceforth be sent to Gansu for punishment.[56]

The embargo against Kokand (1828–31) was of course another important period of government restriction of the rhubarb trade in Xinjiang. Although rhubarb was never traded in such volume as tea, and was therefore less of a concern, most of the actions taken by Nayanceng and others to control the circulation of tea in Xinjiang during this period applied to rhubarb as well, including confiscation of stockpiles, limitation of amounts East Turkestanis could purchase, issuance of licenses, and maintenance of official vigilance in key gateway cities to prevent smuggling of the drug to Zungharia, whence it might be exported by nomads.

Jade

The Chinese word *yu*, translated as "jade," is a very general term, referring to any of a variety of stones suitable for carving. In common speech, it is often used in opposition to *shitou* ("rock")—a piece of stone is either a *shitou* (worthless) or *yu* (valuable). "Jade" in English, although somewhat more specific, is likewise confusing in that it refers to two petrologically distinct materials: nephrite, a silicate of calcium and magnesium with varying amounts of iron in a tightly interwoven, needlelike crystalline structure, and jadeite, a silicate of sodium and aluminum. The latter stone is most valuable when bright green, thus resembling its Chinese namesake, the Southeast Asian kingfisher (*feicui*). Jadeite was not widely known in China until the eighteenth century, when it began to be imported from Burma.[57]

Nephrite (hereafter "jade") carries a much longer pedigree, having been highly regarded in China proper since at least neolithic times. Its hardness and luster made jade a material par excellence for worked funerary objects, scepters, tablets, talismans, chimes, animal figures, wine vessels, sash pendants, and a host of other ritual, ornamental, and functional objects. Neolithic lapidaries probably got nephrite from sources near Lake Tai and in the northeast (from Liaoning to Shandong), but the finest source of jade available to China since antiquity derived from the Kunlun Mountains south of the Tarim Basin. Marco Polo was referring to this material when he noted the plentiful presence in the rivers not far from Khotan and Yarkand of "stones called jasper and chalcedony."[58]

TRIBUTE JADE AND THE UŠŠAQTAL MONOLITHS

After conquering East Turkestan, the Qing took control of the region's jade production, extracting mountain and river jade with corvée labor drawn from the East Turkestani population. The richest deposits of jade lay in Miertai Mountain, a little over 100 kilometers from Yarkand. There East Turkestanis ascended the slopes on yaks loaded with excavating tools to cut enormous boulders from the mountainsides with hammer and chisel (see Figure 6). The best riparian jade came from two rivers that emerge from the Kunlun range south of Khotan and skirt the city on either side before converging north of the city to flow into the Taklamakan as the Khotan River. In the beds of

Figure 6. Jade boulder carved with a scene of jade quarrying, Qianlong period. Note the conical fur hats and boots of the miners, which reveal them to be East Turkestanis or perhaps Kirghiz. Photograph courtesy of the Palace Museum, Beijing.

the Yurongqash (White Jade) River and Qaraqash (Black Jade) River, could be found polished pieces of jade "white as snow, blue-green as the kingfisher, yellow as wax, red as cinnabar, black as ink." The nuggets, ranging from "the size of a fist or chestnut" to "the size of plate or a dipper" and weighing up to 200 kilograms,

> are gathered in this way: one official supervises from the far bank, while a battalion official watches from the near side of the river. A gang of twenty or thirty experienced Muslims are sent to span the river shoulder to shoulder and walk over the stones barefoot. The Muslim knows when he treads on jade. He bows down and lifts it onto the bank. On the shore a guard bangs a gong, and at each crash of the gong the official makes a red mark [in a register]. When the Muslims emerge from the water, the stones are collected in accordance with the [number of] red dots.[59]

TABLE 13
Xinjiang Jade Tribute in the Qianlong and Jiaqing Periods

	Number of Pieces	Weight (catties)
1760	120	—
1771	12	4,044
1779	18,143	—
1806	2,132	3,446
1809	1,956	4,033
1811	2,028	4,775
1813	1,240	2,058

SOURCE: Documents from the Number One Historical Archives, Beijing, cited in Yang Boda, "Qingdai gongting yuqi," pp. 52, 55.

The court initially required that all jade mined and gathered in the Yarkand region each year be shipped to Beijing. Later, an annual tribute quota of 4,000 catties (2,000 kilos) was established, although actual amounts varied somewhat depending on the size of the pieces of rough jade carted to the capital in a given year. Besides these annual shipments (which took five to six months to reach Beijing), the court also dispatched officials to Yarkand to arrange extraordinary consignments every few years, including, for example, material to cut four sets of jade chimes for the Ningshou Gong in 1775. These special orders were generally larger than the tribute quota, one in 1776 weighing 20,000 catties (10,000 kilos). In 1812, because stocks of jade in the Imperial Household Workshop (Zaoban Chu, located within the imperial city) were sufficient, the court lowered Khotan's jade quota to 2,000 catties annually. Later, in a typical display of frugality, the Daoguang emperor eliminated this tribute requirement altogether during the first year of his reign (1821). Although at first Xuanzong had intended only a temporary cessation, on the grounds that palace storerooms were full, the Altishahr jade tribute was never restored.[60] Available jade tribute figures are given in Table 13.

The jade excavated and shipped eastward during the first half century of Qing rule in Xinjiang was more than enough for one empire, however. Perhaps nothing better sums up the character of the Qing at its height under Qianlong, with its remarkable military, logistical, administrative, and artistic skills and grandiose vision, than the court's ability—and desire—to turn Khotanese mountain jade into Beijing's jade mountains, boulder by massive boulder. Several of these monumental jade sculptures were produced, four of them from single pieces of rough jadestone weighing 1,500, 2,000, 2,500, and 4,500 kilograms respectively. The 4,500-kilo boulder arrived in Beijing in 1780; the Imperial Household Workshop drew up a design, modeled after a Song painting on the subject of Great Yu quelling the waters, and the following year shipped the raw jadestone, a four-sided plan, and a wax mock-up to Yangzhou for sculpting[61] under the auspices of the Lianghuai Salt Administration, which paid 7,280 taels for the work. Fearing that the wax model would deteriorate over time, the Yangzhou craftsmen executed a second model in wood before starting in on the jade itself. Completion of the work took six years (over 86,000 work days) and spanned the tenures of two salt commissioners. The finished "Great Yu" jade mountain (later known as "King of the Jades") stood 2.25 meters high and was almost a meter in diameter. The salt administration shipped it over inland waterways back to the capital in 1787, and the following year Gaozong had it inscribed with a poem of his own composition and the pattern of his imperial seal. The piece remains in the collection of the Beijing Palace Museum.[62]

The Qianlong era's predilection for monumental nephrite sculpture left Xinjiang officials a troublesome legacy that endured half a century after Gaozong's death. During the long-lived emperor's final months, Yarkand officials began transporting two enormous pieces of jade along the post road to the east. When these pieces were first excavated, Yarkand superintendent Ji-feng-e had suggested cutting the rocks up, as they were rather severely fractured, but Hešen ordered them shipped whole—clearly, the Jiaqing emperor, Renzong, later declared, for Hešen's own profit.[63] Late in 1798* an official in the field informed Hešen of the hardships endured by the East Turkestani corvée laborers charged with hauling the stones, which were later estimated to weigh a total of 15,000 kilos. Hešen apparently failed to memorialize at this point either and ordered the shipment to proceed. Two weeks after Gaozong's death, Renzong learned of the massive jades still en route from Altishahr and dispatched an express edict to the responsible officials to abandon the boulders wherever they were upon receipt of the order. The new emperor had the begs involved rewarded with bolts of silk and the porters paid in silver to "display sympathetic feelings for our Muslim subjects."[64]

The jade stopped here, but the story does not. Yu-qing, superintendent of Karashahr, discovered the jade boulders on an 1806 inspection trip to Uššaqtal (Wushaketale, now Wushitala), where they had been abandoned seven years before.[65] The superintendent suggested in a memorial that "peddlers and trading merchants who by imperial grace now swarm over the great distances to Yarkand and elsewhere with their money" might be called in to purchase (at the government's price), break up, and haul off the jade pieces, thus yielding a tidy profit in silver for the Xinjiang authorities. The Jiaqing emperor would

---

* Although this was the third year of the Jiaqing reign, at this time Hešen still enjoyed commanding influence in the Qing court. Renzong did not begin to rule in his own right for another four months.

have none of this, however, responding that this idea of profiting from the jade missed the point and forbade Yu-qing from selling the boulders. Later, however, he reconsidered and instructed Yu-qing to look into transporting the two smaller pieces in the autumn with the tribute jade, if this would not involve too much difficulty. Yu-qing zealously set about making the arrangements, requisitioning carts, rope, 50 to 60 horses, and several dozen East Turkestanis. But when the emperor heard of these preparations and learned that even these "small" pieces weighed 1,850 and 3,750 kilograms—each one greater than the annual tribute quota at this time—he was highly displeased and transferred Yu-qing to Yili where Song-yun could keep an eye on him. The jade monoliths remained in Uššaqtal, where Lin Zexu found them east of the post station in the spring of 1845. Lin wrote: "Seeing them [the jade boulders] now, they look like small mountains. They are rough, uncut gems. One face protrudes, a jade green with a crystal lustre. One may look, but it is forbidden to take a chisel to them. It is a mysterious thing." [66] What finally happened to the nephrite monoliths is unknown.

Jade is unique among the items the Qing court shipped to the capital from the New Dominion in that it was the only article with intrinsic commercial value. To be sure, of the over 110,000 kilograms of tribute jade shipped to Beijing between 1760 and 1820, much went to carving the jade mountains and hanging chimes, innumerable ceremonial or display items (archaistic imitations of bronzes, faux-Moghul bowls and teapots, human and animal figures, *ruyi* scepters to be given as gifts to loyal ministers, banquet tableware, jewelry, hair ornaments and trinkets, implements of the scholar's study, tablets, sacrificial vessels, Buddhist and Taoist icons), and even such practical things as flutes, combs, boxes, and backscratchers. But after the best-quality pieces of each grade of jade were selected and carved, much second-quality stone remained in the Imperial Household Workshop and Scepter Warehouse (*Ruyi Guan*). This the imperial household sold off at the Chongwen Men, or through "apportionment" (i.e., forced sale—*tanpai*) to salt administrations, silk factories, or custom houses. In 1804, for example, the Lianghuai and Changlu Salt Administrations; the Suzhou, Hangzhou, and Jiangning silk factories; and six southern customs houses purchased—or were ordered to buy—over 2,600 catties of second-through fifth-grade jadestone from the palace for 1,329 taels. [67]

PRIVATE COMMERCE IN ALTISHAHR JADE:
A TALE OF TWO SUZHOUS

That Yu-qing could consider soliciting merchant help in dispensing with the Uššaqtal monoliths demonstrates that a private market for jade existed in

Xinjiang at this time. Indeed, although Qing authorities in the Yarkand and Khotan area controlled the extraction and gathering of the stone and set up special *karun* to interdict smugglers and illicit miners, possession and traffic in jade was illegal only for a short time during the 1759–1862 period, and then only in Xinjiang. In 1773 the court gave permission for jade extracted from Miertai Mountain to be registered and sold to officials, soldiers, and common merchants after the annual quota of tribute jade had been selected from the year's haul. Such private purchases were limited to 50 catties (25 kilos) and were accompanied by a certificate (*piao*) with which merchants and others could bring their jade along the post road back through the Jiayu Guan to China proper.

After taking up the post of Yarkand superintendent in 1776, Gao Pu revised the system. The jade left over after the tribute had been sent was to be divided up, with 60 percent sold to merchants and the remaining 40 percent retained, supposedly as compensation for the East Turkestani miners, but most probably falling to Gao Pu himself. Gao also raised the individual weight limit on mountain jade to 150 catties, arguing that it was a shame for high-quality boulders to be cut up for the sake of mere legal formalism (but the emperor later ascribed the impetus for this reform to Gao's corrupt scheming).[68]

By this time, the word was out that jade could be purchased legally in Xinjiang and the jade rush was on. The Jiayu Guan, now kept open all day to accommodate the busy westward traffic, saw Chinese merchants pass through en route to Altishahr in unprecedented numbers. Jade was of course particularly attractive to long-distance traders because of its high value relative to weight and volume, and many of the merchants who carried silver or traded silks, tea, rhubarb, and other Chinese products in Xinjiang brought their profits home in the form of jade. Although certified and hence legally importable jade was available only in Yarkand, the Xinjiang jade market most frequented by Chinese merchants was not, as might be expected, in Khotan or Yarkand, but in Aksu, where East Turkestanis sold jadestone in the Muslim city and where the East Turkestani and Chinese shops in the bazaar dealt in rough and carved jade. Silk and other goods traded here were often bartered directly for jade.[69]

With more merchants passing through the Jiayu Guan, and with a growing number of jade certificates to tally, inspections inevitably became cursory and private jade slipped through into Gansu illegally. (Zhang Luan could get through any customs barrier with a few words and a small gift to the inspectors, all of whom were acquainted with him.) Suzhou (Gansu) served as a major entrepôt for Altishahr jade and goods from China proper. Merchants operating between Xinjiang and Gansu, many of them Tungans, could market jade from beyond the Pass in one of Suzhou's many jade shops (*yupu*) whether it had been shipped legally or not. Once a private merchant sold or bartered a consignment of jade in Suzhou, it was "clean": its provenance could not be traced, though everyone knew it came from Khotan.[70] Merchants from south China then purchased or exchanged luxury items for the jade in Suzhou and carried it to other parts of the empire, including the jade carving centers of Beijing, Tianjin, Jiangning, and especially Yangzhou and Soochow (Jiangsu). This latter city was the main center of jade carving and dealing in the Qing, and its street of lapidaries, Zhuanzhu Xiang, received a great fillip from increased supply of jadestone and increased private and official patronage during this period. Wealthy merchants like Zhang Luan set up residences and businesses in Soochow centered on their jade trade. The imperial court farmed out much of its tribute jade to the salt administrations and silk factories for carving, and the commissioners of these imperial household monopolies availed themselves of the talented artisans in the Jiangnan cities to perform the work.[71] One result was an increase in technical and artistic skill in jade carving that clearly impressed contemporaries. From the time of the victories in Zungharia and Altishahr, the scholar Ling Tingkan noted, the skill of Yangzhou's carvers had improved in unprecedented fashion, as could be seen in two large pieces displayed in one of the city's famous Buddhist temples and, on a smaller scale, in the city's famous "Hindustani" (faux-Moghul) jadework, clocks, pipes, snuff bottles, and miniature fire engines (*shuichong*).[72]

A second result of the vastly increased jade supply was a popularization of jade items.* Lin Sumen wrote of the prevalent fashion in Yangzhou around 1805 for rich and poor alike to affect jade mouthpieces on their pipes. Flourishing production of jade assured moderate prices for such items, which were readily available in Yangzhou markets.[73] The Qianlong emperor, who wrote over 800 poems on jade-related subjects, deplored the "vulgarization" that attended the expansion of jade supply, from Xinjiang, and of demand, from rich merchants. Carvers employing over-decoration and flashy new designs

---

* "It was the trade in such small objects as pipes and snuff-bottles that really took off in the eighteenth century, I assume, thanks to the new supplies of Turkestan jade that came in with the conquest of Xinjiang. In the novel *Pinhua baojian*, by Chen Sen, which describes the pleasures of Peking life in the early nineteenth century (c. 1830–49), roving peddlers with trays of jade 'antiques'—commonly pipes, incense-burners, snuff-bottles, and other bric-a-brac—are described hawking their wares to patrons in teahouses and theaters. Presumably, this was the lowest level of a luxury trade concentrated in Peking, Wuhan, and the Jiangnan cities." Steven Shutt, personal communication, January 3, 1993.

to get a better price for their work galled him in particular, and he used his bully pulpit to promote aesthetic conservation of this precious resource.[74]

The uncovering in 1778 of the jade scam perpetrated by Gao Pu, Zhang Luan, Zhao Junrui, and coconspirators marked the end, for the time being, of the Qing court's accommodation of private jade trafficking. The wide-ranging search for Gao Pu's associates and their goods-in-transit netted a host of more modest smugglers, most unconnected to Gao Pu, and in the process revealed the workings of the jade trade in the eighteenth century. These merchants' stories are summarized in Table 14.

Several points emerge from analysis of this sample. The merchants involved fall into two general categories: those based in Xinjiang and the northwest, operating between Xinjiang and Gansu (the first section of the table), and those either from the Jiangnan or traveling between there and the northwest (the second section). There were, in addition, Kokandi merchants buying Altishahr jade. The first group are typical west route traders, leaving their hometowns in Gansu, Shaanxi, and Shanxi to be employed in or run shops or work as laborers throughout Altishahr. They include many Tungans, probably more than are explicitly identified as Muslims in the sources. They operated on a small scale, often spending no more than a few hundred cash to buy a piece or two of refuse jade from Tungans or East Turkestanis, or occasionally from shops, in Altishahr and in Suzhou. Many were tea or cloth traders.

The second group were generally more affluent. Silk merchants journeying between Jiangnan cities and Xi'an, Lanzhou, Suzhou, and other northwest destinations with cargoes of silk and other goods would often exchange them for jade. Some ventured as far as Aksu, but most seem to have traded in Suzhou, often with Tungan suppliers. They dealt in large pieces of high-quality stone; often several merchants would pool capital in a single shipment of jadestones, which they transported by cart and riverboat to Soochow and Yangzhou for sale.

In addition, two more general conclusions are possible. The first is that Tungan middlemen were ubiquitous in the jade trade, whether in Xinjiang or in the jade entrepôt of Suzhou; this is not surprising after what we have already seen concerning these Chinese Muslims. And second, there were no exclusive jade merchants among these "smugglers"; all dealt simultaneously in such other commodities as cotton cloth, tea, and silk. Some of the Shanxi merchants caught up in the Gao Pu investigation claimed as much in their depositions: "Those who go to Soochow to sell jade are by no means specialist dealers in jade. They are all traders who go between Gansu, Suzhou, Aksu, Yarkand, and so forth, selling silk and miscellaneous items and pri-

TABLE 14

Merchants Dealing in Jadestone in Xinjiang and China Proper, 1778-90

Jade Merchants or Smugglers	Place of Origin/ Base of Operations	Place and Manner of Purchase
MERCHANTS BASED IN THE NORTHWEST		
Lei Ying	Shaanxi; partner in Zheng Heng Shop in Hami	Bought jade from Tungan leather shop owner, from sheep broker, and from camel teamster; traveled with over 100 catties to Shaanxi
Sun Quande	Shaanxi; worked at Hami Tian Deng Shop	Hami Tungans who owed Sun money repaid him with jade
Fan Yingji	Shanxi; ran a shop in Suzhou	Purchased jade in Aksu from Zhou Xiuzhong, a Jiangnan man
Four or five unnamed individuals	Apprehended in Jingzhou, Gansu	Supplied by the Tian Xi Dian in Suzhou and by Tungans from Gansu and Shaanxi, now resident in Suzhou
Wei Zhongxiao	Gansu; ran shop in Kashgar	Traded tea for small amount of jade
Wang Ming	Gansu; ran shop in Aksu	Traded cloth and tea for 24 pieces of jade worth 7 taels
Hu Kui (Tungan)	Gansu; had worked as laborer in Ush	Bought small piece of jade from unknown East Turkestani
Cao Zhi	Gansu; sold meat in Yarkand	Bought small pieces of jade in Yarkand
Li Dequan	Shanxi; sold goods in Aksu	Purchased 34 pieces of jade worth 65 taels
Zhang Dakui	Shanxi; ran store in Aksu	Traded cash, cotton cloth, and tea for 15 pieces of jade worth 56 taels
Li Ge	Shanxi; ran store in Aksu	Bought 40 catties of jade worth 23 taels
Zhang Guoyun, Zhang Tizheng, Shi Bingjun	Gansu; did business in Aksu and Yarkand	Traded tea and purchased small pieces of jade
Li Yingfu, Ma Shide, Mu Jun	Did business in Yarkand	Bought small pieces of jade
Hai Shenglian (Tungan)	Active in China proper	Dealt privately in jade
Ma Tianlong (Tungan)	Apprehended in Aksu	Concealed jade in a cart
MERCHANTS FROM OR OPERATING IN THE SOUTH		
Wang Dezhang	Jiangsu; sold silk in Suzhou	Bought jade from Tungan in Suzhou
Mr. Shi	Unknown; had southern accent	Stayed in Xi'an inn with a cart full of jade; fled when discovered
Yang Tianshan, Zhao Shengwu, and 3 partners, in a band of 17 merchants	Jiangsu; traveled to Xi'an and Shuozhou, Gansu, to sell silk	After selling silk to San Yi Dian in Shuozhou, with help of local broker bought several dozen pieces of jade from local Tungans; bought 20–30 pieces from Jin family shop in Lanzhou; apprehended

TABLE 14
(continued)

Jade Merchants or Smugglers	Place of Origin/ Base of Operations	Place and Manner of Purchase
MERCHANTS FROM OR OPERATING IN THE SOUTH		
		while changing boats near Xiangyang, Hubei, en route for Soochow and Yangzhou
Wu Qizhou and seven others		Purchased in Aksu and Suzhou with proceeds from silk sales; received jade in Suzhou, Liangzhou, and Lanzhou in repayment of debts for credit sales in the past; total of 1,367 catties
Zhao Aiyuan, Mr. Peng	Shanxi	Shipped consignment of large white jade pieces from Aksu to Soochow
Xu Jueru	Soochow	In 1773 went to Gansu to sell dry goods; in 1776 to Aksu, then Yarkand; returned to Aksu and Suzhou in 1777, buying jade from a Lanzhou Tungan in Aksu; returned to Soochow in 1778
Li Buan, Fu De		Purchased 1,000 catties of jade worth 14,000 taels in Aksu from Zhao Junrui; two Shanxi men, one living in Suzhou San Yi Dian, bought into the deal
KOKANDI MERCHANTS		
A-bu-la and followers	Kokand	Bought jade illegally in Yarkand

SOURCES: For Lei Ying, Sun Quande, and Fan Yingji, GPSYYSA 25:909a–910b; for the unnamed merchants, GPSYYSA 26:950; for Wei Zhongxiao and Wang Ming, Fu-kang-an, *Zougao, ce* 14, QL49.9.3; for Hu Kui, Cao Zhi, Li Dequan, Zhang Dakui, and Li Ge, Fu-kang-an, *Zougao, ce* 20, QL50.7.26; for Zhang Guoyun et al. and Li Yingfu et al., Fu-kang-an, *Zougao, ce* 24, QL51.5.28; for Hai Shenglian, GZSL 1338:20b–21a, QL54.9 *guiyi*; for Ma Tianlong, GZSL 1363:3, QL55.9 *jiawu*; for Wang Dezhang and Mr. Shi, GPSYYSA 25: 909a–910b; for Yang Tianshan et al., GPSYYSA 21:750b–751a; for Wu Qizhou et al., GZSL 1068:9b–10b, QL43.10 *yiwei* and GPSYYSA 24:868a, 870a; for Zhao Aiyuan and Mr. Peng, GPSYYSA 26:951, 952b–953a; for Xu Jueru, GPSYYSA 26:953b–954a; for Li Buan and Fu De, GPSYYSA 26:950b; for Kokandi merchants, GZSL 1173:6a–7a, QL48.1 *renzi*.

vately carrying jade stones to Soochow to sell. And they all stay at inns— they don't run jade shops."[75] (Zhang Luan, the wealthy jade dealer in collusion with Gao Pu, did own jade shops in Soochow, but he seems exceptional in the breadth and net worth of his business activities.)

When it cracked down on Gao Pu and prohibited all private jade dealings in 1778, the court expressed little concern over the small, independent merchants who traded a little nephrite on the side. Some, indeed, still held certificates when they were caught, and, although the Qing had revoked the jade certification system when it made the trade illegal, where goods and certificates tallied the dynasty took no action. Nor, indeed, did the dynasty punish any merchant not affiliated with Gao Pu, except to confiscate the jade. The emperor likewise realized the futility of trying to chase down all the Chinese merchants implicated in sales and resales of jade items in the northwest during the previous boom years. The 1778 investigation was thus greatly limited in scope. If everyone who had dealt with Gao Pu and his associates were punished, Gaozong pointed out, not one of the Soochow jade shops would be spared. Nevertheless, after this initial display of leniency, for the next 21 years, as long as the restriction against private dealing remained in effect, officials would occasionally apprehend jade smugglers and pronounce sentences as if upon thieves, with the number of heavy bamboo blows based on the value of the jadestone found in the criminal's possession.[76]

In yet another example of how the economy in Qing Xinjiang was increasingly deregulated over time, the Jiaqing emperor lifted restrictions on jade entirely as soon as he came into his own, in 1799. (At the same time, he relaxed laws forbidding private ginseng gathering in the northeast.) Merchants were free to trade in the stone; those being punished for past offenses could have their cases reviewed. Moreover, the Qing government ceased jade mining operations in Khotan, thus freeing up the soldiers and officials who had supervised jade extraction in the past and avoiding the expense of equipping and provisioning the East Turkestani mining crews. Thereafter, the state still managed the selection of tribute jade,[77] but East Turkestanis could sell directly to Chinese merchants. Han and Tungan were still technically required to hold certificates for their jade, subject to inspection in Aksu or at the Jiayu Guan, but it is doubtful how vigilantly this system—which never covered more than a fraction of the privately traded jade in Xinjiang—was enforced in the nineteenth century.[78]

After this almost complete privatization, Chinese merchants made their way to Altishahr in increased numbers. In Kashgar, Councillor Fu-jun noted this fact, attributed it to the lifting of restrictions on jade, and even theorized that the price of copper cash (relative to silver) in Altishahr would thereafter be dependent upon sales of jade in the Jiangnan: as Chinese merchants clamored to buy jade from East Turkestanis, who, Fu-jun claimed, sold only for *pul*, the price of copper money rose not only in Yarkand, but also in Aksu, Kashgar, and Yangi Hisar—presumably because of Chinese merchants' demand for copper money and the amount of silver they dropped into the local economy. If jade did not sell well in China proper, Fu-jun believed, the copper price in Altishahr would fall again.[79]

One puzzling aspect of the commerce between China proper and Xinjiang between 1759 and 1862 is the problem of how Chinese merchants brought profits home. The exports from the Chinese provinces via Xinjiang abroad to Central and South Asia are easily identified: silk, cotton cloth, silver ingots, tea, and rhubarb are frequently discussed in the Qing sources, and the reasons for their demand are easily appreciated. In addition, merchants brought for sale in Xinjiang those items that Han, Tungan, Manchu, and others required from China proper (tea, silk, cloth, china, drugs and food stuffs, copper ware, iron tools). But what could these merchants bring back from Xinjiang that could be sold in China proper? Xinjiang was too far from the urban centers of China proper for most pastoral products—generally bulky and heavy in relation to their value—to be profitable imports. Qi-shi-yi does mention that a fashion in Beijing for coats and hats made of the hide of Bukharan "heavy-boned sheep" created a demand for these skins in the 1770s ("When style creates a taste for something, a place 10,000 *li* away responds like an echo").[80] And we have seen that Zhang Luan shipped a cartload of hides to Shanxi, so there must have been some market for such items. But it would seem that most demand for hides, felts, wool, and even livestock on the hoof could be adequately supplied from closer pastoral regions in Mongolia. Cotton grown in the Eastern March, particularly the Turfan area, was imported profitably to the northwestern provinces, but the same was not true of the produce of Zungharia and Altishahr. Some flax, too, was exported to China proper.[81] However, even taken together, the eastward trade of these items does not seem commensurate with the voluminous westward commerce in tea, rhubarb, silk, and other Chinese products.

Jadestone, on the other hand, was clearly a major eastward trade item, eagerly purchased by Chinese merchants exchanging goods in Xinjiang. Jade must have gone some way toward "balancing" the China proper–Xinjiang trade. We have seen that from the eighteenth to the early nineteenth century, and perhaps still later, there was a direct and sizeable private silk-for-jade trade linking Suzhou in the northwest with Soochow in the Jiangnan, and, moreover, that small-scale tea traders operating in Xinjiang regularly exchanged tea for jade, which they could market in Aksu or back in Gansu. For this reason, above and beyond the anecdotal evidence on jade amassed above, we may assume an important role for jade in the commerce linking Xinjiang with China proper.

Opium

Opium may have played a similar part from the 1830s to the 1850s. Although we know little about the opium trade in this region, within a short time of the implementation of the opium prohibition in Xinjiang in 1839, authorities confiscated almost 160,000 ounces (*liang*) of opium. Most was seized from foreign—especially South Asian—merchants, but Han and Tungan were implicated in these cases as well. Somewhat later, Chinese merchants met the caravans of Tatar merchants who sold opium for its weight in silver outside Yili and Tarbagatai. The volume of opium imports from Kashmir and other Himalayan countries increased in the fifteen years after the Qing prohibition; by the 1840s it was a staple article of trade, with 210 maunds (about 7,854 kilos) smuggled in goatskins into Yarkand yearly. A series of arrests in Urumchi in early 1840 brought in over 30 smokers and dealers; it is likely that the Chinese merchants who purchased opium stocks, whatever their origin, smuggled the drug eastward to Gansu and other provinces of the northwest.[82]

We cannot look entirely to simple formulas (silk-for-jade, silk-for-horses, silver-for-opium) to describe the commercial relations between Xinjiang and China proper. Rather, it seems that most merchants relied on a more complex series of transactions (such as the triangle trade that supplied the Mongol banners in Khobdo and Uliasutai with flour through tea sales in Gucheng) or set up shop for some time in Xinjiang in order to amass profits in monetary form. No doubt the Shanxi firms' remittance services were an aid in the "repatriation" of such earnings. Moreover, although there were long-distance caravans plying the whole route from Yarkand, say, to Guihua, or from Soochow to Aksu, more commonly a rough pattern of relay trade pertained, whereby one group of merchants traded between China proper and gateway cities near the Xinjiang border (Suzhou, Gucheng, Urumchi), and another group, based in Xinjiang cities, conveyed goods from the entrepôts further into the Xinjiang interior for local retail or sale to foreign merchants for re-export. To a great degree, these stages of the relay trade corresponded to the distinct classes of merchants identified in this chapter. Affluent Jiangnan traders and major Shanxi merchants worked the Soochow-Suzhou axis, generally not venturing beyond Gansu. Many Shanxi merchants on the northern route, too, turned back or continued north to trade in Mongolia after selling their goods in Gucheng or Urumchi. The Xinjiang-based merchants included many Tungans, East Turkestanis, and less-highly capitalized Han peddlers and shopkeepers, as well as a smaller number of established name-brand firms. Thus, despite the great influx of Chinese merchants to Xinjiang during this period, the distinction between "inside" and "outside the Pass," enshrined in place-name usage and maintained by the territory's administrative structure, was reflected in private commercial arrangements as well.

This chapter's focus on major trade items and groups of merchants adds complexity to the story, begun in Chapters 2 through 4, of the relationship between Qing empire builders and Chinese merchants in Xinjiang. As the Qianlong emperor had argued, merchants from China proper were indeed critical to the maintenance of Qing outposts in the New Dominion, not only for the commercial taxes and rents they paid, but by supplying tea to Xinjiang garrisons, a variety of other goods to towns throughout Xinjiang, and, indirectly, grain to Mongols and Qing forces in northwestern Mongolia. (As we will see below, they were also a critical source of portage and credit to the Qing military in wartime.) But while the dynasty in principle approved of and relied upon Xinjiang trade, the court and officials often cast a wary eye upon individual Chinese traders, many of whom indeed operated outside the law. Chinese taken abroad as captives, tea and rhubarb dealers flaunting embargoes, smugglers of jade, opium runners, virtually anyone surnamed "Ma"— all at one point or another were perceived as a threat to imperial order in Xinjiang, even as economic networks and ties to China proper (such as those of the Shanxi firms) expanded. In particular, the Tungans fell under scrutiny disproportionate to their minor economic clout, in part because their identity as Muslim Chinese challenged the categories by which the Qing organized its subjects in the New Dominion.

CHAPTER 6

Qing Ethnic Policy
and Chinese Merchants

On arriving in Kashgar, Your ministers entered the city to conduct a reconnaissance. The city wall is over ten *li* in circumference, and over 2,500 households of dog-Muslims live within.

Zhao-hui, Memorial, February 3, 1760

The East Turkestanis metamorphosized from subhuman barbarians into imperial subjects sometime during the third week of February 1760.

The move toward neutral depictions of the Qing's new Xinjiang subjects was early and abrupt, at least in official materials. Memorials from the Zunghar and Altishahr front between 1758 and early 1760 referred to the East Turkestanis, then still a newly conquered and unknown entity, with a derogatory character *hui* ("Muslim") that included the canine radical in conjunction with the phonetic *hui*, thus creating an ethnonym with an effect something like "dog-Muslim." Zhao-hui, Huang Tinggui, and Yang Yingju all used this character in their dispatches of this time. For example, an important policy document sent in by Zhao-hui from Kashgar on February 3d, 1760, contains this character, even in its extensively corrected Grand Council copy. In his series of reports from the cities of Altishahr, Yang Yingju employs the canine-*hui* character in memorials dated February 1st, 2d, and 16th. On February 26th, however, he writes the character without the deprecatory radical, which thereafter does not appear in official Qing sources. Somehow in this ten-day interim the Shaanxi-Gansu governor-general either decided or was ordered no longer to refer to the East Turkestanis in this pejorative manner.[1]

Qing Images of Xinjiang Peoples

Such evidence of official Qing concern over the language used in reference to new Muslim and Mongol subjects forces us to confront a deeply held assumption about Chinese culture and empire, namely, that in Qing times, the

"Chinese empire," was Sinocentric. This is a principal lesson of John King Fairbank's writings on the "Chinese World Order"; according to that paradigm, one would expect "the Chinese" to view those peoples who were culturally non-Chinese as "barbaric." But the evidence from these early dispatches from Xinjiang indicates the emergence of a very different approach to cultural difference among Qing subjects, as well as an official recognition that language mattered in formulating ethnic policy.

To be sure, there was much in Xinjiang that was alien to Han and Manchu alike. Qi-shi-yi, a Manchu traveling in Altishahr in the latter half of the eighteenth century and writing about it in Chinese considers the Arabic script to be a mess of scratchings and wrigglings — hard to make out and outlandishly horizontal: "The Muslim script is like the tracks of birds, like tadpoles. It is read horizontally and linked up. Breaks are particularly difficult to distinguish."[2] Not surprisingly, given the unfamiliarity of the region and its people, and their recent status as enemies, the early unofficial gazetteers of Xinjiang likewise contain examples of chauvinistic and derogatory depictions. One of the harshest may be found in the 1772 *Huijiang zhi*.

> The Muslims' natural character (*fuxing*) is suspicious and unsettled, crafty and false. Hard-drinking and addicted to sex, they never know when they have had enough. They understand neither repentance nor restraint, and wild talk takes the place of shame. They are greedy and parsimonious. If husbands, wives, fathers, or sons have money, they each hide it away for themselves. If even one cash falls into a drainage ditch, they have to drain, sift, and dredge until the coin is retrieved. They enjoy being proud and boastful, exaggerating their reputation. They prefer ease to industry, considering an opportunity for inactivity and sleep a great boon, and a drunken binge from dusk to dawn a great joy. Their character is lethargic, and they lack foresight. They do not know what it is to learn skills or to store grain, thus they must have someone to rely on in order to survive. Still, they have their good side: they can endure hunger and cold, will take any insult, and can be happily frugal.[3]

In a passage on the East Turkestani Islamic marriage system, the authors lingered upon what was to them the outrageous custom of considering children by a man's various wives all to be of equal rank in the inner family, distinguished only by age, and of treating a woman's children by different husbands as consanguineous (*tongbao*). Then they interject an assimilationist note: "Now, because they have come over and submitted and are already part of the realm, they also know to look up to and revere Chinese customs (*huafeng*) and gradually will accept the rituals and proper conduct."[4]

One factor behind this style of description is no doubt simply an author's natural desire to write compellingly about things strange and new. Qi-shi-yi in 1777 records the bizarre information he had "seen and heard" regarding other peoples of the West, such as Kokandis with sheep nine inches tall, or Russian ladies who wear long, double-lined skirts because they lack undergarments. When he discusses people about whom he had firsthand experience, however, his descriptions take on a harder edge. "Now Torghuts and Khoshuuts are settled on this land. It is indeed a pleasant place to dwell, but the people are restless and lazy and cannot apply their energies to cultivation to feed themselves. The men put their efforts into highway robbery, and their women shamelessly into prostitution. They are just a bad type (*lei*) of western people (*rongren*)."[5]

In later gazetteers, however, such as the *Huijiang tongzhi* (1804) and *Xichui zongtong shilue* (1809), pejorative images of the peoples in Xinjiang are generally absent from the ethnographic descriptions.[6] Most significantly, the ethnographic material in the imperially commissioned gazetteers, *Huangyu Xiyu tuzhi* (1782) and *Xinjiang zhilue* (1821) is free of patently defamatory language. The reason for this is stated explicitly in the latter work, compiled under the supervision of Song-yun: "The Muslims of the south and the Oirats of the north have all become subjects (*fuyi*), are equivalent to the registered people (*bianmeng*), and must not be called 'outer barbarians' (*waiyi*)."[7] Thus the *Xinjiang zhilue* distinguishes them clearly from Kazakhs, "Buruts" (Kirghiz), and other nomadic peoples on Xinjiang's borders and beyond.*

Nailene Chou notes a similar contrast in the attitudes expressed in materials on Xinjiang (mostly poetry and articles by exiles) of the middle and late Qing periods. In the late eighteenth and nineteenth centuries, Qing commentators observed the customs of Xinjiang peoples "with interest and amusement"; while they occasionally expressed disapproval, overtly pejorative terms were avoided. "By contrast, in works done in late Ch'ing, say, after the Moslem rebellion in the 1870s [*sic*], references made to the minorities were often phrased in contemptuous ways. This change perhaps reflects the difference between a genuine self-confidence and a nervous chauvinism."[8]

---

* The term *yi* ("foreign, barbarian") was not applied to the native inhabitants of Xinjiang (East Turkestanis, Oirats, Torghuts, and so forth) following the conquest. I have discovered only one instance in which it appeared: in his *Wushi shiyi* (also published under the title *Xinjiang Fuhuacheng zhilue*), a practical handbook for Qing officials in Ush, Bao-da includes a section on the *Huiyi chu*, an office that supervised local Muslim affairs, adjudicated murder cases, and issued road passes for Muslim travel abroad, often in concert with the Ush hakim beg. This agency also handled matters pertaining to foreign Burut or Andijanis, who are referred to as *yi* in other sources. I suspect that by the late date of this gazetteer (1857), the official neutrality of the Qianlong period had given way to a more Sinocentric outlook.

Chou suggests that bitterness over the bloody Tungan rebellion could explain the latter attitude. But, as I suggest below, there seems to be something more deep-seated distinguishing the attitudes of the eighteenth century from those of the late nineteenth, for the Qianlong-era ideology of empire differs profoundly from that held by Han Chinese of the Ming or Republican periods and, indeed, from that attributed to the Qing by the "Chinese world order" paradigm.

Five Nations, Under Heaven: Gaozong's Vision of the Empire

Official terms for and references to the East Turkestanis were sanitized following the dynasty's 1759 military victory in Altishahr. The changed terminology seen in Yang Yingju's official correspondence with the court was but the first step in the ideological promotion of the East Turkestanis from semicanine barbarians to full members of the Qing imperial polity, a process that began no later than 1759. When the Qianlong emperor fully articulated the new imperial vision, East Turkestani joined Han, Manchu, Mongol, and Tibetan as one of the five culture blocs that comprised the principal domains of the Qing realm, a status from which such other peoples as the Miao or indigenous Taiwanese, who lacked writing systems, were excluded.[9] This position in the empire is symbolized, for example, by the inclusion of Turki (in Arabic script) among the languages used on gates and on polyglot steles. Following the Xinjiang conquest, for example, the Qianlong emperor ordered that the main gates at the Chengde summer palace and the Shenyang palace, as well as "dismount here" steles at the Qing ancestral tomb complexes, be recarved in Manchu (*Qing*), Chinese (*Han*), Mongol (*Menggu*), Tibetan (*Xifan*), and Arabic/Turki (*Huizi*). Thus he intended to "proclaim the supremacy of the unified linguistic universality of our dynastic house."[10]

Further evidence may be found in two major multilingual publications: the *Wuti Qingwen jian* (Imperially authorized mirror of the five scripts of Qing letters)[11] and the *(Qinding) Xiyu tongwen zhi* (Imperially commissioned unified-language gazetteer of the Western Regions). The latter work, completed in 1763, is a geographical and genealogical dictionary of Western Region place-names and personal names in Manchu, Chinese, Mongolian, Todo (Oirat Mongol),* Tibetan, and Turki, with Manchu entries primary and

---

* The Todo (from Mongolian for "clear, lucid") script was adapted from the Mongolian in 1684 by Zaya Pandita, a Khoshuut, to represent the pronunciations of western or Oirat Mongolian. Enoki, "Introduction," p. 18.

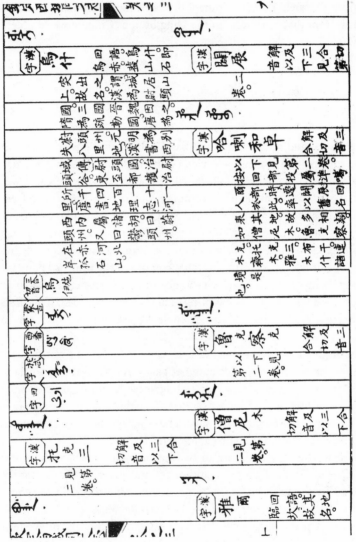

Figure 7. Page from the multilingual gazetteer of the Western Regions (*Xiyu tongwen zhi*). The entry for Ush starts in the top right, beginning with Manchu, "Uši," and proceeding left. Subsequent cartouches indicate Chinese, Chinese pronunciation, Mongolian, Tibetan, Oirat, and Turki (Arabic), respectively. The top and bottom of the page are separate entries.

elevated (see Figure 7). The dictionary was intended principally as an aid in the compilation of the military history of the conquest of Tibet and Xinjiang (*[Qinding] pingding Zhunga'er fanglue*) and the imperial gazetteer of the Western Regions (*[Qinding] huangyu Xiyu tuzhi*). In addition, it served the vital function of standardizing Chinese transliterations of these non-Chinese names, thus avoiding confusion in field dispatches to the court as well as in historiography.[12] Above and beyond this, however, through the collection and codification of genealogies of ruling elites and etymologies of place-names in Zungharia, East Turkestan, Qinghai, and Tibet, it was an exercise in imperial scholarship and scholarly imperialism, a linguistic conquest to consolidate both practically and symbolically the military victories already achieved.

With a well-chosen example in his preface to this work, the Qianlong emperor portrayed the unity of these five peoples "under Heaven" and simultaneously situated himself, in his celestial capacity, as the element unifying the whole.

> Now, in Chinese [*Hanyu*], "Heaven" is called *tian*. In the language of our dynastic house [*guoyu*] it is called *abka*. In Mongolian [*Mengguyu*] and Zungharian [*Zhunyu*] "Heaven" is *tngri*. In Tibetan [*Xifanyu*] it is *nam-mkhah*. In the Muslim tongue [*Huiyu*, i.e., Turki] it is called *asman*. Let a Muslim, meaning "Heaven," tell a Han it is called *asman*, and the Han will necessarily think this is not so. If the Han, meaning "Heaven," tells the Muslim *tian*, the Muslim will likewise certainly think it not so. Here not so, there not so. Who knows which is right? But by raising the head and looking at what is plainly up above, the Han knows *tian* and venerates it, and the Muslim knows *asman* and venerates it. This is the great unity (*da tong*). In fact, once the names are unified, there is nothing that is not universal.[13]

From Gaozong's exalted viewpoint in this passage, Han and East Turkestani cultural entities occupied equivalent positions under a universal heaven —represented by the emperor himself (Gaozong's Manchu reign-name, Abkai Wehiyehe (supported by heaven), contains the word "heaven"— abka—within it). Neither Han Chinese, nor Chinese civilization, enjoys a privileged position within this vision of *da tong*.

The emperor's pluralist configuration of empire, with its implied equivalency for each of the five groups mentioned, stands in contrast to John King Fairbank's depiction in his discussions of "the tributary system" and "the Chinese world order." According to this theory, "Chinese dynasties" understood their relations with "non-Chinese" peoples and countries in terms of a hierarchy of peoples ranging from culturally superior to inferior around the

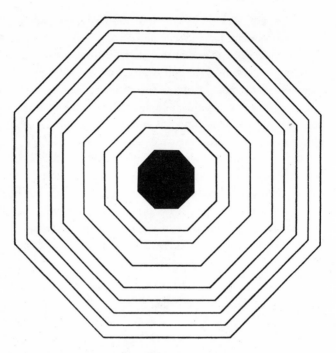

Figure 8. Cover illustration by Hugh Price from John King Fairbank, ed., *The Chinese World Order* (Cambridge: Harvard Univ. Press), © 1968 by the President and Fellows of Harvard College.

Sinic cultural and (to some degree) geographical center. Where, as was often the case, the actual nature of the relationship belied this characterization, the tribute ritual and terminology employed by the court served to maintain the fiction for political and historiographical purposes. To represent this arrangement, Fairbank employed a series of concentric rings, with China at the center and outlying zones extending like pond ripples of progressively attenuated civilization (Figure 8).[14] This image, with its classical precedents in the "Tribute of Yu" and the *Zhou li*, has influenced the way Western scholars of China in the latter half of the twentieth century imagined traditional China's relationship with its neighbors. The schematic is useful as a description of the rhetorical stance adopted by Chinese elites at certain times with regard to *foreign* peoples and accurately characterizes the institutions employed for a period during the Ming.[15] It must however be seriously qualified for each dynasty discussed, a task undertaken by the other articles in the *Chinese World Order* collection; Morris Rossabi and contributors to the volume *China among Equals* have, moreover, challenged the applicability of the Sinocentric model to East and Inner Asia in the tenth through fourteenth centuries. These exceptions lead one to question the model's general utility. In the case of the Manchu Qing dynasty, the question of who and what comprises "Chinese" is problematic. Was Gaozong's weltanschauung really Sinocentric?

Still more seriously, when taken not merely as a characterization of ideology but as a real organizing rubric for foreign relations in East Asia, the "Chinese world order" theory is misleading. This is because it assumes as the norm a static, essentialized—and thus ahistorical—"Chinese culture" at the apex of the hierarchy. Given the longevity of conquest dynasties and the influence of nomadic peoples on the Chinese polity, particularly from the Tang on, it is unreasonable to consider this Inner Asian stream of Chinese history to be somehow episodic or aberrant.

To return, then, to Gaozong's little vocabulary lesson. Did he imagine China and "Chinese culture" to occupy the center of his empire? Were we to map his vision on the empire's ideal structure, based on the passage above, and taking into account the special nature of the relationships between the various groups he mentions and the Manchu imperial house, would such a picture consist of concentric rings? I suggest not and propose my own "map" in Figure 9. In this version, the five linguistic or ethnic blocs exist not in starkly hierarchical, but something more like parallel relationship to each other.[16] Though the empire is centripetal, at the center lies neither an abstract "Chinese civilization," nor even the Confucian Son of Heaven, but rather the Aisin Gioro house, in the person of the many-faceted Qing emperor. The so-called outer domains (*waifan*) are here represented no differently from the

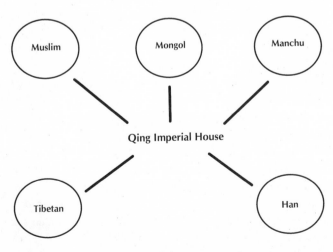

Figure 9.   Gaozong's vision of the empire, mid-Qianlong reign.

Han, in keeping with the implications of the less value-laden Manchu term (outer provinces, Ma. *tulergi golo*—discussed in the last chapter).

The lines connecting each bloc to the imperial house do not represent a merely "tributary" relationship; rather, imagine them to convey any and all of the multifarious means of articulating and producing the emperor-subject relationship: gift exchange, court audiences, intermarriage, autumn hunts, religious patronage, personal communications, imperial tours, sponsored scholarship, and so forth.

One could, moreover, elaborate upon this diagram, by including compartments for bondservants and the eight banners, Han scholars, common Han (*min*), other groups, such as the Yao and Miao, or even the multitude of foreign lords with whom the Qing imperial house interacted on similar terms.[17] I would not want to exaggerate the usefulness of the diagram in Figure 9, however. It is an attempt to represent the views expressed by Gaozong in the preface to the *Xiyu tongwen zhi* and implied by the examples of ostentatious polylingualism given above. Inasmuch as the emperor's views were those of the court, the diagram may be said to reflect the Qing imperial ideology at this moment in the late eighteenth century. I hope the contrast with the ubiquitous, and, for the Qing, inaccurate model of Sinocentric rings will be thought-provoking, but do not pretend to encompass in such a simplistic fashion the manifold differences in status of the groups represented, let alone explain how the positions of those groups relative to the center of power changed over time.

If what I have called the pluralist Qing empire of the latter eighteenth century is not well characterized by concentric rings, the melting-pot would be a still more unfortunate analogy. Though the empire's culture blocs were in theory juxtaposed on an impartial basis, the boundaries between them were nonetheless to be strictly maintained lest excessive, uncontrolled contact lead to trouble. Walled cities, or cantonments within cities, often served this purpose materially. Where Fairbank's map implies assimilation, a gravitational pull toward the Sinic center, the domains in the Qianlong emperor's eyes were to remain culturally discrete, their boundaries vigilantly maintained by the state through administrative structures, laws, the pass system, and so forth.

In practice, however, Chinese merchants who journeyed to Xinjiang transgressed cultural as well as geographic boundaries. They lived both inside and outside the cantonments, frequented bazaars between new and old cities, set up shop in the Muslim part of town and even penetrated remote East Turkestani villages and steppe camps of nomads. Some Tungans intermarried with East Turkestanis. Because of their mobility—and this distinguished them from Chinese agriculturalists on state farms in Xinjiang—they were in frequent contact with East Turkestanis. And because of these merchants' commercial sophistication, the Qing viewed such contact as potentially dangerous, if unavoidable. Hence the laws and edicts governing Chinese merchants in Altishahr focused on various types of interethnic contact. In particular, three kinds of crime were particularly sensitive, because they challenged the normative imperial model directly by blurring the boundaries between peoples of the empire or by threatening to drive the East Turkestanis, through intense exploitation, to the point of rebellion against the Qing. These crimes involved hair, sex, and money.

A New Twist on the Queue

In a "postpacification" memorial from Altishahr, Nayanceng presented the court with what he saw as the typical curriculum vitae of a Gansu Tungan:

> In the province of Gansu three out of ten Tungans (*Hanhui*) have no livelihood; they are almost all ramblers who travel beyond the Pass as far as Altishahr, where the first thing they do is study the Muslim language [i.e., Turki] and rely upon their shared religion to establish their reputation. Men and women do not avoid each other, but fornicate at will. They swindle and cheat—there's nothing [the Tungans] will not do. After a while they take East Turkestani wives and gradually grow closer [to local society]. Before the Jahāngīr affair there were even Tungans who went so far as to cut their queues and act as ākhūnds. Thus their religion leads them to violate the law, causing strife on the frontier.[18]

As this catalog of crimes builds to its crescendo, it follows the young Tungan through experiences of unemployment, vagrancy, language study, networking, sleeping with local women, petty entrepreneurship, miscegenation, and finally cutting off the queue and serving in the religious establishment. This litany charts both a geographical and a cultural journey, as well as what seems a remarkable social leap from rootless vagrant to married pillar of the Altishahr Islamic community. But such hyperbole aside, the emphasis Nayanceng puts on queue cutting in this passage illustrates the particular meanings the Manchu headdress conveyed in Xinjiang: by clipping his braid, such a Tungan severed a last tie to China proper and Chineseness. He was guilty less of sedition per se than of crossing the ethnic boundaries within which the Qing imagined its subjects to exist.

Dorgon's 1645 decree imposed the shaved forehead and queue on the men of the recently conquered Han population of China proper. Ming loyalists viewed it as a demeaning sign of submission, and there was much resistance to the tonsure and much ruthless repression of those who failed to keep their foreheads closely shaven. We know little about how Han (or Tungan) Chinese in the eighteenth and early nineteenth centuries viewed their enforced hairstyle; perhaps they resented it, perhaps they accepted it as a dreary fact of life. But if Philip Kuhn is right, the question of sedition by queue clipping in the mid-1700s was so sensitive that not even the Qianlong emperor could raise it freely in secret communications with his officials.[19]

It is curious, then, that the Qing did not enforce the Manchu headdress on East Turkestanis after the conquest of Altishahr in 1759. Rather than require all to adopt the tonsure and queue as a unifying symbol and visible sign of loyalty, in Xinjiang the Qing made the hairstyle serve as a distinguishing characteristic, a badge of rank and a mark of ethnic identity.

Until after Jahāngīr's jihad, no East Turkestani wore the queue. After the Qing victory, a memorialist suggested that those begs who remained loyal during the 1826 invasion and uprising be given hereditary title to their offices, tax benefits, and *permission* to wear the queue, "to show distinction" (*yi shi qubie*). In 1828 the court bestowed the right to wear a queue upon Isḥaq b. Muḥammad Hudawī and his sons and grandsons, in recognition of this Kashgar hakim beg's successful efforts to capture Jahāngīr.[20] Not long thereafter, other begs and Muslims with hereditary rank began to clamor for the right to display their affection and loyalty to the dynasty in this fashion. Xuanzong thought such avid loyalty deserved reward and first ordered that those who wished could grow queues, while others, for whom the abrupt change might be difficult, could do as they liked. The forever skeptical Nayanceng, however, pointed out that the East Turkestanis viewed the Manchu coiffure as a status symbol and suggested that allowing everyone to adopt it would result in "no distinction whatsoever" and a loss of the queue's cachet. In the end, the relevant substatute in the *Huijiang zeli* permitted nobles (*junwang, gong,* etc.), begs from the hakim down to the fourth rank, and the sons and grandsons of loyal begs to wear the queue *if they wanted to.* Begs below the fourth rank were expressly forbidden from wearing the queue, "in order to demonstrate restraint." What was to Han and Tungan men a common duty, then, was thus to the East Turkestani a rationed privilege.[21]

This distinction cut in at least two ways. Begs and nobles so honored were, on the one hand, set apart from other East Turkestanis and from the mass of lower beg officials who were not invited to the capital for imperial audiences and with whom Manchu authorities in Xinjiang had little direct contact. On the other hand, the queue distinguished men from China proper—the

Han and Tungan merchants and farmers—from South and Central Asians, Kazakhs, Kirghiz, and the majority of East Turkestanis.

One might think that migrants from China proper were clearly identifiable in any case by their dress, speech, and customs, but identification was not the point so much as maintenance of the cultural boundaries by which the Qing organized its subjects. As the Tungans whom Nayanceng found so dangerous illustrate, assimilation in border areas was not one-way; as we have seen, there were cases of Turkicized Chinese just as there were East Turkestanis who spoke Chinese or dressed and wore their hair like Manchu officials. As an externally imposed label, the queue thus served the Qing authorities in Xinjiang, who associated cross-cultural drift with sedition, as a touchstone of Han-ness as well as of loyalty to the dynasty. Chinese merchants were allowed to journey to Qing lands far from their homes within the Pass on the condition that they remain within their cultural frontiers. For this reason, then, cutting off the queue stood near the apex of Nayanceng's hierarchy of Tungan perfidy. Similarly, when prisoners were returned from Central Asia without the ordained pigtail, Xinjiang officials noted that fact in reports and the captives hastened to assure the authorities that they had been shorn involuntarily.[22]

For foreigners, too, the queue immediately identified Chinese merchants. It is unclear why Kirghiz, Kokandis, and the Khojas almost invariably cut the queues of their prisoners from Xinjiang, but the gesture clearly bore symbolic import; perhaps they intended to demean their captives or discourage them from escaping back to suspicious Qing officials. For a while in 1826 and 1827 a band of Kirghiz who pastured their animals near Ush began taking the queues—and scalps—of merchants, soldiers, officials, caravaneers, and other "Chinese" (*neidi ren*) they waylaid in the mountains. In the past these nomads had occasionally stolen a head or two of livestock, leaving people unharmed, but since the beginning of the jihad the herdsmen had greatly escalated the violence of their attacks. Jahāngīr sought the assistance of these Kirghiz in his campaign against Qing rule in Xinjiang, and when Kirghiz presented him with scalps, the attached queue sufficed to prove that the unfortunate victim had indeed been a "Chinese" infidel.[23]

Intermarriage, Fraternization, and Rape

As in any military occupation where large numbers of alien troops are stationed in the midst of a civilian population, sexual relations between the occupying force and local women could be an explosive source of discontent in Xinjiang. This was demonstrated soon after the Qing conquest, when Su-cheng's molestation of East Turkestani women proved a principal factor behind the 1765 rebellion in Ush. In Altishahr, the delicacy of the situation was exacerbated by the fact that not until after 1831 did the Qing permit garrison troops or Chinese merchants to be accompanied by family members. It is thus no surprise that Qi-shi-yi should comment on the plentitude of prostitutes in Kashgar.[24]

Xinjiang authorities viewed intermarriage and fraternization between native East Turkestani women and men of various other groups in Xinjiang as threatening to security. Marriage between Kokandi merchants and East Turkestani women was most common, both before and after the jihad of 1826. In the aftermath of that event, when Nayanceng expelled the Kokandi merchants from Altishahr, he separated them from their wives and forbade such marriages in the future. Song-yun, in his memorial urging the retraction of Nayanceng's disastrous postpacification measures, advised the emperor that Kokandi–East Turkestani marriages should once again be allowed. With the lifting of the embargo in 1831 the merchants returned and were reunited with their wives.[25]

The most serious cases of fraternization with East Turkestani women involved not Chinese merchants but Manchu officials, banner troops, Green Standard soldiers, and exiles enslaved to begs. If we take the behavior specifically prohibited in statutes as a guide to the sort of abuses that actually occurred, then Han soldiers and exiles occasionally took East Turkestani wives. Moreover, both Manchu officials and soldiers brought East Turkestani women into the Qing citadels at night, or spent the night out themselves; some had long-term contractual arrangements with prostitutes. While stationed at the *karun* or while traveling, Manchu soldiers sought female companionship in the East Turkestani villages and towns—a practice that greatly angered the Muslim population.[26]

Because of their powerful position, Xinjiang's Manchu ambans were often able to engage in sexual exploitation; such activity was especially threatening to security on the frontier, as the Ush case made clear. In 1807 Yu-qing was accused of a series of abuses of his position as superintendent of Kara-shahr. Most of these involved extortion and other sorts of peculation, such as misuse of the official price to buy skins and furs from the Torghuts for his personal use. But the investigation also disclosed that Yu-qing had procured a nine-year-old Torghut boy named Manji[27] for his household. During his short time in Yu-qing's yamen, the boy cried each time the amban approached. Although Yu-qing claimed he had only acquired the boy in order to study Mongolian with him and sent him back home soon afterward, the officials on the case suspected the worst.[28]

The most dangerous case of exploitation of East Turkestani women since the Ush affair occurred between 1818 and 1820, just as Jahāngīr began his campaign of incursions into Altishahr. While investigating the cause of the unrest, Qing-xiang discovered that the Qing councillor Bin-jing and a circle of accomplices had been extorting bribes from East Turkestanis. Although Qing-xiang reported that these abuses were unconnected to Jahāngīr, the *Veritable Records* entries warn ominously against revealing the true extent of Bin-jing's crimes to the Muslim masses, lest it turn their hearts against the dynasty. What the *Veritable Records* failed to report (it is unclear whether the court ever learned the full details) was that Bin-jing had "dishonored" the daughter of the Kokand *aqsaqal*, who killed the girl and rushed with her severed head to Bin-jing's yamen to confront the councillor. For whatever reasons, Bin-jing was rapidly removed from the post.[29]

As we have seen, Nayanceng also uncovered several instances of Tungan men marrying East Turkestani women. He separated the couples and forbade the practice; statutes to this effect were thereafter entered into the *Huijiang zeli*.[30] No other specific cases of Han or Tungan marrying East Turkestani women have come to light. Perhaps Chinese merchants, because of their vulnerable position, exercised restraint or simply avoided detection. Still, such associations must have occurred, for the issue arose again in 1846 in diplomatic correspondence between the Qing and Kokand. The Daoguang emperor recalled in a proclamation to the Kokandi *mingbaši*, Mussulman Qulï, that the Kashgar councillor would severely punish Chinese (*zhongyuan ren*) who took East Turkestanis as wives. The Qur'ān prohibits Muslim women from marrying non-Muslims, and thus Mussulman Qulï heartily agreed, adding, "There is no [allowance] for such [marriages] either in the Muslim classics [i.e., the Qur'ān] or in the ways of China. In handling local matters, it would be better if there were no such people." Nai-mai-ti, the Kokandi tax agent in Kashgar, was still more enthusiastic and promised to have "bad Muslim women" (*buhao de Huizi nüren*) bound and brought to his yamen. This was going too far, however, and the emperor, testy about jurisdiction in a city where Qing control over commercial affairs had already been seriously eroded, responded in an edict, "Don't you know the great emperor has local officials, as well as the hakim and other begs, to handle these matters? If ever there is such a woman, they will handle her. There's no cause for you foreigners to tie her up and carry her off. Don't interfere with local affairs."[31] Liaisons between Chinese merchants and East Turkestani women, Xuanzong believed, remained an issue of strategic import in which the dynasty should maintain an active concern, even when the Qing ceded jurisdiction over Kashgar's foreign trade, customs tariffs, and other aspects of commercial affairs to foreign interests.

Chinese Money-lending in Xinjiang

Pawn-broking, money-lending, and selling of goods on credit was a specialty of many north bend traders in Xinjiang, including those trading in areas populated by East Turkestanis and Western Mongols. Such practices easily led to friction between Chinese merchants and the local population and occasionally erupted into violence. Judging from the quantity of such cases, Chinese merchants who engaged in such forms of banking were far more common than those intermarrying with other peoples.

Perhaps because of the devastating effects of Chinese usury in Mongolia, where the rebellions of 1755–58 were to a great degree sparked by popular Mongol enmity toward the Chinese traders to whom they were in debt, the Qing was alert to the potential for similar practices by the Chinese merchants resident in Altishahr. Nayanceng detailed some of the techniques Chinese lenders employed to ensure their profits. In addition to charging high initial interest rates, a favorite trick was the note that came due after a short period—three months or even a week after the loan was made. If the East Turkestanis could not repay the loan, plus interest, by this time limit, the merchant would "change the ticket," refinancing to combine interest and principal into a new, higher loan on which the borrower now owed interest. After a year, these merchants might take houses or land in lieu of repayment for the compounding debt.[32]

Needless to say, in the Southern and Eastern Marches, loans were frequently the cause of disputes. Liu Yingjiang's case is one example. Liu had come from Shanxi to Sanbao, near Turfan, early in the Jiaqing reign. With his uncle, Liu Shisheng, and a third man he opened a drygoods shop in 1804. Over time, he loaned money and extended credit to Hu-da-bai-er-di; because the man was delinquent in repaying, Liu was forced to dun him several times for the debt, which amounted to a little over one tael and three piculs of grain. In 1805 Hu-da-bai-er-di agreed to farm a piece of land by the city moat for Liu for two years as payment of the debt; he then used the land or its proceeds to pay off another debt, enraging Liu Yingjiang, who jumped him one day outside the drygoods shop in town. The two grappled until separated by onlookers.

In the spring of 1806, Hu-da-bai-er-di came to Liu's store. A man named Niyāz, who lived outside of town owed him grain, Hu-da-bai-er-di explained.

If Liu would come with Hu-da-bai-er-di to visit Niyāz he could simply take the grain as repayment then and there. The two rode off, Liu on horseback, Hu-da-bai-er-di on a mule. Near an old beacon tower in a wilderness outside of town, Hu-da-bai-er-di asked exactly how much he owed Liu. Liu dismounted to scratch figures in the sand, and Hu-da-bai-er-di, pretending to go relieve himself, stole up behind Liu, garroted him with a tether-rope, and left the body in a gully. The investigation was hampered by difficulty in identifying this corpse later, as wild animals had ripped off the head and dragged it away, but Hu-da-bai-er-di was eventually caught and himself beheaded.[33]

A similar case arose a few years later in a village outside Kashgar. Liu Wenyuan was owed 2,200 *pul* by an East Turkestani farmer named Ibrāhīm. Liu went to the man's fields to seek repayment, got into a fight with him, and sustained a groin injury from which he died in a few days. Ibrāhīm was sentenced to strangling after the autumn assizes.[34] And around 1850, Liu Xinghu, originally of Shaanxi, died outside Urumchi under similar circumstances. Liu ran a shop outside the lower west gate with his cousin Wang Zhenghai and there they "did the East Turkestani trade" (*zuo chantou maimai*). When an East Turkestani debtor died, the two foreclosed on his debt for nine taels of silver, three piculs of wheat, and two piculs of beans, taking the collateral, a piece of land, in lieu of repayment. Liu and Wang gave the land to two East Turkestanis, Ai-zha-mu-xia and Su-bu-er-gai, who promised to repay the dead man's loan in return. Ai-zha-mu-xia took the loan contract away with him, but many days passed, and he did not return with the money. Eventually Liu rode off to get the contract back. On his return Wang noticed a small cut near his eye, and Liu admitted he had grappled with the two East Turkestanis. By the next day Liu's wound had begun to suppurate, and Wang summoned Ai-zha-mu-xia and Su-bu-er-gai, telling them they would have no cause to beat people up if they simply paid the money they owed. The two agreed to relinquish the land contract. That night Liu's entire face swelled, and he began to groan with pain. A doctor was called, who prescribed some pills. Su-bu-er-gai and Ai-zha-mu-xia returned with the contract the following morning; much chastened by the sight of Liu's condition, Ai-zha-mu-xia even tried to help by draining the wound with a heated china cup, but to no avail. Liu died, and the autopsy determined he had been hit with a wooden object.[35]

Grim indeed were the dangers of infection in nineteenth-century East Turkestan! More than this, however, these cases reveal the extent to which Chinese retail commerce and banking had penetrated East Turkestan's rural communities by the early nineteenth century. Indeed, the shopkeeper and moneylender were often one and the same, selling dry goods as well as lending money and grain to East Turkestanis from villages outside of the cities.

Lin Zexu noted the presence of another such enterprise in 1845, a pawnshop run by Shanxi merchants in a small settlement of mixed Han and East Turkestani population between Karashahr and Bugur.[36]

Resentment at Chinese usury could lead to more serious incidents. About twenty kilometers northwest of Yangi Hisar on the road to Kashgar, in the 1840s there were twenty Chinese shops in an East Turkestani village called Qaraqash. These shops all made high interest, short-term loans, demanding repayment at each weekly bazaar. In early 1845, during a Kirghiz attack on Kashgar, Yangi Hisar, Yarkand, and Khotan, East Turkestanis rebelled in concert with the nomad raiders and killed nineteen of the Han merchants, whose exploitation had earned them the enmity of the locals. When Lin Zexu passed through Qaraqash soon after this incident, the traders' shops still stood empty, a ghostly reminder of the dangers of their former occupants' profession.[37]

When begs became indebted to Chinese merchants, the results could be still more destabilizing. Soon after Wu-er-qing-a first took up his new post as superintendent in Kucha in 1853, his secretary for Muslim affairs presented to him the hakim beg, Mai-ma-si-di-ke, and the other begs and ākhūnds of each village in the Kucha jurisdiction. They explained that they were collectively in debt to the Wan Shun Lei and five other name-brand shops to the amount of 49 silver ingots and already owed interest of 4,260,000 *pul*. The East Turkestani officials originally took out the loan to finance repairs to the *mazar* (tomb complex), public buildings, a bridge, mill, irrigation ditches, post stations, and *karun*, as well as to repay grain debts owed by absconded East Turkestani farmers. (The memorial does not mention this, but the responsibility for these repairs was probably imposed upon the begs by Wu-er-qing-a's predecessor.) Because interest on their debt was accumulating at an alarming rate, the begs pleaded with Wu-er-qing-a to help them refinance. The superintendent refused, insisting that as the problem predated his assignment, he need take no part in its solution. Mai-ma-si-di-ke and his successor, Ibrāhīm, were able to collect 6,965,000 *pul* from the Kucha populace, but continuing exactions to raise the remaining 7,095,000 needed to repay the principal brought the city to the brink of rebellion, and the hard-pressed Kuchaliks went to Yili to file complaints against their begs. These plaintiffs were then sent to the councillor in Yarkand for a hearing, which resulted in an order to the Kucha hakim beg to cease the exactions. He did not, and the people of Kucha rose. Interestingly, although Wu-er-qing-a was cashiered for mismanaging the begs' crisis, the Chinese merchants do not seem to have borne any official blame for this turn of events. In fact, they convinced the government to redeem at least part of their loss: one of the principals in the rebellion, Molla Khoja, owed Guang Taiyi and eleven other merchants a total of over 300,000 *pul* for private loans at the time of his arrest. After the merchants petitioned a captain in the army, He Chaogui, he released 342,000 *pul* of confiscated funds to the merchants. The captain was later punished for this unauthorized dispensation of official property, but the case reveals the increasing influence, even immunity, that Chinese merchants enjoyed by the mid-nineteenth century in Altishahr.[38]

The Growing Influence of Chinese Merchants

Jahāngīr's jihad was the first serious challenge faced by the Qing after 60 years of military rule in Xinjiang. After several years of harassment, in 1826 Jahāngīr organized an invasion and with the help of sympathetic Āfāqī East Turkestanis quickly took the four western cities of Altishahr. The following year a Qing army of around 20,000 troops led by Chang-ling succeeded in putting the Khoja attackers to flight and recovering the cities. Nevertheless, the projected cost of maintaining a sufficient defense force in Altishahr (Chang-ling requested an increase of 8,000 men[39]) worried the emperor, and, hoping to withdraw as many troops as possible, he asked upper-level officials in Xinjiang to consider the alternative of devolving control over these four cities (Kashgar, Yangi Hisar, Yarkand, and Khotan) to native rulers (*tusi*). The response of Kashgar councillor Ulungge (Wu-long-a) summed up precisely the dilemma that plagued the Qing in Altishahr: "If we retain few troops [in western Altishahr], they will be insufficient to defend [the area]. If we retain many, it will be hard to continue financing them."[40] Since the four western cities, hemmed in as they were by hostile foreigners, remained vulnerable, Ulungge thought "the land not worth defending and the people not worth converting to loyal subjects." Rather than "waste useful salaries on useless land," he advocated a retrenchment to the eastern part of Altishahr, which he believed could be much more economically defended. Chang-ling, too, favored granting more autonomy to the western cities and proposed as *tusi* a son of Burhān ad-Dīn named ʿAbd al-Khaliq, whom the Qing had maintained in Beijing for over 60 years. Unlike the Muslim officials employed by the dynasty in Xinjiang, ʿAbd al-Khaliq continued to enjoy the affection of Āfāqīs there, which made this old Khoja the best choice, in Chang-ling's opinion, as native ruler of unruly Altishahr. Having barely concluded a second war with the Makhdūmzāda Khojas, however, the court was not about to deliver western Altishahr over to one of their number. Displeased, the Daoguang emperor stripped both Chang-ling and Ulungge of their ranks (while retaining them in office) and sent Nayanceng to take over the reconstruction effort.[41]

Chang-ling soon redeemed himself in Xuanzong's eyes, however, when Qing forces in Kashgar succeeded in taking Jahāngīr alive. This victory was greeted in the capital with joyous celebration during an otherwise gloomy reign: amid much pomp, the "rebel" Jahāngīr was taken to Beijing for slicing, the generals and their descendants ennobled in perpetuity, and their likenesses enshrined in the Ziguang Ge (the dynasty's gallery commemorating victorious empire builders). Exam questions, moreover, were set celebrating the pacification of the Muslim frontier. All in all, "this heartening victory provided contemporaries with renewed confidence in the imperial power."[42]

In Xinjiang and within decision-making circles of the Qing court, however, the Jahāngīr invasion raised grave concerns that prompted changes in almost every aspect of Qing policy and administration in Xinjiang. For the time being, the court abandoned the idea of retrocession in favor of Nayanceng's more aggressive responses, primarily the trade embargo against Kokand and deportation of the Kokandi merchants from Xinjiang.

In the course of his "postpacification" work in Altishahr, Nayanceng also devoted a considerable amount of time to what he saw as the problems posed by the presence of Chinese merchants in the area. He investigated Chinese merchants for the dangerous forms of interaction with East Turkestanis discussed above: assimilation and abandonment of the queue, fraternization and intermarriage, and rapacious money-lending.[43]

It seems somewhat odd that Nayanceng should in part blame Chinese merchants for the troubles, but his reaction is completely analogous to Mingrui's segregation decree after the Ush uprising. In neither case was there any evidence of direct Chinese merchant involvement, either as provocateurs or coconspirators. But this "round up the usual suspects" approach reflects the fundamental suspicion with which officials in Xinjiang during the first 70 years of Qing rule there viewed the presence of Han and Tungan in regions populated by other peoples.

The cases that Nayanceng brought were entered as substatutes and subsequently published in the *Huijiang zeli*. This small body of laws involving Chinese merchants and Qing soldiers in Altishahr leaves us a record of the normative structure of interethnic relations in Xinjiang under the Qing. The picture that arises from these cases and statutes suggests an imperial state bent on minimizing friction between its subject peoples by reinforcing cultural differences and prohibiting exploitative conduct by military personnel and the Chinese merchants.[44] Moreover, when we recall (see Chapter 4) that in cases involving Han (or Tungan) perpetrators and East Turkestani victims, the Chinese criminals were dealt with according to Muslim law by local begs, it seems that the legal system in Xinjiang was stacked against Han and Tungan from China proper.

By the early nineteenth century, however, Chinese merchants seem to have enjoyed more practical latitude than mere perusal of the laws suggests. We have already seen how Ming-rui's decree segregating Chinese from East Turkestani in Altishahr was never enforced and how, despite prohibitions on usurious loans, Chinese moneylenders in Altishahr cities and rural communities operated with little interference from the authorities, even when debts drove East Turkestanis to murder and mayhem. But the most telling illustration of the strength of the Chinese merchants' position in Xinjiang by the early nineteenth century occurred during the Kokand invasion of 1830, in a little-known incident of open ethnic strife.

A Cover-up in Kashgar

That year, in response to the Qing trade embargo, Muhammad ʿAlī Khan of Kokand staged another invasion of Altishahr, control over which had long been an ambition of the khanate's. The attackers consisted mostly of troops from Andijan and Tashkent, with some Kirghiz tribesmen and a contingent of the "Andijani" merchants whom the Qing had deported after Jahāngīr's invasion of 1826. The khan placed this force under the nominal command of the Khoja Muḥammad Yūsuf, grandson of Burhān ad-Dīn, but real command lay in the hands of Ḥaqq Qulï, the khan's brother-in-law. Soon after the Kokand army moved against Kashgar, Yangi Hisar, and Yarkand in the late summer of 1830, the Muslim sections of these cities fell. When news of the renewed hostilities reached the Qing court, it issued orders to Chang-ling and Yang Fang (whose campaign in 1827–28 had captured Jahāngīr) to return to Xinjiang and once again assume command of the effort to retake western Altishahr. Lengthy logistical preparations for the relief mission were begun in Aksu. Even before the Qing march on Kashgar began, however, early in 1831 Ḥaqq Qulï withdrew on orders from the khan of Kokand, and Yūsuf followed soon after with his men. The Qing citadels in Altishahr never fell.[45]

In midwinter, as soon as the lines of communication with Kashgar had been restored, Yang Fang received some disturbing news from Jalungga (Zha-long-a), the councillor of Kashgar. The text of the dispatch merely reported that the invaders had retreated; Jalungga's real message was conveyed orally by a young Tungan messenger, Chang Fengqing: the Kashgar assistant superintendent, Prince Ishāq b. Muḥammad Hudawī, had conspired with Kokand and planned to turn over the city to the invaders.[46]

This was not the first time rumors had called Ishāq's integrity into question. Two years before, the censor Lu Yixuan had heard accusations that Ishāq had been secretly in contact with Jahāngīr, but that Ishāq had only revealed his intelligence concerning the Khoja leader after Qing victory was assured. Lu heard further that Ishāq had engaged in extortion and colluded with Kashgar moneychangers to profit from exchange rate fluctuations when the Qing army came to town in 1827. Lu heard all these stories from the Kashgar Chinese community whom, he believed, bore no grudges against Ishāq and hence had no reason to slander the Muslim official. But at least one of the Chinese merchants' tales was patently false. They told the censor that Ishāq had ordered his followers to bind his (Ishāq's) hands and feet and lock him in a room during the final days of Jahāngīr's occupation of Kashgar, so that he could claim to the Qing authorities later that the rebels had held him in custody. In fact, Ishāq had only come to Kashgar in 1827 with the Qing army, *after* Jahāngīr and his men had fled. Lu believed all these complaints, however, and suggested that Ishāq be removed from frontier duty; Lu's recommendations were overruled in the capital.[47]

The new allegations were more serious. According to Jalungga's secret report, on returning from a reconnaissance in the mountains in the summer of 1830, Ishāq had spread the false news that a large Qing patrol led by the Manchu officer Ta-si-ha had soundly defeated the Kokandi invaders, when in fact the opposite was true. Furthermore, Ishāq had allegedly urged Jalungga to send out more troops to welcome the returning Qing soldiers home in an attempt to lure the remaining Kashgar banner forces into an ambush. Soon thereafter, Ishāq was supposedly seen in the company of a fifth-rank beg who had been Ta-si-ha's guide during the disastrous mission. A search of Ishāq's yamen revealed Muslims hiding in the yamen buildings and in rooms underground, the messenger told Yang Fang, as well as caches of swords, spears, and other weapons. Jalungga then had the leaders of this evident plot, including Ishāq and his family, held for questioning and put the rest of the fifth columnists to death—their summary executions necessitated, according to Jalungga, by the intense attack already underway from the Kokandi bandits.[48]

Somewhat later, more evidence against Ishāq emerged in Kashgar. Jalungga provided documents alleging that one of the women in Ishāq's Kashgar household had been Jahāngīr's wetnurse.[49] Moreover, a letter surfaced reputedly written by the head of the invading army to Ishāq, claiming that Ishāq and other begs of Kashgar had invited the Khojas to return from Bukhara.

Now I've come, but you haven't kept your word and instead remain in hiding in the Chinese city (*Hancheng*) and haven't come out to greet me. What does this mean? We don't want your land. The big and small ākhūnds say now you're following the Chinese (*zhongyuan ren*). According to the Qurʾān it would be proper for your children to be enslaved. Last night you said several things and had them conveyed to me. Just as you asked, I have waited until today, but again you have not kept your promise. Isḥāq, as a leader you should be true to your word. If you come out, Kucha will be your home. I'll call all your young ones together to be united with you. If you say you have not invited us to come, then what have we come for? I have only come because you and this place allowed it. If by chance what you said does not come to pass, my followers will have your children as slaves. If you come out of the city now, I'll give you your old lands back. We'll go to Aksu, Kucha, Yili! [But] if we take the Chinese city [i.e., by siege, without Isḥāq's assistance], that will be of no benefit to you. You were born a Muslim—why do you insist on being a Chinese (*zhongyuan ren*)? I tell you this according to the rules of Islam. If you have a letter in response, send it out to me.[50]

In 1831 Yang Fang brought these new allegations against Isḥāq to the attention of the court. Perhaps it was imperial sagacity, or perhaps the keen hindsight permitted by the belated compilation of the *Veritable Records*, but in his edict in response the Daoguang emperor expressed doubt at Jalungga's version of events. "Isḥāq may be extremely muddleheaded, but not to this extent." Even if Isḥāq had been a turncoat, it was questionable to whom he could turn. He himself had arranged the ruse that brought about the capture of Jahāngīr two years previously, and as a result the Āfāqiyya hated him.* In

---

* "In 1828 Isḥāq b. Muḥammad Hudawī sent an agent into the mountains with false stories of a Ch'ing withdrawal and bribed Jahāngīr's Kirghiz father-in-law Taylaq, so that the Khoja came back into Sinkiang with 500 men. Realizing that he had been duped, the Khoja fled, but this time the Kirghiz, who feared Ch'ing reprisals, betrayed him, and Yang Fang, a Chinese officer who later played an important role in the Opium War, took him prisoner." Fletcher, "The Heyday," p. 366. Isḥāq (?–1842) was descended from Hudawī (E-dui) of Kucha, who had aided the eighteenth-century Qing conquest of Altishahr. (According to Fletcher, Isḥāq was Hudawī's great-great grandson; Gao Wende et al. and Ji Dachun give the relationship as grandson.) Isḥāq had served as hakim beg in several Xinjiang cities before marching with the Qing army to retake Kashgar in 1827, where he then took up the post of hakim beg. After helping capture Jahāngīr, in 1828 he was appointed assistant superintendent (*bangban dachen*), the first such native appointment to the Qing military government since Iskandar in the eighteenth century. Fletcher, "The Heyday,"

return for this service, the Qing had granted him the noble title of "prince" (*junwang*), the right to wear the queue, and the position of assistant superintendent—a Qing military post with more authority than that of hakim beg, including the right to memorialize the throne. Isḥāq thus seemed to have thrown his lot in firmly with the dynasty. Isḥāq's son Aḥmad (Ai-ma-te), hakim beg of Aksu, donated grain and horses to assist the 1830 war effort and seemed greatly concerned about the welfare of his father in Kashgar. Thus the emperor doubted the conspiracy theory and cautioned Jalungga that he would be held personally responsible for Isḥāq's safety. At the same time, Xuanzong ordered Chang-ling to proceed to Kashgar and get to the bottom of the affair.[51]

The Kashgar Massacre

It was only after long investigation and reinterrogation of witnesses that Chang-ling uncovered what had really happened in the Qing cantonment during the siege of Kashgar. Chang-ling memorialized with his full report in September of 1831.[52]

Over a year earlier, Han and East Turkestanis in the Kashgar hinterland began to pick up hints of impending invasion by the Kokandis. Gao Si, a merchant doing business in the village of Halalike heard early in 1830 of a plot to attack Kashgar. He returned to the city and reported to Councillor Jalungga, but the Manchu ignored his story and sent him back home within the Pass as a punishment for rumor mongering. This dismissive treatment frightened other merchants, who thereafter failed to report the similar stories they heard out in the villages.

By September 1830, the invasion had begun in earnest. Early in the morning of the 25th, Ta-si-ha led 1,600 cavalrymen out to meet the enemy. When a day passed with no word from this force, Jalungga sent his Tungan messenger Chang Fengqing (who apparently spoke Turki) out in East Turkestani dress to reconnoiter; Chang encountered a small party of Isḥāqīs* and a Qing soldier who told how the Qing cavalry had been ambushed by the Kokandis,

---

p. 364; Gao Wende et al., *Zhongguo minzu shi renwu cidian*, p. 150; Ji Dachun, "Yi-sa-ke," in *Xinjiang lishi yanjiu* 1985, no. 2:89; Lu Yixuan, LFZZ MZSW 1294, DG9.2.13.

* As adherents of the Isḥāqiyya faction of the Naqshbandiyya, and rivals of the Āfāqiyya Khojas, the Isḥāqī or "Black Hat Muslims" generally sided with the Qing during Jahāngīr's jihad and the Kokandi invasion. Despite the coincidence of names, Isḥāq b. Muḥammad Hudawī was not connected to the Isḥāqī branch of the Naqshbandiyya. See Fletcher, "The Heyday," p. 364, n. 20.

and his own unit of 40 men cut off and eradicated. Chang hastened back to Kashgar on the 28th with the bad news.[53]

The Kokandis had routed the Qing detachment. Jin-li-bu, a private from a Sibe battalion, was taken prisoner and while in captivity overheard one of the Kokandis surmise that Kashgar would fall easily, since Ishāq would help from within the walls of the citadel. Later, Jin-li-bu was put under guard by men who told him privately that they were "Black Hats" (Ishāqīs) captured during the jihad four years earlier. Their leaders had received eight communications from Ishāq in the intervening period, they said, each promising aid if they would invade Altishahr. The Ishāqī guards gave Jin-li-bu a horse, a bow, and arrows and helped him escape back to Kashgar to warn Jalungga about Ishāq's fifth column activities.

While returning to the city on the twelfth, Jin-li-bu encountered Ha-long-a and Ishāq on patrol. The East Turkestani prince burst into tears upon hearing Jin-li-bu's story, saying it was a plot to frame him. He had already moved his family into the Manchu fort, Ishāq pointed out. Why would he have done that if he planned to betray the city? Later, back in Kashgar, Ishāq grew even more nervous. To Fu-long-a, a Sibe platoon commander, he confided that the relatives and entourage of a Colonel Lai Chonggui, lost with Ta-si-ha, blamed him (Ishāq) for the ambush and were out for his blood. Fu-long-a denied this and tried to reassure Ishāq. "We Manchu soldiers will protect you," he told the prince. Ishāq thereupon gave Fu-long-a and his men three good firearms to use in the upcoming battle—or perhaps to defend Ishāq himself. The next day Ishāq moaned to another officer, surnamed Gui, "This is awful! The people in the city all want to kill me. (*Buhao le! Chengnei de baixing yao sha wo ne!*)" "All of heaven rests on our heads," Gui replied. "And now you add this."[54]

While Ishāq fretted over his precarious position, the Qing city of Kashgar prepared for an onslaught. On the 28th, Chinese merchants began to move inside the cantonment from the Muslim city or from their shops and houses outside the walls. Jalungga realized that, even after recalling all the troops from the Muslim city and a fort on the nearby river, he had only 1,800 bannermen and Green Standard troops remaining—an insufficient number against the sizeable Kokandi army. So he organized the Chinese merchants into militia units of 50 men, each under a merchant headman.[55]

That day and the next, about 200 Ishāqī East Turkestanis, farmers, ākhūnds, and begs who had supported the Qing during Jahāngīr's attack four years earlier brought their dependents to seek sanctuary within the Qing cantonment where with the councillor's approval they gained admission. Some of the Black Hat farmers had brought weapons and agricultural implements, but all were voluntarily disarmed before entering the city. The gates were shut, the city secured, and the merchant outbuildings surrounding the walls torched to clear the line of fire.[56]

The following day, September 29th, the Chinese merchants began to grow concerned about the numbers of East Turkestanis within the cantonment. One owner of a Shaanxi name-brand shop went to the yamen compound of Assistant Superintendent Isḥāq to retrieve a saddle he had lent to a young East Turkestani. He noticed the large number of "Muslims" present and reported to the councillor. Liu Shaojun, manager of a Shanxi name-brand store, dropped by the yamen to borrow a wok to cook in—he had not had time to get together such items before fleeing into the cantonment. In the yamen he too noticed many East Turkestanis, one of whom was having his head shaved. With bandits at the gates why would a man be shaving himself bald? He must be cutting off his queue and planning to rebel, Liu concluded with alarm and rushed to notify the councillor's yamen. Jalungga sent a Manchu secretary and then a Green Standard deputy to investigate. They counted 192 begs and other East Turkestanis in Isḥāq's yamen, whom they divided up and put under separate guard. They also had a large number of horses driven out of the yamen compound.[57]

The Kokandis had already occupied the Kashgar native city, and they attacked the Qing cantonment that afternoon, only to withdraw after several fusillades from the Qing battlements. Just before sunset, three or four Chinese merchants approached Jalungga on the parapet. Someone named Hama-wa-zi and others were hidden in Prince Isḥāq's yamen, they said, and they requested leave to go find them.

"What's the point of catching just two or three bandits (*fei lei*)?" Jalungga asked, and though the merchants failed to respond, he granted them permission to "go ahead, but whatever you do don't cause any trouble (*nao shi*)."

Before these men descended from the wall, however, a tumult arose from the direction of Isḥāq's yamen below, where a crowd of several hundred Chinese merchants had gathered. Jalungga sent Jin Jixian, his correspondence secretary (*yinfang zhangjing*), and a Manchu clerk, Feng-shan, armed with a pennant-arrow,* to quell the disturbance. Jin and Feng-shan managed to head off the mob in a narrow alley leading to Isḥāq's residence and ordered them to disperse. Just then, a foot soldier named Yan Xi emerged from the Muslim prince's yamen at a run, shouting "Bandits (*you zei*)!" The crowd surged past the two Qing functionaries and into the compound, where they attacked any East Turkestanis they could lay hands on. Seeing that the secretary and

---

* The *lingjian*, a triangular flag attached to an arrow, served as a token of conferred official authority.

Manchu clerk were unable to stop the riot, a soldier, Wei Qiming, seized the pennant-arrow and brandished it from a spot beyond the press.

"There's no need to fight!" Wei shouted. "If you're going to riot like this, you'd better kill me first."

"They're all bandits!" the merchants shouted back. Wei ordered them to leave the East Turkestanis for Qing officials to investigate in an orderly fashion, but as he was talking, several East Turkestanis were murdered before his eyes. Three terrified begs, including the hakim beg of Yangi Hisar, and several dozen common Muslims clustered around Wei, begging him to save them. Wei managed to escort them out of the prince's yamen and to the commissary office, where they would be safe—or so he thought. Wei returned to the city walls to defend against the renewed Kokandi onslaught. Later he learned that two of the begs he had saved had been lynched during the night.

Not long after Wei left the mayhem in the Ishāq's yamen, Ma Tianxi, a 51-year-old Tungan brigade commander from Ningxia, arrived on the scene from his post on the walls. Many in the crowd respected "old master Ma" (Ma *da laoye*) and listened as he exhorted them to desist from slaughtering the East Turkestanis.

"You say these Muslims are rebelling, but that's hard to know for sure. Go defend the city—this rioting will not do." After some time he managed to disperse the merchant mob and returned to oversee the city defense.[58]

While Ma, Wei, and the other regular military personnel were occupied fending off the Kokandis throughout the night, a Chinese mob again attacked Ishāq's compound. They pulled the East Turkestanis from haystacks and ice cellars, killed over 200 of them, and set fire to buildings. Ishāq, however, escaped, for Jalungga had early on sent men to smuggle the assistant superintendent and his family to safety in the councillor's quarters. But the merchant gangs continued to search for evidence that would substantiate the rumors of a plot to betray the cantonment to the Kokandis. Stories circulated about what they found: arsenals of guns, stacks of firewood "for burning down the yamen," a mysterious "nine dragon bag," and a magical mirror that rendered its user invulnerable. But depositions later revealed that no one had seen any of these items, except the firewood, firsthand. Nor could anyone confirm that the East Turkestanis had been armed or had wounded Chinese merchants or Qing soldiers. Some of the merchants did stumble upon Ishāq's wardrobe, however, and carted off the expensive silks. Others looted a stash of trade goods belonging to Liang Dashou, a merchant who had come to Kashgar to get back some money Ishāq owed him. While in the city, Liang had taken the opportunity to buy up stock to bring back to Yili. Because he was staying in the prince's yamen, the merchants who stole his goods and money accused Liang of supporting the "bandits." They dragged him off to the Guandi Temple, where they were about to string him from a crossbeam when word came that the Kokandis had renewed their attack on the city. Liang was released and took sanctuary in the barracks of the Manchu bannermen.[59]

The Chinese merchant community in Kashgar clearly distrusted and harbored a grievance against Isḥāq, despite censor Lu Yixuan's belief to the contrary. In their testimony before Chang-ling's tribunal, some of the participants in the events of September and October 1830 mention overhearing merchant complaints against the East Turkestani assistant superintendent. For example, Isḥāq had supposedly confiscated stocks of tea from the Chinese merchants to prevent them from trading in violation of the embargo and then secretly sold the tea to Kokand himself.[60]

Other sources of discord lay in the Chinese merchants' perception of Isḥāq's role in two past incidents. Early in 1830, Qing authorities in Altishahr had grown concerned about the number of "vagrants" in the region who had accompanied the Qing army from China proper in 1826. Mostly porters or foot soldiers, they had remained behind in considerable numbers when the Qing force returned east. Jalungga received court approval to round up these men and send them home along the post road to Jiayu Guan, providing them with accommodations and a catty of noodles at each post station. As we saw in Chapter 5, many merchants in Kashgar had arrived there in 1826 or 1827, often under circumstances strikingly similar to those of the "vagrants." Some may themselves have barely escaped this forced repatriation. For some reason, "the masses of Chinese" blamed Isḥāq for this policy and "used the claim that he was a traitor as an excuse to loot and kill."[61]

The second incident was an attempted robbery of Isḥāq's yamen sometime in the winter of 1828–29. A group of Han planned the raid, but Jalungga learned of the plot and apprehended the six ringleaders. During the night of the massacre, one of the Chinese merchants involved was overheard saying, "Last year we wanted to rob Isḥāq's house. The councillor [Jalungga] found out and punished six of us. You think this time we can let him [Isḥāq] off?"[62]

A DARK DAY FOR "BLACK HATS"

But there was more behind the Kashgar massacre than simple animosity toward Isḥāq, even fueled as it was by rumors of the prince's treachery (rumors that may well have grown from disinformation planted by Kokand in Jin-li-bu and others). The Chinese merchants knew that large numbers of Han and Tungans had perished when Kashgar fell in 1826,[63] and they vented their fear and anger at all East Turkestanis within the cantonment. The merchants did not care to distinguish between Afāqī and Isḥāqī, or even recognize that such a distinction existed. The indiscriminate nature of this violence is well illustrated in the massacre's sequel.

After their determined assault of the 29th, the Kokandis fell back, content to besiege the Qing fort while plundering the old city of Kashgar.[64] Fighting resumed after a brief truce. The Qing soldiers and merchant militia launched several successful sorties over the following weeks and held the city until November 25th, when the Kokandis abruptly disappeared.[65] Wary of a trap, the defenders remained on alert and kept the city secured. On the 27th a group of Isḥāqī East Turkestanis approached the western side of the cantonment, unarmed, bearing gifts of sheep, noodles, eggs, melons, and liquor. They identified themselves as "Black Hat Muslims" and said they had come to offer their congratulations to the amban and the dynasty for successfully withstanding the siege. As the cantonment gates were still shut, the merchants on the walls hoisted these visitors one by one up six meters onto the rampart. As each reached the top, he was taken down out of sight and killed. One of the militia headmen informed a Manchu officer about these goings-on; the officer proceeded to the scene of the killing with a Manchu clerk and, once again, the pennant-arrow. The militia, intent on slaughter, again paid no heed. When Jalungga heard about these killings, he simply conveyed the message, "There's no need to kill them; just take a few alive for questioning." One East Turkestani managed to shout out, before he fell under the knife, that he had saved the lives of several Chinese civilians and soldiers. He then produced a list of their names. Only when these men were summoned and had verified his story was the man released. Finally, a Han who had been trapped in the Muslim city during the siege and had only recently been hoisted into the cantonment himself went to Jalungga and tearfully attested that his own life had been saved by an Isḥāqī and that the merchant militia were thus killing many good Muslims. Jalungga then sent men to stop the carnage, but only after 70 or 80 Isḥāqī men had perished. Later, a lynch mob consisting of "soldiers and people" gathered around the guardhouse where three "Black Hat Muslims" who had been taken alive were locked up. The councillor had men restrain the crowd, saying he still wanted to interrogate the prisoners, but the mob disregarded the councillor's orders and killed the three anyway.

On November 29th, Jalungga sent Chang Fengqing to Yang Fang in Aksu with his message accusing Isḥāq of treason.[66]

MERCHANT INFLUENCE AND JALUNGGA'S QUANDARY

Why did Jalungga cover up this murderous insubordination by the Chinese merchants in Kashgar? Why did he permit it in the first place? Were not the loyal East Turkestanis equally Qing subjects? Ha-long-a, a witness to the bloody events in the city who was also privy to some discussions in the councillor's yamen, analyzed Jalungga's predicament in the following way: the Chinese community (*minren*) in Kashgar hated the prince hakim beg Ishāq, and after Jalungga punished the six Han involved in the raid on Ishāq's yamen earlier in the year, they hated the councillor as well. In the heat of the battle against Kokand, Jalungga had dared not prosecute the merchants for murdering the begs in Ishāq's yamen—he needed their support in the defense of the cantonment. So grateful were the merchants for this leniency that they fought especially bravely. Thereafter, the councillor "loved the merchants dearly." Moreover, it was well known to all soldiers, officials, and commoners in the cantonment that "at this time, the battle to defend the city was *in the complete control of the masses of Han, and not that of the councillor*" (emphasis added).

After the Kokandi retreat, however, Jalungga had to explain to his superiors why Ishāq's yamen had been sacked and burned and how so many East Turkestanis had died within the walls. He found these circumstances exceedingly "difficult to memorialize" (*nanzou*). Because no solid evidence of a plot to betray the Qing city had emerged, Jalungga was forced to suborn witnesses to construct a version of events that justified the merchants' pogrom of East Turkestanis in the besieged cantonment and concealed his own negligence.[67]

Chang-ling penetrated Jalungga's deception and memorialized the throne with the more accurate version of events on which the above narrative is based. The Daoguang emperor meted out the sentences in an edict of August 1831: Jalungga was indicted for failing to obtain advance intelligence of the invasion and thus sending Ta-si-ha and the detachment of cavalry to their deaths; for mismanaging the defense of Kashgar, allowing all the begs to take cover in the Qing cantonment and abandoning the Muslim city to the enemy; for standing by "with hands tied and no plan" as the Han mob rioted; for coddling (*guxi*) these traitorous Chinese (*jianmin*) after the siege ended; and for crediting tales disseminated by bandits, filing a false charge of treason, and memorializing without substantiation. Jalungga "really should be executed in front of the army as a warning to the forces or brought to Beijing for interrogation followed by capital punishment," the emperor opined. "This is really what his crime deserves." But in the end he treated Jalungga leniently in recognition of his service in withstanding the Kokandi siege for three months and postponed his execution until after the autumn assizes. Jalungga did not live to be executed, however; after two months in the cangue in Aksu he died of disease.

Ishāq, although vindicated by Chang-ling's investigation and therefore allowed to retain his ranks and honors, clearly could no longer serve viably in

Altishahr. Xuanzong summoned him to live in Beijing, along with his young-est son, Mai-ma-te. His other son, Aḥmad, enjoyed a long career as Aksu hakim beg.[68]

The Chinese merchants in Kashgar resented the manner in which the case was handled, grumbling that "if Isḥāq is punished [as well as Jalungga] then that's all right. If not, then all the Han (*minren*) are willing to support Jalungga in suing for redress (*da guansi*)." Despite this unrepentant attitude and despite the fact that Jalungga was in part being punished for his failure to deal harshly with these same merchants, the court decided to let them off with a warning. The emperor pronounced: "As for the Han in Kashgar, who when the bandits surrounded the city madly spread rumors, stole property, slaughtered the innocent and who are lawless in the extreme, fundamentally speaking they should all be executed. But given that they have participated in the three-month defense of the city and have earned merit, let them not be killed. In the future, let them settle peaceably in each locality. If they dare to raise the slightest trouble, no matter in what regard, they shall be executed."[69]

Chang-ling, as well as Bi-chang, who was transferred to Kashgar from Yarkand to fill in as councillor pro-tem after Jalungga's dismissal, likewise saw fit to mollify the Chinese merchants. The ambans therefore assembled the merchant community in order to allay their concerns. After promising to reward those who had fought most valiantly, Bi-chang added, "Like me, you've suffered greatly defending your city. . . . Let the common [Han] people ship goods to the neidi; let soldiers ship goods here to make a profit. As for the mistaken killing of Muslims, that was basically a case of picking out the traitors in your midst. You are not guilty in this." Only after thus "settling the people's hearts" (*ding minxin*), Bi-chang believed, could the work of recon-structing the burned-out Muslim city and damaged Qing cantonment begin.[70]

The Defense of Yarkand and Khotan

Bi-chang's own recent experience during the Kokandi attack on Yarkand was surely one reason he was well disposed toward Chinese merchants in Alti-shahr. Han and Tungan played important roles defending Khotan and Yar-kand as well as Kashgar; in Yarkand their spontaneous participation resulted in an early and decisive victory for the Qing.

In Yarkand, predominantly Isḥāqī territory, it was not a foregone conclu-sion that the native populace would support the Kokandis. In fact, the Qing authorities bargained for the people's neutrality. Bi-chang describes how the population of the Muslim city was briefed for the upcoming attack.

> A-bu-du-er-man and the ākhūnds conveyed an edict [to the East Turkestanis]. "If you don't obey the bandits, the bandits will kill you. If you obey the bandits, the officers and troops [of the Qing] will kill you. You're dead in either case." The masses, frightened and weeping, prostrated themselves on the ground. The edict continued, "You should seek life out of death: if the rebels come to meet with you, tell them this time the [Qing] military is formidable and you dare not go along [with the Kokandis]. You can shut yourselves in the Muslim city and watch our side kill the bandits.[71]

With the East Turkestanis secured in the old city of Yarkand under orders not to emerge on penalty of death, the Qing military garrison and Chinese merchant community took up stations within the fortified cantonment one kilometer to the west. Due to the large size of the Kokandi army (reported at 10,000, although this is perhaps an exaggeration), Bi-chang and the other Qing officers decided to weather the attack from within the walls and not send out sorties. When the Kokandis came within range, they were met by a withering barrage of cannon and small arms fire from the parapet, which killed many of their number. The rest fled in confusion to the bazaar by the southern gate of the cantonment. From here Chinese merchant shops and residences extended toward the Muslim city; the Kokandis set these structures on fire.

> At this time, the merchants had all taken refuge within the [new] city, but when they heard that the rebels had destroyed their houses, they grew fierce, wanting to sally forth and join arms. Judging that the people's spirit could be useful, we opened the south gate. They emerged quietly and took formation on the bridge [spanning the moat]. On signal, they attacked as one. As their wills strengthened, they grasped their weapons firmly and charged left and right, crossing the bridge to meet the enemy head-on and kill him. Their shouts rattled heaven, and severed heads lay strewn over the ground. There was not one merchant who was not a match for 100 [Kokandis]. The bandits scattered and fled into the Muslim city, remembering that the Muslims in the past had accepted their covenant.

This time, however, the Yarkandis resisted; men and women fought in the streets, driving the invaders out of the city and taking 300 prisoners. Later the Qing had the East Turkestanis kill a few of these captives, to prove that the Yarkandis had truly been fighting with the Qing and were not engaged in a subterfuge.[72]

Although there were further skirmishes with bands of invaders in the countryside around Yarkand, the city was safe after this event. The Qing rewarded the East Turkestanis with 4,000 taels, distributed by the ākhūnds. Meritorious Chinese merchants as well as East Turkestanis were commended and awarded the blue feather for their bravery. The regular Qing military was chagrined at having remained within the cantonment during the crucial battle. "After this, officers and troops, Han (*min*) and Muslims (*Hui*) were joined into a single entity."[73]

Merchant auxiliaries were important in the defense of Khotan as well. Shu-lun-bao reported from that city that the wall there was defended by merchants and exiles answering to Han officers, as well as by East Turkestani troops under the command of the hakim beg.[74]

The Shift in Qing Ethnic Policy

Although the amity achieved by the effective resistance in Yarkand stands in stark contrast to the divisiveness of the Kashgar massacre, the experiences of both cities are similar in two respects. First, in both Kashgar and Yarkand, Chinese merchants assumed a leading role, taking upon themselves primary responsibility for the city defense (in Khotan, too, their contribution was important.) Although the merchant militia mutinied in Kashgar and merely took initiative in Yarkand, both examples illustrate the strength of the Chinese merchant communities in numbers and in influence with the Manchu authorities.

This leads to the second similarity, the physical location of the merchants during the attack. Theoretically, Han and East Turkestanis all were Qing subjects, and the legal system and official attitude of Qing officials up to this time seems on its surface to have been aimed at protecting East Turkestanis at the expense of Chinese merchants. When faced with invasion, however, like the panicky merchants of Kashgar, the Qing government displayed an implicit distrust of East Turkestanis and left all but a chosen few begs outside the forts, at the mercy of the invaders. Han and Tungan traders, on the other hand, were welcomed into the fortified parts of the city. While this is hardly surprising, given traditional East Turkestani support for the Makhdūmzāda Khojas in Altishahr[75] and the local assistance that Jahāngīr's jihad had garnered, it is significant that despite Gaozong's olympian pronouncements on the "great unity" of the five peoples that composed the Qing empire, in practice, by Daoguang times the interests of Qing officials and Chinese merchants in Altishahr had all but converged, at the expense of East Turkestanis.

Turkestan Reunions

Qing recognition of the Chinese merchants' strategic import in Altishahr led to a major shift in the dynasty's policy toward Han migration to the Southern March. The Qing had encouraged merchants to trade in Altishahr from as early as 1759 but did not allow them to bring their families and settle permanently in the southern part of Xinjiang. However, after the incursion of 1830 revealed the bankruptcy of Nayanceng's reforms and the continued military vulnerability of Qing rule in the area, the court approved permanent migration of Han merchants and began to establish Han agricultural colonies in Altishahr.

This change in imperial policy evolved in the context of a high-level debate over post-Jahāngīr Xinjiang, a debate that revisited the same issues about the costs of empire and Xinjiang's place in the realm first raised in the Qianlong reign (and discussed in Chapter 1). Immediately following the Jahāngīr invasion, it will be recalled, Ulungge had proposed retrenchment from western Altishahr. He was rebuked for the idea in 1827, but, even before the conclusion of the campaign against Muḥammad Yūsuf and Ḥaqq Qulï, the argument reemerged, this time in a memorial from E-shan, the governor-general of Shaanxi and Gansu. Echoing Ulungge's comment of three years earlier that current Qing policy amounted to "using the dynasty's useful expenditure on useless wasteland," E-shan advocated selecting loyal, capable hakim begs as *tusi* chiefs to rule Kashgar, Yangi Hisar, Yarkand, and Khotan and defend the frontier in their own right. In his return edict, the Daoguang emperor, Xuanzong, left the question of retrenchment open. The idea was not entirely dismissed even in 1838, when a detailed field survey by En-te-heng-e determined that a viable line of defense could not be established at Aksu and that retrenchment would simply leave Yili and Urumchi vulnerable to aggression from the west while realizing no actual savings. Indeed, in expanded form, the famous debate in the 1870s over defending continental versus maritime frontiers was simply the continuation of these earlier discussions of Xinjiang retrenchment.[76]

Perhaps to make amends for his impolitic suggestion, Ulungge put forward another idea late in 1827. He proposed that the troops stationed in Altishahr on three-year tours of duty be replaced by soldiers settled there permanently with their families in order to improve morale and realize fiscal savings. Moreover, Chinese merchants and farmers should likewise be allowed to bring dependents to Altishahr and farm unused land. Chinese settlers would expand the tax base and eventually could fill vacancies in the Qing army in Altishahr. "In this way, as the numbers of [Chinese] soldiers and people increase over time, the Muslims' strength will gradually weaken, and naturally they will no longer entertain ulterior aspirations."*

Xuanzong read this proposal but deferred judgment until after Nayanceng had arrived in Kashgar and could confer with Ulungge. Nayanceng, of course, had his own ideas about what should be done. For one thing, he saw Chinese merchants as part of the problem in Altishahr, not the solution. And he believed commercial schemes (commissaries and the tea transit tax) could finance a force of up to 10,000 troops in the region. Ulungge's suggestions were shelved.[77]

In the aftermath of the 1830 invasion, the dynasty decided against retrenchment and hoped to avoid further costly emergency outlays (the rescue campaign in 1830–1831 had cost 8 million taels) by strengthening its permanent force in the Southern March to around 15,000 cavalry and infantry. This increase was financed by a 2 percent across-the-board cut in Green Standard allocations in the provinces of China proper.[78]

Although the court had chosen yet again to grit its teeth and bear the expense of extended empire, it continued to seek ways to make Xinjiang more fiscally self-reliant. Thus officials reconsidered the question of the Chinese merchants, who had provided a valuable supplement to the regular military in Altishahr—in both Kashgar and Yarkand they had in fact proved more effective than bannermen or Green Standard troops. The court began to entertain new proposals to grant permanent residence in Altishahr to Chinese merchants, farmers, and their dependents as a means of consolidating Qing rule in the region and expanding the tax base.

The first such suggestion came early in 1831, when Yu-lin proposed extending the system of state farms worked by soldiers and farmers with their families in the Eastern and Northern Marches to the western four cities of Altishahr. Chinese merchants should be encouraged to settle by the post stations in the west of Altishahr, Yu-lin argued, in order to protect the lines of communication should Kashgar, Yarkand, Yangi Hisar, and Khotan be attacked or rebel again. (The Dolans on the *taizhan* had rebelled in sympathy with the invaders in both 1826 and 1830.) These Chinese merchants should, moreover, be allowed to bring family members.[79]

---

* This is precisely the strategy of which Uyghur and Tibetan separatists accuse the government of the P.R.C. today.

Yu-lin's proposal was superseded by a more wide-ranging reform enacted later in the year. In an edict responding to a memorial by Chang-ling, the Daoguang emperor acknowledged the role of Han (and Tungan) natives of China proper in the defense of Altishahr: "Even the Muslim masses know that the majesty of the military and the strength of the [Chinese] people (*bing wei min li*) is in fact sufficient to defend the region." Xuanzong approved Chang-ling's proposal to allow Han families to come to western Altishahr to farm unused land and even rent land from East Turkestanis, so long as the new farms did not interfere with the livelihood of native Muslims. If this plan proved workable, then the emperor envisioned replacing Green Standard troops, as they rotated out of the south, from this new migrant population, toward an eventual goal of one-half locally settled soldiers and one-half rotating troops. "Naturally, the fiscal savings will not be small."[80]

Once the precedent was set permitting Chinese from within the Pass to settle permanently in western Altishahr, "merchants" (many of the aspiring farmers) elsewhere in Xinjiang pressed for the same privilege. In Karashahr, the Tungans at the post stations and the merchants in Karashahr city proper, who had all been living under conditions of forced bachelorhood, had by 1835 seen many families of "north bend merchants" traveling past, bound for new homes in Barchuk (between Aksu and Yarkand). This spurred them to raise a petition to bring out their own dependents. They complained that, under current rules, either their children's upbringing or their businesses suffered, since they could not be in two places at once. Karashahr superintendent E-le-jin, after first determining that the Han and Tungan families in Karashahr would have little contact with either the Torghut and Khoshuut Mongols pasturing near the city or with the East Turkestani towns of Bugur and Korla, recommended that the petition be approved.[81]

Thereafter, Chinese merchants in other cities presented similar petitions, citing the precedent of the four western cities of Altishahr. In Tarbagatai, which unlike Yili had never before permitted merchant dependents, merchants with property were allowed to settle with families after 1836. Kucha followed suit later in the year. Its petitioning merchants lived in a walled compound, paid their rent monthly, and had no trouble with the local East Turkestanis. The same principles were applied in 1843 when Chinese merchants in Aksu sought permission. After ascertaining that the merchants involved paid rent (to the government) and after conferring with the local hakim beg, the Qing authorities granted family privileges to traders in this city as well. Chinese merchants in Khotan, Yarkand, Yangi Hisar, Kashgar, Barchuk, Aksu, Karashahr, and Tarbagatai could now be legally reunited with their families. Other Xinjiang cities where Chinese merchants were present in force (such as Yili, Urumchi, and points east) had never restricted dependents. By 1843, then, Xinjiang was almost entirely open to permanent migration by Han and Tungans from China proper.[82]

The change in Han settlement policy was closely linked to a massive new land reclamation campaign carried out in Altishahr in the 1830s and 1840s with fiscal and strategic goals. Starting in 1832 the Qing financed irrigation works and established colonies for Han settlers outside the new city in Kashgar and near Barchuk, farther down the Kashgar River. In Kashgar, the "reclaimed" lands were actually the confiscated property of East Turkestanis alleged to have sympathized with the Khojas. The Daoguang emperor was initially somewhat nervous about this new departure.[83] By the early 1840s, however, when Yili General Bu-yan-tai (using the field reports relayed to him by Lin Zexu) promoted reclamation throughout Altishahr, the emperor came to embrace the idea of large-scale Han colonization of East Turkestan. In 1845 the court lifted its limit (previously set at 30 percent) on the numbers of rotational troops allowed to remain in Altishahr to farm after completing their tours of duty. And because there was more newly reclaimed land in the south than people to farm it, exiles, too, were allowed to bring their dependents and settle on the land—likewise a departure from the earlier practice of restricting most exiles to Zungharia. Civil and military officials with exceptional records sending settlers to Altishahr were to be rewarded according to the distance and the number of people they persuaded to relocate. The sentences of cashiered officials who could donate money to the homesteading program were reduced.[84]

Eventually, the Daoguang emperor's zeal for Chinese colonization of southern Xinjiang exceeded even that of Xinjiang officials. In 1844, for example, Xuanzong criticized Aksu superintendent Ji-rui for making 100,000 *mu* of new state-reclaimed land available to local Muslims without memorializing the court first: the emperor had intended the land for Han farmers and their families. The following month, he ordered a halt to reclamation work outside Khotan, pending resolution of these concerns: "Can this piece of land really be opened to cultivation? Will the Muslim households who have been brought in to farm cause trouble in the future? Are there any Han households who could be summoned to reclaim the land?" The emperor only acquiesced to the original plan when Bu-yan-tai informed him that the region in question was "in the middle of nowhere (*pianyu zhong de pianyu*)" and that it was hard enough to force Khotanese Muslims to go, let alone Chinese households.[85]

Because of the distance from China proper, then, the change in settlement policy and the Daoguang period *tuntian* expansion in western Altishahr established sizeable Han colonial footholds only in Kashgar and Barchuk. Farther east, however, new colonies in Karashahr, Turfan, and Hami (where land was "donated" by the jasak prince for the purpose) became home to a considerable influx of Chinese settlers.[86]

As in so many other respects, Jahāngīr's invasion in 1826 and the Kokandi attack led by Muḥammad Yūsuf and Ḥaqq Qulï four years later proved to be a watershed in the ethnic policy the Qing adopted in the region. To be sure, Chinese merchants had been encouraged to trade in Xinjiang from a time immediately following the conquest, and their presence had been welcome inasmuch as it contributed economically to military well-being and as long as it did not encroach upon the East Turkestanis. But Manchu officials like Ming-rui and Nayanceng generally considered Chinese merchants to be predatory by nature, and granting them freedom to travel, reside, and trade in the parts of Xinjiang most densely populated with East Turkestanis was seen as involving an element of risk. The dynasty attempted to contain this risk by maintaining controls on the merchants, such as the pass system, Ming-rui's proposed segregation, and the body of statutes Nayanceng enacted to regulate Chinese merchant behavior vis-à-vis native Muslims.

In the aftermath of the 1830 Kokandi invasion, however, there emerged a new official attitude to the Chinese merchants—now potential farmers—in Altishahr. It was no longer just the goods they brought or tax revenues they generated that justified their presence outside the Pass; their presence in and of itself was now seen to serve a strategic function. Only a few years after Nayanceng accused Chinese merchants of partial responsibility for Jahāngīr's jihad, they enjoyed such influence in Kashgar that they could literally get away with murder. With Qing control over Altishahr threatened, the court as well as officials in the field became eager to accommodate Chinese merchants and farmers in the Muslim regions and less concerned about protecting East Turkestanis from them. By 1838, the fait accompli of the Chinese merchants' presence could itself be used as a strong argument against retrenchment from the western cities of Altishahr:

> Gansu province is a poor place. Impoverished people, ramblers, the unemployed, all come beyond the Pass in search of a livelihood. Moreover, there are no fewer than several tens of thousands of merchants gathered in the cities of Altishahr, trading with the Muslims, with an influence as if joined in a single entity—just as when Kashgar and Yarkand were surrounded in 1830, these merchants resisted the enemy with a will and achieved considerable honor. If we withdraw from the frontier, they would have to be driven back toward China proper. To take a population

of several tens of thousands of frontier drifters, strip them of their livelihoods, and scatter their aspirations would be particularly dangerous.[87]

In 70 years, the Qing government's attitude toward Chinese in Altishahr had evolved away from the wariness reflected in Ming-rui's reflexive urge to segregate after the Ush uprising. Now, the court as well as many officials in the field saw the East Turkestanis themselves as a greater threat to stability in Xinjiang than Han and Tungan merchants from China proper. Chinese traders, moreover, had seized the initiative, effectively circumventing the dynasty's policy to protect East Turkestanis, ignoring with impunity the official status of begs, and securing for themselves the right to reside permanently in Altishahr. We catch a glimpse of the culmination of this process in the observation by a traveler in British employ who described Kashgar in 1860: "The new Chinese Settlement . . . is garrisoned by a Chinese infantry force, numbering 3,000 men. The Chinese shop-keepers, merchants and followers, about 2,000 in number, all reside within the walls. The Kilmak portion of the Chinese force (about 200 sowars), however, have their quarters outside. They are not allowed to live inside, not being trusted by the Chinese."[88] By that date, the Kashgar cantonment had become the almost exclusive domain of Han Chinese—a true "Hancheng"—and the Manchu and other bannermen ("Kilmaks") were banished from their own garrison.

Conclusion:
Toward the Domestication of Empire

My family married me, oh! Off to heaven's far side.
Dispatched to a foreign land, oh! As the Wusun king's bride.
A yurt for a room, oh! A felt for a wall.
Meat serves for my grain, oh! To drink? Kumiss is all.
My homesick heart grieves, oh! To abide here so long.
Were I but a yellow crane, oh! I'd take wing back home.

     Attributed to the "Wusun princess" (Xijun), Han Dynasty

The stones of Dabancheng are hard and flat, hey! The watermelons big
   and sweet,
All of the girls there have long ponytails, hey! And their eyes are
   shiny-bright.
If you want to marry, don't you wed another, hey! You had better
   marry me.
Get your millions in cash, bring your little sister, and drive that horse
   cart here to me!

     "Xinjiang Folksong"[1]

These two different Chinese visions of the exotic, two millennia between
them, reflect the changed sensibilities about the Western Regions following
the Qing westward expansion. The modern Xinjiang folksong, whether au-
thentically Uyghur or not (and the rhythm and melody suggest it is not),
has now joined the canon of popular Chinese folksongs; tropes of long hair,
limpid eyes, riches, and polygamy can now titillate, where images of the life
beyond the Pass only horrified before.

The preceding chapters have described the process that laid the ground-
work for this shift. The Qianlong conquest and establishment of military rule
in Zungharia and Altishahr took place in the context of skepticism from Han
scholars and officials, who saw no point in extending direct rule over lands
they considered barbaric wastelands. They used historical arguments against

expending lives and treasure on distant military campaigns to express opposition to the emperor's imperial endeavors in the far west. In response to this
pressure, the Qianlong court issued repeated justifications of its imperial program, asserting that by advancing the Qing frontiers further north and west,
as opposed to keeping Gansu as first line of defense, the dynasty had in fact
realized great fiscal savings. Having made such claims, the court pressured
the military officials governing the New Dominion to make good on them,
by striving to "use the Western Regions to rule the Western Regions."

Efforts in this regard were only partially successful. The Xinjiang garrisons' needs for grain and livestock were quite rapidly met by opening state
farms in Zungharia and establishing trade relations with the Kazakhs. Salaries
and local purchasing still required money, however, and the military government in Xinjiang thus continued to rely on *xiexiang* silver shipments from
China proper to meet annual needs. Tax levels were kept low in Altishahr to
minimize dissent and demonstrate Qing superiority over the Zunghars and
were primarily applied to the costs of local beg administration. Salt and other
governmental monopolies, important revenue sources in China proper, were
unfeasible in Xinjiang. In order to reduce, if not eliminate, reliance on *xiexiang* silver, then, the court encouraged Xinjiang military officials to under-
take innovative monetary and economic institutions in their districts. These
included collection of East Turkestani tax payments in cotton cloth, for trade
with the Kazakhs up north, and creative shuffling of old tea stocks to provide
for the bannermen. Furthermore, under the imperial mandate against "sticking rigidly to the precedents of China," officials developed an interlocked
network of state commissaries, pawnshops, lumber yards, rental properties,
and endowment funds, the profits from which they applied to extrabudget-
ary needs of the Manchu and Mongol soldiers and their families. Officials
manipulated the complex Xinjiang monetary system and levied commercial
taxes in a manner that far exceeded what was legally permitted their colleagues in China proper.

Official and private commerce thus provided an essential margin of extra
revenues to the Xinjiang government. Whether the state gathered them
through taxation or direct involvement in the market, for the most part these
revenues depended on the activities of Chinese merchants, either as suppliers,
shippers, investment brokers, or sedentary shopkeepers paying government
"rents and taxes." Likewise, loans and cash remittances provided by Chinese
merchants served as a crucial safety net during times of crisis after 1826, since
Qing authorities in Xinjiang were far away from official sources of aid.

The Qianlong emperor had from the start recognized the importance of
Chinese farmers and traders in the business of empire, and he encouraged

them to go to the New Dominion. That importance only grew over the decades. But the presence of Chinese in the predominantly Muslim and Turki-
speaking Western Regions raised problems of local control in a multiethnic
environment.

Although Qing sources never explicitly articulate an ethnic policy as such,
the approach that developed through the first several decades of Qing rule
in Xinjiang reflects what might be called the Qianlong ideology of empire.
Within this scheme, neither Han Chinese nor Chinese culture was granted
privileged position in the Inner Asian parts of the realm. In grand imperial
pronouncements, at least, the loyal Muslims and Mongols of Xinjiang occupied a place in the empire side by side with, or even somewhat superior to
the Chinese. On the practical level, this meant that before the late nineteenth century, the dynasty rarely placed Han Chinese (as opposed to Hanjun
[Han martial] or bondservants) in positions of authority over Inner Asians.
Moreover, while the Qing government permitted and even facilitated Chinese migration and travel to Xinjiang, it monitored their movements with
the road-pass system, prohibited their permanent settlement in the Muslim
south, and attempted to prevent their exploitation of commercially unsophis-
ticated Xinjiang natives. In 1765 Ming-rui suggested mandatory segregation
of Chinese from Muslims in Altishahr urban areas; although in practice no
such plan was implemented, following the 1826 Jahāngīr invasion a rough,
voluntary segregation did result when the western four cities were rebuilt.
Nayanceng believed fraternization across ethnic lines to be a cause of local
unrest and, in his postpacification reforms of those years, developed legal
statutes to limit social interactions of Chinese with Muslims as one means of
preventing future incidents.

The second Khoja invasion, in 1830, marked the beginning of a shift in
Qing policy from official solicitousness for East Turkestanis toward greater
accommodation of the Chinese in Xinjiang. Already the expense of reconquering and protecting the vulnerable four western cities of Altishahr after
1826 had sparked a running debate in the Qing court and among high officials over the intractable security problems posed by Kashgar and the other
western cities. Some Xinjiang ambans, notably Chang-ling and Ulungge, initially advocated a Qing retrenchment, with control over the four western
cities to be devolved to local East Turkestani rulers. Others, in part inspired
by the effectiveness of the Chinese merchant militia during the recent invasions, proposed Han colonization of Altishahr in order to expand the tax base
and provide more men and grain for larger Qing armies in Kashgar and Yarkand. By 1831, the court opted for intensified Chinese colonization, lifting
restrictions on Han settlement in the Tarim Basin, allowing merchants and

homesteaders to settle permanently in the Southern March, and establishing state farms worked by Han soldiers and their families in western Altishahr. Although the numbers of Chinese households who migrated to Altishahr in the years immediately following this policy shift remained relatively small, the dynasty had crossed an important divide in its imperial policy, one presaging a greatly refigured conception of empire.

Epilogue: The Xianfeng Fiscal Crisis

Despite the fiscal margin provided by Chinese economic activity, the Xinjiang government's primary source of revenue remained the biannual shipments of *xiexiang* silver to Xinjiang, which, as was noted in Chapter 2, amounted to around 1 million taels by 1830 and rose quickly over the succeeding decades. Shortage of funds for local use was of course a problem shared by all Qing local administrations, not just those in Xinjiang. But Xinjiang's limited tax base and high degree of reliance on silver from the provinces led to more serious consequences when the silver stipends simply stopped coming following the mid-nineteenth century rebellions in China proper and the imposition of foreign indemnities upon the Qing government. Nor did Chinese colonization of Altishahr prove to be the strategic panacea that proponents of the policy had hoped.

THE SILVER LIFELINE SEVERED

After around 1853, many provinces in China proper, particularly those in the devastated Jiangnan, began to default on their stipend obligations, and silver shipments to cities in Zungharia and Altishahr fell gravely into arrears. Due to this shortfall, in 1854 Yili authorities were forced to halve the pay of officials and Manchu cavalry in order to provide 70 percent of the Manchu infantry's and Green Standard troops' wages and to pay the Solon, Chahar, and Oirat banners in full; by the summer of 1855, all groups were paid at only 30 percent. Tarbagatai received no stipend at all between 1856 and 1861. By 1858, Kashgar and Yangi Hisar had received no *xiexiang* for four years, despite an 1857 attack led by Khoja descendants Walī Khan and Tawakkul. Yili councillor Fa-fu-li entreated the Board of Revenue to send aid and to instruct the governor-general of Gansu and Shanxi to remit the late funds to Altishahr. The board responded that Gansu itself was dependent on funds from other provinces that were themselves overdue. In Yarkand, as the supply of silver *yuanbao* ingots declined, their price on the local market rose from 300–400 *tänggä* to 1,000 *tänggä* around 1860. Foreign traders in the city knew that the troops of the Qing garrison were no longer receiving their pay in silver, but in local coin. By 1860, according to a Board of Revenue estimate, the outstanding stipends owed Gansu and Xinjiang amounted to between 10 and 20 million taels.[2]

Faced with the loss of their principal revenue, Xinjiang officials were left to their own devices. In Yili, officials attempted to compensate by a variety of means. They invested a large amount of official funds with pawnbrokers (see Table 5), but the interest income was still insufficient. Merchant "contributions" between 1853 and 1855 brought in a total of 37,700 silver taels and 300,000 *pul*. Two small copper mines newly opened in the Yili area produced sufficient copper cash to pay 80 percent of the Manchu garrisons' wages. Yili also revived Nayanceng's currency trick (now being implemented throughout China proper) and began minting large denomination, alloyed copper coins (*daqian*), as well as iron coins. Shipments of silk from the Jiangnan had stopped, but Yili was able to sell off several hundred thousand bolts of cotton cloth from storage for 121,400 taels between 1854 and 1855. Ush had saved 10,000 taels from silk sales over the years and drew on this sum in 1855 to make up for shortages in the silver budget.[3]

These were all short-term expedients, however. With the old sources of revenue cut off, cities in Xinjiang, like places in China proper, turned to local commercial and transit taxes to try to prop up their depleted treasuries and replace the steady income the *xiexiang* stipends had provided.

When Gansu first notified Yili councillor Bu-yan-tai in the autumn of 1852 that the provincial *xiexiang* contributions had not arrived that year, he recognized the dire implications of this news. Given the recent deficits run up by the wars in south and central China and the necessity of maintaining a force to defend Beijing, Bu-yan-tai proposed a new tax as a major revenue source not just for Xinjiang, but for the empire as a whole. He suggested that 0.1 tael (1 *qian*) per month be levied on all shops with a signboard in order to tax those sedentary merchants directly affected by neither land taxes nor the new likin local customs tax. He also planned to assess rich money-shops at twice this rate. Such a tax, collected throughout the empire, would raise millions of taels per month, Bu-yan-tai predicted.[4]

Like Šuhede, Nayanceng, and San-cheng, Bu-yan-tai is another example of a Qing official who, when posted to the New Dominion and faced with the budgetary constraints inherent in Xinjiang's fiscal system, turned to the commercial economy for a solution. In essence, his proposal involved extending throughout the empire the tax on shops of sedentary merchants that had long been levied in Xinjiang. His empire-wide scheme was never implemented, of course, but other officials in Xinjiang adopted more modest forms of commercial taxation to substitute for *xiexiang* from China proper.

For example, in 1858 Fa-fu-li introduced a tax on Kashgar's exports of cotton cloth both abroad and elsewhere in Xinjiang. When the proposal was enacted after approval by the Board of Revenue, earnings of one to two *pul* per bolt were explicitly earmarked as "*xiexiang* for officials and soldiers." Military Governor Zha-la-fen-tai hoped such a tax could be implemented everywhere in Altishahr.[5]

The Grand Councilor Peng Yunzhang argued that the Kashgar cloth tax would actually help merchants, since systematized inspection, taxation, and application of official seals would prevent extortion by soldiers at the *karun* and post stations along which commercial packtrains traveled. Nevertheless, as in China proper, local customs taxes in Xinjiang seem to have had a deleterious effect on commerce when adjoining jurisdictions competed for shares of dwindling commercial wealth and multiple taxation squeezed profitability. This was clearly the case with Hami's new internal customs tax (*guanshui*), a form of likin or local customs tax like those being implemented simultaneously in the provinces of China proper.

Hami superintendant Cun-cheng implemented the customs tax in the mid-1850s to help defray some of the costs of hosting official travelers. The complex system (which involved a flat rate per camel or per cart but different definitions of a "camel-load" depending on the value of the goods) had been in operation only seven months before the governor of Gansu and banner commander-in-chief wrote to complain about the effects of the Hami tax on their own jurisdictions and tax base. Gansu's licensed tea merchants were already behind in their payments to the government because of poor sales, the governor explained; he requested that Hami lower its tax rates on tea lest the new tax damage the tea administration and licensing system. Urumchi's commander-in-chief, whose jurisdiction included Turfan, similarly pleaded that Turfani cotton be exempted from Hami customs. Urumchi now taxed Turfan's cotton crop to pay for military grain procurement in the Zhendi Circuit, and the circuit revenues would decline as a result of decreased sales of Turfani cotton in China proper. Cun-cheng eventually agreed to a special rate for tea and cotton caravans, but even after this compromise, the customs tax grossed 10,392 taels between late 1861 and early 1863.[6]

With the outbreak of the Tungan rebellion in Gansu in 1862, however, all three cities lost out. Goods no longer circulated between Xinjiang and Gansu, Shaanxi, or Sichuan. What trade remained between Xinjiang and China proper followed the northern route via Gucheng to Guihua and Zhangjiakou.[7] And Hami, despite the increased burden of expenditures for billeting troops en route to Gansu, received decreased revenues.[8]

DECLINE OF TRADE WITH CHINA PROPER

In fact, Xinjiang's commerce with China proper had been decreasing throughout the decade before the outbreak of the Tungan rebellions. As early as 1850 Sa-ying-a noted that "in recent years" there had been fewer Chinese merchants in Kashgar, bringing fewer goods than formerly. A traveler from India reported to the British government around 1860 that the trade between Yarkand, Leh, and Punjab had declined over "the last 15 years," and that Xinjiang's staple articles of trade, "bullion (gold and silver coins, silver ingots, 'Yamboos' &c.), precious stones, tea, silks, kiriana (valuable drugs, &c.)," were in short supply, with Xinjiang now exporting mostly shawl wool and hashish—products originating in Xinjiang itself. By the late 1850s merchants in the south were "very few," and military officials complained of grain shortages—in the past Chinese merchants had distributed grain from Zungharia and elsewhere to towns of the Tarim Basin. Jade buyers from China proper made it to Khotan until the spring of 1861, and in the year 1860–61 they paid 345 taels in internal customs tax. But later that year there were neither Chinese merchants nor goods from China proper to be found in Khotan; any imports that were available were conveyed by "foreign Muslims" (probably Russian subjects) who journeyed from Aksu.[9]

There are several reasons for the late-Daoguang- and Xianfeng-period decline in the numbers of Chinese merchants in Altishahr. One cause may have been the dangers of operating in a region so prone to rebellion and invasion. Many merchants had died in the 1826 and 1830 attacks on the western cities of Altishahr; others as far away as Urumchi had suffered indirectly when the Qing military commandeered or purchased their grain, livestock, and carts at low official prices. Nor did circumstances improve after 1830. During the 1847 War of the Seven Khojas, the Kashgar *aqsaqal*, together with Kokandi merchants apparently sheltering in the Qing cantonment, opened the gates by night to the invaders, who killed 3,000 Chinese merchants, stole their goods, and carried off their women. When it arrived from Yili and Urumchi 75 days later, the Qing army of Manchu, Sibe, Solon, and Torghut bannermen slew many East Turkestanis in revenge for the massacre of the Chinese traders and settlers, but even so, one imagines few merchants would have hastened to Kashgar after such an event. Even without large invasions, moreover, travel in Altishahr had became increasingly hazardous in these years as the Qing cut back on border patrols and *karun* guards. A caravan of seventeen Chinese merchants was wiped out near Artush, not far from Kashgar, in 1860.[10]

The increased taxation levied on Chinese merchants in Xinjiang by desperate local authorities may have been another factor behind the attenuation of the region's commercial ties with China proper. The plethora of customs duties now owed by merchants traveling from Hami westward would have increased frustration and lowered profits for the long-distance trade.

A British Indian scout in 1860 blamed the shortage of Chinese silver and goods in Yarkand's bazaars on "feuds and dissensions between two Chinese factions, the Majoos and the Kurakhutaees, which have existed for the last 15 years." The Karakhitay had left the Xinjiang stage long before, but the pundit was right that fighting was involved.[11] The primary cause of the decline in the Xinjiang trade was surely the chaos in China proper produced by the Taiping and Nian rebellions, which interrupted supplies of tea, silk, and other goods shipped by private merchants, just as it shut down the Imperial Silk Factories and cut off *xiexiang* stipends.

With stipends from China proper no longer available and Chinese merchants declining in number and wealth, Qing officials in Altishahr were forced to turn increasingly to the East Turkestanis for revenues to feed the garrison troops. This meant allowing the begs to levy new taxes on the native populace, including a new poll tax, a salt tax, a tax on goods sold in the bazaar, and additional levies. The Qing forces were now paid, in some parts of Altishahr at least, by the hakim begs—a trend that boded ill for Manchu power. The authorities also resorted to sale of offices. Chinese merchants and East Turkestanis made contributions and received brevet ranks; those who purchased an office attempted to recover their outlay with exactions from the East Turkestanis.

Such conditions undermined the Qing policy of light imperial taxation that had been in effect in Altishahr since 1759. According to foreign (including Turki-language) accounts, popular discontent with Qing rule heightened through the 1850s, as East Turkestanis grew progressively impoverished from taxes, debt, corvée, and corruption. One French source attests that regularly in Khotan in the 1850s, East Turkestanis indebted to Chinese merchants were thrown into the river.[12]

Furthermore, Qing dependence on local revenue forced officials to give free reign to the begs who could extract it from the populace. For example, in 1857 the Yarkand hakim beg, A-ke-la-yi-du, borrowed over 20,000 taels from Andijani merchants for the defense of the Muslim city from Walī Khan and Tawakkul and then repaid the Andijanis with an advance from Han merchants. Two years later, another beg, Apisi, donated a similar amount after being cashiered. The assistant military governor, Yu-rui, chose not to use this sum to repay the Han merchants, but instead ordered it invested at interest. A-ke-la-yi-du then levied a special exaction (*tanpai*) on Muslim Yarkandliks for 20,000 in silver in order to repay his Chinese creditors. The severity of this demand caused an East Turkestani named Tai-la to attempt suicide. When local ākhūnds petitioned to be exempted from the exaction (Muslim clerics were traditionally exempt from *alban* tax), A-ke-la-yi-du had them put in the cangue. Finally a mob rose in protest; the new assistant governor, Ying-yun, apprehended the mob leaders and had them strangled or beheaded forthwith ("according to the Qur'ān"), without first submitting a request for an imperial judgment as was generally required in capital cases. Fiscal arrangements such as these were clearly not conducive to social stability.[13]

Most ominous was the gradual enervation of the Qing forces in Altishahr. The troops who were permanently settled in the Southern March after the policy shift of 1831 had not proved to be the bastion of Qing strength that Chang-ling and others had originally expected. Far from providing a pool of men to replace rotational troops, the resident Green Standard force was by 1857 in such poor condition that councillor Qing-ying petitioned for the rotational troops presently in Altishahr to be retained on an additional three-year tour of duty. Over the previous eight to ten years, Qing-ying explained, 30 to 40 percent of the settled force had died of disease, and even the healthy ones were now weak and old.[14]

By the time the Tungan rebellions reached Xinjiang, such dire circumstances extended even to bannermen in Yili, formerly the New Dominion's elite force, mere word of whose impending arrival had sufficed two decades earlier to put Kokandis and Khojas to flight. According to a Sibe eyewitness to the 1864 rebellion,

> The Manchus, having lived quietly in cities for a hundred years, lost all their militancy and were physically weakened so much that they could not even pull the bows; the arrows shot by them did not go far and did not penetrate the thickly quilted clothes of the Taranchis. The effeminated Manchu officials neglected teaching soldiers how to use the bows. They dressed fashionably and led a debauched life. In the battle with the Taranchis and the Tungans their bulky clothes hampered their movement. On top of these, the soldiers were starving since there was no food in Hui-yüan ch'eng. . . . The horses of the Manchus were also emaciated from hunger because they could not get fodder. They could not gallop in deep snow. The Taranchis and the Tungans caught the Manchus stuck in snow and killed them.[15]

Soft living may have played a part in the loss of the banners' military efficacy, but it will not explain how sleek Zungharian horses became worthless nags.

More to the point is the observation that the banner rank and file were starving in the walled cities. Deprived of both official and commercial sources of revenue, the defense of the Qing empire in Central Asia now came down to just so many famished men, fumbling with their bows and floundering helplessly astride snowbound horses.

Statecraft Thinkers and Qing Xinjiang

Qing power in Xinjiang was decisively defeated in the 1860s. It has thus always been a bit of a puzzle why, over a decade later, given all its other concerns, the dynasty chose to back Zuo Zongtang's plan to reconquer the troublesome territory. One answer to this problem may be found, however, in the changes of imperial ideology and policy that began in the 1820s and 1830s, when proposals for full-fledged Chinese colonization of Xinjiang first emerged.

Significantly, this new direction in imperial policy reflected ideas from a semiofficial quarter. In 1820, when Qing Xinjiang was still at peace, Gong Zizhen (1792–1841), then a 29-year-old provincial graduate (*juren*), composed an essay calling for Xinjiang to be made a province. Gong had failed the metropolitan examinations twice and was at the time employed at a purchased position as a clerk in the Grand Secretariat. In the essay, Gong addressed a familiar concern: Xinjiang was costing China too much money. But whereas literati critics in the eighteenth century had questioned whether the Western Regions, so expensive to seize and maintain, belonged within the empire at all, Gong favored the inclusion of Xinjiang and explicitly contradicted earlier objections that treasure, effort, or lives expended in the cause of westward expansion constituted waste, toil, or loss. Gong believed that current Qing imperial policy urgently needed reform, but here too differed from earlier critics. It was easy to suggest that the Western Regions be used to rule the Western Regions, he commented, but with the troubles in China proper manifold, and even a province like Guizhou (which had no major military installations) running at a deficit, how could the situation in a remote, strategically vital frontier be expected to be otherwise? Gong thus advocated an initial *increased* investment in Xinjiang, to level land, erect windbreaks, and divert streams for irrigation and to assist large numbers of unemployed Han and idle Manchu bannermen to migrate and establish farms in the region. Once the land was reclaimed, populated with private Chinese farmers, and put under Chinese-style provincial administration, the expanded agricultural base could be properly taxed. Thus, he promised, would "the center give up people to benefit the west, and the west give up wealth to benefit the center."

The return on such an investment would not come for twenty years, Gong predicted, but would be worth the wait.[16]

When first written, Gong's essay was premature; he was not entitled to submit it as a memorial, and it was widely ignored. Its appearance in the 1827 *Huangchao jingshi wenbian*,[17] however, proved timely indeed; in the immediate aftermath of the Jahāngīr invasion, Gong offered a cogent alternative to those proposing retrenchment from western Altishahr. In 1829, when Gong once again took (and, this time, passed) the metropolitan exams, he was able to answer retrenchment advocates directly in his response to an exam question involving frontier policy. Reasoning that Xinjiang's lands had already been incorporated and its peoples made into subjects, he argued that since "center and outer were one family" (*zhongwai yijia*), the situation was unlike that of past dynasties, when distant frontiers could be casually abandoned.[18]

Gong's thoughts on Xinjiang are remarkable for several reasons. While he differs significantly from the earlier (and perhaps contemporary) literati opponents of expansion (he calls them "ignorant scholars with shallow views and degenerate students from squalid hamlets"), he also implicitly repudiates the basis of Qing Xinjiang policy since the Qianlong reign—the maintenance of the territory under military government as a unit distinct from China proper. The bulk of his essay consists of a detailed plan for replacement of Qing military and beg administrative divisions with prefectures (*fu*), departments (*zhou*), and counties (*xian*), each governed by a civil official. In outlining these new administrative divisions, the plan substitutes familiar Chinese or Chinese-style names for the Turko-Mongolian place-names used in Qing official correspondence (Qiangzhou for Yeerqiang, i.e., Yarkand; Langxian for Yurongkashi i.e., Yurongqash; Suzhou/Suxian for Aksu).[19] The military governor, superintendent, banner commander, and other positions in the banner hierarchy were to be abolished, and Manchu and Mongol bannermen would fall under the direct jurisdiction of civil officials. In effect, he proposed dismantling the eight-banner system in Xinjiang. Gong did make two concessions to the elite status of bannermen—they would pay 20 percent less tax than commoners and could not be caned by any official lower than a district magistrate![20]

Gong's essay thus shares a subtext with the eighteenth-century critiques of Qing imperial policy, even while openly propounding an opposite position. Opponents of the Qianlong expansion hinted that the Western Regions were not properly "China" and thus should not be incorporated. Gong argues that the Western Regions must be retained; but he, too, feels they are not "Chinese" enough and proclaims they must be integrated *more* closely. Though he does not make it explicit, there is also an ethnic thrust to his proposal. Not only would Xinjiang be populated more intensively by Han

Chinese; it would be governed by them as well. What civil offices there were already in Xinjiang, such as those in the Urumchi area, were generally filled by Han. In proposing that banner, beg, and jasak government be eliminated and Chinese-style civil administration extended throughout Xinjiang, Gong was proposing the devolution of imperial control from Manchus, Mongols, and East Turkestanis into Chinese hands—the same transition we have seen happening informally in Kashgar after 1830.[21]

Other out-of-office scholars issued proposals on Xinjiang following the 1826 troubles, all opposing retrenchment from the western four cities. Shen Yao (1798–1840), a young Zhejiangese, wrote such an article in 1828. Although Shen was not yet a degree holder (he would never pass the provincial exams), his "Personal Proposal for Xinjiang" (*Xinjiang si yi*) was read by Xu Song, the former Hanlin compiler, Yili exile, co-editor of the *Xinjiang zhilue*, and author of three other works on the New Dominion. Since his return from Yili in 1820, Xu had formed a small but influential salon of scholars in Beijing who shared his interest in frontier studies and taste for mutton. Shen wrote that Qing control over Altishahr could be consolidated by colonizing lands in the western four cities with Muslims imported from elsewhere in Xinjiang or with willing Chinese, who would farm and train as a local militia. He also stressed the importance of eliminating corruption and sexual predation by Qing officials in Xinjiang. Xu Song approved of Shen's ideas.[22]

Wei Yuan, a friend of Gong Zizhen's, likewise held strong opinions on the Western Region empire. His account of the Qianlong conquests, *Sheng wu ji*, can in fact be read as a celebration of high Qing imperialism (see Chapter 3). *Sheng wu ji* was published in 1842, but Wei mustered economic arguments against the advocates of retrenchment as early as 1826, in a letter included in the *Huangchao jingshi wenbian*. "Some say [frontier] lands are vast and useless, that officials' food and soldiers' rations each year cost several hundreds of thousands [of taels], which diminishes the center to serve the frontier. [They say] there are only losses, no gains. . . . Well, to disperse and add is the way of Heaven; to decrease [where there are] many and increase [where there are] few is the warp of governing." In this passage (which appears, slightly modified, in the *Sheng wu ji* as well) Wei alludes to the problem of overpopulation in China proper and then recites the many attractive features and valuable resources of Xinjiang: sparsely settled lands, inexpensive food, fertile and well-watered lands, profitable commerce, not to mention gold mines and low taxes. Poor Chinese who exit the Pass all stay to raise children and grandchildren—not one in a hundred returns. Those who wish to discard such a great resource, he notes, cannot be considered wise.[23]

Like Gong, Wei Yuan believes that the Western Regions have required transformation to render them habitable by men. He alludes to a chapter from Mencius that discusses the successive reclamations of China from natural and manmade chaos in ancient times. "Mencius says: 'The world has existed for a long time, now in peace, now in disorder.' The Western Regions have been disordered for several thousand years, from high antiquity until the present. It is Heaven's wish that the thorny thicket be transformed into busy highroad, the canyon's gloom into brilliant daylight, the teeming jungle into [a populace dressed in proper] caps and robes, the felt tent into village and well."[24]

Wei argues that just as ancient China underwent periods of order and disorder, there would be setbacks in the process of ordering Xinjiang; the present military troubles could be overcome, however. In the first episodes of disorder described in the passage by Mencius, chaos among humankind is accompanied by the encroachment of nature: before Yu drained the floodwaters and leveled the earth, aquatic reptiles forced people to live in nests and caves. Later, the tyrants who rose to power upon the death of Yao and Shun pulled down houses to make ponds and turned fields into parks, thus inviting another infestation of harmful beasts and birds. King Wu punished the tyrants and drove "tigers, leopards, rhinoceroses, and elephants to the distant wilds," at which the empire rejoiced. Mencius clearly equates misrule and wilderness, as does Wei Yuan in the above passage. The restoration of appropriate political control and the taming of nature are one and the same, and Wei proposed that the former could be achieved by means of the latter in Xinjiang, invoking the ideas of Gong Zizhen and other proponents of expanded colonization: "It has been said that the Muslim frontier of the Southern March is also suited to agricultural reclamation by military garrisons, as in the Northern March. To call in Chinese people (*huamin*) and *turn this rich loam into China proper (neidi)* would greatly ease the exercise of our authority and greatly increase our profit. Someday, this idea will have to be implemented" (emphasis added).[25]

The statecraft movement of the nineteenth century, of which Gong Zizhen and Wei Yuan are two of the most famous exponents, is generally understood to have been a response to increasingly apparent fiscal and social troubles domestically and to growing commercial and military pressure along the maritime frontier. Statecraft is thus considered a discourse on national defense. These passages, however, also express a new, expansionistic ideology, for Gong and Wei advise defense by assimilation. Implicit in these arguments is a critique of the Manchu model of empire, under which Xinjiang had not been rendered domestic on the proper terms. That is, the Qing had not created a *Chinese* empire in the Western Regions. The military crisis in

Altishahr from the 1820s, and its origins in the fragile economic basis of Qing imperium in Xinjiang, provided the opportunity for scholars such as Gong and Wei (and, to a lesser degree, Shen Yao as well) to lobby for a radical departure from previous policies. In effect, these statecraft thinkers advocated nothing less than the political, demographic, economic, and even ecological remaking of the Western Regions in China's image.

The Question of Qing Imperialism

In the introduction, I applied the term "imperialism" to the Qing enterprise in Central Asia, defining the word in intentionally general fashion in order to examine the Qing empire on its own terms. We are now in a position to hazard some conclusions about the nature of that imperialism in Xinjiang.

The motives underlying Qing expansion into Central Asia, are, like the motives of imperialism everywhere and at any time, complex and shifting and did not operate in isolation. Most obvious in the Qing case was the strategic goal of neutralizing the Zunghars, whose empire in Inner Asia threatened the Qing across a vast crescent-shaped front. Stable Qing relations with Tibet, Mongol peoples, and Russia depended on resolving the Zunghar threat, and Gaozong's conquest of Zungharia can be seen simply as the culmination of efforts toward this end that began with the Kangxi reign. Nonetheless, one senses other contributing factors as well, especially in the edicts, prefaces, and poems of the Qianlong emperor. His personal frustration with Amursana and chagrin at having withdrawn Qing forces too soon on several occasions seem to contribute to the ferocity of the solution that Zhao-hui found to the Zunghar problem. These, as well as a sense of destiny, consciousness of Han and Tang (and Mongol?) precedents, naked opportunism, and perhaps even a desire to control the major source of nephrite, seem to have spurred on the Qing conquest of Zungharia and annexation of East Turkestan. We cannot discount the influence of the "great man" Gaozong on the course of Qing imperialism.

Economic motives loom large in explanations of European expansion. For the Qing, I have found no justifications of empire that cite extraction of natural resources or commercial wealth as a goal until Gong Zizhen and Wei Yuan suggest this possibility after 1820. Nor does the need to secure markets for Chinese products feature as a reason. In fact, Qing authorities were most interested in making the territory self-sufficient. However, the court did maintain that moving the Qing defense perimeter from Shaanxi-Gansu to the far northwest yielded substantial indirect fiscal savings (the "forward defense dividend"). This economic argument became the core of Qianlong-era justifications for holding Xinjiang. A case could likewise be made that the desire for lebensraum, another motive commonly expressed by imperialists and examined by scholars, motivated the Qing to some degree. Gaozong himself suggested as early as 1760 that the growing Chinese population could profitably expand into the vastnesses of the New Dominion, and similar arguments recurred in nineteenth-century debates over whether to reconquer or relinquish lost areas of Xinjiang.

Was the Qing enterprise in the Western Regions characterized by any particular ideology? In its first phase, Qing imperialism in Xinjiang demonstrates little missionary impulse. Qing authorities in Xinjiang did not greatly interfere with local religion or customs (though Confucian-influenced sentencing within Islamic law is perhaps an exception to this). Although eighteenth- and nineteenth-century Qing sources occasionally refer to native inhabitants of Altishahr and Zungharia as "stupid," the same was said of commoners in China proper. Ranking East Turkestani Qing officials were entitled to wear the queue and participated in state rituals, but this was not required of the non-Chinese commoners of either Altishahr or Zungharia. There was certainly no attempt at sinicization during this phase; rather, the maintenance of cultural boundaries was the goal. The Qing court intended that China and Xinjiang, both components of the empire, remain distinct from each other, even as people flowed relatively easily across the Jiayu Guan.

The new policies in Xinjiang after the second Khoja invasion and the statecraft writings of the early and mid–nineteenth century foreshadow an ideological shift, however. If not yet contemplating cultural or racial assimilation of non-Chinese peoples, both Gong Zizhen and Wei Yuan hope to metamorphosize the landscape and displace Xinjiang peoples with massive Han immigration. The Han colonization efforts undertaken by the Qing in Altishahr after 1830 were a step in that direction, though they remained modest in scope and restrained in their cultural goals. After the Tungan rebellion, however, Zuo Zongtang echoed Gong's blueprint in his own proposals and predicted that following an adjustment period, not only would the new Xinjiang province be less expensive to govern, but that Xinjiang peoples would naturally adopt Chinese language and customs.[26]

And what of the effects of Qing imperialism? First and foremost, by the conquest and occupation of Xinjiang, along with the establishment of control over Mongolia, the Qing precluded any further strategic threat from steppe nomads. Likewise, by eliminating the Zunghars as rival patrons of the dGe-lugs-pa religious establishment, the dynasty strengthened its position vis-à-vis Tibet.

Economically, the results of Qing imperialism are harder to assess. Overall, Qing Xinjiang presents a negative balance sheet: claims of a "forward defense dividend" aside, the immediate costs of the administration and defense of Xinjiang far outstripped tax revenues realized from native Muslims or immigrant Han farmers and merchants. These costs could not be met without annual shipments of silk textiles and bulk silver from China proper. With one exception, the Qing state took little of tangible value out of Xinjiang. During the 1759–1864 period, among the products of the industries the Qing developed in Xinjiang (cotton cloth, staple grains) and the resources the Qing extracted (copper, saltpeter, lumber, iron, sulfur), jade was the only item of economic value transported back to the court in Beijing. But the jadestone shipped from Khotan by the thousands of catties annually between the 1760s and 1821 (mostly with corvée labor) was a valuable commodity indeed—particularly as the jade could be resold by palace offices, the profits accruing to the private treasury of the imperial household. It remains a mystery to exactly what extent these resale revenues, and the prized stone itself, might have compensated Qing emperors for Xinjiang's drain on the general treasury.

Strangely, the Qing never adopted the age-old and seemingly obvious expedient of direct taxation on the caravans that passed through Xinjiang—a departure from the practice of the Tang and other powers that had controlled this hub of the Silk Route. Rather, the dynasty charged only nominal import tariffs, and even these they eventually ceded to Kokand. The main form of Qing commercial taxation in Xinjiang until the 1850s (with the exception of small fees for road passes and the sporadic collection of customs duties at Hami) was directed almost exclusively at sedentary Chinese merchants, whereas much of the region's trade was in tea, rhubarb, and other goods destined for export and thus handled primarily by itinerant traders. Some officials recognized this wealth passing them by. Nayanceng and Bu-yan-tai proposed extensive transit taxes during their postings to Xinjiang; San-cheng sought to raise commercial tax rates and to subject East Turkestani as well as Han merchants to the levies. However, none of these proposals to tap the Xinjiang commercial economy more fully was ever approved.

There was considerable wealth there to be tapped, and private Chinese merchants generally did so more effectively than the Qing government. By the turn of the nineteenth century rich Shanxi houses were well represented in Zungharia and Altishahr, trading tea via Inner Mongolia to Gucheng and Urumchi, whence it was transshipped throughout Xinjiang for export and local consumption. Or they purveyed luxuries to exiles and bannermen in the growing urban centers of Urumchi and Yili. Other "north bend traders," many from well-known firms, opened large shops in Xinjiang cities and profited from retail sales and interest on credit extended to their customers. More impressive for their numbers than for their individual economic stature were the "west road traders," who traveled along the Gansu corridor from the northwest provinces of China proper to sojourn in Xinjiang cities or exchange their goods and return home. This diverse group of peddlers, journeymen, day laborers, teamsters, cash-croppers, shopkeepers, smugglers, and snack vendors included both Tungans fleeing hard times in Gansu and Shaanxi and a few prosperous Jiangnan merchants trading textiles and other products of the Chinese core for Khotanese raw jade. (Other rich merchants from Soochow and elsewhere in central China joined in the Xinjiang trade from the relative convenience of Suzhou, Gansu.) Chinese merchants were present throughout Xinjiang, including some of the more remote villages in Altishahr, and were numerous in the major cities.

Can the Qing imperial presence in Xinjiang, in either its official or its private capacities, be considered exploitative or extractive? Was East Turkestan underdeveloped and colonized by the Qing in the Marxist sense? The record of local economic conditions is inadequate to answer this question in any depth for the 1759–1864 period and answers may in any case depend on the perspective of the researcher. The evidence I have provided here is mixed. On the one hand, Qing taxes in Xinjiang were relatively low, and the stability of *pax Manjurica* was good for trade. Although much of this trade was handled by Chinese and foreign Central Asian merchants, the Xinjiang economy may have been stimulated by this increased commerce, as well as by agricultural expansion and the continuous influx of Qing silver. The gradual rate of inflation, despite increased copper *pul* and bulk silver in circulation in Xinjiang, is an indication that Altishahr's economy grew steadily under Qing rule. Chinese scholars today argue, moreover, that the Qing commutation of the head-tax to cotton cloth in western Altishahr stimulated the cottage weaving industry.

On the other hand, extortion by beg officials, tacitly permitted by the Qing, could be crushing to poor East Turkestani peasants. Moreover, as the cases discussed in Chapter 6 indicate, Chinese loans and sale of goods on credit were a source of hardship. Chinese moneylenders demanded high rates of interest and often expropriated land and other property when East Turkestani debtors defaulted. Although the situation does not seem to have been as severe in Xinjiang as in Qing Mongolia, such economic factors no doubt increased East Turkestani disaffection with the Qing and contributed to the violence of the anti-Han and anti-Manchu rebellions in the early 1860s.

Exploitation or no, it does not appear that superprofits were being repatriated from Xinjiang. The long-distance trade was to a great extent bifurcated, with such border cities as Suzhou and Gucheng acting as entrepôts where merchants based in China proper sold goods that other Chinese merchants, based in Xinjiang, relayed to the interior of Zungharia and Altishahr. The two main trade routes that linked Xinjiang to the metropole, one across Mongolia and the other via the Gansu corridor, carried mostly items of high value relative to weight and bulk (tea, rhubarb, silks, china, medicines, and silver moving westward; jade, silver, medicines, fine hides, and furs moving east), but it was primarily small merchants, working on their own, or at most quasi-independent operators of "name-brand" general stores who moved these goods. The Qing fielded no "Western Regions Company," official or private, to dominate the Xinjiang trade.

A century of Qing imperial control did not integrate Xinjiang's economy closely with the Chinese metropole. In another, less tangible way, however, links were drawn, at least for one party in the imperialist discourse. By this I refer to the psychological effect of Qing imperialism on Chinese elites: a changed notion of "China." This process was not complete by the mid–nineteenth century, when we leave the story, but the beginnings of a significant shift are already evident by the 1820s and 1830s. This study has maintained that the debate over the economic costs of empire, which was a constant refrain running through Xinjiang policy making, often cloaked fundamental differences over the "proper" cultural and environmental limits of the realm. It would be too simplistic to depict this difference over imperial policy as ethnically determined, with Han and Manchu mechanically lining up on either side. Nevertheless, the use of such code words as "inner" and "outer" or "wasteland" by eighteenth-century critics suggests that they assumed the realm should be contiguous with their notion of the natural limits of China, a notion received from history and literature and defined by linked moral and environmental parameters. The Qianlong emperor, on the other hand, envisioned his realm very differently. Gaozong's conception of the empire, which he articulated quite plainly in his preface to the *Xiyu tongwen zhi* and elsewhere, included cultural and territorial China as but one of five main components in an imperial system centripetally focused not on China proper or "Chinese" culture, but on the Qing imperial house. The Jiayu Guan, while still a boundary within this scheme, represented for Gaozong a division between cultural blocs of Qing subjects—not the limits of civilization.

By the end of the third decade of the nineteenth century, however, the ground of this debate had shifted remarkably. Some officials in the Qing court and in Xinjiang could now entertain, for practical reasons, proposals to abandon part of the Western Regions. At the same time, however, two groups of Han Chinese were adopting an aggressive stance with regard to Xinjiang. In

Altishahr, Chinese merchants fought off invaders, massacred native Muslims, and clamored for permission to make permanent homes there. In a very different social venue, but thinking along parallel lines, an elite group of Han scholars adopted the Qing imperial territory as their own and lobbied to transform it into a full-fledged Chinese colony. It is impossible to say how representative the ideas of these statecraft thinkers were of contemporary opinion among other Han groups. But Gong Zizhen, Wei Yuan, and Xu Song and his circle clearly enjoyed some influence at court, for the Qing did not retreat from Western Altishahr, and elements of their statecraft proposals began to be implemented in the 1830s.

It is a well-known aspect of China's modern history that Han Chinese officials, commanding new provincial Chinese armies, successfully repressed the Taiping and other rebellions in China proper and thereafter exercised increasing influence on Qing domestic and foreign affairs. There was a less well known but parallel process underway on the peripheries of the Qing empire, however. Han colonization and implementation of Chinese-style administration of frontier regions, from Xinjiang, Mongolia, and Manchuria to Taiwan, became standard dynastic policy as foreign pressures mounted in the latter half of the nineteenth century. Exactly how this policy was implemented in Xinjiang is properly the subject for another book, but the story may be roughly outlined. Following Zuo Zongtang's reconquest, Xinjiang was made a province in 1884 with its capital in Dihua—the Chinese name officially replacing the old Mongol one, "Urumchi." The first governors (*xunfu*) thereupon implemented reforms like those suggested by Gong Zizhen, and, more recently, by Zuo Zongtang. A new Xinjiang civil administration was created and divided into circuits, which were in turn subdivided into the standard units: prefectures, counties, independent subprefectures, and independent departments. The new officials in charge of these jurisdictions included many Han as well as Manchus—indeed, until after the fall of the Qing, the Xinjiang governors were, with one exception, all Han. The tax structure was revised to make it more like that in the other provinces. Begs, whose assistance was still essential to the minority regime, were placed under greater official supervision and renamed "elders" (*xiangyue*) in the hope that they would function as local gentry in China proper. The civil administration established Confucian free schools throughout the Northern, Southern, and Eastern Marches in an attempt to teach the Chinese written language and didactic texts to East Turkestani children.[27]

Moreover, after Zuo's reconquest Chinese immigration to Xinjiang increased greatly, with groups from Hunan and, later, Yunnan and Tianjin prominent among the new merchants and settlers by the Republican period.

Despite another wave of Muslim resistance in the 1930s, this trend of in-creased Chinese migration has continued to the present day. Han comprised 5.5 percent of the Xinjiang population in 1949; by 1970, they comprised 40 percent. (Many of these are soldiers settled in "Production and Construction Corps"—farms reclaimed near Tarim oases, like the military *tuntian* of Qing times. Others are educated urban Chinese relocated during the Cultural Revolution. Still others are resettled convicts and political prisoners.) Most recently, in a proposal that echoes Gaozong's hope to relieve overpopulation in Sichuan and Gong Zizhen's proposal to have "the center give up people to benefit the west," the Kashgar government announced that it would resettle 100,000 Chinese from poor areas along the Yangzi River who would lose their homes following completion of the Three Gorges Dam project.[28]

During its last decades the Qing dynasty struck a bargain to remain in power in China and for security on the borders. The price of that security might be called "Hanization" of the empire. This was not sinicization, the idealized notion that peoples in propinquity to China spontaneously accul-turated to its superior civilization, but rather a concrete and traceable process by which Han replaced Manchus and Mongols in positions of authority (even in Inner Asia, where Han officials had played little role in high Qing times) and Han Chinese population settled frontier regions in increasing numbers.

The Jiayu Guan retained its complex liminality well after the Qing expan-sion brought lands within and beyond it under a single imperial aegis. This was due in part to the pull of a long Chinese tradition regarding the Western Regions as a terrifying ultima Thule and in part to the Qing imperial ide-ology that maintained cultural barriers between Chinese and non-Chinese subjects, even as it broke down geographic and economic ones. But the Jiayu Guan (like "China") could take on new meanings in new eras, even if the old associations were never entirely sloughed off. To see this, we need only re-visit the Pass at a different, post-Qing moment.

The journalist Fan Changjiang, known for his tough-minded and patriotic reporting, journeyed northwest from Jiuquan early in 1936 on a tour through poverty-stricken Gansu. The Jiayu Guan then served as a tax barrier, where merchants arriving from Xinjiang were forced to pay a "customs" tariff, a fact that made Fan indignant. "Xinjiang is *China's own land*," he snapped. "Cus-toms should be levied at the Chinese-Soviet border. Why have they estab-lished them at Jiayu Guan?"[29] (That Xinjiang was in fact Chinese due to the imperialism of Manchus either did not occur to Fan, or he did not deem it significant enough to mention.)

Fan found the fort itself in sorry shape: the roof had blown off the main tower, and the structure was propped up by a few remaining beams. A large hole pierced the center of the gate, around which were scrawled the graffiti of countless travelers. Good reporter that he was, Fan surveyed these writings. Sure enough, they were verses, nine out of ten on the same old theme—homesickness and the bitter frontier. Fan quotes one such bit of doggerel in his newspaper dispatch, then sarcastically comments, "It's as if the Jiayu Guan were the passage between life and death!" Like Qi Yunshi over a century earlier, Fan combs his memory for poems by Chinese of earlier epochs, but unlike his Qing predecessor, Fan impatiently dismisses their cultivated self-pity. He has no time for timid scholars. "I don't understand," he wonders. "Why do they always want to sit around at home?"

Much more to Fan's taste was a robust verse written by Chinggis Khan's Khitan advisor, Ye-lü-chu-cai, while campaigning in the west.

> The kiss of fermenting wine,
> The sight of olives flowering—
> Fill up on chickens' tongues,
> Share a horse-head melon!
> If a man's belly's full,
> What's to stop a desert crossing?

As he gazed out toward Chinese Xinjiang in the February cold, surrounded by war-wrecked reminders of China's present, Fan could soothe his wounded nationalism with the balm of imperial tradition.

REFERENCE MATTER

A-gui (Agūi)	阿桂	Burhān ad-Dīn	
A-long-a	阿隆阿	(Bu-la-ni-dun)	布拉呢敦
ahong (ākhūnd)	阿訇		
alebatu	阿勒巴圖	caishen	財神
Amursana	阿睦爾薩納	caiyuan	菜園
An-ji-yan (Andijan)	安集延	canzan dachen	參贊大臣
aocha	熬茶	Chama Si	茶馬司
		Chang-liang	常亮
Ba-ha-bu	巴哈布	Chang-ling	長齡
baihao	白毫	Chang-qing	長清
banshi dachen	辦事大臣	changgui	長櫃
bantu	版圖	chantou	纏頭
baojia	保甲	chantou Huizhong	纏頭回眾
bazong	把總	chaojin	朝覲
beg	伯克	chayin	茶引
beile	貝勒	chen	臣
beitaoke	北套客	Cheng-ge	成格
beizi	貝子	chengshou ying	城守營
ben	本	chong	衝
Bi-chang	壁昌	chou	綢
bianmin	編氓	congzhi	從之
Bin-jing	斌靜	Cun-cheng	存誠
bing wei min li	兵威民力		
bingcheng	兵城	da guansi	打官司
bingtun	兵屯	da laoye	大老爺
bitieshi	筆帖士	Da-ling-a	達凌阿
boke Huizi	伯克回子	da tong	大通
Bu-la-ni-dun (Burhān		dacha	大茶
ad-Dīn)	布拉呢敦	dachen	大臣
Bu-lu-te	布魯特	dahuang	大黃
Bu-yan-tai	布彥泰	daixiao zhiyin	帶銷滯引
buhao de Huizi nüren	不好的回子	dangshi	當十
	女人	daqian	大錢
Buhao le! Chengnei de		de	德
baixing yao sha wo ne!	不好了! 城	diandang	典當
	內的百姓要	diding	地丁
	殺我呢!	diguozhuyi	帝國主義

Dihua	迪華	guancha	官茶
ding minxin	定民心	guandi	官地
dingwei	定位	Guandi Miao	關帝廟
dou	斗	guanpu	官鋪
duan	緞	Guanshan Yue	關山月
Duolun	多倫	guanshang	官商
dutong	都統	guanshui	關稅
		guanwai	關外
E-er-gu-lun	額爾古倫	guoyu	國語
E-shan	鄂山	guxi	姑息
En-te-heng-e	恩特亨額		
Encheng Dang	恩成當	Ha-sa-ke (Kazakh)	哈薩克
Enxu Dang	恩恤當	Han shu	漢書
Enyi Dang	恩益當	Hancheng	漢城
		Hanhui	漢回
fan	繁	hanjian	漢奸
fan	藩	Hanjun	漢軍
Fan Changjiang	范長江	Hanyu	漢語
Fan Qinghong	范清洪	He-ning	和寧
Fan Qingkuang	范清曠	He-shen (Hešen)	和珅
fangzu	房租	Heng Sheng Shun	恆盛順
fantun	犯屯	Heng Sheng Xing	恆盛興
fei lei	匪類	Heng Xing Sheng	恆興生
feicui	翡翠	Hešen (He-shen)	和珅
feiqi wuyong zhi ren	廢棄無用之人	hongqian	紅錢
		hua	華
fen	分	huafeng	華風
feng	俸	huamin	華民
fengliu	風流	Huang Tinggui	黃廷桂
fu	府	huangshang	皇商
Fu-de	富德	hui	狪
fu dutong	副都統	Huibu	回部
Fu-heng	傅恆	huibu	回布
Fu-jun	富俊	Huicheng	回城
Fu-ming-a	富明阿	huidui	匯兌
fucha	附 (副) 茶	Huijiang	回疆
fumin tongzhi	撫民同知	Huiren	回人
fuxing	賦性	Huishang	回商
fuyi	服役	huitun	回屯
		Huiwu zhangjing	回務章景
gan daying	趕大營	huiyu	回語
Gao Pu	高樸	Huizi	回子
gong	供	Huizi ying	回子營
Gong Zizhen	龔自珍	humin	戶民
guan	關	Huo-ji-zhan (Khoja Jihān)	霍集佔
guanbupu	官布鋪		

huoshen	火神	kuping	庫平
hutun	戶屯		
		lan'ganr	蘭干兒
Isḥāq (Yi-sa-ke)	伊薩克	lao Mancheng	老滿城
		laomin	勞民
Jalungga (Zha-long-a)	札隆阿	lei	類
jasak (zhasake)	札薩克	li	禮
jian	間	li	里
jiangjie	疆界	Li Hongzhang	李鴻章
jiangjun	將軍	liang	兩
jiangjun fu	將軍府	Lifan Yuan	理藩院
Jiangnan xiang	江南巷	lingdui dachen	領隊大臣
jiangyi ju	匠役局	lingjian	令箭
jianmin	奸民	lishi tongzhi	理事同知
jianshang	奸商	liutong	流通
jiansheng	監生	lougui	陋規
Jiayu Guan	嘉峪關	luodishui	落地稅
Jihāngīr (Zhang-ge-er)	張格爾	lupiao	路票
jin	禁		
jin	錦	majia	馬價
jincha	斤茶	Mancheng	滿城
Jing-ge-li (Jing-e-li)	精格哩, 旌	mangpao	蟒袍
	額禮	maoyi Hanmin	貿易漢民
jingfei	經費	maoyi Huimin	貿易回民
jinshi	進士	maoyi puhu	貿易鋪戶
jiucheng	舊城	maoyi ting	貿易亭
Jiujia Wan	九家灣	Menggu	蒙古
juezhen	絕畛	Mengguyu	蒙古語
jumin	居民	menhuan	門宦
juni zhi louxi	拘泥之陋習	min	民
Junji Chu	軍機處	Ming-rui	明瑞
juntai	軍臺	minren	民人
juntun	軍屯	minren juchu	民人居處
junwang	郡王	mintun	民屯
junxian	郡縣	mo	末
juren	舉人	mu	畝
Kalanggui	喀浪圭	Na-yan-cheng	
kalun (karun)	卡倫	(Nayanceng)	那彥成
kaozheng	考證	nan	難
Kashimier (Kashmir)	喀什米爾	nanzou	難奏
kemin	客民	nao shi	鬧事
Khoja Jihān		nei shu	內屬
(Huoji-zhan)	霍集佔	nei wai zhi jie,	
koupiao	口票	bu ke bu fen	內外之界,
kunqu	崑曲		不可不分

neidi	內地	Sheng wu ji	聖武記
neidi Huimin	內地回民	shengxi yinliang	生息銀兩
neidi minren	內地民人	shenqu	神區
neidi shangren	內地商人	Shiji	史記
Nu-san	努三	shitou	石頭
		Shu-he-de (Šuhede)	舒赫德
Peng Yunzhang	彭藴章	shuichong	水銃
pianyu zhong de		Shun-de-na	順德納
pianyu	偏隅中的偏	sizhu qingdan	四柱清單
	隅	Song-yun	松筠
piao	票	Soochow	蘇州
piaohao	票號	Su-bu-tong-a	蘇布通阿
piaowu chu	票務處	Suzhou	肅州
pu	鋪	Šuhede (Shu-he-de)	舒赫德
puer qian	普爾錢		
		taiji	臺吉
qi	氣	taizhan	臺站
Qi-shi-yi	七十一	tanpai	攤派
Qi Yunshi	祁韻士	Taranchi (Talanqi)	塔蘭奇
qian	錢	tengge'er (tänggä)	騰格爾
qiang	牆	tian	天
Qianlong tongbao	乾隆通寶	tianfu	田賦
qiantun	遣屯	Tianshan beilu	天山北路
Qing	清	Tianshan donglu	天山東路
Qing-gui	慶桂	Tianshan nanlu	天山南路
Qing-xiang	慶祥	ting	廳
qingdan	清單	Tong Tai Xing	同泰興
qinglei	清類	tongbao	同胞
qitun	旗屯	tongshihang	通事行
que	缺	tu ren	土人
		tuntian	屯田
rongren	戎人	Tuo-jin	托津
rujin	入觀	tuoma chu	駝馬處
ruyi	如意	tusi	土司
Ruyi Guan	如意館		
		Ulungge (Wu-long-a)	武隆阿
saiwai	塞外		
San-cheng	三成	waifan	外藩
San Yi Dian	三益店	Waifan Menggu Huibu	
Shang shu	商書	wanggong biaozhuan	外藩蒙古回
shangcha	商茶		部王公表傳
shangmin	商民	waiyi	外夷
shangshui	商稅	Wan Shun Lei	萬順雷
shanhou	善後	wang	王
shazao shu	沙棗樹	wansheng	玩生
Shen Yao	沈垚	Wanshou Gong	萬壽宮

Wei Gong Cun	魏公村
Wei Gong Cun	爲公村
Wei Yuan	魏源
Weiwu Cun	畏兀村
wen	文
Wen-shou	文綬
Wu Dashan	吳達善
Wu-long-a (Ulungge)	武隆阿
Wuti Qingwen jian	五体淸文鑑
wuyi	武彝
Xi you ji	西游記
xia	夏
xialiu	下流
xian	縣
Xiang Tai Long	祥泰隆
xiangpian	香片
xiangyin	餉銀
xiangyue	鄉約
xiao Su Hang	小蘇杭
xiaolongtuan	小龍團
xicha	細茶
xieban dachen	協辦大臣
xiexiang	協餉
xieyin	協銀
xifan	西番
xifanyu	西番語
xiluke	西路客
xin Mancheng	新滿城
Xin-zhu	新柱
xincheng	新城
Xinjiang	新疆
xiucai	秀才
Xiyu	西域
Xiyu tongwen zhi	西域同文志
Xu Song	徐松
xunfu	巡撫
xunjian	巡檢
yancai	鹽菜
Yang Fang	楊芳
Yang Yingju	楊應琚
Yang Yuchun	楊遇春
yanglian	養廉
yao	要
yaopu	藥鋪

yi	夷
Yi-sa-ke (Isḥāq)	伊薩克
Yi-shan	奕山
yi shi qubie	以示區別
yihui	夷回
yin	引
yinfang	印房
yinfang zhangjing	印房章京
yingtang	營塘
yizhan	驛站
Yong-gui (Yunggui)	永貴
Yong Shun Gong	永順公
you zei	有賊
youji	游擊
yu	玉
Yu-qing	玉慶
Yu Qing Gong	余慶公
Yuan Tai Quan	源泰泉
yuanbao	元寶
yuandan	元旦
Yunggui (Yong-gui)	永貴
yupu	玉鋪
yushi	玉石
zacha	雜茶
Zaoban Chu	造辦處
Zha-la-fen-tai	札拉芬泰
Zha-long-a (Jalungga)	札隆阿
zhang	丈
Zhang-ge-er (Jihāngīr)	張格爾
Zhang Luan	張鑾
Zhang Rulin	張汝霖
Zhang Zhiye	張知鄴
Zhao-hui	兆惠
Zhao Junrui	趙均瑞
zhao neidi zhangcheng juni banli	照內地章程 拘泥辦理
zhasake (jasak)	扎薩克
zhasake junwang	扎薩克郡王
zhengfu	正賦
zhifu	知府
zhiqian	制錢
zhizao chu	織造處
zhizhou	知州
Zhongguo	中國

Zhongguo zhi ren   中國之人
zhongqu   中區
zhongtu   中土
zhongwai yijia   中外一家
zhongyuan   中原
zhongyuan ren   中原人
zhou   州
Zhou li   周禮
Zhou Renji   周人驥
Zhuanzhu Xiang   專諸巷
zhulan   珠蘭
Zhunbu   準部
Zhunyu   準語

zidi   子弟
zihao   字號
zihao dianpu   字號店鋪
zihaopu   字號鋪
zisheng yinliang   滋生銀兩
zongdu   總督
zouxiao   奏銷
Zunghar   準噶爾
zuo chantou maimai 做纏頭買賣
Zuo Zongtang   佐宗棠
zuoling   佐領
zushui   租稅

INTRODUCTION

1. This translation of Li Bo's *Guanshan Yue* [The borderland moon] is abbreviated and adapted slightly from that in Herdan, trans., *Three Hundred T'ang Poems*, pp. 60–61.

2. Qi Yunshi, *Wanli xingcheng ji*, pp. 402–3; Qi's biography is given on pp. 383–87. See also Hummel, *Eminent Chinese of the Ching Period*, pp. 134–35.

3. The most influential discussion of boundaries in this sense is Michel Foucault's *The Order of Things*, the introduction of which invokes an outlandish assemblage of categories from a "Chinese encyclopedia" to highlight the importance of categorization in structuring human knowledge. For a stimulating and eclectic exploration of this concept with regard to things Chinese, see Hay, ed., *Boundaries in China*, especially Hay's introduction.

4. Although *yi* has generally been rendered into English as "barbarian," this translation may exaggerate the negative connotations of the term as it was used during Qing times. See Hevia, *Cherishing Men from Afar*, pp. 120–21. Dilip Basu has uncovered a debate over the term among British East India employees and other China hands in the 1830s, with those favoring an aggressive, military approach to trade complaints indignantly translating the term as "barbarian," while others (including Sir George Staunton, a member of the Macartney mission) argued for the more neutral sense of "foreign," citing Robert Morrison's dictionary (1815) as an authority. Dilip Basu, " 'Barbarians,' " pp. 6–8.

5. The exceptions are noteworthy, however, and include Owen Lattimore and Paul Pelliot. Fletcher's foundational work, especially that published in the *Cambridge History of China*, informs and inspires many of the questions considered in this study. More recently, Forbes treats political events in Republican Xinjiang, and Benson analyzes the last Muslim movement for independence from China before the Communist takeover.

6. Lattimore, *Inner Asian Frontiers*, p. 512.

7. Two recent studies revise key aspects of Lattimore's work. Barfield's *The Perilous Frontier* tackles the question of the interaction of steppe peoples with China on a Lattimorian scale and with a similar overarching

model modified to stress the importance of the northeast (Manchuria) in this interaction. However, Barfield affords greater significance to the eighteenth-century conquests and implementation of a rigid administrative structure on Inner Asia by the Qing. Barfield credits such factors as the successful cooptation of the Chinggisid aristocracy, the spread of monastic Buddhism, and Chinese economic exploitation—not firearms or modern transport—with effecting the permanent decline of the Mongols as a military threat to China. He thus dates the breakdown of the pattern of steppe-Chinese interaction a century earlier than Lattimore. Waldron's *The Great Wall of China* argues forcefully that walls were a device deployed by Chinese states only at certain periods as defensive expedients, not an eternal, emblematic feature of Chinese history and culture. Although Lattimore is always careful to distinguish between the Great Wall frontier and the Wall itself, he essentializes and dehistoricizes the concept of the Great Wall in such general statements as "The Great Wall may therefore be described as an effort on the part of the state to fix this Frontier and to limit the proper field of Chinese activity as well as to exclude the peoples of the steppe" (*Inner Asian Frontiers*, p. 471).

8. On tradition/modernity and impact/response, see Cohen, *Discovering History*. On sinicization, see Crossley, "Thinking about Ethnicity." On the tribute system and Chinese world order, see Hevia, *Cherishing Men from Afar*, especially pp. 9–15, chaps. 2 and 5, as well as his "A Multitude of Lords" and "Lamas, Emperors and Rituals"; see also Rossabi's introduction in Rossabi, ed., *China among Equals*. Wills has been refining notions of the tribute system for some time (see his *Embassies and Illusions*) and has recently contributed a forceful critique of the notion: see "How We Got Obsessed" and "Tribute, Defensiveness, and Dependency." On Qing frontier studies in Chinese and American scholarship, see Millward, "New Perspectives on the Qing Frontier."

9. The *Chinese World Order* statement recognizes more directly the important role that military force played in the Qing order. In Fairbank's most recent, and final, synthesis of Chinese history, he writes that the maintenance of the tributary system ideology was one of the requirements of Manchu Son-of-Heavenship in China proper, but does not argue that this worldview characterized Manchu relations with Inner Asian territories. See Fairbank, *China: A New History*, pp. 149, 201. For summaries of the tribute system theory, see Rossabi, ed., introduction to *China among Equals*, pp. 1–4, and Hevia, *Cherishing*, pp. 9–15.

10. Fairbank, "A Preliminary Framework," p. 11.

11. Fairbank and Teng, "On the Ch'ing Tribute System," p. 238.

12. Fairbank, "A Preliminary Framework," Tables 1 and 2, pp. 11, 13.

13. Fairbank, "A Preliminary Framework," pp. 3, 13.

14. Cohen, *Discovering History*, pp. 164–66.

15. Skinner, "Regional Urbanization in Nineteenth-Century China," p. 213; Skinner, Hsieh, and Shigeaki, *Modern Chinese Society*, p. xvii.

16. Skinner, "Marketing and Social Structure in Rural China," p. 17.

17. Skinner, "Introduction: Urban and Rural in Chinese Society," in *The City in Late Imperial China*, pp. 264–69.

18. Skinner, "Cities and the Hierarchy of Local Systems," in *The City in Late Imperial China*, p. 322.

19. These approaches characterize many of the papers presented recently at the "Conference on Ethnic Identity and the China Frontier" at Dartmouth in May 1996. One of the insights to emerge most strongly from this conference was that on frontiers in south China the distinction between Han and others was not as clear-cut as has generally been imagined. Lattimore, of course, portrayed the boundary between Chinese and steppe nomad as permeable and given to defections in either direction.

20. In framing the discussion of the philosophical links between Han thinkers of the late Ming and late Qing in this way, I have substantially followed Crossley, *A Translucent Mirror*, "Postscript." See also Dreyer's analysis of Sun Yat-sen in *China's Forty Millions*, pp. 15–17.

21. I discuss the various ideological justifications of the inclusion of non-Han peoples and Inner Asian territories in the modern Chinese nation-state in Millward, "A Uyghur Muslim," pp. 446–48.

22. In treating national identity as discursively constructed, I am of course following Anderson. In *Siam Mapped*, Thongchai goes further than Anderson in stressing that the concrete physical dimension of nations is itself a cultural as well as a political artifact, one with a history of changing shapes and meanings. Also germane here is Duara's point (stressed in *Rescuing History from the Nation*) that historical narratives of modern nation-states, as teleological accounts of the emergence of a national subject, suppress other counter-narratives. In treating the Chinese nation as unified through time and the Chinese state's current boundaries as primordial, what is suppressed is none other than the narrative of a Qing—as opposed to Chinese—imperial expansion.

In a concise summing up of the problem of defining China, Wang Gungwu recognizes that "the Chineseness of China" is not something historians may take for granted. No definition, whether it treats China as a place, as a people, or as a civilization, is adequate unless change over time and variation over space is taken into account. Rather, "Our understanding of Chineseness must recognize the following: it is living and changeable; it is also the product of a shared historical experience whose record has continually influenced its growth; it has become increasingly a self-conscious matter for China; and it should be related to what appears to be, or to have been, Chinese in the eyes of non-Chinese." (*The Chineseness of China*, p. 2.)

23. Macartney's and Marx's metaphors for the late Qing may be found in J. L. Cranmer-Byng, ed., *An Embassy to China: Being the Journal Kept by Lord Macartney during his Embassy to the Emperor Ch'ien-lung*, (London: Longmans, Green and Co., 1962), pp. 212–13, and Dona Torr, ed., *Marx on China, 1853–1860: Articles from the "New York Daily Tribune"* (London, 1951), pp. 1–4. Both are cited in Spence, *The Search for Modern China*, pp. 123, 182.

24. Important discussions of these concepts by anthropologists include Barth, Bentley, and Keyes. For applications to the Qing and China, and more bibliography, see Crossley, *Orphan Warriors* and "Thinking about Ethnicity"; Elliott, "Resident Aliens"; Gladney, *Muslim Chinese*; Harrell, "Introduction"; and Lipman, *Familiar Strangers*.

25. A complete list is impossible, but some scholars whose work has shaped this emerging approach to the Qing include Chia, Crossley, Di Cosmo, Elliott, Fôret, Hevia, Lipman, Newby, Perdue, and Rawski (much of their work is still in progress; available references are in the bibliography.) The 1994 NEH Summer Institute on the Qing retreat at Chengde, in which several of the above were participants, did much to focus my thinking along these lines. Nor am I the first to use the term "Qing-centered" (see Elliott, "Resident Aliens," p. xx); in her masterful essay on the state of the Qing field ("Presidential Address"), Rawski uses "Manchu-centered," a term similar in intent if different in nuance. Finally, I have not mentioned here the many Japanese scholars of Qing China and Inner Asia for whom my heralding of this paradigm shift will seem little more than a statement of the obvious. They are acknowledged in the notes and bibliography.

26. For a handy compendium of theories of imperialism, see Harrison Wright, *The "New Imperialism."*

27. On the debate over imperialism in China, see "Imperialism: Reality or Myth?" in Cohen, *Discovering History*, pp. 97–147.

28. See collections edited by Gruen and by Harris for examples of Romanists reclaiming the concept of imperialism.

29. In his *Culture and Imperialism*, Said takes up the "cultural resistance" to European imperialism, a subject he "left out of *Orientalism*" (p. xii). For a trenchent critique of Said's work, especially *Orientalism*, see Ahmad, "*Orientalism* and After." For a brief and accessible survey and critique of the practitioners and intellectual genealogy of postcolonial theory, see Jacoby, "Marginal Returns." For a rumination on the applicability of the notion of subalternity to the China field, see Hershatter, "The Subaltern Talks Back."

30. A truly comparative history of imperialisms or empires will require a chronologically general definition and improved specific knowledge of such non-European empires as the Qing or the Ottoman. Eisenstadt took such a general approach but went astray in adopting an ahistorical, grossly generalized concept he called "the Chinese Empire from the Han period to

the Ch'ing" as a principal analytical archetype. For Europe during the same period he distinguishes the Hellenistic and Roman empires; the Byzantine Empire; Western, Central, and Eastern European states from the fall of feudal systems to the rise of absolutism; and European conquest empires outside Europe—yet he assumes China to have remained essentially changeless over 2,000 years. Eisenstadt, *The Political Systems of Empires,* p. 10.

31. The application of "empire" to the political unit ruled by the Qing dynasty at its height seems acceptable to everybody. The Qing patently exhibits most of the characteristics cited in definitions of empire, including territorial vastness, strong centralized power, bureaucratic administration, universalist systems of legitimation, and inclusion of multiple culturally or politically distinct territories in an overarching political formation. For two definitional essays on "empire," see R. A. Seligman, Alvin Johnson, et al., eds., *Encyclopaedia of the Social Sciences* (New York: Macmillan, 1937), pp. 497–506, and David L. Sills et al., eds., *International Encyclopedia of the Social Sciences* (New York: Macmillan, 1968), pp. 41–49.

32. Anderson, *Imagined Communities,* p. 86.

CHAPTER 1

1. The term *Xinjiang* came into common official use within a few years of the conquest; it appears in memorial by 1768 (Wu Dashan memorial, QL33.2.16, GZZZ vol. 28, pp. 654–55). A dispatch in 1778 defines it nicely: "*Jiayu Guan wei Xinjiang menhu*" (Jiayu Pass is the gateway to Xinjiang). Le-er-jin memorial, QL43.12.16, GZZZ vol. 46, pp. 130–31.

2. Material on Xinjiang geology and tectogenesis may be found in Norin, "Tarim Basin"; Wang Gongque, "Geologic Overview"; and Molnar et al., "Geologic Evolution." I am grateful to John Olsen for these references.

3. See, for example, map 52–53 in Tan et al., eds., *Zhongguo lishi ditu ji.* The ambiguities over Chinese territorial claims in this region have roots in the Qing period.

4. There is evidence of agricultural settlements in Zungharia dating from as early as the late Bronze and early Iron Ages. Di Cosmo, "Ancient Inner Asian Nomads," pp. 1105, 1108.

5. Hedin, *My Life as an Explorer,* pp. 138–79; Polo, *Travels,* p. 54.

6. Xi, "Luobu Bo," p. 16; Zhao Songqiao and Xia, "Evolution of the Lop Desert," p. 320; Hu, "Ershi shiji Takelamagan."

7. Ren, Yang, and Bao, comps. *An Outline of China's Physical Geography,* chap. 13. A map compiled by the Royal Geographical Society and the Mount Everest Foundation (*The Mountains of Central Asia*) includes the Tarim Basin and surrounding ranges. Map 1 is derived in part from the map of Xinjiang in Tan et al., eds., *Zhongguo lishi ditu ji* vol. 8 (Qing dynasty), pp. 52–53.

8. Lattimore, *Inner Asian Frontiers,* p. 172. The desert may be crossed

from north to south (and vice versa) along the channels of the Aksu and Yarkand Rivers, which reach the Tarim when in flood. The rest of the year, the dry riverbeds provide a flat route through the dunes suitable for travel on foot. Herders and merchants willing to share with their camels the water from desiccating pools may make the trip from Aksu to Khotan, for example, as late as October.

9. Yü, "Han Foreign Relations," pp. 405–21; Yü, *Trade and Expansion,* 135–50. See also Loewe, *Crisis and Conflict in Han China,* pp. 214–31.

10. Although Chinese sources gloss over this fact, Tibet seems to have controlled the Tarim Basin oasis states from 670 to 692 (Beckwith, *The Tibetan Empire,* pp. 37–54).

11. Based primarily on Wechsler, "T'ai-tsung (Reign 626–49) the Consolidator," pp. 219–31; Twitchett and Wechsler, "Kao-tsung (Reign 649–83) and the Empress Wu," pp. 279–87; and Twitchett, "Hsüan-tsung (Reign 712–56)," pp. 433–38. For a closely researched account of the ebb and flow of Central Asian empires in this period, see Beckwith, *The Tibetan Empire,* whose non-Chinese perspective, and skepticism about Chinese sources, is refreshing.

12. For a recent study of the Torghuts' experience in Russia, see Khodarkovsky, *Where Two Worlds Met.*

13. On these events and the influence of Naqshbandī Islam in Xinjiang, Gansu, and Qinghai, see Fletcher, "Ch'ing Inner Asia," pp. 74, 87–90, and "The Naqshbandiyya in Northwest China."

14. On the Zunghar trade at Suzhou and *aocha* missions, see Zhang Yuxin, "Suzhou maoyi kaolue," Cai, "Shiba shiji zhongye Zhunga'er," and Ye, "Cong maoyi aocha kan Qianlong qianqi."

15. Edict to the Grand Secretariat, QL20.6.7, from Zhongyang yanjiu yuan, *Ming Qing shiliao,* geng bian, vol. 10, p. 918, cited in Zhuang, *Qing Gaozong,* pp. 40–41. The emperor identifies Ce-leng and Šuhede (Shu-he-de) as the cowards, but at least one other official (Chen Hongmou) had earlier expressed concern about attacking Dawachi. See the section "Literati Dissent, Imperial Response," below.

16. For useful surveys of the historical interactions between China and Inner Asia outlined above, see Rossabi, *China and Inner Asia,* and Mano, Nakami, Hori, and Komatsu, *Nairiku Ajia.*

17. On the circumstances surrounding the production of the engravings of the Qianlong conquests, see Beurdeley and Beurdeley, pp. 79–88; Pelliot, "Les 'conquêtes de l'empereur de la chine' "; and Enoki, "Researches in Chinese Turkestan," Appendix 1.

18. General accounts of the Zunghar wars and conquest of Xinjiang may be found in Barfield, *The Perilous Frontier,* pp. 277–94, and Rossabi, *China and Inner Asia,* pp. 141–49. See also Hummel, *Eminent Chinese,* 9–11, and Halkovic, *The Mongols of the West.* Other important works in Western

languages include Courant, *L'Asie centrale aux XVIIe et XVIIIe siècles,* and Zlatkin, *Istoria Dzhungarskogo khanstva, 1635-1758.* See also the English notice of this book, Zlatkin, "The History of the Khanate of Dzhungaria," which includes a discussion of the Mongol, Kalmuk, and Russian sources.

The basic Chinese source is Fuheng et al., comps., *(Qinding) pingding Zhunga'er fanglue,* which assembles official communications from the Kangxi, Yongzheng, and Qianlong campaigns. Several of the major Xinjiang gazetteers contain capsule histories of this period, such as Song-yun, "Zhun-ga-er quanbu jilue," in *(Qinding) Xinjiang zhilue* juan shou: 57b-64a. Wei Yuan (*Sheng wu ji*) and Zeng (*Zhongguo jingying Xiyu shi*) offer longer versions. Zhuang's highly detailed narrative is based on archival documents as well as the published Qing sources (the account of the Qing conquest of Altishahr given here is primarily based on Zhuang's). The "Weilate Menggu jianshi" bianxie zu ("Concise History of the Oirat Mongols" editorial group) presents an official P.R.C. line, which winds carefully between admiration of the Oirat and Zunghar *minzu* (which suffered "nationality oppression and class oppression" at the hands of the Qing) and criticism of Zunghar leaders. The group's bibliography includes Russian, Oirat, Mongolian, and Tibetan works, in addition to Chinese published and archival sources.

In Japanese, Haneda's *Chūō Ajia shi kenkyū* provides informative coverage. Chiba's *Kara Būran* is a popular history of the Kangxi, Yongzheng, and Qianlong Zunghar campaigns and the Qing conquest of Zungharia and East Turkestan, presented in a dramatic style.

19. On the beg administrative system, see Saguchi, *18-19 seiki Higashi Torukisutan,* chap. 3; Haneda, "Iminzoku tōchijō"; and articles by Sanada.

20. The Qing likewise introduced Chinese civil administration on the Taiwan frontier as a control measure only after Han settlement there was established. See Shepherd, *Statecraft and Political Economy,* pp. 198-208. A similar pattern arose in Manchuria, where *zhou, xian,* and *ting* governments were established alongside the military government to accommodate an expanding Han civilian population. See Lee, *The Manchurian Frontier,* pp. 71-74.

21. *Jasak* (Mo. *jasaǧ;* Ch. *zhasake*) was the Manchu term used by the Qing for the heads of the eight Mongol banners and other hereditary chiefs. Fuller descriptions of Qing administration in Xinjiang may be found in Fletcher, "Ch'ing Inner Asia," pp. 58-81; Zeng, *Zhongguo,* part 2, chap. 2; Luo Yunzhi, chaps. 3-5; and Kataoka, *Shinchō Shinkyō,* pp. 59-75.

22. Saguchi argues that Jahāngīr escaped and acted independently of Kokand's control ("Revival of the White Mountain Khwājas," pp. 15-19). Fletcher maintains that the khan of Kokand initially unleashed him intentionally and later denied any alliance with him ("The Heyday," p. 361).

23. Hummel et al., *Eminent Chinese,* pp. 584-87; NWYGZY juan 73-80.

24. Fletcher, "The Heyday," p. 377.

25. Yu-lin, ZPZZ MZSW 556-12, DG11.2.25; En-te-heng-e, ZPZZ MZSW 0093-1, DG18.5.2.

26. On the Makhdūmzādas, the best sources are Fletcher, "The Heyday," pp. 360–95, and Saguchi, "Revival of the White Mountain Khwājas." On Russian influence in nineteenth-century Xinjiang, see Fletcher, "Sino-Russian Relations," pp. 325–32. On Ya'qūb Beg, see Kim, "The Muslim Rebellion and the Kashgar Emirate," as well as Boulger, *The Life of Yakoob Beg*.

27. *Huangshu*, 1a–2b, translated in De Bary, Chan, and Watson, comps., vol. 1:544–45.

28. Dikötter, *Discourse of Race*, p. 27. For a somewhat more detailed analysis of Wang's thought on these questions, tending to the same conclusions, see Langlois, "Chinese Culturalism," pp. 361–65.

29. Waldron, *The Great Wall*, p. 58.

30. Confucius, *The Analects*, 9:13 and 13:14, translated in Chan, *A Sourcebook in Chinese Philosophy*, pp. 36, 41. See, however, Tillman, "Proto-Nationalism," pp. 425–26 for a discussion of the *limits* of cosmopolitanism in Zhu Xi's philosophy.

31. Legge, trans., "The Tribute of Yu," in *The Shoo King*, pp. 142–51. The relevant sections of the *Zhouli* are books 29 and 33.

32. See, for example, Waldron, *The Great Wall*, p. 42.

33. Tillman, "Proto-Nationalism," p. 407 passim.

34. Waldron, *The Great Wall*, pp. 42–43.

35. Gaozong took punitive action against Liu Tongxun, recalling him to the capital, arresting him and his sons, and confiscating the family property. Liu learned his lesson; after the emperor pardoned him the following year, he redeemed himself in a variety of important positions. *Qingshi liezhuan*, j. 18 (vol. 5, p. 1392); Hummel et al., *Eminent Chinese*, p. 533; Enoki, "Researches in Chinese Turkestan," pp. 6–7.

36. *GZSL* 543:12a–16a, QL22.7 *dingwei*. I have been unable to locate any further information on Zhang Zhiye. The *Guochao qixian leizheng* contains a biography of a Zhang Rulin (1708?–69), a native of Hengcheng county, Anhui province. In 1735 Zhang was put forward as a tribute student (*gongsheng*) by the local Confucian school and the following year was recommended for a post as district magistrate. He served in several Guangdong counties and enjoyed a career full of typical magistrate's concerns (water conservancy, restraining powerful families, quelling unrest) and a few less typical ones, including instructing Hainanese in agriculture and proper marriage rituals and dealing with Western traders in Macao. His request to remain in Macao upon retirement was denied, and he returned to Hengcheng. (Li Huan, comp., *Guochao qixian leizheng* j. 253, pp. 36a–37a.) This account does not mention the memorial regarding the Zunghar campaigns—although we would not necessarily expect a formal biography to do so. It may concern the same man.

37. Sima Qian, *Records of the Grand Historian*, chap. 30, "The Treatise on the Balanced Standard," vol. 2, pp. 61–85. My thanks to Nicola Di Cosmo for pointing me to this reference. "Emperor Wu's excessive expansionistic policy incurred severe posthumous criticism at the court. Even the expansionistic emperor himself issued a decree toward the end of his life expressing his regrets" (Yü, *Trade and Expansion*, p. 2).

38. *GZSL* 612:19b–22a, QL25.5 *renzi;* Hua, "Qingdai Xinjiang nongye kaifa shi," p. 46. See also her "Qianlong nianjian yimin chuguan."

39. *GZSL* 649:34, QL26.11 *jiazi.* See also *GZSL* 612:19b–22a, QL25.5 *renzi.*

40. *GZSL* 920:23a–24a, QL37.11 *guimao.*

41. See Goodrich, *The Literary Inquisition*, pp. 47–49.

42. Song-yun et al., comps., *(Qinding) Xinjiang zhilue* 2:2b–3a.

43. Ibid.

44. Wei Yuan, in his *Sheng wu ji*, cites the Qianlong edict of 1772 (*GZSL* 920:23a–24a, QL37.11 *guimao*) to assert Xinjiang's profitability (*Sheng wu ji*, 4:10b).

45. On the maritime/frontier debate, see Hsu, "The Great Policy Debate in China," and Kwang-Ching Liu and Smith, "The Military Challenge: The North-west and the Coast."

CHAPTER 2

1. *HYXYTZ* 39:2a, *bingfang.*

2. Huang Tinggui, ZPZZ QL23.12.10, quoted in Lü Xiaoxian, "Qianlong chao . . . sichou maoyi," p. 5. *GZSL* 557:11a–12a, QL23.2 *dingchou,* 556:19, QL23.2 *gengwu.*

3. On Tea and Horse Agencies (*Chama Si*) in the Song, see Smith, *Taxing Heaven's Storehouse;* on the Ming border trade, see Rossabi, "Tea and Horse Trade," and Kano, "Chama bōeki no shūmatsu." Millward, "The Qing-Kazakh Trade and the 'Tribute System,'" includes a brief comparative discussion of frontier horse markets from Tang through Qing times.

4. The Imperial Silk Factories were monopolies of the Imperial Household Agency (*Neiwu Fu*), locally managed by Manchu bondservants in much the same fashion as the salt administrations in Yangzhou and Changlu. With origins in the Yuan Dynasty, the three Jiangnan factories were the last of around 25 such centers that had operated throughout China during the Ming, when silk played a more important role in dynastic financial and taxation systems. In early Qing times, the three factories were employed primarily in the production of silk for use by the imperial clan as well as of satin and brocade tributary "gifts in return." After 1759, however, the factories were mobilized to produce trade silks, and from then on almost all the silk exchanged officially for Kazakh livestock was processed through the three factories, although only luxury fabrics were actually manufactured in-house, the more common varieties being produced through an outsourc-

ing system. Lillian Li, *China's Silk Trade*, pp. 38–45; Fan Jinmin, "Qingdai Jiangnan," p. 31 ff.

5. *GZSL* 550:10b–13a, QL22.11 *guiyi*.

6. Wu Dashan memorial, QL33.2.16, *GZZZ* vol. 28, pp. 654–55.

7. The preceding section is based on a longer discussion in Millward, "The Qing Trade with the Kazakhs" and "Beyond the Pass," chap. 1.

8. See, for example, Mancall's argument that the dynamic approach toward foreign trade suggested by the early Qing grain imports from Korea gave way before the onslaught of "sinicization," and thus "the [Kangxi] emperor's death at the end of 1722 marked the end of experimentation and encouragement in the field of foreign trade for well over a century." Mancall, "The Ch'ing Tribute System," p. 87.

9. Giuseppe Castiglione, *Hasake gongma*, painted 1757, cat. 23, in Musée Guimet, Paris. Partial reproductions in Beurdeley and Beurdeley, *Giuseppe Castiglione*, pp. 102–5, 166.

10. *GZSL* 577:29b–30a, QL23.12 *gengchen*.

11. See Hevia, *Cherishing Men from Afar*.

12. A ritual preceded the trade between the Qing and Manchu tribal peoples in Jilin c. 1809. Before real trade commenced, the chiefs of the tributary peoples gathered in a wooden fenced enclosure where Qing officials were seated on a raised dias. The chiefs kowtowed before them, presented the finest sable pelts, and received in return gifts in descending order of quality depending on their rank: a clan chief received a roll of brocade, a village chief one of damask, others lengths of cotton cloth. Lee writes that "the core of the [northeastern trading] system was the sable tribute," but was not this tribute ceremony merely coincident with, and not a cover for, direct trade? The ritual exchange of gifts was clearly politically important in this example—more so than in Zungharia. But it was not—as tribute has so often been said to be—trade by another name. The two forms of exchange were distinct, and all concerned understood them to be so. Lee, *The Manchurian Frontier*, pp. 44–46.

I do not deny that there was a ritual component to Qing relations with bordering peoples and with elites within Inner Asian territories. There certainly was, though it was greatly attenuated in the Kazakh trade. Di Cosmo discusses this ritual aspect—he calls it the "tribute environment"—with regard to nineteenth-century Xinjiang in his "Trade, Tribute, and the Qing Occupation of Xinjiang." My point is that trade and tribute were distinct and were treated as such by Qing authorities.

13. Fairbank, "A Preliminary Framework," p. 25.

14. Tsiang, "China and European Expansion"; Fairbank and Teng, "On the Ch'ing Tribute System," p. 141. On Tsiang and his influence on Fairbank, see Hevia, *Cherishing Men from Afar*, pp. 239–40.

15. The principal gazetteers, as well as the *Veritable Records*, *PDZGEFL*,

and of course documentary holdings at the Number One Historical Archives in Beijing all contain much primary information on Qing agricultural reclamation (*tuntian*) in Xinjiang and the northwest. There is also a sizeable secondary literature. Saguchi, Zeng, and Luo's general studies of Xinjiang in the eighteenth and nineteenth centuries all contain useful sections on agricultural development. More recently, monographic works from the People's Republic and Taiwan have established this subfield. In addition to books by Fang Yingkai and Wang Xilong (on which my account is primarily based), see Lin Enxian, *Qingdai Xinjiang kenwu yanjiu*, and Hua "Qingdai Xinjiang nongye kaifa shi," a dissertation based on archival material. There are many recent articles on various aspects of agricultural colonies in Xinjiang: Chen Shenglin and Guo, "Lin Zexu yu Yili tunken"; Hua, "Qianlong nianjian yimin chuguan" and "Daoguang nianjian Tianshan nanlu bingtun"; Wang Xilong, "Qingdai shibian Xinjiang" and "Qingdai Wulumuqi tuntian"; Wu Yuanfeng, "Qing Qianlong nianjian Yili tuntian." Zhao Yuzheng, *Xinjiang tunken*, brings the story up to the present, with an account of the work of the Production Construction Corps under the Chinese Communist Party. In English, see Borei's "Economic Implications of Empire-building" and Perdue's "Military Mobilization in Eighteenth-Century China, Mongolia, and Russia."

16. Fang, *Xinjiang tunken shi*, p. 570.

17. *GZSL* 534:18a–19a, QL22.3 *bingwu*.

18. According to Saguchi, the term *taranči* was originally a Chaghatai Turkish term meaning "farmer"; it appears in Qing Chinese sources as *taliyaqin*, perhaps reflecting influence of the Mongolian (Saguchi calls it Oirat) *tariya-či* (fieldhand, farmer). Note that the Oirat equivalent of *tariya* was *tarā(n)*, thus also yielding *taranči*. Modern Chinese transliterates the term as "*talanqi.*" For the history of the Taranchis in Yili, see Saguchi, *Shinkyō minzoku shi kenkyū*, pp. 239–40; cf. Krueger, *Materials for an Oirat-Mongolian to English Citation Dictionary*, "*tarān*"; "*taranči*" is not cited in this lexicon.

19. Fang, *Xinjiang tunken shi*, p. 571.

20. *GZSL* 604:15a–17b, QL25.1 *gengshen*; see also *GZSL* 612:19b–22a, QL25.5 *renzi*.

21. Yang Yingju suggested and received court approval for the homesteading policy in 1762. (Wang Xilong, *Qingdai Xibei tuntian*, p. 179, citing *Wulumuqi zhenglue*.) I have used Wang Xilong's estimate of the Han homesteader population in 1803, based on gazetteer data (*Qingdai Xibei tuntian*, p. 179). A 1787 census of Chinese in the two prefectures of Zhenxi and Dihua (including Urumchi and outlying settlements of Changji, Fukang, Suilai, Qimusa, and Hutubi) counted 114,348 individuals, which more or less corroborates Wang's later and more extensive figure (Le-bao memorial, QL53.2.9, *GZZZ* vol. 67, p. 264). Compare Fletcher's estimate, following

Zeng Wenwu, that by 1800 the 1775 population of just under 17,200 [Chinese] civilian households (approx. 72,000 persons) [in Xinjiang] "must have doubled several times over" ("Ch'ing Inner Asia," pp. 65–66). Hua writes that approximately 52,250 people migrated from Gansu and Shaanxi to Xinjiang in the Qianlong period (Hua, "Qianlong nianjian yimin," p. 124, cited in Borei, "Beyond the Great Wall," p. 32).

The East Turkestani households figure is from the Jiaqing edition of the *(Qinding) Daqing huidian shili*, 742:11a–12a, cited in Chia, "The Li-fan Yuan in the Early Ch'ing Dynasty," p. 134. A population figure for 1761, also cited by Chia, gives 58,744 households and 205,292 individuals, which works out to only about 3.5 members per registered household.

22. On Lin's work to expand *tuntian* in Altishahr, see Gu and Cai, eds., *Lin Zexu zai Xinjiang*, and Lin's own diary, *Yiji riji*.

23. Fang, *Xinjiang tunken shi*, p. 607; Hua, "Lin Zexu yu Nanjiang," p. 156.

24. Fang, *Xinjiang tunken shi*, p. 608; Wang Xilong, *Qingdai Xibei tuntian yanjiu*, p. 256. Fang cites figures used by Zeng to show that Xinjiang's grain tax by late Qianlong times sufficed to feed the officials and troops, with a considerable surplus.

25. Yong-bao and Xing-zhao, *Ta'erbahatai shiyi*, 2:2a.

26. Fang, *Xinjiang tunken shi*, p. 607.

27. This is Xu Bofu's estimate ("Qingdai qianqi Xinjiang diqu de huobi zhidu," p. 43). Zeng, whose estimates run high, gives the figure 30 million taels for the Qianlong campaigns and 70 million for the Kangxi- and Yongzheng-period excursions against the Zunghars (*Zhongguo jingying Xiyu shi*, p. 256).

28. *GZSL* 614:9, QL25:6 *dingchou*.

29. In 1712 the Kangxi emperor fixed the corvée assessment in perpetuity at 1711 levels. Because the population of male adults subject to the labor-service levy fluctuated, while the *ding* quota was now fixed, some local and provincial officials soon sought to consolidate the land and corvée taxes in order to ease collection. Sichuan and Guangdong actually carried this out around 1716. The Yongzheng emperor implemented the tax merger throughout China proper between 1723 and 1729, and by 1735 most districts had carried out the reform. Huang, *Autocracy at Work*, pp. 263–65; Yeh-chien Wang, *Land and Taxation*, p. 10 et passim.

30. Saguchi, "Kashgaria," p. 69; Xu Bofu, "Qingdai . . . fushui zhidu," pp. 65–67; Fletcher, "Ch'ing Inner Asia," pp. 73–74.

31. Xu Bofu, "Qingdai . . . fushui zhidu," pp. 67–68; Yong-bao, *ZTYLSY*.

32. *GZSL* 572:11, QL23.10 *yimo*, 593:11a–16a, QL24.7 *gengwu*. Zhaohui noted that the high Zunghar quotas had often remained unfulfilled.

33. For breakdowns of the various categories and amounts assessed c. 1795, see He-ning, ed., *Huijiang tongzhi*, j. 7–9 or *HYXYTZ* j. 34–35.

34. Around 1777 the Qing collected 36,000 *tänggä*, but only about 3,110 *patman* (approx. 14,000 piculs) of grain; by this time, a portion of the Altishahr grain tax had been converted to a levy of cotton cloth. *XYWJL* 2:31a.

35. Yong-bao, *ZTYLSY* p. 153. Hōri has determined that the amount of land tax Altishahri peasants were assessed rose from the mid–eighteenth to mid–nineteenth century, but the head-tax remained the same ("Shinchō no Kaikyō tōchi").

36. Yong-bao, *ZTYLSY* p. 193; Adshead, "China in Islam," pp. 9–11. Tu Lien-che's biography of Song-yun in Hummel et al., *Eminent Chinese*, contains a slight error related to salt: Tu writes that Song-yun was demoted by the Jiaqing emperor in 1800, soon after Renzong had appointed him military governor of Yili, because of repeated memorials proposing to lift the ban on private production of salt and coinage "in that region." In fact, Song-yun's memorials suggested the privatization of salt production and minting not in Xinjiang, but throughout the realm. He resubmitted this proposal the last time, in person to the Jiaqing emperor, in the intercalary fourth month of JQ5 (1800). At this point, he had not yet traveled to Yili to take up his position. Song-yun's disfavor did not last long; after brief service at a lower rank, he was again raised to military governor in 1802. See *Qingshi liezhuan*, 32:1a.

37. *GZSL* 578:4b–5b, QL24.1 *jiashen*, 603:13b–14b, QL24.12 *dingyou*, 602:10b–11b, QL24.12 *xinyi*.

38. *YJJZ* p. 259; Yeh-chien Wang, *Land and Taxation*, p. 9.

39. ZPZZ MZSW 75-22, n.d. *pian* (enclosure).

40. Cheng-ge, ZPZZ MZSW 0526-3, DG10.8.22; E-shan, ZPZZ MZSW 0541-15, DG10.9.21; Cheng-ge, ZPZZ MZSW 541-14, DG10.9.20; Yang Yuchun and E-shan, ZPZZ MZSW 0540-13, DG10.10.22; Chang-qing, ZPZZ MZSW 0541-31, DG10.10.29.

41. Sa-ying-a, ZPZZ MZSW 0528-1, DG10.9.8; Sa-ying-a, 0541-9, DG10.9.8; Sa-ying-a, ZPZZ MZSW 0541-29, DG10.10.11; Cheng-ge, ZPZZ MZSW 0541-8, DG10.9.2; Rong-an and Chang-qing, ZPZZ MZSW 0540-3, DG10.9.21; ZPZZ MZSW 0535-4, DG10.9.11.

42. The northeast (Manchurian) territories, too, were dependent on remissions of silver from China proper. "In the case of Kirin nearly 80 percent of the expenditures, and in the case of Heilongjiang practically all the expenditures were paid by the central government." (Lee, *The Manchurian Frontier*, pp. 75–76.)

43. Yeh-chien Wang, *Land and Taxation*, p. 18.

44. In the first three months of 1759, merchant communities in Lianghuai, Zhejiang, and Changlu and Shandong paid "contributions" of 1,000,000, 200,000, and 300,000 taels, respectively, to celebrate the Qing victory in the Western Regions (*GZSL* 578:4, QL24.1 *jiashen*, 581:29a–30b,

QL24.2 *yimao*, 582:6a–7b, QL24.3 *xinyi*). Contributions by merchants from China proper were raised at times of particular need in Xinjiang during the Jiaqing and Daoguang reigns. In the Xianfeng and early Tongzhi periods, as the court and provincial governments suffered ever more severe fiscal deficits, contributions and sales of offices became an increasingly important source of Xinjiang's revenue. See Qi Qingshun, "Qingdai Xinjiang xiexiang," p. 79.

45. Zeng, *Zhongguo jingying Xiyu shi*, p. 314; Yi-xin et al., eds., *(Qinding) pingding Shaan Gan Xinjiang*. Fletcher cites this amount as the total cost of military salaries ("Ch'ing Inner Asia," p. 60) but adopts the figure 1.2 million for the amount of silver coming from China proper annually (p. 61).

46. Xinjiang's tight *xiexiang* budget included no allocation for expenses at the lowest levels of local government and no funds for the benefit or relief of indigenous Eastern Turkestanis. The various begs received emoluments in the form of grain grown by serfs (Tu. *yänchi*) on land granted to the begs by the Qing; the highest-ranked begs received *yanglian* stipends as well, paid by their Altishahri subjects. These ranged from 5,000 to 30,000 *pul*, but apparently these sums left begs' integrity undernourished, as abuses were rampant. In order to pay the expenses of running their yamens, fund travel on official and private business, and to provide food for their household establishments, begs at every level levied two additional taxes on Muslim households. The first, called in Chinese *keliekalike* (Tu. *qirqliq*, "fortieth"?), was an "apportioned exaction" (*tanpai*), a flat charge of 25 *pul* per household per month. The second, which varied in amount, was a supplementary tax, the *seliq* ("tax, contribution"). Though such exactions were illegal, begs were levying them around 1828 and probably, under one name or another, before and after that as well. There were also cases of corruption among Manchu officials involving embezzlement, loans or sales on credit to Muslims (an illegal practice), and accepting gifts and services from begs. (Examples may be found in He-ning, ZPZZ MZSW 70-2, JQ11.4.6; LFZZ MZSW 1374, DG8; *NWYGZY* 77:19 ff.) The cost of goods and services provided by begs to the Manchu overlords were, of course, passed on to the East Turkestani people.

47. These estimates were obtained by totaling attested *xiexiang* amounts for each city in Table 1. Where multiple amounts are recorded, their average value was used to calculate the general estimate. For the post-1828 period, I found no *xiexiang* data for Tarbagatai, Urumchi, Karashahr, Kucha, or Aksu; for the estimate I employed the pre-1828 amounts for these cities.

48. Based on the average of the three available data for Urumchi's stipend listed in Table 1.

49. En-te-heng-e, ZPZZ MZSW 93-1, DG18.5.2. Cf. Xu Bofu, "Qingdai . . . huobi zhidu," where he gives 1,135,800 (1,136,800 is a misprint— personal communication) as Xinjiang's annual *xiexiang* budget after 1759.

Qi Qingshun ("Qingdai Xinjiang xiexiang," p. 80) writes that Urumchi alone "before the Xianfeng period" received an annual 1,080,000 taels from China proper. That these two careful scholars, both of the Xinjiang Academy of Social Sciences in Urumchi, could reach disparate conclusions merely demonstrates that study of this problem must be chronologically specific.

50. All of Xinjiang's *xiexiang* passed through Hami, which was responsible for shipping the silver; Hami officials applied for reimbursement of transport costs on the basis of the exact amount transported. Thus this figure is given with great precision—to five decimal places. But it may have been somewhat out of date by the time the gazetteer was published. Zhong Fang, *Hami zhi*, 20:1a, 3a.

51. In 1879, in response to a memorial from Zuo Zongtang advocating provincial status for Xinjiang, officials in the Board of Revenue searched for records of Xinjiang's subsidy in former times, before the Tungan rebellion. The three figures given here were all they could find: other records had apparently been destroyed in a fire. Yi-xin et al., eds., *(Qinding) pingding Shaan Gan Xinjiang*, 310:9b–10b, 17a–23a, cited in Chou, "Frontier Studies," pp. 225–26.

52. *PDZGEFL xu*, 5:6b–7b, QL25.7 *yihai*; *NWYGZY* 77:3a–b.

53. Davies, *Report*, p. 29, cxci (Appendix 24); Wathen, "Memoir," pp. 657–96. On the stoppage of Chinese silver shipments to Xinjiang in the 1850s, see Conclusion.

54. King, *Money and Monetary Policy*, pp. 141–42; Yan, *Zhongguo jindai jingji*, pp. 27–33. I have worked primarily with Chen Zhaonan's graph, the scale of which allows for finer observation of exchange rate fluctuations (*Yongzheng Qianlong nianjian*, p. 12, figure between pp. 20 and 21). Vogel's more complete data series displays the same trends ("Chinese Central Monetary Policy," pp. 6–7, p. 43, Graph 1.)

55. Vogel, "Chinese Central Monetary Policy," pp. 10, 48–49.

56. Yeh-chien Wang, *Land and Taxation*, Table 4.1, p. 70. Tax quotas are based on Wang's estimates for 1753. Xu Bofu, "Qingdai . . . huobi zhidu," p. 43.

57. *GZSL* 606:18a–19a, QL25.2 *chouwei*. Imperial exhortations against, literally, "sticking in the mud" (*juni*) appear frequently in *Veritable Records* items relating to Xinjiang during this time.

58. Šuhede (Shu-he-de), *ZPZZ MZSW* 80-2, QL37.2.29. Šuhede was defending his plan to collect a stamp tax on livestock sales in Yili.

59. *GZSL* 593:11b–16b, QL24.7 *gengwu*; Tuo-jin et al., *(Qinding) Huijiang zeli*, 6:4a–b; *PDZGEFL xu* 8:5a–6b, QL25.12 *bingzi*, 14:11b–12a, QL26.10 *xinyi*, 75:36b–37a, QL24 intercalary 6, *gengwu*; *HYXYTZ* 35:5a–b. For photographs of the Qing *pul*, see Peng, *Zhongguo huobi shi*, Plate 83 between pp. 756 and 757.

60. Xu Bofu, "Qingdai . . . huobi zhidu," p. 38; *HYXYTZ* 35:2b–3a.

276

Notes to Pages 65–73

61. The Baoyi continued to mint cash in Yili until the mid-1860s. However, the small annual run (between 1,000 and 2,000 strings) makes Yili cash among the rarest of Qing coins. On the Yili mint, and for illustrations of coins, see Wei Jing, "Baoyiju" and Mu, "Zai tan Baoyiju."

62. *YJHL* 77–79, "*qianfa*"; Hōri, "Shindai Kaikyō no kahei," p. 586 (table); *HJTZ* 9:14a–b. On mining in Qing Xinjiang, see Wang Zhizhong, "Qingdai . . . kuangye."

63. *GZSL* 612:22a–23b, QL25.5 *renzi*. That there was some uncertainty over this policy in the Qing court is suggested by Gaozong's comment six months later: "We must fix the market price. This will benefit official (*gong*) and private (*si*) alike." Yet the emperor clearly did not oppose adjusting the official rate to match the market—his goal was rather that "all in all neither officials, soldiers or Muslims should be shown favoritism" (*GZSL* 625:14b–15b, QL25.11 *guihai*). On official rates in China proper, see Vogel, "Chinese Central Monetary Policy," pp. 5–6, 43 (Graph 1).

64. *HYXYTZ* 35:4a.

65. Ch'u, *Local Government*, pp. 28, 135.

66. *HYXYTZ* 34:24b; *GZSL* 757:1b–2a, QL313.3, *yiyou*.

67. Fu-jun, Fu-ming-a, ZPZZ MZSW 0075-3, JQ6.4.19.

68. *HJTZ* 9:4a–b, 9:12b–13a, 10:10b–11a.

69. From 1759 to 1761, before official rates caught up to market rates, Altishahr peasants benefitted from the discrepancy. In 1765 the *pul*-tael exchange rate for tax payment in Yarkand may have been higher than the market rate, but in Aksu in 1804 commercial property taxes were calculated at a rate equal to that used for calculating soldiers' food stipends (220:1), i.e., close to the market rate.

70. *RZSL* 287:9a–10a, JQ19.3 *jihai*; *HJTZ* 8:6a–b.

71. In 1762, Amīn Khwāja was serving in Yarkand. For his assistance during the Qing campaigns in Zungharia and Altishahr the Qing had made this Turfani ruler a prince (*junwang*) of the imperial clan. The splendid mosque built with a grant from the Qianlong emperor in Amīn Khwāja's memory by his son, Sulaymān, still dominates the fields outside Turfan. See Lawrence G. Liu, *Chinese Architecture*, pp. 141–43 for photos and a brief description.

72. Xin-zhu et al., Manchu document (*yuezhe dang*), QL27.3.3, quoted in Wang Xi and Lin, "Qing . . . Xinjiang de 'Huibu,'" pp. 113–14; *PDZGEFL xu*, 16:16a–17a, QL27.4 *gengwu*.

73. Wang Xi and Lin, "Qing . . . Xinjiang de 'Huibu'", pp. 119–20; Yong-bao and Xing-zhao, *Ta'erbahatai shiyi*, 2:2b; E-shan, ZPZZ MZSW 72-7, DG7.2.1.

74. *HYXYTZ* 35:1b *qianfa*; *HJTZ* 9:14a–b.

75. LFZZ MZSW *pian* (enclosure) 1217, c. DG8; Wei Jing, "Baoyiju," p. 91; *XZSL* 108:27b–28b, DG6.10 *guiyou*, 177:5b–6a, DG10.10 *bingshen*.

76. Yi-shan, *Yi-shan Xinjiang zougao*, 1:4b–5a, DG27.8.26. For a discussion of these monetary events from a different perspective, see Fletcher, "The Heyday of the Ch'ing Order," pp. 386–87.

77. *NWYGZY* 76:43a–45b, DG8.3.25. An illustration of the silver *pul* may be found in Peng, *Zhongguo huobi shi*, Plate 101, following p. 792.

78. *NWYGZY* 76:43a–45b, DG8.3.25; 76:46a–47b, DG8.4.22; *XZSL* 135:29b–30a, DG8.4 *xinmao*; *NWYGZY* 76:51b–53b, DG8.11.22.

79. Kuznetsov derides the 2,200 tael savings as "meaningless," but the significance of Nayanceng's reform lies in its exploitation of the dual currency system to pay for a greater military presence without any further expenditure of metals. Kuznetsov, *Ekonomicheskaia Politika Tsinskoga Pravitel'stva v Sintsziane v Pervoi Polovine XIX Veka* [Economic policy of the Qing government in Xinjiang in the first half of the nineteenth century] (AN SSSR, Institut Dal'nego Vostoka, Moscow: Nauka, 1973), p. 153; cited in Hōri, "Shindai Kaikyō no kahei seido," p. 596.

80. Zhao Erxun et al., eds. *Qingshi gao* 124: *zhi* 99, *shihuo* 5 (pp. 3646–47); Wei Jing, "Baoyiju," p. 92.

CHAPTER 3

1. Qi Yunshi and Wang Ting Kai, *Xichui zongtong shilue*, 2:5b–6b. The principal Yili garrisons were destroyed during the Tungan and Taranchi rebellions that spread to Yili in 1864 and during the subsequent Russian invasion of 1870. The Russian forces made Ningyuan (the former Muslim town) their headquarters. Today's Yining City (Ğulja) is built on this site. In Huocheng, 30 kilometers away, a drum tower and a section of wall (enclosing the former military governor's yamen, now a Chinese People's Liberation Army base) are all that remain of Huiyuan, the former Xinjiang capital. The adjoining village is, incidentally, the hometown of Wuer Kaishi (Urkesh), a prominent student leader during the 1989 Chinese student movement.

2. Hummel et al., *Eminent Chinese*, p. 7.

3. *XCYL* 2:13a–30a. On the migration and settlement in Yili of the Sibe banners, see Tong, ed., *Xibozu* and Zhongguo diyi lishi dang'an guan, ed., *Xibozu dang'an shiliao*.

4. Nayanceng, *NWYGZY* 76:51a–b.

5. Upon their return to Zungharia from the Volga region, some Torghut Mongols were given lands near Karashahr while others were incorporated within the existing Oirat banners. All were granted by special imperial dispensation a stipend of cash and grain. *XCYL* 2:16a–b.

6. *XCYL* 2:14b–15a.

7. *PDZGEFL zheng* 72:17a–b, QL24.5 *renwu*; Wu Dashan, LFZZ QL24.5.21 in *QDDA* pp. 45–46; *GZSL* 591:24b–25b, QL24 intercalary 6, *yiyi*.

8. *GZSL* 614:20, QL25.6 *guimo*. Mule trains were very costly. In 1760, the Qing purchased mules in Gansu for 15 taels each and outfitted them with saddlery and pack frames at market price in preparation for the journey to Aksu. On the road, each mule consumed three pints of beans and a ten-catty bale of hay per day. A team of 80 mules required a military escort under command of a brigade commander, 2 attendants, and 40 soldiers; their combined salaries came to 2.82 taels daily. Zhang Yinjin, LFZZ QL25.11.28 in *QDDA* p. 57.

9. Yang Yingju, LFZZ QL30.1.3 (rescript date) in *QDDA* pp. 89–90; Wen-shou ZPZZ MZSW 79-1, QL36.6.15; Zhuo-ke-tuo et al. ZPZZ SYMY 0356 4-72, QL40.

10. *GZSL* 487:28, QL20.4 *guiyou*, 668:14, QL27.8 *renyin*, 699:13b–15a, QL28.11 *dingchou*; Yang Yingju memorial, QL28.12.26, *GZZZ* vol. 20, pp. 171–72.

11. On the Song system, see Smith, *Taxing Heaven's Storehouse*. On the Ming tea-horse trade, see Rossabi, "The Tea and Horse Trade," and Hou, "Frontier Horse Markets." On Qing practice, see Gardella, "Qing Administration of the Tea Trade."

12. Kano, "Chama bōeki no shūmatsu."

13. *GZSL* 487:28, QL20.4 *guiyou*.

14. Yong-bao and Xing-zhao, eds., *Ta'erbahatai shiyi*, 2:2.

15. *GZSL* 854:1b–2a, QL35.3 *gengchen*. In this edict, the emperor refers to an earlier exchange with Ming-rui, without specifying the date.

16. *Yili luezhi*, pp. 289, 292; *ZTYLSY* pp. 192–93. These accounts differ slightly as to the exact date of foundation and source of the *guanbupu* capital.

17. *Yili luezhi*, p. 292; *ZTYLSY* p. 192. The monthly interest rate of 2 percent (i.e., 24 percent annual interest, 26 in years with intercalary months) was high. Annual rates of return on imperial household funds invested in imperial pawnshops (*huangdang*) in the Beijing area were commonly no more than 8 percent, 10 to 15 percent at the highest—although this concealed peculation by officials, and actual rates charged borrowers were generally higher (Wei Qingyuan, "Lun Qingdai de 'huangdang,'" pp. 90, 110). Xinjiang's official investments with Shanxi firms, as we shall see below, yielded only 12 to 13 percent annually. (Wei Qingyuan gives interest figures in annual terms, while my sources provide monthly interest rates. I assume here that the interest in Xinjiang's official pawnshops did not compound monthly and thus reason that 2 percent monthly is equivalent to 24 percent, or 26 percent, annual interest.)

Yili's official pawn operations do not seem extortionary, however, in comparison with pawnshops in the United States in the 1990s. According to a Goldman, Sachs analyst, the largest pawnbroking chain in the U.S., Cash America, makes "20 percent gross profit on defaulted loans and *205 percent interest* on loans repaid" (*New York Times*, Nov. 13, 1991, pp. D1, 10; my emphasis).

18. *Yili luezhi*, pp. 292–93; *ZTYLSY* p. 193.

19. Qi Qingshun, "Qingdai Xinjiang de guanpu," p. 78; *Qingdai chouban yiwu shimo* (*Xianfeng chao*), 1:3:3–4.

20. ZPZZ MZSW 0071-2, QL38.10.19; Qing-gui et al., ZPZZ MZSW 0071-3, QL39.8.20; Ya-de, Shen-bao, ZPZZ MZSW 0071-5, QL41.4.19; Ma-xing-a, Dun-fu, A-er-sa-lang, ZPZZ MZSW 0071-8, QL44.6.15.

21. *SZJL* pp. 144–46.

22. *SZJL* pp. 145–47; Yong-bao et al., *Wulumuqi shiyi*, p. 79.

23. Yong-bao and Xing-zhao, *Ta'erbahatai shiyi*, 2:1a–3a.

24. *SZJL* pp. 148–49.

25. Zelin, *The Magistrate's Tael*, p. 281.

26. *GZSL* 854:1b–2a, QL35.3 *gengchen*.

27. *GZSL* 979:12, QL40.3 *wuchen*.

28. *GZSL* 1324:15b–16a, QL54.3 *jiazi*.

29. *XZSL* 119:13a–14a, DG7 intercalary 5, *wuchen*.

30. Yong-bao, *ZTYLSY* pp. 191, 196.

31. *GZSL* 1362:12b–13a, QL55.9 *guimo*.

32. Yong-bao et al., *Wulumuqi shiyi*, p. 7b.

33. *XJZL* 10:13b–14a.

34. Wei Qingyuan, "Qingdai Qianlong shiqi 'shengxi yinliang,'" pp. 231–32 et passim. Wei's series of articles, based on extensive archival research, provide the best account of Yongzheng and Qianlong imperial investments and local use (and misuse) of *shengxi yinliang* funds. As part of a longer examination of pawn-broking in the Qing, Abe discusses the importance of imperially capitalized pawnbrokers in "Shindai ni okeru tentōgyō no sūsei." Elliott, *Resident Aliens*, pp. 360–69, discusses similar banner garrison investments in China proper in the Yongzheng period. Zelin includes a brief discussion of *shengxi yinliang* in *The Magistrate's Tael*. Zelin makes two important points: that commercial forms of generating wealth were acceptable to the Qing government in the eighteenth century and that the existence of such an institution as *shengxi yinliang* points to a key difference between the economies of Europe and Japan and that of China at the time. In eighteenth-century China, it was the state, not merchant houses, that provided the primary source of liquid capital (pp. 281–83).

35. Wei Qingyuan, "Qingdai Qianlong shiqi 'shengxi yinliang,'" p. 254.

36. *HJTZ* 9:3b–4a. The Number One Historical Archives holds a series of cover memorials that accompanied lists of Qing sales of tea, silk, etc., in Altishahr (ZPZZ MZSW 0071-5, 6, 13, 14, 15, 19, all dating from QL40 until the end of the reign). The lists themselves, originally sent to the Board of Revenue, do not seem to have survived, or are filed elsewhere.

37. *HYXYTZ*, cited in Xie Zhining, "Qianlong shiqi," p. 10.

38. *NWYGZY* 76:51a–b.

39. *NWYGZY* 80:82a–88a, DG8.4.19. The idea for the embargo, according to Nayanceng, originated with Song-yun, Mongol elder statesman and scholar of foreign and border territorial affairs. In the winter of 1827, as Nayanceng prepared to leave the capital to take up his posting as imperial commissioner in Altishahr, Song-yun advised him to cut off Kokand's trade because of the khanate's arrogance and continued support for "the rebels." When this policy backfired and a Kokand-sponsored force invaded again in 1828, Nayanceng was punished for the failure (*NWYGZY* 77:6a, DG8.9.3; Hummel et al., *Eminent Chinese*, p. 586).

40. *NWYGZY* 77:1a–2b, DG8.8.3; *XZSL* 142:4, DG8.9 *gengzi*.

41. *NWYGZY* 80:83a–84b, DG8.7.19; 77:3b, DG8.8.3; LFZZ MZSW 1232 n.d. The Qing was forced in 1832 to compensate Kokand for the goods and land lost by Kokandi merchants after their deportation. But the compensation paid, 10,000 taels (according to the Qing *Veritable Records*), was much lower than the value of confiscated property. Cf. Fletcher, "The Heyday," p. 373.

42. *NWYGZY* 77:5a, DG8.9.3; Ulungge (Wu-long-ga), E-er-gu-lun, Isḥāq (Yi-sa-ke), ZPZZ MZSW 0081-1, DG9.2.19.

43. Ulungge (Wu-long-ga), E-er-gu-lun, Isḥāq (Yi-sa-ke), ZPZZ MZSW 0081-1, DG9.2.19; *NWYGZY* 77:7a–b, DG8.11.3.

44. *NWYGZY* 77:3b, DG8.8.3, 80:17a–b, DG8.12.28. On Qing relations with Kirghiz (Burut) tribes, see Di Cosmo, "Reports from the Northwest," pp. 8–9, texts 5 and 9.

45. *XZSL* 157:26, DG9.6 *jichou*.

46. Jalungga, E-er-gu-lun, Isḥāq (Yi-sa-ke), ZPZZ MZSW 0081-2, DG9.11.9.

47. Jalungga, E-er-gu-lun, Isḥāq (Yi-sa-ke), ZPZZ MZSW 0081-2, DG9.11.9; *XZSL* 163:10b–11b, DG9.12 *xinmo*; ZPZZ MZSW 0074-3, n.d. (c. DG9.12.)

48. Adshead, *China in World History*, pp. 22–24. Adshead's argument is based on the extreme cost of moving goods overland, particularly in rugged, dangerous, highly taxed Turkestan, and on the fact that, despite the rhetorical denunciations in Roman sources, Chinese silk could be little more than a novelty in the vast Roman economy.

49. Zeng, *Zhongguo jingying Xiyu shi*, p. 177.

50. PDZGEFL *zheng*, 83:21b–22a, QL24.12 *dingyou*; HYXYTZ 34: 17b–18a; HJTZ 7:8b, 9:5a; Li Hongzhang et al., *(Qinding) Da Qing huidian shili*, j. 983, n.p., "Menggu minren maoyi"; *NWYGZY* 77:12b–14a, DG9.1.12; *XZSL* 209:18, DG12.4 *wuzi*; Wathen, "Memoir," p. 661; Naqshbandī, "Route from Kashmir, via Ladakh, to Yarkand," p. 382; Tuo-jin et al., *(Qinding) Huijiang zeli*, 6:10; Fletcher, "The Heyday," pp. 373, 379. See also Fletcher, "Ch'ing Inner Asia," p. 83; Pan and Wang, "Qing qianqi Kashiga'er Ye'erqiang duiwai maoyi," p. 26. Fletcher ("Ch'ing Inner Asia"

and "The Heyday") and Pan (*Zhongya Haohanguo*) give the best accounts of Qing-Kokand relations and trade issues.

Precise records of customs revenues in Xinjiang have not come to light, but they were not large and were not itemized or, sometimes, not even included in the accounts of city budgets in Altishahr. Ush in 1804 took in "between ten and twenty strings of cash" (45–90 taels) annually, which the local tax bureau used for general maintenance and to purchase sacrificial items, candles, and incense.

51. Zhong Fang, *Hami zhi*, j. 21. This brief gazetteer entry is puzzling in several respects. First of all, it is unclear which *guan* is meant: the Hami tax barrier, one of the Hami city gates (known as *beiguan, dongguan*, etc.) or the Jiayu Guan. The words *chuguan* and *ruguan* in the passage might merely indicate direction of travel, that is, west or east, and thus iron-rim carts arriving in Hami from the east paid 3 taels, then another 2 taels upon departure toward Turfan or Barkol—which seems excessive. The permits (*koupiao*) mentioned seem to be the documents issued by many cities under the road-pass system. (Waley-Cohen takes this view; *Exile in Mid-Qing China*, p. 105 n. 5.; cf. chap. 4, n. 22, below). But why are they not called road passes (*lupiao*) as in other sources? Moreover, how could Hami alone enjoy the privilege of taxing carts as well as travelers? Were the jade import permits needed for passage through the Jiayu Guan sold only in Hami? These taxes were presumably being collected c. 1844, the publication date of the *Hami zhi*, but we do not know when they first came into effect.

52. LFZZ MZSW 1447-2, QL27.

53. LFZZ MZSW 1447-2, QL27. The commercial tax rates were initially standard throughout Xinjiang. By the early nineteenth century Urumchi divided commercial farmland into categories for taxation purposes, the highest rate being 0.35 taels per *mu* annually (*SZJL* pp. 120–21). Towns in Altishahr likewise eventually adopted slightly different rates for taxing shops, some even employing a five-grade scale (ZPZZ MZSW 0080-7, JQ16.4.5).

54. *ZTYLSY* pp. 191–92; *Wulumuqi zhenglue*, pp. 130–31; Yong-bao et al., *Wulumuqi shiyi*, p. 7a. A practice analogous to Qing renting out of government real estate exists in contemporary China, where state work units (*gongzuo danwei*) rent out retail space to small private businesses (*getihu*). The space occupied by these booksellers, grocers, restaurateurs, hair stylists, and so on are often literally holes-in-the-wall—niches in or sheds abutting the compound walls of work units. The urban landscape created by the reforms in the command economy today must resemble that produced by the economic policies of Manchu garrison communities in eighteenth-century Xinjiang. Both arose from the conjunction of state and private economies and an affinity for walls.

55. Yili's stamp tax took effect in 1772; Karashahr's was the latest, not being implemented until 1849. Šuhede (Shu-he-de), ZPZZ MZSW 0080-2, QL37.2.29; Sa-ying-a, ZPZZ MZSW 0080-11, DG29.10.15.

56. "Bazaars and vegetable farms are assessed rent, and camels, horses, cattle, and sheep are taxed. From this comes the term *zushui*" (*SZJL* p. 104).

57. *YJJZ* pp. 18b–19a; Bao-da, *Wushi shiyi*, p. 6a; Yong-bao and Xing-zhao, *Ta'erbaghatai shiyi*, 2:5b; *Wulumuqi zhenglue*, pp. 99–100. Bao-da's *Wushi shiyi*, in the edition listed in the bibliography is essentially identical (except in pagination) to his *Xinjiang Fuhuacheng zhilue*, for which a reprint edition published in Taiwan is available. References are given here to the generally less accessible P.R.C. reprint, however, because I own a copy.

58. San-cheng, ZPZZ MZSW 0080-5, JQ15.12.22; Tie-bao, ZPZZ MZSW 0080-6, JQ16.1.10; *RZSL* 239:15b–16b, JQ16.2 *guiyi*; LFZZ MZSW 1447-3, JQ16.2.25; LFZZ MZSW 1447-10, JQ16.2.28.

59. *NWYGZY* 77:45a, DG8.7.19.

60. *NWYGZY* 77:44b–46a, DG8.7.19.

61. *NWYGZY* 77:52a–53b, DG8.10.5; Rong-an, ZPZZ MZSW 518-7, DG9.9.20. The Kangxi emperor in 1720 initiated the practice of licensing Han merchants who traded in Mongolia in an attempt to limit their number. At first, the permits were available only in Beijing. After 1792 merchants could obtain them in Inner Mongolia as well. See Sanjdorj, *Manchu Chinese Colonial Rule*, pp. 33–34.

62. The point-of-sale tax rates (*luodishui*) in Yili and Tarbagatai were to be broken down to account for the different types of tea: "big catty tea," "small catty tea," and *fucha* (tea licensed for sale by merchants in return for shipping official tea). "Fine tea" and "loose tea" could not legally be shipped to Yili or Tarbagatai because of the embargo on Kokand: it was feared that Kazakhs or merchants traveling from Zungharia would resell tea to the khanate.

63. *NWYGZY* 77:45b–46a, DG8.7.19, 49a–53b, DG8.10.5.

64. *NWYGZY* 77:45b, DG8.7.19.

65. *NWYGZY* 77:55a, DG8.10.5.

66. *NWYGZY* 77:68a–69a, DG9.2.14.

67. Wang's research shows that in 1753, 73.5 percent of Qing tax revenues derived from the land tax, but by 1908 only 35.1 percent did. Yeh-chien Wang, *Land and Taxation*, p. 80, Table 4.8.

68. Mann, *Local Merchants*, p. 7.

69. The analogy between Qing-Kokand relations in the 1830s and Qing-British relations in the 1840s is the insight of Fletcher ("The Heyday," pp. 382–85). In the immediate aftermath of the first Opium War, the Qing court appointed Yi-shan, Yang Fang, and Bi-chang to top positions in southern coastal provinces. These officials had all played important roles in handling the Jahāngīr and Kokandi troubles in Altishahr.

CHAPTER 4

1. Wu Aichen, comp., *Lidai Xiyu shichao*, p. 12; Ji Yun, *Wulumuqi za shi*, p. 1, stanza 2 (*fengtu* 2). In 1768 Ji Yun (1724–1805), a native of Zhili, was

serving as a reader in the Hanlin academy when he learned that Lu Jianzeng, the grandfather of his son-in-law and a retired salt commissioner, was to be implicated in the Lianghuai Salt Administration bribery case. Ji tipped off his relative before official charges were brought, and for this interference was himself cashiered. He spent 1769-71 in exile in Xinjiang, which inspired his *Random Verses of Urumchi*, a sort of tourist guide in 160 verses describing the scenery, institutions, customs, products, excursions, and mysterious matters of Urumchi and environs. Pardoned in 1771, Ji returned to the capital, where in 1773 he was appointed one of the chief editors of the *Siku quanshu* imperial library. Hummel et al., *Eminent Chinese*, p. 120; Lidai Xiyu shi xuanzhu editorial group, ed., *Lidai Xiyu shi xuanzhu*, pp. 96-97.

2. *Qingchao tongzhi* (Comprehensive gazetteer of the Qing reign), j. 93, "shihuo lue" (economy) 13, cited in Xu Bofu, "Qingdai . . . shangye wanglai," p. 203; Yang Yingju, ZPZZ MZSW 0473-5, QL24.12.15.

3. *GZSL* 494:9a-10b, QL20.8 *gengxu*.

4. Fuheng, ZPZZ SYMY 4, n.d. (1756); *GZSL* 513:20, QL21.5 *bingshen*.

5. *GZSL* 580:11b-12a, QL24.2 *bingchen*.

6. *GZSL* 604:15b-17a, QL25.1 *gengshen*.

7. *GZSL* 610:5b-6b, QL25.4 *jimao*.

8. *Wulumuqi zhenglue*, pp. 92-98.

9. Yang Yingju, ZPZZ SYMY 0074, box 2, QL27.3.21; *PDZGEFL xu*, 16:1, QL27.3 *jiawu*.

10. *GZSL* 656:1b-2a, QL27.3 *jiawu*.

11. Fletcher, "Ch'ing Inner Asia," p. 76. Fletcher indicates that the only Han Chinese supposed to be in Altishahr before the 1830s were Green Standard soldiers on rotating tours of duty and some Gansu tea concessionaires. He also mentions Jiangsu, Zhejiang, and Shaanxi traders who got to Yarkand illegally but reiterates that "Han Chinese traders were, as a matter of policy, excluded from Altishahr" (p. 82). One cause of confusion may be the fact that the sources seldom refer to Han (or Tungan) as such, but simply as *min* (common people), in contrast to East Turkestanis, who were *Huizi*.

One item in the *Veritable Records* has been interpreted to imply that merchants from China proper were in fact excluded from Altishahr (*XZSL* 169:11b, DG10.5 *yichou*). An ambiguously worded edict to the Grand Secretariat in 1830 orders that "of Chinese (*minren*) from China proper who exit the Pass, whereas the prohibition (*jin*) of the former edict should be exercised with regard to those destined for cities in the south, those bound for the north who, in conformity with the old precedent, have had their securities verified and been given passes in Suzhou, should be let pass." The "prohibition of the former edict" would seem to mean a prohibition against travel by Han merchants along the southern route, i.e., Altishahr. However, the item continues that in order to prevent merchants sneaking south from Zungharia, a guard post in Toksun (the first city on the road south) be established. Those found without proper passes were to be arrested and punished—implying that some merchants at least could travel to the south, provided they were properly documented. A better translation for *jin* here might in fact be "restriction" or "control," rather than "prohibition," and the edict may refer simply to the pass system. The exact precedents referred to in this item are not clear; in any case, however, we have an overwhelming amount of other evidence to the effect that Han merchants and laborers were allowed and even officially welcomed in the south. For example, a statute published in 1842, twelve years after the edict just quoted, states that Han laborers in Altishahr without a proper pass must be returned to their place of origin in China proper—again implying that with the right papers Han could travel freely in Altishahr. Tuo-jin et al., *(Qinding) Huijiang zeli,* 8:13.

12. Yang Yingju and Ming-de memorial, QL29.7.11, *GZZZ* vol. 22, pp. 157–58. On the character designations of official posts, see Skinner, "Cities and the Hierarchy of Local Systems," in *The City in Late Imperial China,* pp. 314–15.

13. Wen-shou, "Chen Jiayu Guan wai qingxing shu," 81:6a. Wen-shou had just been banished to the northwest from Sichuan; see Waley-Cohen, *Exile in Mid-Qing China,* p. 81.

14. *GZSL* 615:13a, QL25.6 *dingyou,* 608:1b–2b, QL25.3 *dingwei*; Forsyth, *Report of a Mission to Yarkund in 1873,* p. 43.

15. Wen-shou, "Chen Jiayu Guan," 81:6a.

16. Little is known about Qi-shi-yi, whose account of Altishahr in 1777 (*XYWJL*) comprises such an important source for this early period of Qing rule in Xinjiang. He was a member of the Plain Blue Banner and passed the metropolitan examination in 1754. Chou, "Frontier Studies," pp. 40, 333, n. 37.

17. *GZSL* 542:4a–5a, QL22.7 *xinmao,* 556:14, QL23.2 *dingmao*; Wen-shou, "Chen Jiayu Guan," 81:5a; *XYWJL* 7:107a, "za lu." Ji Dachun defines *lan'ganr* as an intermediate post station, or *yaozhan* (*Xinjiang lishi yanjiu* 1985, no. 2: 99, item on *lan'ganr* by Ji Dachun). One example of a *länggär* place-name is Andi'er Lan'ganr, on the Endere River east of Khotan, where four enormous poplars date from the Qing period.

18. On the Xinjiang *taizhan* functions and routes, see Jin, "Qingdai Xinjiang Xilu taizhan," parts 1 and 2. Yi-keng-e, ZPZZ MZSW 0060-3, JQ15.7.2, mentions the various official functions of the post stations in Altishahr and their utility to merchants.

19. Jin, "Qingdai Xinjiang Xilu taizhan," part 2, p. 93.

20. Jin, "Qingdai Xinjiang Xilu taizhan," part 2, p. 93; *GZSL* 613: 21b–22a, QL25.5 *renshen*; Yu Jin'ao, ZPZZ MZSW 0088-1, QL41.6.22; Yi-keng-e, ZPZZ MZSW 0060-3, JQ15.7.2; Yu-lin, ZPZZ MZSW 0556-12, DG11.2.25.

21. Michell and Michell, trans., *The Russians in Central Asia,* Appen-

dix 3. Ma Tianxi ("Ma-tiang-shi") and several other merchants from China proper were captured by Jahāngīr's forces in 1826 and enslaved in Central Asia. This account was recorded by Russians who repatriated the merchants after they escaped to Orenburg (see Chapter 5). The merchants' own statements as taken by Qing officials appear in Yang Yuchun, ZPZZ MZSW 0513-1, DG12.7.10. For verification of travel times, see Wathen, "Memoir on Chinese Tartary and Khoten."

22. Li Hongzhang et al., *(Qinding) Da Qing huidian shili*, j. 983, n.p., "Menggu minren maoyi"; *XZSL* 53:29a, DG3.6 *wuwu*. 'Izzat Allāh, "Travels Beyond the Himalaya," pp. 306–7; *XYWJL* 2:27a; *HJTZ* 7:24a, 31a–b. The issuance fee for the road pass in Altishahr was formally abolished in 1823.

According to Haneda, pass holders entering Xinjiang via the Jiayu Guan exchanged their passes (*lupiao*) at the Hami commandant's yamen for new passes (*yinpiao*) made out for specific Xinjiang destinations ("Iminzoku tōchijō," p. 166).

23. Yin Jiaquan, ZPZZ MZSW 0072-2, QL36.10.20.

24. GPSYYSA 23:824a. On the Gao Pu case in general, see Saeki, "Shindai Shinkyō ni okeru gyokuseki mondai"; McElderry, "Frontier Commerce: An Incident of Smuggling"; and Torbert, *The Ch'ing Imperial Household Department*, appendix.

25. *Xinjiang lishi yanjiu* 1985, no. 2: 95, item on *xiangyue* by Qi Qingshun. According to Qi, *xiangyue* were appointed to East Turkestani and Kirghiz communities only after 1887. A memorial from 1788 implies that the position of *xiangyue* was established among Gansu Tungans only in 1781 (Le-bao memorial, QL53.1.8, *GZZZ* vol. 67, p. 10), but in his testimony, the Tungan Zhao Junrui indicates that he was a *xiangyue* elder in Yarkand sometime before 1778 (see Chapter 5, section titled "Tungan Merchants").

On the Sacred Edict (*shengyu*) and village lectures in China proper, see Mair. Such lectures were used to popularize the *Sacred Edict* among the Yao (Mair, "Language and Ideology," pp. 332–33), but I have found no evidence of such an application in Altishahr during the first epoch of Qing rule there.

26. *GZSL* 608:16a–17a, QL25.3 *dingyi*. The city of Hami apparently remained under the jurisdiction of Gansu even for routine criminal matters until 1774, when authorities there too were granted authority to handle noncapital and other less serious cases itself. Le-er-jin memorial, QL39.7.25, *GZZZ* vol. 36, p. 176.

27. *HJTZ* 11:8a, 7:17b–18a; the quote is from Li Hongzhang et al., *(Qinding) Da Qing huidian shili* j. 996: n.p.; the statute itself cites an edict of 1792.

28. *GZSL* 612:31b–32a, QL25.5 *wuxu*; *Qingdai chouban yiwu shimo*, Xianfeng reign, p. 6, Sa-ying-a, enclosure, DG30.3 *guichou*. The principles behind and implementation of the dual legal system in Qing Xinjiang comprise an important but little-studied subject. I have found very few

Chinese-language documents involving Xinjiang legal cases in the Number One Historical Archives in Beijing. Because of Xinjiang's special administrative status, its legal affairs were not handled by the Board of Punishments, but locally or, for the most important matters, directly through the Grand Council, in consultation with the Muslim Affairs Section of the Court of Colonial Affairs (Lifan Yuan). Thus there is no hoard of *xingke tiben* records concerning Xinjiang cases (although there may be a few among the records for the Shaanxi-Gansu jurisdiction). Lifan Yuan documents from this period that were stored in Beijing have been almost entirely lost. I have not had the opportunity to survey local archive collections in Xinjiang for Qing period legal records in any language. Scattered among the palace memorial and Grand Council reference collection documents (*zhupi zouzhe* and *lufu zouzhe*), however, there are a few Xinjiang legal cases of considerable interest.

On the implementation of Islamic law in Xinjiang, specifically the sentences of beheading and severing of fingers for robbery, see GZSL 628: 13a–14b, QL26.1 *guichou*. On Qing legal treatment of Muslims (primarily the Tungans) in general, see Kataoka, "Kei'an shiryō yori mitaru Shinchō no Kaimin seisaku," and two follow-up notes, "Kei'an shiryō yori mitaru Shinchō no Kaimin seisaku: hosetsu" and " 'Shinchō no Kaimin seisaku' no mata kentō."

29. GZSL 1437:3b–4a, QL58.9 *bingwu*; Tuo-jin et al., *(Qinding) Huijiang zeli*, 8:11–12.

30. GZSL 1075:11b–13b, QL44.1 *dingwei*, 1366:8b–9a, QL55.11, *renwu*. Zhang's stock was confiscated, and he was sent to his original place of registration in China proper for punishment. From 1785 to 1792, the Qing shut down the Russian trade at Kiakhta due to a border dispute. See Chapter 5, section titled "Xinjiang's Tea and Rhubarb Trade."

31. Li Hongzhang et al., *(Qinding) Da Qing huidian shili*, j. 983, n.p., "Menggu minren maoyi."

32. Ibid. One such merchant prisoner is Ma Tianxi, whose description of travel from Turfan to Kashgar was summarized above. Other cases are described in Chapter 5.

33. GZSL 1464:1a–3a, QL59.11 *yibing*; Tuo-jin et al., *(Qinding) Huijiang zeli*, 6:11a–12b. There was considerable intercourse between Turkestanis in Kashgar and Kokand. One poor Kashgarlik, Ta-li-pu, worked as a camel puller crossing the Pamirs for Andijani merchants. He delivered letters and cash contributions to Jahāngīr in Kokand before the Khojas' attack on Altishahr (LFZZ MZSW 1217).

34. Narrow-leaved oleaster, *Elaeagnus angustifolia*.

35. There has been some confusion about the date of the Ush rebellion, for which we again apparently have Wei Yuan to thank. Wei sets his account in Qianlong 29 (1764), a year early, and has been followed by Zeng, Lin

Enxian, and others. (*Sheng wu ji*, 4:32, "Qianlong Xinjiang hou shiji"; Zeng, *Zhongguo jingying Xiyu shi*, p. 299; Lin Enxian, *Qingchao zai Xinjiang de Han Hui geli zhengce*, p. 207.) The actual date of the outbreak is QL30.2.14 (March 5, 1765); it was first reported in QL30 intercalary 2 *yimao* (*GZSL* 730:12a–13a). A fuller account, which Wei Yuan's version resembles (except for the date), is in He-ning, ed., *Huijiang tongzhi*, 12:4b–5a. The earliest narrative record of the story regarding Su-cheng and his son appeared in Qi-shi-yi, *Xiyu wenjian lu*, 2 *xia*: 79a ff., in 1777. Judging from some similarity of wording, He-ning may have drawn upon this work, or both may share a common source.

The late nineteenth century *Tārīkh-i Ḥamīdī* by Mollā Mūsa Sayrāmī associates the forced shipments of oleaster (*jigdä*) with an East Turkestani girl sent to Beijing as concubine for the Qianlong emperor—a model for the famous "Fragrant Consort," Xiang Fei (Sayrāmi, *Tarixi Hamidi*, pp. 204–6). On Xiang Fei, see Millward, "A Uyghur Muslim."

36. *PDZGEFL xu* 32:25a–b, QL30.10 *jiayin*.

37. See Sanjdorj, *Manchu Chinese*, p. 22, and Bawden, *The Modern History of Mongolia*, p. 83.

38. See Haneda, "Iminzoku tōchijō," especially pp. 164–74; Lin Enxian, *Qingchao . . . Han Hui geli zhengce*; and Luo Yunzhi, *Qing Gaozong tongzhi Xinjiang zhengce de tantao*, pp. 293–321.

39. Hešen (He-shen), memorial, QL49.4.28, cited in Hua Li, "Qing zhongye Xinjiang yu neidi de maoyi wanglai," p. 302. Hešen held a position as grand councillor from 1776 until his overthrow early in 1799, the fourth year of the Jiaqing reign.

40. Wu Aichen, comp., *Lidai Xiyu shichao*, p. 140. Similar lonely sentiments characterize Li Bai's poems *Guanshan yue* (Pass mountain moon) and *Saixia qu* (At the frontier). Ibid., pp. 10–12; see Obata, *The Works of Li Po*, pp. 77–78, 140, for English translations.

41. *XYWJL* 2:29a–b.

42. On Ming relations with Hami and Turfan, see Zeng, *Zhongguo jingying Xiyu shi*, chap. 6; on Turfan's early contacts with the Qing in the context of the Zunghar threat, see Saguchi, "Formation of the Turfan Principality."

43. Lin Enxian, *Qingchao . . . Han Hui geli zhengce*, pp. 204–5.

44. *XYWJL* 1:4; *HJTZ* 11:14b–15a; Zhong, *Hami zhi*, j. 14, 15:1a–3b. Map 4 is the frontispiece to *Hami zhi* (between *fanlie* and *mulu*).

45. *HYXYTZ* 14:2b.

46. In 1806 the Turfan commandant mooted a plan to rent unused land in the Turfan area (near Ya'er Lake and Putaogou) to "merchants" from China proper. Although he claimed he could raise 300 taels per year on 1000 *mu* of land in this manner, He-ning advised against the proposal on the grounds that the land technically belonged to the Turfan jasak prince and

that opening it to Chinese farmers might upset heretofore amicable relations between Han and Muslims in Xinjiang's Muslim regions (He-ning, LFZZ MZSW 1435-3, JQ11.12.24). Some Chinese merchants did own land in the Turfan area, however (Qi-chen, ZPZZ MZSW 0655-6, JQ10. intercalary 6.25).

47. In 1789 a Yarkandi merchant named Yu-de-ke bought rhubarb from a local Han or Tungan in Turfan (*GZSL* 1322:16b–18a, QL54.2 *yiwei*). When petitioning for permission to repair the Turfan city walls in 1835, Meng-xun used as justification the fact that traders from foreign tributary countries, as well as their official embassies to Beijing, passed through Turfan (Ming-xun, ZPZZ MZSW 0092-3, DG15.5.2). Meng-xun completed his project with over 600 taels in contributions from local merchants, an indication, perhaps, that these merchants enjoyed the custom of foreign traders.

48. *HJTZ* 11:5b; Forsyth, *Report of a Mission to Yarkund*, pp. 50–51; Ji Yun, *Wulumuqi za shi*, p. 12, stanza 70 (*minsu* 37); Davies, *Report*, pp. cxcii, ccxxi–ccxxii, 14; Cun-cheng, Yu-qi, ZPZZ MZSW 0080-13, XF7.4.22. On Turfan's cotton production and trade, see Hua Li, "Qing zhongye Xinjiang yu neidi de maoyi wanglai," p. 296.

49. A-bu-du-lu-pu was sentenced to strangulation according to the statute on brawling and manslaughter; the execution was postponed until after the autumn assizes. Ming-liang, ZPZZ MZSW 0655-2, JQ8.3.28.

50. *GZSL* 578:20b–21a, QL59.1 *bingshen*; Qi Yunshi, comp., *Xichui yaolue*, 2:6a; Wen-shou, "Chen Jiayu Guan," 81:5a, *GZSL* 911:37, QL37.6, 152:22a–23a, DG9.2 *guiyi*; Yan Xuchang, Gao Yaonan, et al., *Zhenxi ting xiangtu zhi*, "shang," in Ma Dazheng et al., *Xinjiang xiangtuzhi gao*, p. 212.

51. Ming-shan, ZPZZ MZSW 0077-1, QL34.8.4.

52. *XYWJL* 1:6a; *Wulumuqi zhenglue*, 114; Wang Dashu, *Xizheng jicheng*, 2:7b; Yong-bao et al., *Wulumuqi shiyi*, 8a; Qi Yunshi, comp., *Xichui yaolue*, 2:3b; Wan Ma, ed., *Huashuo Wulumuqi*, appendix, pp. 171–79. Gaubatz includes a similar account of Urumchi's history along with historical maps of the city walls in her *Beyond the Great Wall*, pp. 71–73.

53. For an example, see Luo Yunzhi, *Qing Gaozong*, pp. 293–94.

54. Ji Yun, *Wulumuqi za shi*, p. 1, stanza 1.

55. Hong, *Tianshan kehua*, p. 381; see also his mention of the Guandi Temple in Huiyuan (p. 378). On the Guandi cult, see Duara, *Culture, Power, and the State*, pp. 139–48 passim, and Feuchtwang, "School Temple and City God." On Roman amphitheaters and empire building, see Futrell, "Circles Across the Land."

56. *XYWJL* 1:6b. On the *zihao* stores, mostly branches of Shanxi firms, see Chapter 5.

57. Wang Dashu, *Xizheng jicheng*, 2:7b; Yong-bao et al., *Wulumuqi shiyi*, 8a.

58. *GZSL* 647:17, QL27.11 *wuchen*. On commercial taxation, see Chapter 3.

59. Yong-bao et al., *Wulumuqi shiyi*, pp. 23a–24a. The *baojia* figures for civilians (*humin*) were drawn from a catchment area including Dihua Zhou, the counties of Changji, Suilai, Fukang, Qimusa, and Hutubi, the Zhenxi area (including Yihe and Jitai), Toutun, Lucaogou, and Taxihe. There is some ambiguity regarding the merchant figures; they may be *in addition to* those for civilian households (*humin*) and not a subsegment of the civilian population.

Civil administration had been implemented in Urumchi at the subprefectural (*ting*) level in 1760 when a magistracy (*tongzhi*) was established there; military administration organized as in China proper soon followed for the Eastern Circuit, with a commander-in-chief (*tidu*) posted to Barkol in charge of regional Green Standard forces after 1762. Manchu bannermen remained under the jurisdiction of the military governor in Yili, however, even after Urumchi was upgraded to the status of department (*zhou*), with a department magistrate (*zhizhou*) answerable to the governor of Gansu.

60. Ji Yun, *Wulumuqi za shi*, p. 8, stanza 42 (*minsu* 9). Other verses referred to in these two paragraphs: p. 7, stanza 34 (*minsu* 1), stanza 38 (*minsu* 5); p. 11, stanza 64 (*minsu* 31); p. 13, stanza 72 (*wuchan* 1), stanza 75 (*wuchan* 4); p. 15, stanza 87 (*wuchan* 16); p. 24, stanza 147 (*youlan* 9); p. 25, stanzas 152–55 (*youlan* 14–17).

61. Liangzhou and Ganzhou were both cities in Gansu province. Ibid., p. 12, stanza 67 (*minsu* 34); p. 7, stanza 37 (*minsu* 4). Xu Bofu, himself a resident of Urumchi, tells us that merchants from China proper had by 1779 already built native-place association halls (*huiguan*) outside the west gate of old Dihua. Xu Bofu, "Qingdai qianqi Xinjiang diqu de chengzhen jingji," p. 100.

62. *PDZGEFL xu*, 26:1a–2a, QL29.7 *jiazi*.

63. *GZSL* 791:1b–2b, QL32 intercalary 2, *wushen*; Šuhede (Shu-he-de), *ZPZZ MZSW* 0080-2, QL37.2.29.

64. The term "Muslims" (*Huizi*) in this instance probably refers not only to East Turkestanis but also to Kokandi merchants who came north to trade with the Kazakhs. A survey taken in 1828 produced the figure of 1,500 "Andijanis" in Yili (Cao Zhenyong et al., comp., *(Qinding) pingding Huijiang jiaoqin niyi fanglue*, 68:9b). After 1800, Russian subjects also came to Yili and Tarbagatai on trading missions, starting with Tatars and Siberians, followed by Tashkentis. See Fletcher, "Sino-Russian Relations," p. 320.

65. *GZSL* 1100:3, QL45.1 *xinhai*; Xie Zhining, "Qianlong shiqi Qing zhengfu dui Xinjiang de zhili yu kaifa," p. 29. *Tongzhi* usually refers to a magistrate in charge of a subprefecture (*ting*) and serving as assistant to a prefect (*zhifu*). However, in Yili during the period 1759–1864 there were no

prefectures in place under the military government. I have thus employed the translation "civil commissioner," used by Brunnert and Hagelstrom for such officials in the somewhat analogous locale of Guihua. Brunnert and Hagelstrom, *Present Day Political Organization of China*, §§849, 849a, 894.

The functions of these civil commissioners seem to have shifted over time. According to an 1809 gazetteer, the *fumin tongzhi* administered livestock, mines, mints, land and building rents, taxes, and public works, in addition to adjudicating in all murders and robberies involving merchants or Green Standard troops in the nine cities of the Yili region. The *lishi tongzhi*, on the other hand, handled murders and robberies involving Manchus, nomadic tribal peoples (Sibe, Solon, Oirat, etc.), and Muslims in the two Manchu banner garrisons. Qi Yunshi and Wang, *Xichui zongtong shilue*, 4:4 (203).

66. *RZSL* 194:1b–2b, JQ13.4 *dingmao*. On other diversions for exiles in Yili, see Hong, *Tianshan kehua*, p. 380.

67. Yong-bao and Xing-zhao, *Ta'erbahatai shiyi*, 2:5b; Xian-fu, ZPZZ MZSW 0061-9, JQ24.11; Da-ling-a, ZPZZ, MZSW 0061-13, DG9.11.12.

68. (Gen-chu-ke-ze-bang?), ZPZZ MZSW 0085-4, c. 1834–35.

69. Adshead notes that Central Asian urban topography reflects a sociopolitical tripartition between townspeople, native officials/clergy, and alien conquerors. "Frequently, there was a new city or citadel for the ruler, his governor, his garrison, his tax office, physically separate, often by a few miles, from the native old city of religious foundations, guilds and artisans, with the major market, which served both, and also longer distance trade, in between. . . . This tripartite division is clearest in Chinese Turkestan, but there are signs of it at Herat." *Central Asia*, p. 23.

Research by Gaubatz has discovered a preponderance of mainly orthogonal, twin, or double-walled cities (cities divided by internal defensive walls) in north China, northwestern China, and Xinjiang, as opposed to more irregular and round-walled cities in eastern and southern China. Gaubatz concludes from this that "frontier cities seem to better fulfill the ideals that originated in the core area than do those of the core itself. . . . This probably reflects the character of frontier forms as simplified replications of the ideal." (*Beyond the Great Wall*, pp. 170–71. See the entire chapter "City Forms on the Frontiers," for her complete argument.) Although this is an interesting thesis, one would like to see more specific evidence that core Chinese "ideals" informed the design of these Manchu garrison citadels, as opposed to the more immediately apparent factors of strategic necessity and greater room to build than in the densely populated and cultivated parts of China proper. As we will see below, the circumstances underlying the construction of many of Altishahr's twin cities (not discussed by Gaubatz) suggest that strategic reasons were primary. Nonetheless, the influence of geomantic principles on Qing city building in Xinjiang is not to be discounted, as

Gaubatz rightly points out and illustrates with the case of Urumchi (p. 136). Forêt has written a detailed analysis of the geomancy of Chengde, another Qing frontier city ("Making an Imperial Landscape").

70. On the Torghuts, see Chapter 2, footnote on p. 55.

71. *XYWJL* 2:18a–20b.

72. Nayanceng, ZPZZ MZSW 0057-5, JQ12.5.8; Guang-hou, ZPZZ MZSW 0057-2, JQ12.3.15; Song-yun, ZPZZ MZSW 0057-14, JQ12.6.21.

73. Guang-hou, ZPZZ MZSW 0057-2, JQ12.3.15.

74. *RZSL* 231:17b, JQ15.6 *jibing*; Tie-bao, ZPZZ MZSW 0080-70, JQ16.4.5. The numbers of shops were assessed in the unit *jian* and taxed on a five-tier scale depending on the size of the establishment. See Chapter 3 on commercial taxation in Xinjiang.

75. *HJTZ* 10:2b; Tie-bao, ZPZZ MZSW 0080-7, JQ16.4.5; Forsyth, *Report*, p. 43.

76. *XYWJL* 2:26b–27a.

77. *HJTZ* 9:11a; *GZSL* 1070:17a–19b, QL43.11 *jichou*; *NWYGZY* 76:1b–2a, DG8.3.25; Tie-bao, ZPZZ MZSW 0080-7, JQ16.4.5; Forsyth, "Report," p. 42; Qi Yunshi, comp., *Xichui yaolue*, 2:9.

78. Bao-da, *Xinjiang Fuhua zhilue* 1:7a–9b, 2:24b–25a.

79. *HJTZ* 9:2, 7b–8a; Bao-da, *Xinjiang Fuhua zhilue* 1:15b–16a. Forsyth, *Report*, p. 42; Tie-bao, ZPZZ MZSW 0080-7, JQ16.4.5; Bao-da, *Wushi shiyi*, p. 9b; Cao et al., comp., *(Qinding) pinding Huijiang*, 64:9b–10a. Shawl wool from Ush became an important export product via Yarkand to Leh and Kashmir. On the international market for and struggle to control the supply of "Toorfanee" (i.e., from Ush Turfan) wool—one of the principal wools used in the traditional manufacture of "Kashmiri" shawls—see Fletcher, "The Heyday," pp. 399–402.

80. Yang Yingju, LFZZ MZSW 1440-2, QL25.2.27; Yunggui, Gu, and Se-er-de, *Huijiang zhi*, pp. 37–39; *HJTZ* 7:2b–3a; Qi Yunshi, comp., *Xichui yaolue*, 2:6b–7a; Tie-bao, LFZZ MZSW 1447-1, JQ16.1.10; LFZZ MZSW 1447-2, c. JQ14–15. Sections of the old Laining city wall may still be seen in the western part of Kashgar today, not far from the Seman Hotel.

81. *XYWJL* 2:31b; 'Izzat Allāh, p. 320.

82. *HJTZ* 7:2b–3a, 17b. Lin Enxian cites Yong-bao's 1794 real estate venture as evidence of implementation of the 1765 segregation order (*Qingchao . . . Han Hui geli zhengce*, p. 207).

83. *HJTZ* 7:2b–3a, 17b; LFZZ MZSW 1447-2, c. JQ14–15; Ha-lang-a, Yang Fang, ZPZZ MZSW 0561-1, DG11.1.3.

84. Jalungga (Zha-long-a), LFZZ MZSW 1222-6, DG9.6.27.

85. LFZZ MZSW 1232, n.d. (1829–30); *NWYGZY* 76:12a–14a; Davies, comp., *Report*, p. cccxv (Appendix 29a). In his 1848 memoir of events of 1830, Bi-chang called the second Qing cantonment in Kashgar "Hancheng" (Bi-chang, *Ye'erqiang shoucheng jilue*, p. 4b). By Xianfeng times, this usage

was common (e.g., Qing-ying, ZPZZ MZSW 0599-1, XF7.6.4). Such a term may have been used prior to this time, but I have found no reference to it.

86. After the 1835 accord between Kokand and the Qing, true control over Kashgar's foreign commerce lay in the hands of Kokand's *aqsaqal* representatives. Whereas in 1828 Nayanceng found 715 households of "Andijanis" (Kokandis) in Kashgar, of whom he expelled 108 families, by the 1850s foreign merchants and their dependents comprised one quarter of Kashgar's population of 145,000, and there were 6,000 Andijanis alone. Valikhanov, cited in Pan and Wang, "Qing qianqi Kashiga'er Ye'erqiang duiwai maoyi," p. 2. On Kokand's rising influence in Altishahr through the early nineteenth century, see Fletcher, "The Heyday," pp. 361–95.

87. *HJTZ* 7:28a; Qi Yunshi, comp., *Xichui yaolue*, 2:7; Davies, *Report*, p. cccxvi (Appendix 29a); Wathen, "Memoir," p. 656.

88. Tie-bao, ZPZZ MZSW 0080-7, JQ16.4.5; Tie-bao, LFZZ JQ16.5.9, cited in Hua Li, "Qing zhongye Xinjiang yu neidi de maoyi wanglai," p. 290; Ha-lang-a, ZPZZ MZSW 0544-8, DG10.12.13. Main exile colonies in Xinjiang (*qiantun*) were situated in Barkol, Hami, Tarbagatai, Urumchi, and Yili; see Waley-Cohen, *Exile in Mid-Qing China*, pp. 166–69, et passim.

89. Forsyth, *Report*, pp. 37–38; LFZZ MZSW 1232, n.d. (1829–30); NWYGZY 76:12b–13a, DG8.11.3, 76:3b–4b, DG 8.4.19; Davies, *Report*, p. cccxvi (Appendix 29a). The name Yangi Hisar (*yängi hisar*), meaning "new castle," should not be confused with yängi šähär, "new city." The latter term was used in many places to refer to the Qing fortress, which was of course always new compared to the existing Muslim city.

There is a schematic map of the new Qing cantonment in Yangi Hisar in (Nayanceng?), LFZZ MZSW 1236, n.d. (DG8-9), but it does not show the cantonment in relation to the older city nearby.

90. Qi Yunshi, comp., *Xichui yaolue*, 2:7b; *HJTZ* 8:3a, 4a; NWYGZY 76: 3b–4a.

91. NWYGZY 76:3b–4b, DG8.4.22, 76:6b, DG8.5.15, 76:13a, DG8.11.3; LFZZ MZSW 1232, n.d. (1829–30).

92. Yi-jing, Sai-shi-ya-le, ZPZZ MZSW 0092-5, DG25.2.1.

93. *XYWJL* 2:29a–b; 'Izzat Allāh, pp. 302–3; Pundit Munphool, "Geographical Description of Turkish China," in Davies, *Report*, Appendix 29a, cccxii, cccxxiii–iv; Kuropatkin, *Kashgaria*, p. 52.

94. *XYWJL* 2:29b; 'Izzat Allāh, p. 303; Wathen, "Memoir," p. 655.

95. Forsyth, *Report*, p. 36.

96. Kuropatkin, *Kashgaria*, p. 52. Another British agent commented on the general contentment of the Yarkandis under Qing rule in the early 1850s, attributing this to light taxation (Naqshbandī, "Narrative of the Travels," p. 349). An additional reason underlying Yarkandis' apparent satisfaction with Qing rule lies in the fact that the majority of East Turkestanis in the Yarkand area were affiliated with the Ishāqiyya branch of the Makhdūm-

zāda Sufi brotherhood. Burhān ad-Dīn, Khoja Jihān, and the later Khojas harrassing the Qing in Altishahr belonged to the rival Āfāqiyya branch of the family. After 1828, Yarkandis remained neutral or actively opposed attacks on the city by the Khojas and their followers. See Fletcher, "The Naqshbandiyya in Northwest China."

97. Tie-bao, ZPZZ MZSW 0080-6, JQ16.1.10; LFZZ MZSW 1447-9 n.d. (c. JQ16); LFZZ 1447-9 *qingdan*, n.d. (c. JQ16); Na-yan-bao, LFZZ MZSW 1447-5, JQ16.2.24; Jalungga (Zha-long-a) LFZZ MZSW 1222-6 (new no. 8053-59), *pian*, rescript DG9.6.27; Bi-chang, Chang-li, et al., ZPZZ MZSW 0555-1, DG10.11.17; cf. Na-yan-bao, LFZZ JQ16.3.28, cited in Hua Li, "Qing zhongye Xinjiang yu neidi de maoyi wanglai," p. 290. Duo-lie-su-pi produced this figure while in the custody of Kokandi invaders who clipped his queue, cut him, and tortured him on a rack—at least, this is what he told Qing officials when they interrogated him later about his capture. The figure does seem reasonable in light of earlier and later data, and for this reason is provided here.

98. Wathen, "Memoir," p. 654; Davies, *Report*, Appendix 29a, pp. cccxxiii–iv; Forsyth, *Report*, p. 36.

99. *HJTZ* 8:11a; Qi Yunshi, comp., *Xichui yaolue*, 2:8a.

100. Fu-kang-an, Liu Bingtian, et al., *Zougao*, *ce* 20, QL50.7.29; LFZZ MZSW 1307-1, XF7.8.28; *NWYGZY* 76:13a–b, DG8.11.3; Tie-bao, ZPZZ MZSW 0080-7, JQ16.4.5; LFZZ MZSW 1232, n.d. (DG9–10); Forsyth, *Report*, p. 33; *Hetian zhili zhou xiangtuzhi* (Khotan sub-prefectural local gazetteer), in Ma Dazheng et al., *Xinjiang xiangtuzhi gao*, p. 680 (*dili lei—zhisuo*).

101. See, for example, Lin Enxian, *Qingchao . . . Han Hui geli zhangce* chap. 4.1, and Table 4-1.1 on p. 271; or Zeng, *Zhongguo*, p. 312. In each, Qing citadels of the Qianlong era and the period after Jahāngīr alike are erroneously called "Hancheng." By contrast, Nayanceng—who built many of the citadels in question—uses the terms "Mancheng" and "Huicheng" (Muslim city) to describe the divisions of Yangi Hisar and Yarkand before 1828 and the new cantonments built in these cities and in Kashgar after that date (*NWYGZY* 76:3b–4b, DG8.4.22, 76:6b, DG8.5.15, 76:12, DG8.11.3). See also LFZZ MZSW 1490 (see Map 3), where the Kashgar cities are clearly labeled in Chinese "Mancheng" and "Huicheng."

102. Wei Yuan, *Sheng wu ji*, 4:48b, "Daoguang chongding Huijiang ji." Although not explicit in this excerpt, that Wei means the *Han* merchants were excluded from the "Hancheng" is evident both from his use of the term *shangmin* and the phrase "mixed among the Muslim houses."

103. Xinjiang shehui kexueyuan minzu yanjiusuo, ed., *Xinjiang jianshi*, vol. 1, p. 298. It is of course incorrect that the Qing prohibited Chinese merchants from going to Altishahr.

CHAPTER 5

1. Davies, *Report*, p. 14.

2. The two earliest instances contrasting *Zhongguo* to Xinjiang that I
have encountered both appear in unofficial writings. A marginal comment in
the Qingzhao tang congshu edition of Qi-shi-yi's *Xiyu wenjian lu* remarks
that in Xinjiang the fermentation of grains is "surprisingly similar to that
in China (*Zhongguo*)" (7:91a); this was perhaps added by Qi-shi-yi or a
contemporary in the 1770s, or may date from 1835 when the work was
republished in a collectanea. Ji Yun, in describing an ancient city outside
Jimusa (*Wulumuqi za shi*, p. 3, stanza 15, *fengtu*), comments how its design
resembles that of cities in *Zhongguo*. In the 1770s, then, *Zhongguo*, like
neidi, meant the provinces of China proper in contrast to imperial holdings
outside and beyond.

Other parts of Inner Asia could also be designated in Chinese by reference to their position outside passes and gates. Mongolia was commonly
known as *kouwai* (beyond the Gubeikou or Shahukou Pass) or *saiwai*
(beyond the strategic strongpoint), while *guanwai* was also a term for Manchuria, alluding to the Shanhai Guan, where the Ming long wall meets the
North China Sea.

3. Jalungga (Zha-long-a), LFZZ MZSW 1222-6, DG9.6.27.

4. Tuo-jin, LFZZ MZSW 1221, n.d.

5. Jing-shun, ZPZZ MZSW 0656-1, GX8.7.16; Qi Yunshi and Wang,
Xichui zongtong shilue, 10:22a. In the initial months after the conquest,
official correspondence used the character *hui* with a dog radical to refer
pejoratively to East Turkestanis; see Chapter 6.

6. Slightly adapted from a poem collected from a Khotanese informant
in 1935. The young woman demands a variety of fancy Chinese textiles and
cosmetics from her suitor, which he obtains from Beijing or the bazaar. In
the end, however, she brushes him off as too effeminate. Jarring, *Materials
to the Knowledge of Eastern Turki*, vol. 1, pp. 123–25.

7. Togan, "Inner Asian Muslim Merchants at the Closing of the Silk
Route (17th Century)," pp. 18–24, et passim. Fletcher has described the
penetration of Naqshbandī brotherhoods into the northwest of China proper
in "The Naqshbandiyya in Northwest China." For references to Chinese
sources on pre-Qing commercial activity of East Turkestani merchants in
Altishahr, Hami and Turfan, Gansu, Tibet, and Khalkha, see Feng Jiasheng,
Cheng, and Mu, eds., *Weiwuer zu shiliao jianbian*, vol. 2, pp. 259–65.

8. Fletcher, "Ch'ing Inner Asia," pp. 82–83. On Xinjiang's import duties,
see Table 8. On the rules governing East Turkestani travel beyond the *karun*
and within Xinjiang, see *GZSL* 464:1a–3a, QL59.11 *yibing*, and Tuo-jin
et al., *(Qinding) Huijiang zeli*, 8:6. One group of rich East Turkestani merchants apparently survived the Qing conquest: sources refer to a group of

caravan traders, the "Bo-de-er-ge," in Khotan (or, according to another source, Kashgar), who paid the Qing a tax of ten gold taels annually. There were 10 Bo-de-er-ge households in Khotan in 1759; a later source mentions 80 households "at first in Kashgar"—this may be an error for Khotan or Altishahr—and 400 households in 1780. *GZSL* 602:10b–11b, QL24.12 *xinyi*; Xu Ke, *Qingbai leichao*, 36:28 (*zhongzu lei*, Bo-de-er-ge).

9. Saguchi, *18–19 seiki higashi Torukisutan*, pp. 310–11; *GZSL* 629:15a–16b, QL26.1 *jiyi*; *NWYGZY* 77:38a–39b, DG9.3.5; Wathen, "Memoir on Chinese Tartary and Khoten," p. 658.

10. Ji Yun, *Wulumuqi za shi*, p. 12, stanza 70 (*minsu* 37); NWFLW MZSW 5, *bao* 1720, box 2, JQ8.10.25; Wathen, "Memoir," pp. 658, 662–63.

11. Luo Yunzhi, *Qing Gaozong tongzhi Xinjiang zhengce de tantao*, p. 191; *XYWJL* 2:25a–b. A similar rotational schedule of imperial audiences was in effect for the rulers of other Qing subjects in border regions, including the non-Manchu banners of Qinghai, Yili, Khobdo, and Chahar; jasaks and lamas of Inner and Outer Mongolia, Rehe, Fengtian, and Wutaishan; and Sichuan's tusi. Xu Ke, *Qingbai leichao*, 13:3 (*chaogong lei, nianban chaojin*). Documents on Zhao-hui's return from Xinjiang and the elaborate preparations made at each stop along the way for the entertainment of the East Turkestani nobles are in ZPZZ MZSW 0469.

12. *GZSL* 1217:6a–7b, QL49.10 *xinchou*. Figures from Jue-luo Chang-lin, NWFLW MZSW 1720, box 2, JQ2 intercalary 6.21. An identical description appears in Xu Ke, *Qingbai leichao*, 13:4 (*chaogong lei, nianban jinjing suodai xingli renyi*).

13. Tuo-jin, LFZZ MZSW 1355, JQ21.2.3; Xu Ke, *Qingbai leichao*, 13:3 (*chaogong lei, nianban chaojin*). Embassies from Kokand caused the same problems. One such mission, returning after an imperial audience in 1810, acquired so much tea, silk, and china along the way that officials were obliged to add one or two carts to the train at each post station. Even so, by the time they reached Gansu the Kokandis' carts were so overloaded that the single horse pulling each could not surmount a steep wooden bridge. Chinese merchants, too, had attached themselves to the entourage. Nayanceng, LFZZ MZSW 1450-4, JQ15.10.13.

14. Fairbank, "A Preliminary Framework," pp. 9–10.

15. Chia, "The Li-fan Yuan in the Early Ch'ing Dynasty," pp. 19–20.

16. For an examination of Han dynasty foreign relations that relies upon the tribute system model, see Yü, *Trade and Expansion*.

17. *GZSL* 609:19a–20a, QL25.3 *gengwu*, cf. *GZSL* 610:1b, QL25.4 *yihai*; Zhang Yuxin, "Qingdai Beijing de Weiwuer zu," pp. 92–95. On the Khojas in Beijing, see also Saguchi, *18–19 seiki Higashi Torukisutan*, pp. 80–89, 700–702.

18. More than a simple military officer, the banner captain (Ch. *zuoling*; Ma. *niru janggin*) was the hereditary leader of a *niru* ("company," liter-

ally, "arrow"; the Chinese term *zuoling* also refers to this unit). Not only Manchus, but also Han who submitted early to the Qing, as well as "clan villages of tribal peoples" were organized into this basic building block of the banner system. The banner captain was thus "military officer in wartime, civil administrator in peacetime, and enforcer of clan rules and moral code." Lee, *The Manchurian Frontier*, p. 27. For a synthetic discussion of the origins of the banner system that focuses on the importance of the *niru* unit in the hunt, see Elliott, "Resident Aliens," pp. 8–21.

19. NWFLW MZSW 1719, QL57.5.1; Zhang Yuxin, "Qingdai Beijing de Weiwuer zu," pp. 92, 95–96. For the stories about the *Huizi ying* and Xiang Fei, see Millward, "A Uyghur Muslim," and Yu and Dong, eds., *Xiang Fei*. There were several old mosques in the region south of Nanhai, including one associated with the *Huizi ying*, just across the avenue from Xinhua men; Yuan Shikai had this razed in 1913 (Beijing shi diming bangongshi, *Beijing diming mantan*, p. 182–83). The stories about Xiang Fei and the *Huizi ying* remain current today: see *Beijing wanbao*, Oct. 23, 1990, "Daogu shuojin: Hua Beijing, Beijing de Weiwuer zu."

A recently reconstructed map of Qianlong-era Beijing situates the "Muslim Camp" in the northwestern quadrant of the city, north of Fucheng Men Dajie and west of Xi Da Shi Jie on the Huizi Ying Hutong (now Anping Xiang). This locates the "Muslim Camp" in the block now defined by Da Chaye Hutong, Xiao Chaye Hutong, and Qingfeng Hutong (Zhongguo shehui kexueyuan kaogu yanjiusuo, comp., *Ming Qing Beijingcheng tu*).

20. NWFLW MZSW 1720, box 2, JQ8.10.25. Another part of Beijing commonly associated with East Turkestanis—known today as the "Uyghur nationality"—is Wei Gong Cun, the site of the Zhongyang Minzu Daxue (Central University of the Nationalities) today. During the Yuan period, the village was inhabited by Uyghurs—the Buddhist Uyghur people best known for their relations with the Tang dynasty. At that time the village was named "Weiwu Cun" (see characters in the glossary). Later one of the Uyghurs was posthumously granted the title *weiguo gong*, and because of this the name became "Duke of Wei's Village" or "Wei Gong Cun" (Matsumoto, *Pekin chimei kō*, p. 305). During the cultural revolution, this neighborhood's name was again changed, this time in punning and progressive fashion to "For the Public Village" (Wei Gong Cun); the characters have now been restored to "Duke of Wei." By a fitting coincidence, there is a large Uyghur (East Turkestani) population in the area today due to the proximity of the Nationalities University. However, I have found no information to link the site with East Turkestanis present in Beijing during the Qing.

21. Ji Yun, *Wulumuqi za shi*, p. 12, stanza 69 (*minsu 36*).

22. Terada's *Sansei shōnin no kenkyu* covers the Shanxi merchants during the Ming period; though there has been to my knowledge no book-length study of their development in the Qing, there are, however, several

good articles. Saeki's "Shinchō no kōki to Sansei shōnin" and Wei Qingyuan and Wu's "Qingdai zhuming huangshang Fan shi de xingshuai" discuss the dynastic relationship with Shanxi merchant houses, particularly for the early Qing. Pang and Qu, "Lun Qingdai Shanxi tuobang de dui E maoyi," discusses the merchants' tea trade with Russia. On the Shanxi traders' Mongolian activities, see Kong Xiangyi, "Qingdai beifang zuida de 'tongshihang': Dashengkui"; Saeki, "Shindai saigai ni okeru Sansei shōnin"; and *Lü Meng shang Dashengkui.*

23. For a similar description of the recruitment and employment system of Shanxi merchants in Manchuria, see Lee, *The Manchurian Frontier*, p. 99.

24. Li Hua, "Shilun qingdai qianqi de Shanxibang shangren," p. 320; Saeki, "Saigai ni okeru Sansei shōnin," p. 373; Ji Xiaogang, *Yuehui caotang biji*, j. 23, quoted in Saeki, "Saigai ni okeru Sansei Shōnin," p. 371; conversation with Chang Baoyu, Alashan Left Banner (Bayin Khota), July 1990.

25. Conversation with Chang Baoyu, Alashan Left Banner (Bayin Khota), July 1990. The diagram in Figure 5 is based on the Xiang Tai Long store, which stood in Bayin Khota until 1984, when it was replaced by the Lenin Department Store. For a 1923 photograph of a similar trading post, also in Alashan, see Alonso, *China's Inner Asian Frontier*, p. 65.

26. On the Gao Pu case, see McElderry "Frontier Commerce"; Saeki, "Shindai Shinkyō ni okeru gyokuseki mondai"; and Torbert, *The Ch'ing Imperial Household Department*, pp. 136–71.

27. GPSYYSA 19:670b–671a, 20:707b–708a, 22:784–785a, 23:823a, 25: 903, 26:948b, 28:9b–10b.

28. Fu-kang-an, Liu Bingtian, et al., *Zougao*, II 13 B 182, *ce* 20, QL50.7.26; Li Shaokang's *gong* (deposition), LFZZ MZSW 1296-31, c. DG11; Liu Shaojun's *gong* (deposition), LFZZ MZSW 1296-30, c. DG11; Yang Guozhen, *Lin Zexu shujian* (Lin Zexu's letters), pp. 198–206, quoted in Lin Min, "Luelun Lin Zexu," pp. 226–27. Branch stores seem often to have altered one character of the home firm's name to create a name of their own that could nonetheless reflect the link to the home company. There also seem to have been cases of imitators employing similar sounding names in hopes of attracting custom. In 1836, just a few years before Lin's arrival in Yili, there was a stabbing in the Heng Xing Sheng shop in that city. Two characters of this name are identical to those of the Heng Sheng Xing Lin mentions, and the third a near homonym; the order of the characters was slightly rearranged. Te-yi-shun-bao, ZPZZ MZSW 0069-3, DG16.10.9.

29. Wang Zhizhong, "Qingdai Gan-Ning-Qing," p. 59.

30. Tie-bao, *fupian* (enclosure), JQ16, quoted in Hua Li, "Qing zhongye Xinjiang yu neidi de maoyi wanglai," p. 295.

31. GPSYYSA 25:909a–910b; Fu-kang-an, Liu Bingtian, et al., *Zougao, ce* 14: QL49.9.3; *ce* 20: QL50.7.29, QL50.7.26; Xing Sheng's *gong*

(deposition), LFZZ MZSW 1296; Liang Dashou's *gong* (deposition), LFZZ MZSW 1296-14; Zhang Bao's *gong* (deposition), LFZZ MZSW 1296-32; Yan Lianggui's *gong* (deposition), LFZZ MZSW 1296-29.

32. Yang Yuchun, ZPZZ MZSW 0513-1, DG12.7.10. More than a few Chinese merchants were taken as prisoners to Kokand after the 1826 and 1830 invasions. Two Shaanxi merchants were sold as slaves to the Tajiks after Jahāngīr took Kashgar in 1826. The Tajik beg, Ku-bu-te, sent them back as peace offerings to the Qing the following year (Chang-ling, Yang Yuchun, Ulungge [Wu-long-a], ZPZZ MZSW 0490-4, DG7.5.27). In 1832 a mission arrived in Kashgar from Kokand with a train of returned prisoners, including seven begs, six ākhūnds, 763 East Turkestani commoner men and women, two Manchu bannermen, fourteen Green Standard soldiers, a Han exile, and twenty Chinese merchants (*minren*). All had been taken to Kokand in 1826 or 1830 and had survived during the intervening years by begging (Cheng-duan, ZPZZ MZSW 0555-4 *pian* (enclosure), DG12 intercalary 9.6).

33. The major Shaanxi and Gansu Tungan (Hui) rebellions were those of Mi-la-yin (1648), Su Sishisan (1781), Tian Wu (1784), the Shaanxi Eighteen Battalions (1860s), Ma Hualong (1860s), Ma Zhan'ao (1860s), and Ma Yong-rui (1895). See Wakeman, *The Great Enterprise*, pp. 799–895, for an account of the Mi-la-yin rebellion and an introduction to the Chinese bibliography; for the nineteenth- and twentieth-century history of the Hui, see Lipman, *Familiar Strangers*.

34. On the role of Tungans (today's Hui nationality) in commerce in Qing Inner Asia and northwestern China, see Lai, *Huizu Shangye shi*, pp. 174–207 et passim.

35. Based on a conversation with Yang Huaizhong and others in the Ningxia Academy of Social Sciences, July 1990, and interviews with care-takers or directors of the Lanzhou Si, Suzhou Si, Shaanxi Da Si, Hezhou Si, Ninggu Si, Balikun Si, Sala Si, Qinghai Da Si and Dongfang Si, September 1990. For a description of several of Urumchi's mosques and their architectural features, see Gaubatz, *Beyond the Great Wall*, pp. 223–28.

36. GPSYYSA 20:715b–716, 24:870b–871b, 25:911a–912a; Saguchi, *Shinkyō minzoku shi kenkyū*, pp. 293–94.

37. NWYGZY 79:13a–14a; Chang Fengqing's *gong* (deposition), LFZZ MZSW 1294, n.d. (c. DG11), deposition; XZSL 158:10b–12a, DG9.7 *jihai*.

38. Fletcher, "The Naqshbandiyya in China," pp. 21–22, 42–48. See also Lipman, *Familiar Strangers*, chap. 3, sec. 10.

39. Fu-kang-an, Liu Bingtian, et al, *Zougao, ce* 20, QL50.3.29; GZSL 1217:6a–7b, QL49.10 *xinchou*; GZSL 1228:16b–17a, QL50.4 *yichou*. See Saguchi, *Shinkyō* minzoku shi kenkyū, p. 295.

40. GZSL 1218:22a–23a, QL49.11, *renxu*.

41. XZSL 73:8a–9a, DG4.9 *yiwei*; Saguchi, *Shinkyō minzoku shi kenkyū*, pp. 301–2.

42. *NWYGZY* 79:12b.

43. *NWYGZY* 79:14, 77:43; Tuo-jin et al., *(Qinding) Huijiang zeli,* 8:14.

44. *NWYGZY* 79:12.

45. Bi-chang, *Shoubian jiyao/Ye'erqiang shoucheng jilue* 1848 joint edition, p. 29a, cited in Saguchi, *Shinkyō minzoku shi kenkyū,* p. 302.

46. The Russian explorer Valikhanov in the 1850s corroborated these Qing officials' observations of poor relations between East Turkestanis and Tungans in Altishahr. Cited in Saguchi, *Shinkyō minzoku shi kenkyū,* p. 304.

47. Ji Yun, *Wulumuqi za shi,* p. 12, stanza 68 (*minsu* 35).

48. Lin Yongkuang and Wang, *Qingdai Xibei minzu maoyi shi,* pp. 74–75; *NWYGZY* 77:44, DG8.7.19.

49. The figure is based on a survey conducted by Nayanceng in early 1828, prefatory to implementation of the embargo on Kokand (*NWYGZY* 77:44). The original figures were quoted in *feng,* or bundles of tea. Each *feng* of *fucha* weighed three catties; a *feng* of "mixed tea" (*zacha*) contained five catties.

50. De-ying-a, Rong-an, LFZZ MZSW 1451-5, DG8.7.2; Yu-lin, Bu-yan-tai, ZPZZ MZSW 558-1, DG10.12.19.

51. *Wulumuqi zhenglue,* pp. 108–9; Su-er-de et al., *Xinjiang Huibu zhi,* p. 22; Cao Zhenyong et al., comp., *(Qinding) pingding Huijiang jiaoqin niyi fanglue,* 68:6b–7b; YJJZ p. 17.

52. XZSL 56:12, DG3.8 *gengzi,* 60:25b–26b, DG3.10 *dingyi,* 71:18b–19b, DG4 intercalary 7, *jiachen.* See also Xu Bofu, "Qingdai . . . shangye wang-lai," p. 197. Fletcher ("The Heyday," p. 368), probably following Kuznetsov, dates the establishment of the tea customs station in Gucheng to 1826, with successful taxation of "mixed tea" beginning in 1828.

53. Jacques Savary des Bruslons, *Dictionnaire universel de commerce,* 3 vols., Paris: J. Estienne, 1723–30; trans. by Malachy Postelthwayt, as *The Universal Dictionary of Trade and Commerce,* 2 vols., London: J. and P. Knapton, 1751–55. Quoted in Foust, *Muscovite and Mandarin,* p. 164. See also Foust, *Rhubarb: The Wondrous Drug.* The earliest known citation of rhubarb in English dates from the beginning of the fifteenth century (*Oxford English Dictionary,* "rhubarb"). From 1605 we have Shakespeare's line, "What Rubarb, Cyme, or what Purgative Drugge / Would scowre these English hence?" (*Macbeth,* V:3:55.)

54. Pan and Wang, "Qing qianqi Kashiga'er Ye'erqiang duiwai Maoyi," p. 25; Foust, *Muscovite and Mandarin,* pp. 170–83; XYWJL 3:43.

55. GZSL 1320:7b–9b, QL54.1 *xinyou;* cf. GZSL 1322:16b–18b, QL54.2 *yiwei,* 1323:32, QL54.2 *guichou.*

56. GZSL 1323:30b–32a, QL54.2 *guichou,* 1361:35b–36b, QL55.8 *dingchou.*

57. Ward, "Jade: Stone of Heaven," pp. 290, 293; Watt, "Jade," p. 41. Top-quality jadeite, primarily from Burma, is now more valuable than the best nephrite and has all but supplanted it on the market in Hong Kong.

58. Schafer, *The Golden Peaches of Samarkand*, pp. 223–27; So, "Chinese Neolithic Jades"; Marco Polo, *Travels*, pp. 52; Olschki, *Marco Polo's Asia*, p. 163. The word *jade* in European languages dates from after the Spanish encounter in Mesoamerica with the *piedra de ijada*, "colic stone" or "flank stone" worn by indigenous Americans for its magical prophylactic qualities.

59. *XYWJL* 2:29b–30b.

60. *GZSL* 602:10b–11b, QL24.12 *xinyi*; *XZSL* 17:26b–27a, DG1.4 *yiyi*; Yang Boda, "Qingdai gongting yuqi," pp. 52, 58. Because the jade was imperial property, shipping it was delicate work above and beyond the physical difficulties involved. When officials of the Zijing and Miyun customs stations discovered in 1781 that pieces of rough jade passing through Luancheng (in Zhili, southwest of Beijing) en route to the capital had sustained damage, they were at pains to locate the source of the problem anywhere but within their jurisdictions. A piece weighing a kilogram had cracked along an original fault line and broken off from a boulder of 650 kilos. This must have happened on the rough roads of Shaanxi province, they reported to the Imperial Household Agency. The jade had come from Yarkand packed in leather sacks atop a wooden cart, which itself was inadequate: it had only a few boards laid across the frame to serve as a floor, and was held together by a piece of rope. NWFLW MZSW 1719, QL46.1.16. Thomas Buoye recently informed me that the Neiwu Fu *yuezhe dang* monthly reports (held in the Number One Historical Archives) contain detailed accounts of jade received or sold by the Zaoban Chu and Ruyi Guan.

61. At 6 to 6.5 on the Mohs scale, nephrite is too hard to be carved with metal tools. Rather, it was worked with abrasive pastes composed of harder minerals, such as quartz sand. So, "Chinese Neolithic Jades," p. 1.

62. Yang Boda, "Qingdai gongting yuqi," p. 57; Chen Zhongnan and Xia, "Qiaoduo tiangong de Yangzhou yuqi," p. 107. A photo of the "Great Yu Quells the Waters" jade mountain may be found in Ward, "Jade," p. 294, and in Yang Boda, "Jade," p. 91.

63. As superintendent of customs and octroi at the Chongwen Gate (Chongwen Men *shangshui shiwu jiandu*) (Hummel et al., *Eminent Chinese*, p. 288) for an unusually lengthy term (1778–86), Hešen must have had ample opportunity to profit personally from sales of jade. Consider the following item in a Neiwu Fu monthly report of QL45.7 from Neiwu Fu Amban Hešen: "The Ruyi Guan transferred clothing accessories, dishes, and other large and small items of green jade and mountain jade; the total was sold for 16,323,717 taels" (Neiwu Fu *yuezhe bao* 413, QL45.7). One wonders how many such transactions went unreported.

64. *RZSL* 38:9b–10a, JQ4.1 *wuyin*, 41:11b–12a, JQ4.3 *dingchou*. Gaozong died on February 7, 1799 (JQ4.1.3).

65. There were three boulders at this point, not two, but Yu-qing states clearly that this is the same jade originally shipped on Hešen's orders. One of the pieces may have split in transit along a preexisting fracture.

66. Yu-qing, ZPZZ MZSW 0078-2, JQ11.8.8; *RZSL* 170:15a–17a, JQ11.10 *xinchou*; Lin Zexu, *Yiji riji*, p. 153.

67. Yang Boda, "Qingdai gongting yuqi," pp. 52, 55. On Moghul-style jade ware in the Qing court, see Zhou, "Hengdusitan yu qi suo zao yuqi kao." On the Chongwen Men as retail outlet for imperial household overstock, see Torbert *The Ch'ing Imperial Household Department*.

68. GPSYYSA 26:949.

69. *GZSL* 1070:3a–5b, QL43.11 *dinghai*, 1070:17a–19b, QL43.11 *jichou*. On the open Jiayu Guan policy, see Wen-shou, "Chen Jiayuguan wai qingxing shu," 81:6a, and Chapter 4.

70. GPSYYSA 26:949, 22:791, 21:758a. The Qianlong emperor was well aware of and only mildly concerned about the jade smuggling going on before Gao Pu elevated the practice to new heights of perfidy (*GZSL* 1068: 10b–13a, QL43.10 *jiwei*). On one of his southern tours Gaozong noted that the finely sculpted pieces in the Soochow and Yangzhou jade markets were all carved from Khotanese jade (Yang Boda, "Qingdai gongting yuqi," p. 53).

71. Yang Boda, "Qingdai gongting yuqi," pp. 50, 53.

72. The comment appears in a letter to Ruan Yuan regarding Li Dou's *Yangzhou Huafanglu*, in which Ling argues that a section on jade should have been included in this history of Yangzhou (Ling Tingkan, "Yu Yuan Boyuan gexue lun *Huafang lu* shu," 23:12b–13a). Ling Tingkan (1757–1809) spent the years 1779–81 in Yangzhou, before passing the civil service exams. It was here that he met the scholar-official Ruan Yuan (Hummel et al., *Eminent Chinese*, p. 515). My thanks to Stephen Shutt for this and the following reference.

73. Lin Sumen, *Hangjiang sanbai yin*, 7:4. Lin (fl. 1780–1810) was Ruan Yuan's maternal uncle and a member of his circle in Yangzhou.

74. Yang Boda, "Jade," pp. 84–86.

75. GPSYYSA 26:952b–3a.

76. Mu-xing-a, ZPZZ MZSW 0078-1, QL44.8.24; *GZSL* 1070:40b–42a, QL43.11 *bingshen*, 1068:10b–13a, QL43.10 *jiwei*; Fu-kang-an, Liu Bingtian, et al., *Zougao, ce* 15, QL49.9.3.

77. With jade extraction no longer a government monopoly, it is unclear how the collection of high-quality tribute jade was accomplished. Authorities in Yarkand did maintain some controls on river jade, at least, even in the 1840s, well after the Daoguang emperor stopped the tribute shipments. A foreign observer reported in 1843 that jade in a river near Yarkand was

gathered exclusively by the Qing government. ʿIzzat Allāh, "Travels Beyond the Himalaya," p. 303.

78. *RZSL* 39:8, JQ4.1 *wuyin*, 43:20b–21a, JQ4.4, memorial by Khotan superintendent Xu Ji and assistant superintendent En-chang; Ji-feng-e, LFZZ MZSW 1443-2, JQ4.4.10.

79. Fu-jun and Fu-ming-a, ZPZZ MZSW 0075-3, JQ6.4.19. In 1842 Wei Yuan suggested that since Khotan was now part of China, the Qing should adopt the jade standard of ancient times as a hedge against the falling value of copper in China proper. Cited in Waley, *The Opium War*, p. 25.

80. *XYWJL* 4:60b.

81. Hua Li, "Qing zhongye Xinjiang yu neidi de maoyi wanglai," p. 296; Cun-cheng, Yu-qi, ZPZZ MZSW 0080-13, XF7.4.22; Davies, *Report*, p. 14.

82. (Ji-hui?) LFZZ MZSW 1458-1, rescript DG19.12.23; *XZSL* 329:23b–24a, DG19.12 *xinji*, 329:31b–32b, DG19.12 *yiyou*, 330:29, DG20.1 *gengshen*, et passim; Davies, *Report*, pp. ccv–ccvi, 12, 28. See also Fletcher, "The Heyday," p. 382, and Li Hongzhang, et al., *(Qinding) Da Qing huidian shili*, j. 775.

CHAPTER 6

1. Huang Tinggui, ZPZZ MZSW 0458-6, QL23.7.2; Zhao-hui, LFZZ MZSW 1201-2 (new no. 8049-36), QL24.12.17; Yang Yingju, ZPZZ MZSW 0473-1 through 0473-13, QL24.9.5 through 25.12.27; Yang Yingju, LFZZ MZSW 1440-1, QL24.12.30. The nonderogatory *hui* character first appears in ZPZZ MZSW 0473-8, QL25.1.10. Unfortunately, the extant documents bear no rescripts that might explain the change in usage.

The canine *hui* character may have continued in popular use or re-emerged after the rebellions of the 1860s. According to Yang Huaizhong of the Ningxia Academy of Social Sciences, a meeting of Republican authorities in Gansu in 1912 proscribed use of the insulting version of the character in reference to Tungans (personal conversation, July 1990).

2. *XYWJL* 7:105b.

3. Yunggui (Yong-gui), Gu, and Su-er-de, *Huijiang zhi*, pp. 64–65. The Taiwanese reprint of this gazetteer, based on a manuscript edition, lists its author as "unknown" and date simply as "Qianlong period." However, scholars at the Xinjiang Academy of Social Sciences, in a study of the Xinjiang gazetteers, attribute the initial version of this work (also called *Xinjiang Huibu zhi*) with essentially the same contents, to Yunggui and Gu Shiheng. Yunggui, a Manchu of the plain white banner, was managing Altishahr affairs as senior Manchu head of the censorate (*zuobu yushi*) and president of the Board of Rites in 1761 when he compiled this gazetteer with Gu. Before the book was complete, Yunggui was reassigned and the Ush councillor Su-er-de took over command of Altishahr and supplemented and reorganized

the *Huijiang zhi*, finally completing it in 1772. Ji Dachun et al., "Xinjiang xiancun fangzhi gailan," p. 5.

4. Yunggui, Gu, and Su-er-de, *Huijiang zhi*, pp. 55–56.

5. *XYWJL* 2:20.

6. See Qi Yunshi and Wang, *Xichui zongtong shilue*, 12:19a–21b, for a nonjudgmental account of Altishahri culture. He-ning's *Huijiang tongzhi* does contain three brief negative passages; see 12:23 (on the pugilistic East Turkestani character and untrustworthiness of Muslim headmen) and 12:18a (on the sexual initiation of Altishahri boys with a she-ass). I am inclined to attribute this last account more to authorial credulity than to malice.

7. *XJZL* 12:1a. *Waiyi* might be better translated simply as "foreigner" here; see the discussion in the introduction, n. 4.

8. Chou, "Frontier Studies," pp. 76–77.

9. My thinking on the Qianlong ideology of empire in this section has been greatly influenced by the works of Crossley and Hevia. Specific citations can illustrate this debt only inadequately, but see for example Crossley, "The Qianlong Retrospect," pp. 64 and 99, on universal empire, taxonomy, and "sectors" within the empire, and "*Manzhou yuanliu kao*," pp. 780–81; as well as Hevia, "A Multitude of Lords" (or the chapter by that name in *Cherishing Men from Afar*).

10. *Donghua xulu* 317:46, cited in Zhang Yuxin, "Qingchao qianqi de bianjiang zhengce," p. 317. The "dismount here" steles outside the Donghua and Xihua gates of the Forbidden City in Beijing are still in place; the Turki reads, "*bu yärdä atdin.*"

11. This encyclopedic glossary contains lexical items on a variety of subjects ranging from ornithology to personal and family relationships. The "five scripts" are Manchu, Chinese, Mongolian, Tibetan, and Arabic (Turki). The Qianlong period edition was reprinted in 1957 by the Minzu chubanshe (Nationalities Press) in Beijing. Crossley refers to this example in "*Manzhou yuanliu kao*" p. 780.

12. An example of such a confusion, resolved by the *Xiyu tongwen zhi*, may be found in the quotation at the head of this chapter: Kashgar, which Zhao-hui here transcribed into Chinese as "Hashiha'er," would later come to be transliterated as "Kashiga'er."

13. Fuheng et al., comp. *(Qinding) Xiyu tongwen zhi*, preface, 2a. On the significance of the *Xiyu tongwen zhi*, see Enoki, "Introduction," and "Researches in Chinese Turkestan." Enoki argues that on the ideological level, the *Xiyu tongwen zhi* was an attempt to show the equivalency of various cultures and their means of expression. He suggests that *tongwen*, or "linguistic universality" was "one of the basic elements in the cultural policy of the Ch'ing dynasty" ("Researches in Chinese Turkestan," p. 23). My thanks to Ethan Goldings for help rendering the Chinese *na-mu-ka* back into Tibetan.

14. See his "A Preliminary Framework" for the most developed state-ment of the model. As Wills has pointed out ("How We Got Obsessed with the 'Tribute System' "), the image of concentric zones, each containing a people progressively less civilized than its inward neighbor, is evoked in the "Tribute of Yu" chapter of the *Shangshu*. Legge includes a diagram of these relationships as concentric squares in the notes to his translation. Legge, trans., *The Shoo King*, "The Tribute of Yu," vol. 3, pp. 147–49. This diagram of the Nine Domains of the Zhou is apparently drawn from a seventeenth-century reconstruction based on the *Zhou li*. See Henderson, "Chinese Cosmographical Thought," p. 207, fig. 8.3.

15. Wills argues that the "tribute system" only truly functioned as "a unified set of institutions and precedents" for 125 years (c. 1425–1550) during the Ming. "How We Got Obsessed with the 'Tribute System,' " p. 3.

16. For my use of "ethnic," please see the discussion in the footnote on page 14 in the introduction.

17. Hevia's concept of "a multitude of lords" raises an interesting prob-lem, which I do not directly address here: to what extent did the Qing distinguish foreign and domestic in its ideology of hegemony? It is a key point of Fairbank's model that the Qing did not appreciate the concept of equally sovereign states, but rather envisioned all peoples as lying along a hierarchical continuum that included Koreans and Annamese further in, East Turkestanis and Mongols in the next tier, and British and Dutch in the chilly outer circle. While he disputes much of Fairbank's model, Hevia seemingly follows this approach in suggesting that to the Qing court domes-tic and foreign relations were conceptually and ritually identical, that the difference between Macartney, say, and a Mongol prince was one of relative distance achieved by the "centering process" and not of substantive division between "us" and "them" (*Cherishing Men from Afar*). Yet from the sources on Xinjiang, it is clear that by the eighteenth century Qing officials and the court clearly recognized, and for many purposes drew sharp distinctions between, peoples who were Qing subjects (Chahars, Oirats, East Turkestanis) and those who were not (Kazakhs, Andijanis), even when all visited Rehe or Beijing, exchanged gifts, and joined in hunts. For example, Qing sources from this period call East Turkestanis *minhui* (including the character *min* for "populace," and Kokandis *yihui* (with the character for foreign, bar-barian). Were we to adapt Figure 9 to reflect a foreign/domestic distinction, perhaps we might draw a dotted border around the diagram and place the bubbles occupied by Qing subjects inside, and those of foreign lords outside, this perimeter.

18. *NWYGZY* 79:12b.

19. For a discussion of the implementation of the tonsure decree in the seventeenth century and Han resistance to it, see Kuhn, *Soulstealers*, pp. 53–

59. On official and imperial reticence concerning potential defiance of the tonsure order, see pp. 80 and 92.

20. Only the queue, and not the shaved forehead, is mentioned in this and other documents about begs' adoption of the hairstyle; the term usually used is "grow the queue" (*xuliu fabian*). The tonsure is probably implied, however.

21. LFZZ MZSW 1222-4, n.d. (c. 1827–28); Nayanceng, LFZZ MZSW 1373-1, DG8.8.20; Tuo-jin et al., *(Qinding) Huijiang zeli*, 8:2. Apparently the rule against begs lower than fourth rank affecting the queue was not always enforced: Duo-lie-su-pi of Yarkand, although only a fifth rank beg, wore a queue. He lost it in 1830 when he was captured by a band of 400 Kokandi "bandits," who cut his hair before torturing him. Bi-chang, Chang-li, et al., ZPZZ MZSW 0555-1, DG10.11.17.

22. We saw examples of this in Chapter 5, in the case of the seven Chinese merchants captured during the fall of Kashgar in 1826 who made their way to Kiakhta seven years later. The queues of the 300 officers and troops taken prisoner during the Jahāngīr invasion likewise were cut off. NWYGZY 73:10a, DG7.12.8.

23. Duo-gui, Na-yan-bao, and Qi-shen, ZPZZ MZSW 0499-1, DG7.3.12.

24. Qi-shi-yi, *Xiyu wenjian lu*, 2:31b. For Xinjiang's Oirat bannermen, the Qing went so far as to import brides. In 1764 the dynasty provided with clothing and transported 420 Mongol slave women and girls between the ages of 15 and 40 to live among the Oirat banners in Zungharia. The total cost, not including transport, amounted to 6,912 taels, of which 2,412 was the price paid to various owners for the women's freedom. Bawden, *Modern History of Mongolia*, pp. 138–39.

25. NWYGZY 77:40a, DG9.3.5; Tuo-jin et al., *(Qinding) Huijiang zeli*, 8:7; Song-yun, ZPZZ MZSW 0556-13, DG11.6.7.

26. NWYGZY 77:41, DG9.3.5; Tuojin et al., *(Qinding) Huijiang zeli*, 6:16, 8:8–9.

27. *Manji*, in Oirat, means "novice monk."

28. Nayanceng, ZPZZ MZSW 0057-5, JQ12.5.8; (Nayanceng?) ZPZZ MZSW 0057-6 *pian* (enclosure), n.d. (c. JQ12.5.8); Song-yun, ZPZZ MZSW 0057-14, JQ12.6.21. Yu-qing might not have been a pederast, but merely a slave runner. The Central Asian trade in boys and girls created a market for Xinjiang slaves, especially Torghuts, who were exported to Central Asia or purchased by East Turkestanis. An 1827 edict strictly prohibiting "the private support in [official] households of male or female youths or children" may have been aimed at preventing Xinjiang authorities from trafficking in East Turkestani or Torghut slaves. The family of a former commandant of Khotan, De-hui, almost ran afoul of this rule in 1832. De-hui had brought a servant back with him from Khotan when he retired as commandant in

1830. He had obtained the young man, named Ba-hai, several years earlier from another amban, who had in turn gotten him from Ulungge in Kashgar. Ba-hai had entered Ulungge's household at the age of eleven. Because the youth, sixteen years old in 1832, dressed in Han clothes and cap and wore the queue, everyone, himself included, believed he was Han. But one spring day in 1832 in the Xi'an market Ba-hai saw an East Turkestani man traveling in the entourage of Ishāq, en route to the capital, and immediately recognized him as his uncle. Ba-hai could not accompany the man to Beijing right away and, not knowing his name, was forced later to make official inquiries to the court. De-hui had since died, but his son was closely interrogated as to how the family came to have an East Turkestani servant. The son barely managed to convince the investigators that because of Ba-hai's flawless Chinese, no one had suspected his real origins. Xu Kun, Ming-chan, and Tu-ming-a, ZPZZ MZSW 0512-1, DG12.9.10.

29. *XZSL* 9:19, JQ25.11 *gengchen*, 10:18b–20b, JQ25.12 *renchen*, 12:31b–32b, DG1.1 *renshen*, 13:40a–41b, DG1.2 *jiyou*; Fletcher, "Ch'ing Inner Asia," p. 86. Fletcher, who cites no source for this anecdote, gives the year as 1808. However, Bin-jing served as councillor in Kashgar between 1818 and 1820, and the event must have occurred during that time.

30. Tuo-jin et al., *(Qinding) Huijiang zeli*, 8:14.

31. Mu-su-man Ku-li, LFZZ MZSW 1330-8, n.d. (c. DG26); Xuanzong, LFZZ MZSW 1330-9, n.d. (c. DG26).

32. *NWYGZY* 77:42b, DG9.3.5. Although a statute prohibiting such loans appeared in the *(Qinding) Huijiang zeli* after Nayanceng's investigation in the 1820s (Tuo-jin et al., 8:12), the practice continued: Lin Zexu commented on it in 1845 (*Yiji riji*, p. 175).

33. Qi-chen, ZPZZ MZSW 0655-6, JQ10 intercalary 6.25.

34. Bin-jing, 0655-12, JQ25.5.13.

35. Wang Zhenghai, LFZZ MZSW 1501, *gong* (deposition), n.d. (c. DG30).

36. Lin Zexu, *Yiji riji*, p. 155. In this town, known as Yangsar Tai (Yangsar station), Chinese rented and grew crops on East Turkestani land.

37. Lin Zexu, *Yiji riji*, p. 175. The Kirghiz coordinated their attack with the ākhūnds of the four cities of western Altishahr. Despite the aid of these fifth columnists, however, the Kirghiz were quickly repulsed. *XZSL* 417: 2a–3a, DG25.5 *renxu*; 417:6a–7a, DG25.5 *yichou*, 417:12b–13b, DG25.5 *jiyi*.

38. Qing-ying, ZPZZ MZSW 0639-11, XF8.4.15.

39. By the time Nayanceng took up office in Kashgar, it had been decided to increase the numbers of troops defending "the five cities including Kashgar" by 6,500 Green Standard infantry. These were to be progressively reduced by 2,000 in two year's time and by another 2,000 after five years, though the Muhammad Yūsuf invasion took place first. An edict of early

1829 mentions that there were then a total of 10,600 Green Standard troops stationed in Altishahr. *NWYGZY* 75:28, DG9.2.14; 75:26a, DG9.1.12.

40. Ulungge (Wu-long-a) memorial, in Cao et al., comps., *(Qinding) pingding Huijiang jiaoqin niyi fanglue,* 55:7a–10b, DG7.12 *guiyou.*

41. Ibid., 49:17b–32b, DG7.8 *guimo;* Wei Yuan, *Sheng wu ji* 4:40 ("Daoguang chongding Huijiang ji"); Hummell et al., *Eminent Chinese,* p. 68; *XZSL* 125:12b–14a, DG7.9 *xinhai.*

42. Chou, "Frontier Studies," p. 85 and n. 5.

43. Nayanceng discusses Chinese merchant business practices in *NWYGZY* 77:42, DG9.3.5, and 77:44a, DG8.7.19.

44. Most of the substatutes in the *Huijiang zeli* concern appointment, transfers, numbers, ranks, stipends, rewards, imperial audiences, and other matters involving the beg officials; there are some items similarly regulating tribute missions and imperial compensation for Kazakhs and, rather incongruously, Kham (Jinchuan) tribesmen. Other substatutes define Xinjiang weights, measures, and currency values. The laws on the queue, intimate relations between Manchu or Han and East Turkestanis, and commercial interaction fall for the most part in the final *juan* of the collection.

45. Bellew, "History of Kashgar," p. 184; Fletcher, "The Heyday," pp. 369–72.

46. Chang Fengqing had worked in Yili until 1826, at which time he made his way south as a militiaman in the army dispatched against Jahāngīr. When Kashgar was again peacefully under Qing control, he went into business there, but kept up his official contacts and was thus able later to provide an insider's testimony on occurrences within the besieged city. Chang Fengqing's *gong* (deposition), LFZZ MZSW 1294.

Materials on this incident are contained primarily in LFZZ MZSW 1293 through 1296, all large *bao* in which documents have not been individually numbered. Where possible, I have provided a document number in addition to the *bao* number (e.g., "1296-23") based on my own count—this is necessarily approximate, however, because in the microfilm versions it is not always clear where one document ends and another begins. Moreover, this *lufu zouzhe* collection has since been renumbered and re-microfilmed and I do not know whether the original order has been maintained. (Scholars who have worked in the Number One Archives more recently than I report that the difference between old and new microfilms is often substantial.) Another difficulty lies in the fact that the depositions that comprise the bulk of these documents were originally transmitted to the court as enclosures with memorials and thus were not individually dated. Unfortunately, the direct association with a dated memorial has not been maintained on the microfilms. From other evidence, however, we know that the depositions condemning Ishāq were probably submitted to the court early in DG11

(1831), while the ones vindicating him came later in the year, perhaps accompanying Chang-ling's DG11.7.23 memorial.

47. Lu Yixuan, LFZZ MZSW 1294, DG9.2.13.

48. *XZSL* 181:24a–26b, DG10.12 *jiawu*.

49. Sha-mi-xu-ding's deposition, LFZZ MZSW 1296-55; A-na-ya-te's deposition, LFZZ MZSW 1296-40. The woman was said to have been among a group of servants captured from Jahāngīr's retreating forces by the Qing in 1826 and later sold or given to begs and officials as slaves.

50. LFZZ MZSW 1294, "*Jinjiang zeimu song gei Yi-sa-ke laizi*" (letter to Isḥāq from the chief of the bandits encroaching on the frontier). This letter, in vernacular Chinese, is labeled a "translation." Although the Number One Historical Archives does contain some correspondence in Turki, no original of this letter has been discovered so far.

51. *XZSL* 181:24a–26b, DG10.12 *jiawu*.

52. Chang-ling, LFZZ MZSW 1296-1, DG11.7.23. My thanks to Lü Hui-tz'u for transcribing the Lufu copy of this memorial.

53. Chang Fengqing's deposition, LFZZ MZSW 1294.

54. Ha-long-a's deposition, LFZZ MZSW 1296-8; Fu-long-a's deposition, LFZZ MZSW 1296-24.

55. There seems to have been no special criteria for selecting merchant commanders in this crisis. Yan Lianggui, 34 years old, was put in charge of 50 men; he had only come to Kashgar in 1827 and worked as a small businessman from that time on. He happened to be in town in September because he had traveled in from his outlying home to find out the current grain price and decided to stay once he heard of the imminent Kokandi attack. Yan Lianggui's deposition, LFZZ MZSW 1296-29.

56. Jalungga and Duo-long-wu, ZPZZ MZSW 0528-8, DG10.17.11; Yi-sa-ke's deposition, LFZZ MZSW 1296-9; Fu-kui's deposition, LFZZ MZSW 1296-11; Ma Tianxi's deposition, LFZZ MZSW 1296-12.

57. Li Shaokang's deposition, LFZZ MZSW 1296-31; Liu Shaojun's deposition, LFZZ MZSW, 1296-30; Fu-kui's deposition, LFZZ MZSW 1296-11.

58. Ha-long-a, LFZZ MZSW 1296-8, *gong* (deposition); Jin Jixian, LFZZ MZSW 1296-15, *gong* (deposition); Wei Qiming, LFZZ MZSW 1296-22, *gong* (deposition); Ma Tianxi, LFZZ MZSW 1296-12, *gong*, (deposition).

59. Ma Tianxi's deposition, LFZZ MZSW 1296-12; Xing Sheng's deposition, LFZZ MZSW; LFZZ MZSW 1296-5, "*Jin jiang Zha-long-a zhe nei zhuceng genjiu ge yuanyou kailie qingdan*" (List displaying each detail of Jalungga's memorial respectfully examined in succession); Liang Dashou's deposition, LFZZ MZSW 1296-14; Chang Fengqing's deposition, LFZZ MZSW 1294.

60. Hei-wa-zi (Pa-la-ti), deposition, LFZZ MZSW 1294-29.

61. *XZSL* 166:4b–5a, DG10.3 *jiawu;* Yang Yingjian's deposition, LFZZ MZSW 1296-23.

62. In late 1829 or early 1830 a band of desperadoes led by the exile Gao Liansheng attacked the prince's yamen again and made off with clothing and silver ingots (*yuanbao*). They initially succeeded in eluding the Qing authorities. Jalungga apprehended them later, however, in connection with an armed raid on the commissary office. *XZSL* 166:5a–6a, DG10.3 *jiawu;* Zhou Pengling's deposition, LFZZ MZSW 1296-13; Ha-long-a's deposition, LFZZ MZSW 1296-8.

63. Jalungga (Zha-long-a), LFZZ MZSW 1222-6 (new number 8053-59), *pian* (enclosure). The dynasty recognized 887 "merchants and Tungans" to commend posthumously for their defense of the city in 1826.

64. It was a trying time for those Han or Ishāqīs unlucky enough to be caught outside the Manchu city. One Ishāqī camel driver, named "Blacky" (Hei-wa-zi, a.k.a. Pa-la-ti), secretly brought food to several Chinese merchants who had been taken captive by the Kokandis. One of the traders, Zhang Fengming, turned over all the silk and cotton cloth he had hidden in the Muslim town to the "Andijanis," who in turn removed his fetters and set him to work feeding their chief's horses. Blacky himself was later locked up in a compound with his whole family and only avoided being sold into slavery by presenting his captors with six gold pieces. Hei-wa-zi (Pa-la-ti), deposition, LFZZ MZSW 1294-29.

65. The siege's most dramatic moment occurred a few days after the initial attack, when a contingent of Kokandi merchants advanced to just beneath the Qing walls, shouting, "Don't shoot! We've got something to say!" The Kokandis, who had been surrounding the city, all knelt down by the side of the moat. A spokesman pleaded their case in Chinese: "We are Andijanis driven out of Kashgar, Aksu, and Yili. We are all servants of the great [Qing] emperor. We traded for many years within the *karun* and did not support Jahāngīr's rebellion—all the East Turkestanis, soldiers, and officials know this. Last year suddenly all our tea and rhubarb was taken from us without compensation. We were driven out of the *karun*, and we can no longer see our wives. And we've lost our lands and property. We've no livelihood outside the *karun*—we're just waiting for death. Then the Kirghiz came to our camp with good tea, bragging that the great emperor had bestowed it upon them. We grew still more angry, and that's why we entered the *karun*, and near the *karun* when the officials and soldiers encountered us, they killed us, and we killed them." All they wanted, claimed the Kokandi merchants, was their tea and rhubarb back, the resumption of trade, and a promise that the Qing would not take reprisals on local East Turkestanis. When these demands were relayed to Jalungga, he replied that the tea and rhubarb had been confiscated during the tenure of his predecessors and had nothing to

do with him and told the "Andijani" traders to return to Kokand and submit a formal petition. Such fruitless negotiations continued until nightfall, when the Kokandis got up off their knees, withdrew to their battle lines and resumed firing on the fort with cannon and small arms. Chang Fengqing's deposition, LFZZ MZSW 1294; cf. Ha-long-a's deposition, LFZZ MZSW 1296-8.

66. Ha-long-a's deposition, LFZZ MZSW 1296-8; Fu-long-a's deposition, LFZZ MZSW 1296-24; Chang Fengqing's deposition, LFZZ MZSW 1294.

67. Chang Fengqing's deposition, LFZZ MZSW 1294; Ha-long-a's deposition, LFZZ MZSW 1296-8. Jalungga's associates, including some beg officials, collected a body of false testimony to demonstrate Ishāq's guilt. Even Ishāq's servant Ai-sa was coerced into implicating his master. An interpreter taught him by rote the Chinese sentences to utter at the inquest. Ai-sa's deposition, LFZZ MZSW 1296-39.

68. *XZSL* 193:8b–12a, DG11.7 *guiyou*; Sun Wenliang et al., *Manzu da cidian*, p. 135. Because of illness, Ishāq returned to Kucha after only three years in the capital. When he died in 1842, his son Aḥmad inherited the *junwang* title. Aḥmad enjoyed a long career governing for the Qing in Aksu and Yarkand, his record tarnished only by two convictions for extortion of East Turkestanis (in 1852 and 1860) and one incident when he was found to be in private communication with foreigners, after which he retired. His loyalty seems unquestionable: during the rebellion of 1864 in Kucha he refused to serve as figurehead for the new Islamic regime and was killed by the insurgents. Gao Wende et al., eds., *Zhongguo minzu shi renwu cidian*, p. 458.

69. Liang Dashou's deposition, LFZZ MZSW 1296-14; *XZSL* 193: 8b–12a, DG11.7 *guiyou*.

70. Bi-chang, *Ye'erqiang shoucheng jilue*, p. 6a. In an administrative shuffle prompted by the Qing realization of Kashgar's vulnerability to attack from Kokand, the councillorship was relocated to Yarkand in November of 1831 (DG11.10). The Kashgar post was thereafter downgraded to commandant until 1858, when the councillorship returned to this westernmost city.

71. Ibid., p. 3.

72. Ibid., pp. 3b–4a; Bi-chang, Chang-feng, Cheng-duan, ZPZZ MZSW 0524-7, DG10.8.27.

73. Bi-chang, *Ye'erqiang shoucheng jilue*, p. 4a.

74. Shu-lun-bao, ZPZZ MZSW 0524-5, DG10.8.23.

75. This support waned, in fact, after the 1830 Kokand invasion. The brutality of the invaders and the lack of any substantial role for Muḥammad Yūsuf undermined Makhdūmzāda prestige in Altishahr. See Fletcher, "The Heyday," p. 371.

76. *XZSL* 178:36–37, DG10.10 *jiayin*; En-te-heng-e, ZPZZ MZSW

0093-1, DG18.5.2. Xuanzong's rescript on this memorial is equivocal: "What you have memorialized is not without interest."

77. Cao et al., comps. *(Qinding) pingding Huijiang jiaoqin niyi fanglue,* 55:7a–10b, DG7.12 *guiyou; XZSL* 131:2b, DG7.12 *guiyou; NWYGZY* 77: 45b, DG8.7.19. On Nayanceng's faith that commercial schemes could finance increased troop strength see *NWYGZY* 75:26a–b, DG9.1.12.

78. *XZSL* 182:18b–19b, DG10.2 *wushen;* Wei Yuan, 4:48a–b; cf. Fletcher, "The Heyday," p. 374. Again, Wei Yuan's numbers are problematic. He writes that 3,000 cavalry from Yili and 4,000 Green Standard troops from Shaanxi-Gansu were added to the 6,000 troops originally in the "Western four cities" of Altishahr but gives the total of "new and old troops" as "12,000, not including 1,000 each in Aksu and Ush." (Fletcher apparently assumed 12,000 to be a misprint for 13,000, hence yielding his total of 15,000.) Wei also lists individual figures for postreform troop allocations for Kashgar, Yangi Hisar, Barchuk, Khotan, and Yarkand as well as Aksu and Ush; these add up to 16,000, and I have followed these figures here.

Fletcher adds, citing Wathen, that "as late as 1835 none of these [15,000 Altishahr troops] appears to have been a Tungan, because the government feared that Tungans, being Muslims, might join in an insurrection if one should arise." There were in fact many Tungans among the Green Standards; we have met "old master Ma" in Kashgar. See also Bi-chang's discussion of Tungans quoted in Chapter 5.

79. Yu-lin, ZPZZ MZSW 556-12, DG11.2.25.

80. *XZSL* 197:17b–20b, DG11.9 *wuyin.*

81. E-le-jin, ZPZZ MZSW 0082-1, DG15.4.24; *XZSL* 267:3b–4a, DG15.4.24.

82. Chang-ling, LFZZ MZSW 1456-3 (new no. 8096-31) DG16.1.14; Geng-fu, LFZZ MZSW 1456-4 (new no. 8096-32) DG16.9.26; Ji-rui ZPZZ MZSW 0082-2, DG23.10.15.

83. *XZSL* 252:24–25, DG14.5 *dinghai,* 254:9–11, DG14.7 *gengwu,* 255: 38–40, DG14.8 *xinyou.*

84. *XZSL* 423:7b–8b, DG25.11 *renxu;* cf. Hua Li, "Qingdai Xinjiang nongye kaifa shi yanjiu," pp. 205–6. See also Fletcher, "The Heyday," pp. 385–86.

85. *XZSL* 409:21, DG24.9 *dinghai,* 410:3, DG24.10 *dingyou,* 419:18–19, DG25.7 *dingchou.*

86. Saguchi provides a fine account of the 1840s reclamation and Han and East Turkestani settlement of the newly opened lands, on which I have based my discussion of Daoguang policy here (*18–19 seiki Higashi Torukisutan,* pp. 226–60). Mincing no words, Saguchi calls the policy "colonialist" in its conception (if not entirely successful as such). Reviewing Qing agricultural reclamation in Xinjiang over the long term, Wang Xilong makes much the same point, though he calls the enterprise *shibian,* "consolidating

the frontier" and blames its ultimate failure on China's own victimization by semicolonialism and semifeudalism ("Qingdai shibian Xinjiang shulue").

The Qing employed Han migration and colonization as an explicit policy on other frontiers as well. In the late seventeenth century, concern over Russian encroachment forced the Kangxi court to open parts of the northeast (Manchuria) below the willow palisades to Han farmers and to bring in exile laborers to construct communications infrastructure needed for frontier defense. But it was not until after 1860 that Heilongjiang began to be opened to legal Han settlement, again with the strategic goal in mind of blocking foreign encroachment by establishing Han population on the frontiers. The process culminated with the lifting of settlement restrictions for the entire Kirin province in 1902 and for Heilongjiang in 1904 (Lee, *The Manchurian Frontier*, pp. 103, 112–15).

For a case where the Qing restricted Han settlement in order to protect indigenous peoples (as in Altishahr prior to 1831), see Shepherd on Taiwan (*Statecraft and Political Economy*, especially pp. 182–191, 226–30).

87. En-te-heng-e, ZPZZ MZSW 0093-1, DG18.5.2.

88. Davies, *Report*, p. cccxv (Appendix 29a). "Kilmak" (*Qalmaq*, Kalmak, Kalmyk, etc.) here does not refer to Torghuts. The term was used by the East Turkestanis as a general term for Mongol or nomadic peoples: Oirat, Mongol, Kazakh, Sibe, Solon, and Manchu. Such usage resembles that of the word "Tartar" in English, which can mean variously Mongol, Turk ("Tartary"), Manchu ("Tartar City"), and even Tibetan.

CONCLUSION

1. Wusun gongzhu [Wusun princess], "Song," in Wu Aichen, comp., *Lidai Xiyu shichao*, pp. 1–2; also quoted in Fan Changjiang, *Zhongguo de xibei jiao*, chap. 4.8 ("Jiayu guan tou"), p. 144, where the poem is entitled "Song of the Yellow Crane" and attributed to Wang Xijun, a young woman sent to the old Wusun chief during the reign of Han Wudi in order to forge an alliance against the Xiongnu. The "Xinjiang Folksong," translated from Chinese, is well known in mainland China and Taiwan; a version is printed .n Guo Shanlan, comp., *Ni xiaide Zhongguo minge*, pp. 166–67. Dabancheng lies along the road between Urumchi and Turfan.

On the exoticization and eroticization of non-Han minorities in China, see Gladney, "Representing Nationality," and Millward, "A Uyghur Muslim."

2. YJJZ p. 26b; WZSL 351:2, XF11.5 *wuzi*; Peng Yunzhang, LFZZ MZSW 1513, XF8.7.4; Davies, *Report*, pp. cxci (Appendix 24) and p. 28; WZSL 313:16b–18a, XF10.3 *xinhai*. Other cities in Xinjiang suffered similar *xiexiang* shortfalls; see Bao-da, *Wushi shiyi*, p. 6a; Chang-liang, ZPZZ CZGS, XF11.12.16 (microfilm 22–27). On the Xianfeng fiscal crisis in Xinjiang, see Qi Qingshun, "Qingdai Xinjiang de xiexiang gongying he caizheng weiji."

3. *YJJZ* pp. 17, 23a–24b, 21b–22a; Bao-da, *Wushi shiyi*, p. 6a.

4. Bu-yan-tai, *Bu-yan-tai Ye'erqiang zougao*, pp. 26b–27b.

5. Peng Yunzhang, LFZZ MZSW 1513, XF8.10.13.

6. This tax seems to be Cun-cheng's innovation and bears no relationship to the obscure Hami customs tax discussed in Chapter 3. Cun-cheng and Yu-qi, ZPZZ MZSW 80-13, XF4.22. Figures for Hami customs tax revenues for the period XF11.11 to TZ2.4 may be found in Mu-lu, Xing-tai, et al., ZPZZ CZGS, TZ1.3.24, TZ1.6.3, TZ1 intercalary 8.6, TZ1.11.8, TZ2.2.13, TZ2.4.22 (microfilm 32, pp. 49–50, 62–63, 81–82, 97–98, 115–116, 132–133).

7. With the growing Russian presence in Zungharia, particularly after the signing of the Treaty of Kulja in 1851, tea became an increasingly important export from Yili and Tarbagatai. See Fletcher, "Sino-Russian Relations," pp. 329–32.

8. Xing-tai and Duan-chang, ZPZZ MZSW 80-15, TZ1.9.22.

9. *Qingdai chouban yiwu shimo (Xianfeng chao)*, pp. 5–6 (Sa-ying-a, *pian* [enclosure], DG30.3 *guichou*); Davies, *Report*, pp. cxc–cxcii (Appendix 24); Qing-ying and Gu-qing, ZPZZ MZSW 0090-8, XF7.11.15; Chang-liang, ZPZZ CZZS microfilm 32, pp. 22–27, XF11.12.16.

10. Kuropatkin, *Kashgaria*, pp. 144–45; Bellew, "History of Kashgar," pp. 186, 189.

11. Davies, *Report*, pp. cxc–cxcii (Appendix 24).

12. LFZZ MZSW 1307-1, XF7.8.28; Davies, *Report*, p. cccxxxix; Kim, "The Muslim Rebellion," p. 46. Kim's account relies heavily on Muslim sources. He cites the French report, *Mission Scientifique dans la Haute Asie, 1890–1895* (3 vols., Paris, 1989) vol. 3, pp. 52–53, on the drowning of indigent East Turkestanis in Khotan.

13. Yi-xin et al., LFZZ MZSW 1348, n.d. (c. TZ1.4.19).

14. Qing-ying, ZPZZ MZSW 0090-8, XF7.11.15.

15. "Vospominaniia Iliiskago Sibinitsa o Dungansko-Taranchinskom vozstanii v 1864–1871 godakh v Iliiskom krae," *Zapiski Vostochnogo otde-leniia Russkogo Arkheologicheskogo Obshchestva* 18 (1907–8), p. 249. Kim ("The Muslim Rebellion," p. 42) cites this Russian translation of a Manchu language account written by a Sibe contemporary.

16. Gong Zizhen, "Xiyu zhi xingsheng yi," 81:6b–7a,9a (pp. 2888–89, 2893); Hummell et al., *Eminent Chinese*, pp. 431–34.

17. Gong's essay was published in 1827 in the famous *Huangchao jingshi wenbian*, a compendium of statecraft writings undertaken by Wei Yuan under He Chang-ling's name. It also appeared around this time in a collection of Gong's own writings, the *Zike ben ding'an wenji*. For an excellent discussion of Gong and other scholars' contributions to the debate over Xinjiang, in the context of the statecraft movement, see Kataoka, *Shinchō Shinkyō*, pp. 90–111.

18. Cited in Kataoka, *Shinchō Shinkyō*, pp. 95, 108–9, n. 38.

19. See Kataoka, *Shinchō Shinkyō*, for a chart of Gong's plan. The

Huangchao jingshi wenbian edition of Gong's essay does not include the sinicized names in his list of prefectures and districts. The names are included in the version in *Gong Zizhen chuanji*, vol. 1, (Beijing: Zhonghua shuju, 1986), pp. 105–12. On place-name politics, see Chou, "Frontier Studies," p. 49.

20. Gong Zizhen, "Xiyu zhi xingsheng yi," 81:8b (p. 2892).

21. In somewhat contradictory fashion, given the overall assimilationist and integrative thrust of this piece, Gong stipulates that an inspector be established at Jiayu Guan to tax outgoing commerce and to allow only grain, salt, tea, rhubarb, and cotton and silk textiles to be exported. No "marvelous and corrupting" Chinese goods could exit the Pass, in order to bolster "their" (the Muslims?) culture. Nor could anything besides leather goods or melons be imported from Xinjiang, in order to "enrich their" economy. Gong Zizhen, 871:8a (2891).

22. Shen Yao and his essay are discussed in Kataoka, *Shinchō Shinkyō*, pp. 97–100; On Xu Song, see Hummell et al., *Eminent Chinese*, pp. 321–22. On Xu Song's Beijing coterie and frontier studies, see Chou, "Frontier Studies," p. 86.

23. Wei Yuan, "Da ren wen," p. 2a (2849); cf. *Sheng wu ji* 4:10a.

24. *Sheng wu ji*, 4:10b. The quote is from Mencius 3b:9; Lau, p. 113.

25. Wei Yuan, *Sheng wu ji*, 4:13a. Wei began the *Sheng wu ji* in 1829 and completed it in 1842 (Leonard, *Wei Yuan*, pp. 16–17). It seems clear that he refers in this passage to the colonization plans of Gong Zizhen and others, but it is uncertain exactly when he wrote this section of the book.

26. Chou, "Frontier Studies," pp. 224–25; Zuo's memorial is in Yi-xin et al., *(Qinding) pingding Shaan Gan Xinjiang Huifei fanglue*, 310:1a–9a.

27. For an analysis of the post-1884 reforms in Xinjiang administration, see Kataoka, *Shinchō Shinkyō*, chaps. 3 and 4.

28. Dillon, "Xinjiang," pp. 31–32. The Kashgar proposal was quickly retracted, following "a national and international outcry."

29. My emphasis. Fan Changjiang, *Zhongguo de xibei jiao*, pp. 141–44 (bk. 4, "Qilianshan bei de lüxing," chaps. 8 and 9).

Abe Takeo. "Shindai ni okeru tentōgyō no sūsei" (Pawn-broking tendencies in the Qing dynasty). In *Tōyōshi ronsō*, Haneda memorial volume.
Haneda Hakushi kanreki kinen kikai, 1950.

Adshead, S. A. M. *Central Asia in World History*. London: Macmillan, 1993.

———. "China in Islam: The Salt Administration in Sinkiang, 1900–1950."
In *Proceedings of the Sixth International Symposium on Asian Studies 1*
(1984): 9–14. Hong Kong: Asian Research Service, 1985.

———. *China in World History*. 2d ed. London: Macmillan, 1995.

Ahmad, Aijaz. "*Orientalism* and After: Ambivalence and Metropolitan
Location in the Work of Edward Said." In Aijaz Ahmad, *In Theory:
Classes, Nations, Literatures*, pp. 159–220. London: Verso, 1994.

Alonso, Mary Ellen, ed. Text by Joseph Fletcher. *China's Inner Asian Fron-
tier: Photographs of the Wulsin Expedition to Northwest China in 1923*.
Cambridge, Mass.: Peabody Museum of Archaeology and Ethnology,
Harvard University, 1979.

Anderson, Benedict. *Imagined Communities*. Rev. ed. London and New York:
Verso, 1991.

Bao-da (Bao-heng). *Wushi shiyi* (Affairs of Ush Turfan). 1857. Repr.,
Zhongguo minzu shidi ziliao congkan, ed. Wu Fengpei, no. 30. Beijing:
Zhongyang minzu xueyuan tushuguan, 1982.

———. *Xinjiang Fuhua zhilue* (Gazetteer of Ush). Preface 1857. Repr.,
Zhongguo fangzhi congshu, Xibu difang, vol. 19. Taipei: Chengwen, 1968.

Barfield, Thomas. *The Perilous Frontier: Nomadic Empires and China*.
Cambridge, Mass.: Basil Blackwell, 1989.

Barth, Fredrik. *Ethnic Groups and Boundaries: The Social Organization of
Culture Difference*. Boston: Little, Brown, 1969.

Bartlett, Beatrice. *Monarchs and Ministers: The Grand Council in Mid-
Ch'ing China, 1723–1820*. Berkeley: University of California Press, 1991.

Basu, Dilip. " 'Barbarians': Construction of Chinese Xenology and the
Opium War." Paper presented at the conference "Beyond Orientalism?"
held at the University of California, Santa Cruz, Nov. 12–13, 1993.

Bawden, C. R. *The Modern History of Mongolia*. 2d rev. ed. New York:
Kegan Paul International, 1989.

Beckwith, Christopher I. *The Tibetan Empire in Central Asia: A History* of the Struggle for Great Power among Tibetans, Turks, Arabs, and Chinese During the Early Middle Ages. Princeton: Princeton University Press, 1987.

Beijing shi diming bangongshi, Beijing shidi minsu xuehui (Beijing city place-names office and Beijing geography, history, and popular customs association), eds. Beijing diming mantan (Chats on Beijing place-names). Beijing: Beijing chubanshe, 1990.

Bellew, Henry Walter. "History of Kashgar." In T. D. Forsyth, ed. Report of a Mission to Yarkund in 1873, under Command of Sir T. D. Forsyth, K.C.S.I., C.B., Bengal Civil Service, with Historical and Geographical Information Regarding the Possessions of the Ameer of Yarkund. Calcutta: Foreign Department Press, 1875.

Benson, Linda. The Ili Rebellion: The Moslem Challenge to Chinese Authority in Xinjiang, 1944–1949. Armonk, N.Y.: M. E. Sharpe, 1990.

Bentley, G. Carter. "Ethnicity and Practice." Comparative Study of Society and History 29, no. 1 (Jan. 1987): 24–55.

Beurdeley, Cécile, and Michel Beurdeley. Giuseppe Castiglione: A Jesuit Painter at the Court of the Chinese Emperors. Rutland, Vt.: Tuttle, 1972.

Bi-chang (Xingyuan). Ye'erqiang shoucheng jilue (A record of the defense of Yarkand). 1848. Mimeograph repr. ed., Wu Fengpei ed., Zhongguo minzu shidi ziliao congkan, no. 27. Beijing: Zhongyang minzu xueyuan tushuguan, 1982.

Borei, Dorothy V. "Beyond the Great Wall: Agricultural Development in Northern Xinjiang, 1760–1820." In Jane Kate Leonard and John R. Watt, eds., To Achieve Security and Wealth: The Qing Imperial State and the Economy 1644–1911, pp. 21–46. Ithaca, N.Y.: Cornell East Asia Series, 1992.

———. "Economic Implications of Empire-building: The Case of Xinjiang." Central and Inner Asian Studies 5 (1991): 22–37.

———. "Images of the Northwest Frontier: A Study of the Hsi-yü Wen Chien Lu." The American Asian Review 5, no. 2 (summer): 26–46.

Boulger, D. C. The Life of Yakoob Beg. London, 1878.

Brunnert, H. S., and V. V. Hagelstrom. Present Day Political Organization of China. A. Beltchenko and E. E. Moran, trans. Rev. ed., 1911; repr. Taipei: Chengwen, 1978.

Bussagli, Mario. Cotton and Silk Making in Manchu China. New York: Rizzoli, 1980.

Bu-yan-tai. Bu-yan-tai Ye'erqiang zougao (Bu-yan-tai's memorials from Yarkand). Mimeograph repr. ed., Wu Fengpei, ed., Zhongguo minzu shidi ziliao congkan, no. 22. Beijing: Zhongyang minzu xueyuan tushuguan, 1982.

Cai Jiayi. "Shiba shiji zhongye Zhunga'er tong zhongyuan diqu de maoyi wanglai lueshu" (Commercial relations between Zungharia and China

proper in the middle of the eighteenth century). In Zhongguo shehui kexueyuan lishi yanjiusuo Qingshi yanjiushi, ed., *Qingshi luncong* (Articles on Qing history), vol. 4, pp. 241–55. Beijing: Zhonghua
shuju, 1982.

Cammann, Schuyler. "The Making of Dragon Robes." *T'oung Pao* 40, livr.
4–5 (1951): 297–321.

———. "Presentation of Dragon Robes by the Ming and Ch'ing Court for
Diplomatic Purposes." *Sinologica* 3 (1953): 193–202.

Cao Zhenyong et al., comps. *(Qinding) pingding Huijiang jiaoqin niyi fanglue* (Imperially commissioned military history of the pacification of the
Muslim frontier and apprehension of the rebels' descendants). Preface,
1830; repr. entitled *(Qinding) pingding Huijiang jiaoqin nifei fanglue*.
Jindai Zhongguo shiliao congkan, no. 851. Taipei: Wenhai, 1965.

Chan, Wing-tsit, trans. and comp. *A Sourcebook in Chinese Philosophy*.
Princeton: Princeton University Press, 1963.

Chang, Hsin-pao. *Commissioner Lin and the Opium War*. Cambridge,
Mass.: Harvard University Press, 1964.

Chen Qinglong. "Lun Huijiang de shangtou" (On the *aqsaqals* of Altishahr).
Shihuo yuekan (Economics monthly) 1, no. 12 (Mar. 1972): 630–35.

———. "Qingdai Tianshan nanbei de maoyi" (Trade north and south of the
Tianshan in the Qing dynasty). *Shihuo yuekan* (Economics monthly) 6,
no. 3 (June 1976): 85–94.

Chen Shenglin and Guo Xiaodong. "Lin Zexu yu Yili tunken" (Lin Zexu and
land reclamation by troops stationed in Yili). *Xinjiang daxue xuebao* no. 4
(1987): 34–40.

Chen Zhaonan. *Yongzheng Qianlong nianjian de yinqian bijia biandong*
(Fluctuations in silver-copper exchange rates in the Yongzheng and
Qianlong periods). Taipei: Shangwu, 1966.

Chen Zhongnan and Xia Linbao. "Qiaoduo tiangong de Yangzhou yuqi"
(Yangzhou's superbly crafted jades). *Yangzhou wenshi ziliao* (Historical
materials on Yangzhou) no. 9 (1990): 104–10.

Chia, Ning. "The Lifanyuan and the Inner Asian Rituals in the Early Qing
(1644–1795)." *Late Imperial China* 14, no. 1 (June 1993): 60–92.

———. "The Li-fan Yuan in the Early Ch'ing Dynasty." Ph.D. diss., Johns
Hopkins University, 1991.

Chiba Muneo. *Kara būran: kuroi saran* (Qara buran: Black tempest). Tokyo:
Kokusho kankōkai, 1986.

Chou, Nailene Josephine. "Frontier Studies and Changing Frontier Administration in Late Ch'ing China: The Case of Sinkiang, 1759–1911." Ph.D.
diss., University of Washington, 1976.

Ch'u, T'ung-tsu. *Local Government in China under the Ch'ing*. Cambridge,
Mass.: Harvard University Press, 1962.

Chu, Wen-djang. *The Moslem Rebellion in Northwest China, 1862–1878*.
The Hague: Mouton, 1966.

Cohen, Paul A. *Discovering History in China: American Historical Writing on the Recent Chinese Past.* New York: Columbia University Press, 1984.

Courant, Maurice. *L'Asie centrale aux XVIIe et XVIIIe siècles: Empire kalmouk ou empire mantchou?* Lyon: 1912.

Creel, H. G. "The Role of the Horse in Chinese History." *American Historical Review* 70 (1965): 641–42.

Crossley, Pamela K. "*Manzhou yuanliu kao* and the Formalization of the Manchu Heritage." *Journal of Asian Studies* 46, no. 4 (Nov. 1987): 761–90.

————. *Orphan Warriors: Three Manchu Generations and the End of the Qing World.* Princeton: Princeton University Press, 1990.

————. "The Qianlong Retrospect on the Chinese-Martial (*hanjun*) Banners." *Late Imperial China* 10, no. 1 (June 1989).

————. "The Rulerships of China." Review article, *American Historical Review* 97, no. 5 (Dec. 1992): 1468–83.

————. "Thinking about Ethnicity in Early Modern China." *Late Imperial China* 11:1 (June 1990): 1–35.

————. *A Translucent Mirror: History and Identity in Qing Imperial Ideology.* Berkeley: University of California Press, forthcoming.

Davies, R. H., comp. *Report on the Trade of Central Asia.* London: House of Commons, 1864.

De Bary, Wm. Theodore, Wing-tsit Chan, and Burton Watson, comps. *Sources of Chinese Tradition.* 2 vols. New York: Columbia University Press, 1960.

De Quincey, Thomas. *Flight of a Tartar Tribe.* (Original title, "Revolt of the Tartars," 1837.) Milton Haight Turk, ed. Riverside Literature Series, no. 110. Boston: Houghton Mifflin, 1897.

Di Cosmo, Nicola. "Ancient Inner Asian Nomads: Their Economic Basis and Its Significance in Chinese History." *Journal of Asian Studies* 53, no. 4 (Nov. 1994): 1092–1126.

————. "Reports from the Northwest: A Selection of Manchu Memorials from Kashgar." Indiana University, Research Institute for Inner Asian Studies, Papers on Inner Asia, no. 25. Bloomington: Research Institute for Inner Asian Studies, 1993.

————. "Trade, Tribute, and the Qing Occupation of Xinjiang." Paper prepared for the panel "Rethinking Tribute: Concept and Practice," Annual Meeting of the Association for Asian Studies, April 1995.

Dikötter, Frank. *The Discourse of Race in Modern China.* Stanford: Stanford University Press, 1992.

Dillon, Michael. "Xinjiang: Ethnicity, Separatism and Control in Chinese Central Asia." Durham East Asian Papers, 1. Durham, England: Department of East Asian Studies, University of Durham, 1995.

Dreyer, June. *China's Forty Millions: Minority Nationalities and National*

Integration in the People's Republic of China. Cambridge, Mass.: Harvard University Press, 1976.

Duara, Prasengit. *Culture, Power, and the State: Rural North China, 1900–1942*. Stanford: Stanford University Press, 1991.

———. *Rescuing History from the Nation: Questioning Narratives of Modern China*. Chicago: University of Chicago Press, 1995.

Eisenstadt, Shmuel N. *The Political Systems of Empires*. New York: The Free Press, 1963.

Elliott, Mark. "Resident Aliens: The Manchu Experience in China, 1644–1760." Ph.D. diss., University of California at Berkeley, 1993.

Enoki Kazuo. "Introduction." In Tōyō Bunko, ed., *Seiiki tōbun shi*, Tokyo: 1961–64.

———. "Researches in Chinese Turkestan during the Ch'ien-lung Period, with Special Reference to the Hsi-yü-t'ung-wen-chih." *Memoirs of the Research Department of the Tōyō Bunko*, 14 (1955): 1–46.

Fairbank, John King. *China: A New History*. Cambridge, Mass.: The Belknap Press of Harvard University Press, 1992.

———. "A Preliminary Framework." In John King Fairbank, ed., *The Chinese World Order: Traditional China's Foreign Relations*. Cambridge, Mass.: Harvard University Press, 1968.

———. *Trade and Diplomacy on the China Coast: The Opening of the Treaty Ports, 1842–1854*. 1953. Repr. Stanford: Stanford University Press, 1969.

———, ed. *The Chinese World Order: Traditional China's Foreign Relations*. Cambridge, Mass.: Harvard University Press, 1968.

Fairbank, John King, and Ssu-yü Teng. "On the Ch'ing Tribute System." *Harvard Journal of Asiatic Studies* 6 (1941): 135–246; Repr. in John King Fairbank and Ssu-yü Teng, *Ch'ing Administration: Three Studies*, Cambridge, Mass.: Harvard University Press, 1960.

Fan Changjiang (Fan Xitian). *Zhongguo de xibei jiao* (China's northwest corner). 1936. Repr., Chongqing: Xinhua chubanshe, 1980.

Fan Jinmin. "Qingdai Jiangnan yu Xinjiang diqu de sichou maoyi" (Silk trade between south China and the Xinjiang region during the Qing period). Paper presented at the International Conference on Qing Regional Socio-economic History and Fourth National Conference on Qing History, Nanjing, November 1987. Published in Nanjing daxue xuebao, ed., *Zhexue shehui kexue youxiu lunwen ji* (Collected Superior Articles in Philosophy and Social Science), pp. 173–203. Nanjing: Nanjing daxue xuebao, 1988.

Fang Yingkai. *Xinjiang tunken shi* (History of agricultural reclamation in Xinjiang). 2 vols. Urumchi: Xinjiang qingshaonian chubanshe, 1989.

Farquhar, David M. "Emperor as Bodhisattva in the Governance of the Ch'ing Empire." *Harvard Journal of Asiatic Studies* 38, no. 1 (June 1978): 5–34.

Feng Chengjun, comp. Rev. Lu Junling. *Xiyu diming* (Western Regions place-names). Beijing: Zhonghua shuju, 1982.

Feng Jiasheng, Cheng Suluo, and Mu Guangwen, eds. *Weiwuer zu shiliao jianbian* (Concise compilation of historical materials relating to the Uyghur nationality). 2 vols. Beijing: Minzu chubanshe, 1981.

Feuchtwang, Stephen. "School Temple and City God." In G. W. Skinner, ed., *The City in Late Imperial China*, pp. 580–608. Stanford: Stanford University Press, 1967.

Fletcher, Joseph. "Ch'ing Inner Asia c. 1800." In John King Fairbank, ed., *The Cambridge History of China*, vol. 10, *Late Ch'ing, 1800-1911, part 1*, pp. 35–106. Cambridge, Engl.: Cambridge University Press, 1978.

―――. "The Heyday of the Ch'ing Order in Mongolia, Sinkiang and Tibet." In John King Fairbank, ed., *The Cambridge History of China*, vol. 10, *Late Ch'ing, 1800-1911, part 1*, pp. 351–408. Cambridge, Engl.: Cambridge University Press, 1978.

―――. "The Naqshbandiyya in Northwest China." In Joseph F. Fletcher, *Studies on Chinese and Islamic Central Asia*, Jonathan Lipman and Beatrice Forbes Manz, eds., Variorum Collected Studies Series. Aldershot, Hampshire: Variorum, 1995.

―――. "Sino-Russian Relations, 1800–62." In John King Fairbank, ed., *The Cambridge History of China*, vol. 10, *Late Ch'ing, 1800-1911, part 1*, pp. 318–50. Cambridge, Engl.: Cambridge University Press, 1978.

Forbes, Andrew D. W. *Warlords and Muslims in Chinese Central Asia: A Political History of Republican Sinkiang 1911-1949.* Cambridge, Engl.: Cambridge University Press, 1986.

Forêt, Philippe. "Making an Imperial Landscape in Chengde, Jehol: The Manchu Landscape Enterprise." Ph.D. diss., University of Chicago, 1992.

Forsyth, Sir T. D. *Report of a Mission to Yarkund in 1873, Under Command of Sir T. D. Forsyth, K.C.S.I., C.B., Bengal Civil Service, with Historical and Geographic Information Regarding the Possessions of the Ameer of Yarkund.* Calcutta: The Government Press, 1875.

Foust, Clifford. *Muscovite and Mandarin: Russia's Trade with China and its Setting, 1727-1805.* Chapel Hill: The University of North Carolina Press, 1969.

―――. *Rhubarb: The Wondrous Drug.* Princeton: Princeton University Press, 1992.

Fuheng (Fu-heng) et al., comps. *(Qinding) huangyu Xiyu tuzhi* (Imperially commissioned gazetteer of the Western Regions of the imperial domain). 1782. Repr. Guji shanben congshu, Wu Fengpei, ed. Beijing: Zhongyang minzu xueyuan tushuguan, 1986.

―――― et al., comps. *(Qinding) pingding Zhunga'er fanglue* (Imperially commissioned military history of the pacification of the Zunghars). 3 vols. *(qian, zheng, xu)*. 1768. Repr., Xizang Hanwen wenxian huike

(Tibet Chinese language imprints), 4 vols., Xizang shehui kexue yuan Xizangxue hanwen wenxian bianjishi (Tibetan Academy of Social Sciences, Chinese language materials on Tibetan studies editorial office), ed. Beijing: Quanguo tushuguan wenxian suowei fuzhi zhongxin, 1990.

———— et al., comps. *(Qinding) Xiyu tongwen zhi* (Imperially commissioned unified-language gazetteer of the Western Regions). 1763. *Siku quanshu* edition, 1782. Repr. Minzu guji congshu, 2 vols., Wu Fengpei, ed. Beijing: Zhongyang minzu xueyuan chubanshe, 1984.

Fu-kang-an, Liu Bingtian, et al. *Zougao* (Memorials). Tōyō bunko collection (Tokyo), catalog no. II 13 B 182.

Futrell, Alison. "Circles Across the Land: The Amphitheatre in the Roman West." Ph.D. diss., University of California at Berkeley, 1991.

"Gao Pu si yu yushi an" (The case of Gao Pu's illegal private jade sales). *Shiliao xunkan* (Historical materials tri-monthly), nos. 19–28 (Feb. 1930 to Mar. 1931).

Gao Wende et al., eds. *Zhongguo minzu shi renwu cidian* (Dictionary of historical biography of Chinese nationalities). Beijing: Zhongguo shehui kexue yuan, 1990.

Gardella, Robert. "Qing Administration of the Tea Trade: Four Facets over Three Centuries." In Jane Kate Leonard and John R. Watt, eds., *To Achieve Security and Wealth: The Qing Imperial State and the Economy 1644–1911*, pp. 97–118. Ithaca, N.Y.: Cornell East Asia Series, 1992.

Gaubatz, Piper Rae. *Beyond the Great Wall: Urban Form and Transformation on the Chinese Frontiers*. Stanford: Stanford University Press, 1996.

Ge Beng'e. *Yijiang huilan* (Survey of the Yili River region). 1775. Manuscript edition, n.d., Gansu provincial library.

Gladney, Dru C. *Muslim Chinese: Ethnic Nationalism in the People's Republic*. Cambridge, Mass.: Harvard University Press, Council on East Asia, 1991.

————. "Representing Nationality in China: Refiguring Majority/Minority Identities." *Journal of Asian Studies* 53, no. 1 (Feb. 1994): 92–123.

Gong Zizhen. "Xiyu zhi xingsheng yi" (A proposal for establishing the Western Regions as a province). In He Changling, comp., *Huangchao jingshi wenbian* (Collection of Qing dynasty statecraft writings). 1826. Repr., Jindai Zhongguo shiliao congkan 731:6:81:6b–9a (pp. 2888–93). Taipei: Wenhai, 1965.

Gongzhong dang Qianlong chao zouzhe (Secret palace memorials of the Qianlong period). Compiled by the Palace Museum, Documents Section. Taipei: Guoli gugong bowuyuan, 1982.

Goodrich, Luther Carrington. *The Literary Inquisition of Ch'ien-Lung*. 1935. Repr., New York: Paragon Book Reprint Corp., 1966.

Gruen, Erich S., ed. *Imperialism in the Roman Republic*. New York: Holt, Rinehart and Winston, 1970.

Gu Bao. "Cong tianma dao Yilima" (From heaven-horse to Yili-horse). In
    Xinjiang lishi conghua (collected stories on Xinjiang history), pp. 39–45.
    Urumchi: Xinjiang renmin chubanshe, 1985.
Gu Bao and Cai Jinsong, eds. *Lin Zexu zai Xinjiang* (Lin Zexu in Xinjiang).
    Urumchi: Xinjiang renmin chubanshe, 1988.
Guo Shanlan, comp. *Ni xiaide Zhongguo minge* (The Chinese folksongs you
    love). Tainan, Taiwan: Daxia chubanshe, 1977.
Hahn, Reinhard. *Spoken Uyghur*. Seattle: University of Washington
    Press, 1991.
Halkovic, Stephen A., Jr. *The Mongols of the West*. Ural and Altaic Studies,
    vol. 148. Bloomington: Indiana University Press, 1985.
Hamada Masami. "Supplement: Islamic Saints and Their Mausoleums." *Acta
    Asiatica* 34 (1978): 79–98.
Haneda Akira. *Chūō Ajia shi kenkyū* (Research on Central Asia). Kyoto:
    Rinsen Shoten, 1982.
———. "Iminzoku tōchijō kara mitaru Shinchō no Kaibu tōchi seisaku"
    (Qing Dynasty ruling policy in the Muslim Region from the point of
    view of rule over alien peoples). In Tō-A kenkyūjo, ed., *Iminzoku no
    Shina tōchi kenkyū, Shinchō no henkyō tōchi seisaku* (Research on rule
    over the alien peoples of China: The Qing Dynasty policy for rule of
    border regions), pp. 101–213. Tokyo: Shibuntō, 1944.
Harrell, Stevan. "Introduction: Civilizing Projects and the Reaction to
    Them." In Stevan Harrell, ed., *Cultural Encounters on China's Ethnic
    Frontiers*. Seattle: University of Washington Press, 1995.
Harris, W. V. ed. *The Imperialism of Mid-Republican Rome*. Rome: Ameri-
    can Academy, 1984.
Hay, John. *Boundaries in China*. London: Reaktion Books, 1994.
He-ning, ed. *Huijiang tongzhi* (Comprehensive gazetteer of Altishahr). 1804.
    Repr., Zhongguo bianjiang congshu, vol. 67. Taipei: Wenhai chuban, 1966.
———, ed. *Sanzhou jilue* (Cursory record of three prefectures: Hami, Tur-
    fan, and Urumchi). Preface 1805; repr., Zhongguo fangzhi congshu, Xibu
    difang, vol. 11. Taipei: Chengwen, 1968.
Hedin, Sven. *Jehol, City of Emperors*. London: Kegan Paul, Trench, Trubner
    and Co., 1932.
———. *My Life as an Explorer*. Alfhild Huesh, trans. Garden City, N.Y.:
    Garden City Publishing, 1925.
Henderson, John B. "Chinese Cosmographical Thought: The High Intellec-
    tual Tradition." In J. B. Harley and David Woodward, eds., *The History
    of Cartography*, vol. 2, bk. 2, *Cartography in the Traditional East and
    Southeast Asian Societies*, pp. 203–27. Chicago: University of Chicago
    Press, 1994.
Herdan, Innes, trans. *Three Hundred T'ang Poems*. 3d ed. Taipei: The Far
    East Book Company, 1981.

Hershatter, Gail. "The Subaltern Talks Back: Reflections on Subaltern Theory and Chinese History." *Positions* 1, no. 1 (Spring 1993): 103–30.

Hevia, James L. *Cherishing Men from Afar: Qing Guest Ritual and the Macartney Embassy of 1793.* Durham, N.C.: Duke University Press, 1995.

———. "Lamas, Emperors and Rituals: Political Implications in Qing Imperial Ceremonies." *Journal of the International Association of Buddhist Studies* 16, no. 2 (1993): 243–78.

———. "A Multitude of Lords: Qing Court Ritual and the Macartney Embassy of 1793." *Late Imperial China* 10, no. 2 (Dec. 1989): 72–105.

———. "Sovereignty and Subject: Constituting Relations of Power in Qing Guest Ritual." In Angela Zito and Tani E. Barlow, eds., *Body, Subject, and Power in China.* Chicago: University of Chicago Press, 1994.

Hong Liangji. *Tianshan kehua* (Tales of a traveler in the Tianshan). c. 1800. Repr. in Yang Jianxin, et al., eds., *Gu xi xing ji xuanzhu* (Selected and annotated westward travel accounts of the past). Yinchuan: Ningxia renmin chubanshe, 1987.

Hōri Sunao. "18–20 seiki Uiguru zoku no doryōkō ni tsuite" (Uyghur units of measurement from the eighteenth to the twentieth centuries). *Otemae joshi daigaku ronshū* (Collected articles from Otemae Women's College) 12 (Oct. 1978): 57–67.

———. "Shinchō no Kaikyō tōchi in tsuite no ni, san no mondai" (Two or three questions concerning the Qing dynasty's control over Altishahr). *Shigaku zashi* 88, no. 3 (March 1979): 1–36, 137–38.

———. "Shindai Kaikyō no kahei seido—puru chūzōsei ni tsuite" (The currency system in Eastern Turkestan under Qing rule: The pūl minting system). In *Nakajima Satoshi sensei koki kinen ronshū* (Festschrift on the occasion of Professor Nakajima Satoshi's seventieth birthday), vol. 1, pp. 581–602. Tokyo: Namafuru shoyin, 1980.

Hou Jen-chih. "Frontier Horse Markets in the Ming Dynasty." In John De Francis and E-tu Zen Sun, eds., *Chinese Social History*, pp. 309–32. Washington, D.C.: American Council of Learned Societies, 1956.

Hsu, Immanuel C. Y. "The Great Policy Debate in China, 1874: Maritime Defense vs. Frontier Defense." *Harvard Journal of Asiatic Studies* 25 (1965): 212–28.

Hu Wenkang. "Ershi shiji Takelamagan shamo huanjing ji bianqian" (The Taklamakan Desert environment and its changes in the twentieth century). Paper presented at the International Conference on Exploration and Research of the Western Regions in the Twentieth Century, Urumchi, Oct. 1992.

Hua Li. "Daoguang nianjian Tianshan nanlu bingtun de yanbian" (The evolution of military agricultural colonies in southern Xinjiang during the Daoguang reign). *Xinjiang shehui kexue*, no. 2 (1988): 99–105.

———. "Lin Zexu yu Nanjiang tunken" (Lin Zexu and land reclamation in

Altishahr). In Gu Bao and Cai Jinsong, eds., *Lin Zexu zai Xinjiang*, pp. 146–66. Urumchi: Xinjiang renmin chubanshe, 1988.

———. "Qianlong nianjian yimin chuguan yu Qing qianqi Tianshan beilu nongye de fazhan" (Migration to Xinjiang in the Qianlong period and agricultural development in north Xinjiang during the early Qing). *Xibei shidi*, no. 4 (1987): 119–31.

———. "Qing zhongye Xinjiang yu neidi de maoyi wanglai" (Commercial relations between Xinjiang and China proper during the mid-Qing). In Ma Ruheng and Ma Dazheng, eds., *Qingdai bianjiang kaifa yanjiu*, pp. 275–304. Beijing: Zhongguo shehui kexue chuban, 1990.

———. "Qingdai Xinjiang nongye kaifa shi yanjiu." Ph.D. diss., Zhongguo Renmin Daxue (China People's University), n.d.

Huang, Pei. *Autocracy at Work: A Study of the Yung-cheng Period, 1723–1735*. Bloomington: Indiana University Press, 1974.

Huijiang zhi. See Yong-gui.

Hummel, Arthur W., et al. *Eminent Chinese of the Ch'ing Period (1644–1912)*. Washington, D.C.: U.S. Government Printing Office, 1943; repr., Taipei: Ch'eng-wen, 1970.

ʿIzzat Allāh, Mīr. "Travels Beyond the Himalaya, by Mir Izzet Ullah." 1825. Repr., *Journal of the Royal Asiatic Society of Great Britain and Ireland* 7, no. 14 (1843): 283–342.

Jacoby, Russell. "Marginal Returns: The Trouble with Post-Colonial Theory." *Lingua Franca* 5, no. 6 (Sept./Oct. 1995): 30–37.

Jagchid, S., and C. R. Bawden. "Some Notes on the Horse Policy of the Yüan Dynasty." *Central Asiatic Journal* 10, nos. 3–4 (1965): 246–68.

Jarring, Gunnar. *Materials to the Knowledge of Eastern Turki*. Vol. 1. Lund: C. W. K. Gleerup, 1951.

Ji Dachun et al. "Xinjiang xiancun fangzhi gailan" (Extant gazetteers of Xinjiang). Photocopy from *Xinjiang shehui kexue yanjiu* (Research on social sciences in Xinjiang, an internal circulation journal). n.d.

Ji Yun. *Wulumuqi za shi* (Random verses of Urumchi). 1771. Repr., Congshu jicheng chubian, ed. Wang Yunwu, vol. 2307, pp. 1–26. Shanghai: Shangwu, 1937.

Jin Feng (Altan-Orghil). "Qingdai Xinjiang Xilu taizhan" (Postal stations along the Western Route in Xinjiang in the Qing Period). Parts 1 and 2. *Xinjiang Daxue Xuebao* no. 1 (1980): 60–73 and no. 2 (1980): 93–101.

Kano, Naoshi. "Chama bōeki no shūmatsu—Yōsei jidai no chahō no jittai o megutte" (The end of the tea-horse trade: The situation of the tea laws in the Yongzheng period). *Tōyōshi kenkyū* 22, no. 3 (1963): 73–93.

Kataoka Kazutada. "Kei'an shiryō yori mitaru Shinchō no Kaimin seisaku" (The Muslim policy of the Qing dynasty: A look from the perspective of criminal cases.) *Shigaku kenkyū* 136 (June 1977): 1–24.

———. "Kei'an shiryō yori mitaru Shinchō no Kaimin seisaku: hosetsu"

(The Muslim policy of the Qing dynasty: A look from the perspective of criminal cases—supplement). *Rekishi kenkyū* (Ōsaka kyōiku daigaku) 21 (June 1986): 137–45.

————. "'Shinchō no Kaimin seisaku' no mata kentō—Shinshitsuroku o chūshin ni" (Another study of the "Muslim policy of the Qing dynasty": Focus on the Qing Veritable Records). *Rekishi kenkyū* (Ōsaka kyōiku daigaku) 13 (Mar. 1976): 59–79.

————. *Shinchō Shinkyō tōji kenkyū* (Researches on Qing dynasty rule in Xinjiang). Tokyo: Yū San Kaku, 1991.

Keyes, Charles F. "The Dialectics of Ethnic Change." In Charles F. Keyes, ed., *Ethnic Change*. Seattle: University of Washington Press, 1981.

Khodarkovsky, Michael. *Where Two Worlds Met: The Russian State and the Kalmyk Nomads, 1600–1771*. Ithaca: Cornell University Press, 1992.

Kim, Ho-dong. "The Muslim Rebellion and the Kashghar Emirate in Chinese Central Asia, 1864–1874." Ph.D. diss., Harvard University, 1986.

King, Frank H. H. *Money and Monetary Policy in China, 1845–1895*. Cambridge, Mass.: Harvard University Press, 1965.

Kong Xiangyi. "Qingdai beifang zuida de 'tongshihang': Dashengkui" (The largest "interpreter company" of the Qing dynasty: The Dashengkui). *Shanxi wenshiziliao* 34, no. 4 (1984): 154–62.

Krueger, John R. *Materials for an Oirat-Mongolian to English Citation Dictionary*. Parts 1–3. Bloomington, Ind.: Publications of the Mongolia Society, 1978–84.

Kuhn, Philip A. *Soulstealers: The Chinese Sorcery Scare of 1768*. Cambridge, Mass.: Harvard University Press, 1990.

Kuropatkin, A. N. *Kashgaria (Eastern or Chinese Turkestan): Historical and Geographical Sketch of the Country: Its Military Strength, Industries, and Trade*. Trans. Walter E. Gowan. London: W. Thacker and Co., 1882.

Kuznetsov, V. S. "British and Russian Trade in Sinkiang, 1819–1851." *Central Asian Review* 13, no. 2 (1965): 149–56.

————. "Tsin Administration in Sinkiang in the First Half of the Nineteenth Century." *Central Asian Review* 10, no. 3 (1962): 271–84.

Lai Cunli. *Huizu Shangye shi* (History of Hui [Tungan] commerce). N.p.: Zhongguo shangye chubanshe, 1988.

Langlois, John D. "Chinese Culturalism and the Yüan Analogy: Seventeenth-Century Perspectives." *Harvard Journal of Asiatic Studies* 40, no. 2 (Dec. 1980): 355–98.

Lattimore, Owen. *Inner Asian Frontiers of China*. 1940. Repr., Hong Kong and New York: Oxford University Press, 1988.

Lee, Robert H. G. *The Manchurian Frontier in Ch'ing History*. Cambridge, Mass.: Harvard University Press, 1970.

Legge, James, trans. *The Shoo King (Shangshu)*. In *The Chinese Classics, with a translation, critical and exegetical notes, prologomena, and copi-*

ous indexes. 1867–76. 5 vols. Repr., Hong Kong: Hong Kong University Press, 1960.

Leonard, Jane. "Ch'ing Perceptions of Political Reality in the 1820s." *The American Asian Review* 5, no. 2 (Summer 1987): 63–97.

————. *Wei Yuan and China's Rediscovery of the Maritime World.* Cambridge, Mass.: Harvard University Council on East Asian Studies, 1984.

Li Hongzhang et al. *(Qinding) Da Qing huidian shili* (Imperially commissioned statutes and precedents of the Qing dynasty, Guangxu edition). 1899.

Li Hua. "Shilun qingdai qianqi de Shanxibang shangren—Qingdai difang shangren yanjiu zhi er" (A preliminary discussion of the Shanxi gang merchants in the early Qing dynasty: Study number two of regional merchants during the Qing). *Lishi luncong* 3 (Apr. 1983): 304–32.

Li Huan, comp. *Guochao qixian leizheng chubian* (Classified collection of biographies of famous men of our dynasty). 1884–90.

Li, Lillian. *China's Silk Trade: Traditional Industry in the Modern World, 1842–1937.* Cambridge, Mass.: Harvard University Press, 1981.

Lidai Xiyu shi xuanzhu editorial group, ed. *Lidai Xiyu shi xuanzhu* (Collected and annotated poems of the Western Regions through history). Urumchi: Xinjiang renmin chubanshe, 1981.

Lin Enxian. *Qingchao zai Xinjiang de Han Hui geli zhengce* (The Han-Muslim segregation policy in Xinjiang during the Qing Dynasty). Taipei: Taiwan shangwu yinshu guan, 1988.

————. *Qingdai Xinjiang kenwu yanjiu* (Research into land reclamation in Xinjiang in the Qing period). Repr. in 3 parts. Taipei: Zhonghua wenhua chubanshe, 1972.

Lin Enxian, et al., eds. *Jindai Zhongguo bianjiang lunzhu mulu* (Index to articles and books on the modern Chinese frontier). Taipei: Guoli Zhengzhi Daxue Bianzheng Yanjiusuo, 1986.

Lin Min. "Luelun Lin Zexu qianshu Xinjiang shiqi de jiashu" (A brief discussion of Lin Zexu's letters home from exile in Xinjiang). In Gu Bao and Cai Jinsong, eds., *Lin Zexu zai Xinjiang*, pp. 224–41. Urumchi: Xinjiang renmin chubanshe, 1988.

Lin Sumen. *Hanjiang sanbai yin* (Three hundred poems of the Han River [Yangzhou]). 1808. Repr., Yangzhou: Guangling guji keyinshe, 1988.

Lin Yongkuang. "Cong yi jian dang'an kan Xinjiang yu neidi de sichou maoyi" (A look at the silk trade between Xinjiang and China proper based on one document). *Qingshi yanjiu tongxun* no. 1 (1983): 23–26.

Lin Yongkuang and Wang Xi. "Hangzhou zhizao yu Qingdai Xinjiang de sichou maoyi" (The Hangzhou Imperial Silk Factory and silk trade with Xinjiang in the Qing dynasty). *Hangzhou daxue xuebao* 16, no. 2 (June 1986): 108–16.

————. "Jiangnan san zhizao yu Qingdai Xinjiang de sichou maoyi" (The three south China Imperial Silk Factories and silk trade with Xinjiang in the Qing dynasty). *Liaoning shifan daxue xuebao (shehui ban)* no. 3 (1986): 67–73.

———. "Qian Jia shiqi neidi yu Xinjiang de sichou maoyi" (Silk trade between China proper and Xinjiang in the Qianlong and Jiaqing reigns). *Xinjiang daxue xuebao* no. 4 (1985): 45–54.

———. "Qianlong shiqi neidi yu Xinjiang Hasake de maoyi" (Trade between China proper and the Kazakhs in Xinjiang in the Qianlong period). *Lishi dang'an* no. 4 (1985): 83–88.

———. "Qingdai Jiangning zhizao yu Xinjiang de sichou maoyi" (The Jiangning Imperial Silk Factory and silk trade with Xinjiang in the Qing dynasty). *Zhongyang minzu xueyuan xuebao* no. 3 (1987): 76–78.

———. "Qingdai Qian Jia nianjian Suzhou yu Xinjiang de sichou maoyi" (Silk trade between Soochow and Xinjiang during the Qianlong and Jiaqing reigns). *Suzhou daxue xuebao (zhexue shehui kexue xuebao)* no. 4 (1985): 9–14.

———. *Qingdai Xibei minzu maoyi shi* (Inter-nationality trade in the Northwest during the Qing period). Beijing: Zhongyang minzu xueyuan chubanshe, 1991.

Lin Zexu. *Guimao riji* (Diary of Daoguang 23 [1843]). In Chen Xiqi et al., eds., *Lin Zexu zougao, gongdu, riji bubian* (Supplementary collection of Lin Zexu's memorials, official documents, and diaries), pp. 118–44. Guangdong: Zhongshan daxue chubanshe, 1985.

———. *Yiji riji* (Diary of Daoguang 25 [1845]). In Chen Xiqi et al., eds., *Lin Zexu zougao, gongdu, riji bubian* (Supplementary collection of Lin Zexu's memorials, official documents, and diaries), pp. 145–93. Guangdong: Zhongshan daxue chubanshe, 1985.

Ling Tingkan. "Yu Yuan Boyuan gexue lun *Huafang lu* shu" (Letter to Ruan Yuan on *Yangzhou Huafang lu*). In *Jiaolitang wenji* (Collected prose from the Jiaoli Hall). 23:12b–13a, n.d. (c. 1797).

Lipman, Jonathan. *Familiar Strangers: A Muslim History in China.* Seattle: University of Washington Press, 1998.

Liu Ge and Huang Xianyang, eds. *Xiyu shidi lunwen ziliao suoyin* (Index of articles on Western Regions history and geography). *Zhongguo bianjiang shidi yanjiu ziliao congshu* series, Zhongguo bianjiang shidi yanjiu zhongxin, ed. Urumchi: Xinjiang renmin chubanshe, 1988.

Liu, Kwang-Ching, and Richard Smith. "The Military Challenge: The North-west and the Coast." In John K. Fairbank, ed., *Cambridge History of China*, vol. 11, *Late Ch'ing, 1800–1911, part 2*, pp. 235–50. Cambridge, Engl.: Cambridge University Press, 1980.

Liu, Laurence G. *Chinese Architecture.* New York: Rizzoli International Publications, 1989.

Liu Ziyang, et al. *Qingdai difang guanzhi kao* (Research on the system of local officials in the Qing dynasty). Beijing: Zijing cheng, 1988.

Loewe, Michael. *Crisis and Conflict in Han China, 109 B.C.–A.D. 9*. London: George Allen and Unwin, 1974.

Lü Meng shang Dashengkui (The Dashengkui, traveling merchants in Mongolia). *Nei Menggu wenshi ziliao* 12 (1984): entire issue.

Lü Xiaoxian. "Qianlong chao neidi yu Xinjiang de sichou maoyi gaishu" (A summary of silk trade between China proper and Xinjiang during the Qianlong reign). Paper presented at the International Conference on Qing Regional Socio-economic History and Fourth National Conference on Qing History, Nanjing, Nov. 1987.

Luo Yunzhi. *Qing Gaozong tongzhi Xinjiang zhengce de tantao* (Investigation into the Qing's Qianlong-period control policies in Xinjiang). Taipei: Liren zhuju, 1983.

Ma Dazheng and Ma Ruheng. *Piaoluo yiyu de minzu: 17 zhi 18 shiji de Tuerhute Menggu* (A nationality adrift in foreign lands: The Torghut Mongols in the seventeenth to eighteenth centuries). Beijing: Zhongguo shehui kexue chubanshe, 1991.

Ma Dazheng et al. *Xinjiang xiangtuzhi gao* (Local gazetteers of Xinjiang). Zhongguo bianjiang shidi ziliao congkan, Xinjiang juan (Chinese border history and geography series, Xinjiang volume). Beijing: Quanguo tushuguan wenxian suowei fuzhi zhongxin, 1990.

Macartney, George C. I. E. "Eastern Turkestan: The Chinese as Rulers over an Alien Race." *Proceedings of the Central Asian Society* (10 March 1909). London: Central Asian Society, 1909.

Mackerras, Colin. "The Uighurs." In Denis Sinor, ed., *The Cambridge History of Early Inner Asia*, pp. 317–36. Cambridge, Engl.: Cambridge University Press, 1990.

Mair, Victor. "Language and Ideology in the Written Popularizations of the Sacred Edict." In David Johnson, Andrew Nathan, and Evelyn Rawski, eds., *Popular Culture in Late Imperial China*, pp. 325–59. Berkeley: University of California Press, 1985.

Mancall, Mark. "The Ch'ing Tribute System: An Interpretive Essay." In John K. Fairbank, ed., *The Chinese World Order: Traditional China's Foreign Relations*, pp. 63–89. Cambridge, Mass.: Harvard University Press, 1968.

Mann, Susan. *Local Merchants and the Chinese Bureaucracy, 1750–1950*. Stanford: Stanford University Press, 1987.

Mano Eiji, Nakami Tatsuo, Hori Sunao, and Komatsu Hisao. *Nairiku Ajia* (Inner Asia). Chi'iki kara no sekaishi (World history by region), no. 6. Tokyo: Asahi Shinbunsha, 1992.

Matsumoto Tamio. *Pekin chimei kō* (Research on Beijing place-names). Tokyo: Hōyū shoten, 1988.

McElderry, Andrea. "Frontier Commerce: An Incident of Smuggling." *The American Asian Review* 2 (Summer 1987): 47–62.

Mencius (Meng Ke). *Mencius*. D. C. Lau, trans. London: Penguin Books, 1970.

Michael, Franz. *The Origin of Manchu Rule in China: Frontier and Bureaucracy as Interacting Forces in the Chinese Empire*. Baltimore: Johns Hopkins Press, 1942.

Michell, John, and Robert Michell, comps., trans. *The Russians in Central Asia: Their Occupation of the Kirghiz Steppe and the Line of the Syr-Daria; Their Political Relations with Khiva, Bokhara, and Kokan, also Descriptions of Chinese Turkestan and Dzungaria*. London: E. Stanford, 1865.

Millward, James A. "Beyond the Pass: Commerce, Ethnicity, and the Qing Empire in Xinjiang, 1759–1864." Ph.D. diss., Stanford University, 1993.

———. "New Perspectives on the Qing Frontier." In Gail Hershatter, Emily Honig, Jonathan N. Lipman, and Randall Stross, eds. *Remapping China*. Stanford: Stanford University Press, 1996.

———. "The Qing-Kazakh Trade and the 'Tribute System.'" Unpublished paper, 1995.

———. "The Qing Trade with the Kazakhs in Yili and Tarbagatai, 1759–1852." *Central and Inner Asian Studies*, 7 (1992): 1–42.

———. "A Uyghur Muslim in Qianlong's Court: The Meanings of the Fragrant Concubine." *Journal of Asian Studies* 53, no. 2 (May 1994): 427–58.

Molnar, Peter, et al. "Geologic Evolution of Northern Tibet: Results of an Expedition to Ulugh Muztagh. *Science* 235, no. 4786 (16 Jan. 1987): 299–305.

Moses, Larry W. "T'ang Tribute Relations with the Inner Asian Barbarian." In John Curtis Perry and Bardwell L. Smith, eds., *Essays in T'ang Society: The Interplay of Social, Political and Economic Forces*, pp. 61–89. Leiden, Netherlands: E. J. Brill, 1976.

Mu Yuan. "Zài tan Baoyiju de jige wenti" (Several questions regarding the Baoyiju, reconsidered). In *Xinjiang jinrong* (Xinjiang finance), second meeting of the Xinjiang Numismatics Society, special number (1991): 100–102.

Naqshbandī, Ahmad Shāh. "Narrative of the Travels of Khwajah Ahmud Shah Nukshbundee Syud Who Started from Cashmere on the 28th October, 1852, and Went Through Yarkund, Kokan, Bokhara and Cabul, in Search of Mr. Wyburd." *Journal of the Asiatic Society of Bengal* 25, no. 4 (1856): 344–58.

———. "Route from Kashmir, via Ladakh, to Yarkand by Ahmad Shah Nakshahbandi." J. Dowson, trans. *Journal of the Royal Asiatic Society of Great Britain and Ireland* 12 (1850): 372–85.

Nayanceng (Na-yan-cheng). *Nawen yigong zouyi* (Memorials of Nayen-ceng). Rong-an, ed. 1834. Repr., n.p., 1904.

Netton, Ian Richard. *A Popular Dictionary of Islam.* London: Curzon Press, 1992.

Newby, Laura. "Xinjiang: The Literary Conquest." Paper presented at the panel "Travel Writing in Late Imperial China," Annual Meeting of the Association for Asian Studies, March 1997.

———. "Xinjiang: In Search of an Identity." In T. T. Liu and David Faure, eds., *Unity and Diversity: Local Cultures and Identities in China.* Hong Kong: Hong Kong University Press, 1996.

Nivison, David S. "Ho-Shen and His Accusers: Ideology and Political Behavior in the Eighteenth Century." In David S. Nivison and Arthur F. Wright, eds., *Confucianism in Action,* pp. 208–43. Stanford: Stanford University Press, 1959.

Nordby, Judith, comp. *Mongolia.* World Biographical Series, vol. 156. Oxford: Clio Press, 1993.

Norin, Erik. "The Tarim Basin and Its Border Regions." In K. Andrée, H. A. Brouwer, and W. H. Bucher, eds., *Regionale Geologie der Erde,* vol. 2. Leipzig: Akademische Verlagsgesellschaft, 1941.

Obata, Shigeyoshi. *The Works of Li Po, the Chinese Poet.* New York: E. P. Dutton, 1922.

Olcott, Martha Brill. *The Kazakhs.* Stanford: Hoover Institution Press, 1987.

Olschki, Leonardo. *Marco Polo's Asia.* John A. Scott, trans. Berkeley: University of California Press, 1960.

Pan Zhiping. "Lun Qianlong Jiaqing Daoguang nianjian Qing zai Tianshan nanlu tuixing de minzu zhengce" (Regarding the nationality policy followed by the Qing dynasty in Altishahr during the Qianlong, Jiaqing, and Daoguang reigns). *Minzu yanjiu* (Nationality studies), no. 6 (1986): 37–41.

———. *Zhongya Haohanguo yu Qingdai Xinjiang* (The Central Asian Khanate of Kokand and Qing Xinjiang). *Zhongguo bianjiang shidi yanjiu congshu* series, Zhongguo bianjiang shidi yanjiu zhongxin, ed. Beijing: Zhongguo shehui kexue chubanshe, 1991.

Pan Zhiping and Wang Xi. "Qing qianqi Kashiga'er Ye'erqiang duiwai maoyi" (The foreign trade of Kashgar and Yarkand in the early Qing period). *Xinjiang shehui kexue yanjiu* joint number 7–8 (1988): 18–31.

Pang Yicai and Qu Shaomiao. "Lun Qingdai Shanxi tuobang de dui E maoyi" (Regarding the Shanxi camel gang's trade with Russia during the Qing dynasty). *Jinyang xuekan* 16, no. 1 (1983): 12–21.

Park, Nancy. "Tribute and Official Corruption in Eighteenth Century China." Paper prepared for the panel "Rethinking Tribute: Concept and Practice," Annual Meeting of the Association for Asian Studies, April 1995.

Pelliot, Paul. "Les 'conquêtes de l'empereur de la chine.'" *T'oung Pao* 20 (1921): 183–247.

Peng Xinwei. *Zhongguo huobi shi* (The history of Chinese currency). 2 vols. Shanghai: Renmin chubanshe, 1958.

Perdue, Peter. "Military Mobilization in Eighteenth-Century China, Mongolia, and Russia." *Modern Asian Studies* 30, no. 4 (1996): pp. 757–93.

Polachek, James M. *The Inner Opium War*. Cambridge, Mass.: Harvard University Press, 1992.

Polo, Marco. *The Travels of Marco Polo*. R. E. Latham, trans. Harmondsworth, Middlesex: Penguin Books, 1958.

Qi Qingshun. "Qingdai Xinjiang de guanpu he duiwai maoyi zhengce" (The Qing dynasty policy toward Xinjiang's official shops and foreign trade). *Xinjiang shehui kexue* 46, no. 3 (June 1990): 75–84.

———. "Qingdai Xinjiang de xiexiang gongying he caizheng weiji" (Qing Xinjiang's supply of silver subsidies and the financial crisis). *Xinjiang shehui kexue* 43, no. 3 (1987): 74–85.

———. "Qingdai Xinjiang xiangyin de laiyuan he qian'e" (Origins and deficits of Xinjiang's Qing period provincial shared-revenue). *Xinjiang lishi yanjiu* no. 3 (1985): 77–84.

Qi Yunshi. *Wanli xingcheng ji* (Record of a 10,000-*li* journey). In Yang Jianxin et al., eds., *Gu xi xing ji xuanzhu* (Selected and annotated westward travel accounts of the past), pp. 388–413. Yinchuan: Ningxia renmin chubanshe, 1987.

———, comp. *Xichui yaolue* (Survey of the Western borders). 1807. Repr. of 1837 woodblock edition, Zhongguo fangzhi congshu, Xibu difang, 2, Taipei: Chengwen, 1968.

Qi Yunshi and Wang Tingkai. *Xichui zongtong shilue* (General affairs of the Western borders). Song-yun, general ed. 1809. Repr., Zhongguo bianjiang congshu, vol. 12. Taibei: Wenhai, 1965.

(Qinding) huangyu Xiyu tuzhi. See Fuheng.

(Qinding) pingding Huijiang jiaoqin niyi fanglue. See Cao Zhenyong.

(Qinding) pingding Shaan Gan Xinjiang Huifei fanglue. See Yi-xin.

(Qinding) pingding Zhunga'er fanglue. See Fuheng.

(Qinding) Xinjiang zhilue. See Song-yun et al.

Qingdai chouban yiwu shimo (Xianfeng chao) (Complete record of the management of barbarian affairs, Xianfeng reign, 1851–61). 1930 (based on Qing court manuscript edition). Repr., 8 vols. Beijing: Zhonghua shuju, 1979.

Qingshi liezhuan (Arranged biographies from Qing history). 1928. Repr., annotated by Wang Zhonghan, 20 vols. Shanghai: Zhonghua shuju, 1987.

Qi-shi-yi (Chunyuan). *Xiyu wenjian lu* (Record of things heard and seen in the Western Regions). 1777. Repr., Qingzhao tang congshu, vol. 95, 1835.

Rawski, Evelyn S. "Presidential Address: Reenvisioning the Qing: The Significance of the Qing Period in Chinese History." *Journal of Asian Studies* 55, no. 4 (Nov. 1996): 829–50.

———. "Qing Imperial Marriage and Problems of Rulership." In Rubie S. Watson and Patricia Buckley Ebbrey, eds., *Marriage and Inequality in Chinese Society*, pp. 170–203. Berkeley: University of California Press, 1991.

Ren Mei'e, Yang Renzhang, and Bao Haosheng, comps. *An Outline of China's Physical Geography*. Beijing: Foreign Languages Press, 1985.

Ross, Sir E. Denison, and Rachel O. Wingate. *Dialogues in the Eastern Turki Dialect on Subjects of Interest to Travellers*. London: The Royal Asiatic Society, 1934.

Rossabi, Morris. *China and Inner Asia: From 1368 to the Present Day*. London: Thames and Hudson, 1975.

———. "The Tea and Horse Trade with Inner Asia during the Ming." *Journal of Asian History* 4, no. 2 (1970): 136–68.

———, ed. *China among Equals: The Middle Kingdom and Its Neighbors, 10th–14th Centuries*. Berkeley: University of California Press, 1983.

Rowe, David Nelson, et al., eds. *Index to the Ch'ing-tai ch'ou pan i wu shih mo*. Hamden, Conn.: Shoe String Press, 1960.

The Royal Geographical Society and the Mount Everest Foundation, comp. *The Mountains of Central Asia, 1:3,000,000 Map and Gazetteer*. London: Macmillan, 1987.

Saeki Tomi. "Shinchō no kōki to Sansei shōnin" (Shanxi merchants and the rise of the Qing dynasty). *Shakai bunka shigaku* 1 (Mar. 1966): 11–42.

———. "Shindai saigai ni okeru Sansei shōnin" (Shanxi merchants in the northern border regions during the Qing). In Tōhō gakkai, ed., *Tōhō gakkai sōritsu shūnen kinen tōhōgaku ronshū* (Memorial collection of articles in Asian studies on the occasion of the 25th anniversary of the founding of the Asian Studies Association), pp. 361–75. Tokyo: Tōhō gakkai, 1972.

———. "Shindai Shinkyō ni okeru gyokuseki mondai" (The jade question in Qing Xinjiang). *Shirin* 53, no. 5 (1970): 27–54 (609–36).

Saguchi Tōru. "The Eastern Trade of the Khoqand Khanate." *Memoirs of the Research Department of the Tōyō Bunko* 24 (1965): 47–114.

———. *18–19 seiki Higashi Torukisutan shakai shi kenkyū* (Researches on the history of eighteenth- to nineteenth-century Eastern Turkestan society). Tokyo: Yoshikawa Kōbunkan, 1963.

———. "The Formation of the Turfan Principality under the Qing Empire." *Acta Asiatica (Bulletin of the Institute of Eastern Culture)* 41 (Dec. 1981): 76–94.

———. "Kashgaria." *Acta Asiatica (Bulletin of the Institute of Eastern Culture)* 34 (1978).

———. "The Revival of the White Mountain Khwājas, 1760–1820 (from

Sarimsāq to Jihāngīr)." *Acta Asiatica (Bulletin of the Institute of Eastern Culture)* 14 (1968): 7–20.

———. *Roshia to Ajia sōgen*. Yūrashia bunka shi sensho, no. 3. Tokyo: Yoshikawa Kōbunkan, 1967.

———. *Shinkyō minzoku shi kenkyū* (Researches on the history of the peoples of Xinjiang). Tokyo: Yoshikawa Kōbunkan, 1986.

———. "Shinkyō ni okeru kaimin" (Tungans in Xinjiang). In Saguchi Tōru, *Shinkyō minzoku shi kenkyū* (Researches on the history of the peoples of Xinjiang), pp. 292–306. Tokyo: Yoshikawa Kōbunkan, 1986.

Said, Edward W. *Culture and Imperialism*. New York: Vintage Books, 1994.

———. *Orientalism*. New York: Pantheon Books, 1978.

Sanada Yasushi. "Kashugariya no hakkoku no shihairyoku ni tsuite" (On the control exercised by the Kashgarian begs). *Hakusan shigaku* 18 (Mar. 1975): 72–73.

———. "Sōsekki Shin hakkokusei kara mita Kashugariya oashisu shakai" (Oasis society in Kashgaria as seen from the Qing beg administrative system at the time of its foundation). In *Nairiku Ajia, nishi Ajia no shakai to bunka*, pp. 437–58. Tokyo: Sansen shuppansha, 1983.

Sanjdorj, M. *Manchu Chinese Colonial Rule in Northern Mongolia*. Trans. and annotated by Urgunge Onon. New York: St. Martin's Press, 1980.

Sayrāmi, Mollā Mūsa (Mullā Mūsa Sairāmī). *Tarixi Hamidi*. Anwar Baytur, ed. Modern Uyghur critical edition. Beijing: Millätlär Näšriyat, 1986.

Schafer, Edward H. *The Golden Peaches of Samarkand: A Study of T'ang Exotics*. Berkeley: University of California Press, 1963.

Shepherd, John Robert. *Statecraft and Political Economy on the Taiwan Frontier, 1600–1800*. Stanford: Stanford University Press, 1993.

Shih Min-hsiung. *The Silk Industry in Ch'ing China*. E-tu Zen Sun, trans. Michigan Abstracts of Chinese and Japanese Works on Chinese History, no. 5. Ann Arbor: Center for Chinese Studies, University of Michigan, 1976.

Sima Qian. *Records of the Grand Historian: Han Dynasty*. 2 vols. Burton Watson, trans. Rev. ed. New York and Hong Kong: Columbia University Press, 1993.

Sinor, Denis. "Horse and Pasture in Inner Asian History." *Oriens Extremus* 19 (1972): 1–2.

Skinner, G. William. "Marketing and Social Structure in Rural China." Part 1. *The Journal of Asian Studies* 24, no. 1 (Nov. 1964): 3–43. Repr., AAS Reprint Series No. 1. Tucson: University of Arizona Press, n.d.

———. "Regional Urbanization in Nineteenth-Century China." In G. W. Skinner, ed., *The City in Late Imperial China*, pp. 211–49. Stanford: Stanford University Press, 1977.

Skinner, G. William, ed. *The City in Late Imperial China*. Stanford: Stanford University Press, 1977.

Skinner, G. William, Winston Hsieh, and Shigeaki Tomita, eds. *Modern Chinese Society: An Analytical Bibliography*. Stanford: Stanford University Press, 1973.

Smith, Paul J. *Taxing Heaven's Storehouse: Horses, Bureaucrats, and the Destruction of the Sichuan Tea Industry 1074-1224*. Cambridge, Mass.: Harvard University Council on East Asian Studies, 1991.

So, Jenny F. "Chinese Neolithic Jades." Pamphlet. Washington, D.C.: Freer Gallery of Art, Smithsonian Institution, 1993.

Song-yun, Wang Tingkai, Qi Yunshi, and Xu Song, comps. *(Qinding) Xinjiang zhilue* (Imperially commissioned gazetteer of Xinjiang). Beijing: Wuying Dian, 1821.

Spence, Jonathan D. *The Search for Modern China*. New York: W. W. Norton, 1990.

———. *Ts'ao Yin and the K'ang-Hsi Emperor: Bondservant and Master*. New Haven: Yale University Press, 1966.

Stanley, John C. *Late Ch'ing Finance: Hu Kuang-yung as an Innovator*. Cambridge, Mass.: Harvard University Press, 1961.

Su-er-de et al. *Xinjiang Huibu zhi* (Gazetteer of the Muslim region of Xinjiang). Qianlong period manuscript. Repr., Zhongguo fangzhi congshu, xibu difang, no. 10. Taipei: Chengwen, 1968.

Sun Wenliang, et al. *Manzu da cidian* (Large dictionary of the Manchu nationality). Shenyang: Liaoning daxue chubanshe, 1990.

Ta'erbahatai shiyi. See Yong-bao and Xing-zhao.

Ta'erbahatai zhilue (gazetteer of Tarbagatai). Qianlong period. Repr., Zhongguo minzu shidi ziliao congkan, Wu Fengpei, ed., no. 29. Beijing: Zhongyang minzu xueyuan, 1982.

Tan Qixiang et al., eds. *Zhongguo lishi ditu ji* (Historical atlas of China). 8 vols. Shanghai: Ditu chubanshe, 1987.

Terada Takanobu. *Sansei shōnin no kenkyū* (Research on Shanxi merchants). Tokyo: Tōyōshi kenkyū sokan no. 25, 1972.

Thongchai Winichakul. *Siam Mapped: A History of the Geo-Body of a Nation*. Honolulu: University of Hawaii Press, 1994.

Tillman, Hoyt Cleveland. "Proto-Nationalism in Twelfth-Century China? The Case of Ch'en Liang." *Harvard Journal of Asiatic Studies* 39, no. 2, (Dec. 1979): 403–28.

Togan, Isenbike. "Inner Asian Muslim Merchants at the Closing of the Silk Route (17th Century)." Paper presented at the UNESCO Integral Study of the Silk Roads International Seminar, Urumchi, August 1990.

Tong Keli, ed. *Xibozu lishi yu wenhua* (History and culture of the Sibe nationality). Urumchi: Xinjiang renmin chubanshe, 1989.

Torbert, Preston M. *The Ch'ing Imperial Household Department: A Study of Its Organization and Principal Functions, 1662-1796*. Harvard East Asian

Monographs, no. 71. Cambridge, Mass.: Harvard University Council on East Asian Studies, 1977.

Tsiang T'ing-fu. "China and European Expansion." *Politica* 2 (1936): 1–18.

Tuo-jin et al. *(Qinding) Da Qing huidian shili* (Imperially commissioned statutes and precedents of the Qing dynasty, Jiaqing edition). 1818.

———. *(Qinding) Huijiang zeli* (Imperially commissioned collection of the substatutes of Muslim Xinjiang). 1842. Repr. as *Menggu Zeli, Huijiang zeli,* Zhongguo bianjiang shidi shiliao congkan, Lü Yiran, Ma Dazheng, et al., eds., "general" volume. Beijing: Quanguo tushuguan wenxian suowei fuzhi zhongxin, 1988.

Twitchett, Denis. "Hsüan-tsung (Reign 712–56)." In Denis Twitchett, ed., *The Cambridge History of China,* vol. 3, *Sui and T'ang China, 589–906,* part 1, pp. 333–463. Cambridge, Engl.: Cambridge University Press, 1979.

Twitchett, Denis, and Howard Wechsler. "Kao-tsung (Reign 649–83) and the Empress Wu: The Inheritor and the Usurper." In Denis Twitchett, ed., *The Cambridge History of China,* vol. 3, *Sui and T'ang China, 589–906,* part 1, pp. 242–89. Cambridge, Engl.: Cambridge University Press, 1979.

Viraphol, Sarasin. *Tribute and Profit: Sino-Siamese Trade, 1652–1853.* Cambridge, Mass.: Harvard University Press, 1977.

Vogel, Hans Urlich. "Chinese Central Monetary Policy, 1644–1800." *Late Imperial China* 8, no. 2 (Dec. 1987): 1–52.

Wakeman, Frederic, Jr. *The Great Enterprise: The Manchu Reconstruction of Imperial Order in Seventeenth-Century China.* Berkeley: University of California Press, 1985.

Waldron, Arthur. *The Great Wall of China: From History to Myth.* Cambridge, Engl.: Cambridge University Press, 1990.

Waley, Arthur. *The Opium War through Chinese Eyes.* Stanford: Stanford University Press, 1982.

Waley-Cohen, Joanna. *Exile in Mid-Qing China: Banishment to Xinjiang, 1758–1820.* New Haven: Yale University Press, 1991.

Wan Ma, ed. *Huashuo Wulumuqi* (Urumchi tales). Urumchi: Xinjiang renmin chubanshe, 1989.

Wang Dashu. *Xizheng jicheng* (Record of a westward march). C. 1788. Repr. in Wu Fengpei, ed., *Gan-Xin you zong huibian* (Collected accounts of travels in Gansu and Xinjiang). Beijing: Central Nationalities Institute Library, 1983.

Wang Gongque. "Geologic Overview of Xinjiang." *California Geology* (June 1986): 139–42.

Wang Gungwu. "Introduction." In *The Chineseness of China: Selected Essays,* 1–7. Hong Kong: Oxford University Press, 1991.

Wang Jianmin. *Qingdai Hasake de dongfang maoyi guanxi* (The Kazakhs' eastward trade relations in the Qing dynasty). Master's thesis, Zhongyang minzu xueyuan, minzuxue yanjiu zhongxin, 1985.

Wang Xi. "Qianlong shiqi Kashiga'er de guanfang sichou maoyi" (Official silk trade in Kashgar in the Qianlong period). Paper presented at the International Conference on Qing Regional Socio-economic History and Fourth National Conference on Qing History, Nanjing, November 1987.

Wang Xi and Lin Yongkuang. "Jianlun Qingdai Wulumuqi Hasake maoyi sheli de yuanyin yu jingguo" (A brief discussion of the reasons and course of the establishment of the Urumchi Kazakh trade in the Qing dynasty). *Minzu yanjiu* (Nationality studies) no. 5 (1990): 103–10.

———. "Qing Qianlong nianjian Xinjiang de 'Huibu' maoyi wenti" (The question of "Muslim cloth" in Xinjiang during the Qianlong period of the Qing dynasty). *Xinjiang shehui kexue* no. 5 (1987): 113–32.

Wang Xilong. "Qingdai shibian Xinjiang shulue" (Brief account of the Qing dynasty policy of consolidating the Xinjiang frontier through settlement). *Xibei shidi* (Northwest history and geography), no. 4 (1985): 62–71.

———. "Qingdai Wulumuqi tuntian shulun" (A brief account of Urumchi's agricultural land reclamation in the Qing dynasty). *Xinjiang shehui kexue* no. 5 (1989): 101–8.

———. *Qingdai Xibei tuntian yanjiu* (Research on agricultural reclamation in the Western Regions in the Qing dynasty). Lanzhou: Lanzhou Daxue chubanshe, 1990.

———. "1755–1860 nianjian Qing zhengfu dui Hasake de zhengce he Sha'e de kuozhang" (Qing government policy toward the Kazakhs and the Tsarist expansion). Master's thesis, Lanzhou Daxue, Department of History, 1982.

Wang, Yeh-chien. *Land and Taxation in Imperial China, 1750–1911.* Cambridge, Mass.: Harvard University Press, 1973.

Wang Zhizhong. "Qingdai Gan-Ning-Qing shichang dili kao" (A study of the market geography of Gansu, Ningxia, and Qinghai in the Qing period). *Xibei shidi* (Northwest history and geography) no. 3 (1986): 54–62.

———. "Qingdai Xinjiang kuangye shulue" (Survey of the mining industry in Qing Xinjiang). *Shehui kexue (Gansu)* no. 6 (1986).

Ward, Fred. "Jade: Stone of Heaven." *National Geographic Magazine* 172, no. 3 (Sept. 1987): 282–315.

Wathen, W. H. "Memoir on Chinese Tartary and Khoten." *Journal of the Asiatic Society of Bengal* 4, no. 48 (Dec. 1835): 652–64.

Watt, James C. Y. "Jade." In Wen C. Fong and James C. Y. Watt, eds., *Possessing the Past: Treasures from the National Palace Museum, Taipei,* pp. 41–71. New York: The Metropolitan Museum of Art and Taipei: The National Palace Museum, 1996.

Wechsler, Howard. "Kao-tsung (Reign 649–83) and the Empress Wu: The Inheritor and the Usurper." In Denis Twitchett, ed., *The Cambridge His-*

tory of China, vol. 3, *Sui and T'ang China*, 589–906, *part 1*, pp. 242–89. Cambridge, Engl.: Cambridge University Press, 1979.

———. "T'ai-tsung (Reign 626–49) the Consolidator." In Denis Twitchett, ed., *The Cambridge History of China*, vol. 3, *Sui and T'ang China*, 589–906, *part 1*, pp. 188–241. Cambridge, Engl.: Cambridge University Press, 1979.

Wei Jing. "Baoyiju ji qi zhuqian gaishuo" (About the Baoyiju and its minting operations). *Xinjiang jinrong* (Xinjiang finance), proceedings of the Second Meeting of the Xinjiang Numismatics Society, special number (1991): 90–99.

Wei Qingyuan. "Lun Qingdai de diandangye yu guanliao ziben" (On Qing dynasty pawn-broking and official capital). *Qingshi luncong* no. 8. Repr. in *Mingqing shi bianxi* (Ming and Qing history dispute and analysis), pp. 128–65. Beijing: Zhongguo shehui kexue, 1989.

———. "Lun Qingdai de 'huangdang'" (On Qing dynasty "imperial pawnshops"). In *Xianggang Daxue 1985 nian guoji Ming-Qing shi yanjiu yantaohui lunwenji*. Repr. in *Mingqing shi bianxi* (Debate and analysis of Ming and Qing history), pp. 70–112. Beijing: Zhongguo shehui kexue, 1989.

———. "Lun Qingdai de 'shengxi yinliang' yu guanfu jingying de diandang ye" (On "investment silver" and government-managed pawn-broking in the Qing dynasty). *Zhonghua wenshi luncong*, no. 2 (1986). Repr. in *Mingqing shi bianxi* (Ming and Qing history dispute and analysis), pp. 113–27. Beijing: Zhongguo shehui kexue, 1989.

———. "Qingdai Kangxi shiqi 'shengxi yinliang' zhidu de chuchuan he yunyong" (The creation and application of the "investment silver" system in the Qing Kangxi period). *Zhongguo shehui jingji shi yanjiu*, no. 3 (1986). Repr. in *Mingqing shi bianxi* (Ming and Qing history dispute and analysis), pp. 166–85. Beijing: Zhongguo shehui kexue, 1989.

———. "Qingdai Qianlong shiqi Shengjing dichu de 'shengxi yinliang' he guandian" ("Investment silver" and official shops in the Shengjing [Mukden] region during the Qing Qianlong period). *Shehui kexue jikan* no. 4 (1987). Repr. in *Mingqing shi bianxi* (Ming and Qing history dispute and analysis), pp. 257–88. Beijing: Zhongguo shehui kexue, 1989.

———. "Qingdai Qianlong shiqi 'shengxi yinliang' zhidu de shuaibai he 'shouche'" (The decline and "withdrawal" of the Qing Qianlong-period "investment silver" system). In *Mingqing shi bianxi* (Ming and Qing history dispute and analysis), pp. 229–56. Beijing: Zhongguo shehui kexue, 1989.

———. "Qingdai Yongzheng shiqi 'shengxi yinliang' zhidu de zhengdun he zhengce yanbian" (Reorganization and policy development of the "investment silver" system during the Qing Yongzheng period). *Zhongguo shehui jingji shi yanjiu* no. 3 (1987). Repr. in *Mingqing shi bianxi* (Ming and Qing history dispute and analysis), pp. 186–228. Beijing: Zhongguo shehui kexue, 1989.

Wei Qingyuan and Wu Qiyan. "Qingdai zhuming huangshang Fan shi de xingshuai (The rise and fall of the famous Fan family, imperial merchants of the Qing dynasty). In Wei Qingyuan, *Dangfang lunshi wenbian* (Collection of historical discussions from the archive room), pp. 42–69. Fuzhou: Fujian renmin, 1983.

Wei Yuan. "Da ren wen xibei bianyu shu" (A letter in response to a question on frontier regions). In He Changling, comp., *Huangchao jingshi wenbian* (Collected writings on statecraft in the reigning dynasty), 731:6:80:1–2a. 1826. Repr., Jindai Zhongguo shiliao congkan, vol. 74. Taipei: Wenhai, 1965.

————. *Sheng wu ji* (Record of imperial military achievements). Preface 1842. Repr., Jindai Zhongguo shiliao congkan, vol. 102. Taipei: Wenhai, 1965.

"Weilate Menggu jianshi" bianxie zu ("Concise History of the Oirat Mongols" editorial group). *Weilate Menggu jianshi* (Concise History of the Oirat Mongols). Urumchi: Xinjiang renmin chubanshe, 1992.

Wen-shou. "Chen Jiayu Guan wai qingxing shu" (Report on circumstances outside the Jiayu Guan). In He Changling, comp., *Huangchao jingshi wenbian* (Collected writings on statecraft in the reigning dynasty), 731:6:81:4b–6a. 1826. Repr., Jindai Zhongguo shiliao congkan, vol. 74. Taibei: Wenhai, 1965.

Wiens, Harold J. "Cultivation Development and Expansion in China's Colonial Realm in Central Asia." *Journal of Asian Studies* 26, no. 1 (Nov. 1966): 67–88.

Wills, John E., Jr. *Embassies and Illusions: Dutch and Portuguese Envoys to K'ang-hsi, 1666–1687*. Cambridge, Mass.: Harvard University Council on East Asian Studies, 1984.

————. "How We Got Obsessed with the 'Tribute System' and Why It's Time to Get Over It." Paper presented at the panel "Rethinking Tribute: Concept and Practice," Annual Meeting of the Association for Asian Studies, April 1995.

————. "Tribute, Defensiveness, and Dependency: Uses and Limits of Some Basic Ideas about Mid-Ch'ing Foreign Relations." *American Neptune* 48 (1988): 225–29.

Wright, David. "Translation of (Gong Zizhen's) 'A Proposal for Establishing a Province in the Western Regions.'" Seminar paper, Princeton University, n.d.

Wright, Harrison M., ed. *The "New Imperialism": Analysis of Nineteenth Century Expansion*. 2d ed. Lexington, Mass.: D. C. Heath, 1976.

Wu Aichen, comp. *Lidai Xiyu shichao* (Western Regions poems through history). Urumchi: Xinjiang renmin chubanshe, 1982.

Wu Yuanfeng. "Qing Qianlong nianjian Yili tuntian shulue" (An overview of agricultural reclamation in Yili during the Qianlong reign of the Qing dynasty). *Minzu yanjiu* no. 5 (1987): 92–99.

Wulumuqi zhenglue (Gazetteer of Urumchi). Manuscript edition in Gansu Provincial library. 1778.

Xi Guojin. "Luobu Bo qianyi guocheng ji qi yanjiu de xin faxian" (The movement process of Lop Nor and new discoveries in its research). Paper presented at the International Conference on Exploration and Research of the Western Regions in the Twentieth Century, Urumchi, Oct. 1992.

Xie Zhining. "Qianlong shiqi Qing zhengfu dui Xinjiang de zhili yu kaifa" (The Qing government's rule and development of Xinjiang in the Qianlong period). Master's thesis, Beijing University, 1990.

Xinjiang lishi yanjiu (Historical research on Xinjiang) no. 2 (1985): entire issue. Special number containing excerpts on Xinjiang from the *Zhongguo lishi da cidian* (Large dictionary of Chinese history).

Xinjiang shehui kexueyuan lishi yanjiu suo (Historical Research Institute, Xinjiang Academy of Social Sciences), ed. *Xinjiang difang lishi ziliao xuanji* (Collected materials on Xinjiang local history). Beijing: Renmin chubanshe, 1987.

Xinjiang shehui kexueyuan minzu yanjiusuo (Nationalities Research Institute, Xinjiang Academy of Social Sciences), ed. *Xinjiang jianshi* (Concise history of Xinjiang). Vol. 1. Urumchi: Xinjiang renmin chubanshe, 1980.

Xu Bofu. "18–19 shiji Xinjiang diqu de guanying xumuye" (Government pastoral production in Xinjiang in the 18th and 19th centuries). *Xinjiang shehui kexue* no. 5 (1987): 103–12.

———. "Qingdai qianqi Xinjiang diqu de chengzhen jingji" (The Xinjiang region's urban economy in the early Qing period). *Xinjiang shehui kexue* no. 5 (1988): 98–107.

———. "Qingdai qianqi Xinjiang diqu de fushui zhidu" (Xinjiang's tax system during the early Qing period). *Xinjiang lishi yanjiu* no. 3 (1985): 65–76.

———. "Qingdai qianqi Xinjiang diqu de huobi zhidu" (Xinjiang's currency system during the early Qing period). *Xinjiang lishi yanjiu* no. 4 (1985): 37–47.

———. "Qingdai qianqi Xinjiang diqu de mintun" (Xinjiang's civilian agricultural colonies during the early Qing period). *Zhongguo shi yanjiu* no. 2 (1985): 85–95.

———. "Qingdai qianqi Xinjiang yu zuguo neidi de shangye wanglai" (Commercial exchange between China proper and Xinjiang during the Qing period). In Xiyu shi luncong editorial group, ed., *Xiyu shi luncong 1*, pp. 182–204. Urumchi: Xinjiang renmin, 1985.

Xu Ke. *Qingbai leichao* (Categorically arranged unofficial sources on the Qing). Shanghai: Shangwu, 1917.

Yan Zhongping. *Zhongguo jindai jingji: shi tongji shiliao* (Selected statistical data on China's modern economic history). Beijing: Kexue chubanshe, 1955.

Yang Boda (Yang Po-ta). "Jade: Emperor Ch'ien Lung's collection in the Palace Museum, Peking." Li Wailing, trans. *Arts of Asia* 22, no. 2 (Mar.–Apr. 1992): 81–94.

———. "Qingdai gongting yuqi" (Court jades of the Qing period). *Gugong bowuyuan yuankan* no. 1 (1982): 49–61.

Yang Jianxin et al., eds. *Gu xi xing ji xuanzhu* (Selected and annotated westward travel accounts of the past). Yinchuan: Ningxia renmin chubanshe, 1987.

Yang Zhaoyu (Yang Chao-yü). *The Pawnshop in China*. T. S. Whelan, trans. Ann Arbor: Center for Chinese Studies, University of Michigan, 1979. (Originally published as *Zhongguo diandang ye*; Shanghai: The Commercial Press, 1929.)

Ye Zhiru. "Cong maoyi aocha kan Qianlong qianqi dui Zhunga'er bu de minzu zhengce." (The nationality policy of the early Qianlong period seen from the tea-brewing trade trips). *Xinjiang daxue xuebao* no. 1 (1986): 62–71.

———. "Qianlong shi neiwufu diandangye gaishu" (A brief account of the Imperial Household Agency pawnshops during the Qianlong period). *Lishi dang'an* 18, no. 2 (1985): 92–98.

Yijiang jizai (Record of the Yili River area). 1862. Repr., Zhongguo minzu shidi ziliao congkan, Wu Fengpei, ed., no. 30. Beijing: Central Nationalities Institute, 1982.

Yili luezhi (Survey of Yili). Guan Xingcai, trans. C. 1848. Repr., *Qingdai Xinjiang xijian shiliao huiji* (Collection of rare historical materials from Qing Xinjiang), Zhongguo bianjiang shidi shiliao congkan, Lü Yiran, Ma Dazheng, et al., eds. Xinjiang vol., pp. 277–98. Beijing: Quanguo tushuguan wenxian suowei fuzhi zhongxin, 1990.

Yi-shan. *Yi-shan Xinjiang zougao* (Yishan's Xinjiang memorials). 2 vols. Zhongguo minzu shidi ziliao congkan, Wu Fengpei, ed., no. 23. Beijing: Central Nationalities Institute, 1982.

Yi-xin et al., eds. *(Qinding) pingding Shaan Gan Xinjiang Huifei fanglue* (Imperially commissioned military history of the pacification of the Muslim Rebels in Shaanxi, Gansu, and Xinjiang). Preface 1896.

Yong-bao. *Zongtong Yili shiyi* (Comprehensive survey of affairs in Yili). C. 1795. Repr., *Qingdai Xinjiang xijian shiliao huiji* (Collection of rare historical materials from Qing Xinjiang). Zhongguo bianjiang shidi shiliao congkan, Lü Yiran, Ma Dazheng, et al., eds., Xinjiang vol., pp.

125–276. Beijing: Quanguo tushuguan wenxian suowei fuzhi zhong-xin, 1990.

Yong-bao and Xing-zhao. *Ta'erbahatai shiyi.* (Affairs of Tarbagatai). 1805. Repr., Bianjiang congshu xubian, Wu Fengpei, ed., no. 4. Beijing: n.p., 1950.

Yong-bao et al. *Wulumuqi shiyi* (Affairs of Urumchi). 1796. Repr., Bianjiang congshu xubian, Wu Fengpei, ed., no. 6. Beijing: n.p., 1950.

Yu Shanpu and Dong Naiqiang, eds. *Xiang Fei.* Beijing: Shumu wenxian chubanshe, 1985.

Yü, Ying-shih. "Han Foreign Relations." In Denis Twitchett and Michael Loewe, eds., *Cambridge History of China*, vol. 1, *The Ch'in and Han Empires, 221 B.C.–A.D. 220*, pp. 377–462. Cambridge, Engl.: Cambridge University Press, 1986.

———. *Trade and Expansion in Han China: A Study in the Structure of Sino-Barbarian Economic Relations.* Berkeley: University of California Press, 1967.

Yunggui (Yong-gui), Gu Shiheng, and Se-er-de. *Huijiang zhi* (Gazetteer of the Muslim frontier). 1772. Repr., Zhongguo fangzhi congshu, xibu difang no. 1. Taipei: Chengwen, 1968.

Zelin, Madeleine. *The Magistrate's Tael: Rationalizing Fiscal Reform in Eighteenth Century Ch'ing China.* Berkeley: University of California Press, 1984.

Zeng Wenwu. *Zhongguo jingying Xiyu shi* (History of China's manage-ment of the Western Regions). Shanghai: Shangwu, 1936. Repr. Xinjiang Weiwu'er zizhiqu zongbian shi, 1986.

Zhang Bofeng, comp. *Qingdai gedi jiangjun dutong dachen deng nianbiao, 1796–1911* (Chronological tables of regional generals, military lieuten-ant governors, and other Qing-dynasty ambans, 1796–1911). Beijing: Zhonghua shuju, 1977.

Zhang Wei. "*Song Lu Ju shi Heyuan*" (Seeing off Lu Ju on Embassy to Heyuan). In Wu Aichen, comp. *Lidai Xiyu shichao* (Western Regions poems through history), p. 12. Urumchi: Xinjiang renmin chubanshe, 1982.

Zhang Yuxin. "Qingchao qianqi de bianjiang zhengce" (The frontier policy of the early Qing dynasty). In Ma Dazheng, ed., *Zhongguo gudai bian-jiang zhengce yanjiu* (Researches on premodern Chinese frontier policy), pp. 315–53. Zhongguo bianjiang shidi yanjiu congshu, Zhongguo bian-jiang shidi yanjiu zhongxin, ed. Beijing: Zhongguo shehui kexueyuan chubanshe, 1990.

———. "Qingdai Beijing de Weiwuer zu" (Beijing's Uyghurs in the Qing period). *Xinjiang shehui kexue* no. 4 (1984): 92–97.

———. "Suzhou maoyi kaolue" (Survey of the Suzhou trade). Parts 1–3.

Xinjiang daxue xuebao no. 3 (1986): 24–32; no. 4 (1986): 48–54; no. 1 (1987): 67–76.

Zhao Erxun et al., eds. *Qingshi gao* (Draft official history of the Qing Dynasty). 1928. Repr., Beijing: Zhonghua shuju, 1991.

Zhao Songqiao and Xia Xuncheng. "Evolution of the Lop Desert and the Lop Nor." *The Geographical Journal* 150, no. 3 (Nov. 1984): 311–21.

Zhao Yuzheng. *Xinjiang tunken* (Xinjiang agricultural reclamation). Urumchi: Xinjiang renmin chubanshe, 1991.

Zhong Fang. *Hami zhi* (Gazetteer of Hami). 1846 manuscript edition. Repr. of 1937 Yugong xuehui ed., with afterword by Wu Fengpei, Bianjiang fangzhi no. 20. Taipei: Xuesheng shuju, 1967.

Zhongguo renmin daxue Qingshi yanjiusuo (People's University of China, Qing History Research Center) and Zhongguo shehui kexueyuan Zhongguo bianjiang shidi yanjiu zhongxin (Chinese Academy of Social Sciences, Chinese Borderlands History and Geography Research Center), eds. *Qingdai bianjiang shidi lunzhu suoyin* (Index of books and articles on Qing-period borderland history and geography). *Zhongguo bianjiang shidi yanjiu ziliao congshu* series. Beijing: Zhongguo renmin daxue chubanshe, 1988.

Zhongguo diyi lishi dang'an guan (Number One Historical Archives of China), ed. "Qianlong chao neidi yu Xinjiang sichou maoyi shiliao" (Materials on silk trade between China proper and Xinjiang in the Qianlong reign). In *Qingdai dang'an shiliao congbian* 12, pp. 44–214. Beijing: Zhonghua Shuju, 1987.

———, ed. "Qianlong nianjian Xinjiang sichou maoyi shiliao" (Materials on the Xinjiang silk trade in the Qianlong years). Parts 1 and 2. *Lishi dang'an* no. 1 (1990): 33–43; no. 2 (1990): 13–22.

———, ed. *Xibozu dang'an shiliao* (Archival materials on the Sibe nationality). 2 vols. Shenyang: Liaoning minzu chubanshe, 1989.

Zhongguo shehui kexueyuan kaogu yanjiusuo (Archaeological Research Institute of the Chinese Academy of Social Sciences), comp. *Ming Qing Beijingcheng tu* (Map of the Beijing walled city in the Ming and Qing periods). Beijing: Ditu chubanshe, 1986.

Zhou Nanquan. "Hengdusitan yu qi di suo zao yuqi kao" (A study of jade ware produced in Hindustan). *Gugong bowuyuan yuankan* no. 1 (1988): 60–66.

Zhuang Jifa (Chuang Chi-fa). *Qing Gaozong shiquan wugong yanjiu* (Research on Qing Gaozong's "ten military achievements"). Taipei: Gugong bowuguan, 1982. Repr., Beijing: Zhonghua shuju, 1987.

Zlatkin, I. Ia. "The History of the Khanate of Dzhungaria." *Central Asian Review* 13, no. 1 (1965): 17–30.

———. *Istoria Dzhungarskogo khanstva, 1635–1758.* 2d ed. Moscow: Nauka, 1983.

In this index an "f" after a number indicates a separate reference on the next page, and an "ff" indicates separate references on the next two pages. A continuous discussion over two or more pages is indicated by a span of page numbers, e.g., "57–59."

Millward, James A.
Beyond the pass : economy, ethnicity, and empire in Qing Central Asia, 1759–1864 /
James A. Millward.
p.   cm.
Includes bibliographical references and index.
ISBN 0-8047-2933-6 (alk. paper)
1. Sinkiang Uighur Autonomous Region (China)—History.   2. Sinkiang Uighur
Autonomous Region (China)—Commerce—History.   3. Ethnicity—China—Sinkiang
Uighur Autonomous Region.   4. China—History—Ch' ien lung, 1736–1795.
5. China—History—1795–1861.   I. Title.
DS793.S62M535   1997
951'.6—dc21   97-35503

Original printing 1998
Last figure below indicates year of this printing:
06 05 04 03 02 01 00 99 98